Advances in Comparative-Historical Analysis

Against the backdrop of an explosion of interest in new techniques for data collection and theory testing, this volume provides a fresh programmatic statement about comparative-historical analysis. It examines the advances and distinctive contributions that CHA has made to theory generation and the explanation of large-scale outcomes that newer approaches often regard as empirically intractable. An introductory essay locates the sources of CHA's enduring influence in core characteristics that distinguish this approach, such as its attention to process and its commitment to empirically grounded, deep case-based research. Subsequent chapters explore broad research programs inspired by CHA work; new analytic tools for studying temporal processes and institutional dynamics; and recent methodological tools for analyzing sequences and for combining CHA work with other approaches. This volume is essential reading for scholars seeking to learn about the sources of CHA's enduring influence and its contemporary analytical and methodological techniques.

James Mahoney is Gordon Fulcher Professor in Decision-Making and Professor of Political Science and Sociology at Northwestern University.

Kathleen Thelen is Ford Professor of Political Science at the Massachusetts Institute of Technology.

Strategies for Social Inquiry

Advances in Comparative-Historical Analysis

This new book series presents texts on a wide range of issues bearing upon the practice of social inquiry. Strategies are construed broadly to embrace the full spectrum of approaches to analysis, as well as relevant issues in philosophy of social science.

Published Titles

John Gerring, *Social Science Methodology: A Unified Framework*, 2nd edition
Michael Coppedge, *Democratization and Research Methods*
Thad Dunning, *Natural Experiments in the Social Sciences: A Design-Based Approach*
Carsten Q. Schneider and Claudius Wagemann, *Set-Theoretic Methods for the Social Sciences: A Guide to Qualitative Comparative Analysis*
Nicholas Weller and Jeb Barnes, *Finding Pathways: Mixed-Method Research for Studying Causal Mechanisms*
Andrew Bennett and Jeffrey T. Checkel, *Process Tracing: From Metaphor to Analytic Tool*
Diana Kapiszewski, Lauren M. MacLean, and Benjamin L. Read, *Field Research in Political Science: Practices and Principles*
Peter Spiegler, *A Constructive Critique of Economic Modeling*

Forthcoming Titles

Jason Seawright, *Multi-Method Social Science: Combining Qualitative and Quantitative Tools*

Advances in Comparative-Historical Analysis

Edited by

James Mahoney
Northwestern University

and

Kathleen Thelen
Massachusetts Institute of Technology

CAMBRIDGE
UNIVERSITY PRESS

CAMBRIDGE
UNIVERSITY PRESS

University Printing House, Cambridge CB2 8BS, United Kingdom

Cambridge University Press is part of the University of Cambridge.

It furthers the University's mission by disseminating knowledge in the pursuit of education, learning and research at the highest international levels of excellence.

www.cambridge.org
Information on this title: www.cambridge.org/9781107525634

© Cambridge University Press 2015

First published 2015

Printed in the United Kingdom by TJ International Ltd. Padstow Cornwall

A catalogue record for this publication is available from the British Library

Library of Congress Cataloguing in Publication data
Advances in comparative-historical analysis / edited by James Mahoney and Kathleen Thelen.
    pages   cm. – (Strategies for social inquiry)
Includes index.
ISBN 978-1-107-11002-1 (hardback) – ISBN 978-1-107-52563-4 (paperback)
1. Social sciences – Research – Methodology.   I. Mahoney, James, 1968– author editor of compilation.   II. Thelen, Kathleen Ann, author editor of compilation.
H61.A3933   2015
300.72 – dc23   2015005501

ISBN 978-1-107-11002-1 Hardback
ISBN 978-1-107-52563-4 Paperback

Contents

Part I   Introduction

Part II   Agenda-setting work

Part III   Tools for temporal analysis

Figures

Tables

Contributors

Giovanni Capoccia is Professor of Comparative Politics at the University of Oxford and currently holds a Leverhulme Trust Major Research Fellowship. His research interests include the theory of institutional development, historical approaches to the study of democracy and democratization, and comparative European politics. He is the author of many articles on these subjects and of *Defending Democracy: Reactions to Extremism in Interwar Europe* (2005), which received the award for the Best Book in European Politics by the American Political Science Association. He is the coeditor (with Daniel Ziblatt) of *The Historical Turn in Democratization Studies* (special double issue of *Comparative Political Studies*, 2010). Professor Capoccia is currently completing a book, tentatively titled *Reshaping Democracy After Authoritarianism: Legacies, Institutions, and Responses to Neo-Fascism in Western Europe After 1945*, on how Western European democracies have dealt with Fascist legacies.

Tulia G. Falleti is the Class of 1965 Term Associate Professor of Political Science and Senior Fellow of the Leonard Davis Institute for Health Economics at the University of Pennsylvania. She is the author of *Decentralization and Subnational Politics in Latin America* (Cambridge University Press, 2010), which earned the Donna Lee Van Cott Award for the best book on political institutions by the Latin American Studies Association. Her articles on federalism, decentralization, authoritarianism, and qualitative methods have appeared in the *American Political Science Review*, *Comparative Political Studies*, *Publius*, *Studies in Comparative International Development*, *Qualitative Sociology*, among other journals and edited volumes. She is the coeditor, with Orfeo Fioretos and Adam Sheingate, of *The Oxford Handbook of Historical Institutionalism* and is currently working on a book manuscript on new participatory institutions in Latin America.

Jane Gingrich is Associate Professor of Comparative Political Economy at the University of Oxford and a tutorial fellow at Magdalen College. Her research interests broadly include comparative welfare state and education reform, in particular, the introduction of markets, private actors, and competition into public services. She is author of *Making Markets in the Welfare State: The Politics of Varying Market Reforms* (Cambridge University Press, 2014) as well as several articles on this subject. She currently is working on a number of projects examining the consequences of state marketization for democratic politics. This new work investigates how changes in the architecture of public service provision and benefits have affected both citizen demands and behaviors, and it charts the changing relationship among state actors, citizens, and organized groups.

Jacob S. Hacker is Stanley Resor Professor of Political Science and Director of the Institution for Social and Policy Studies at Yale University. An expert on the politics of US health and social policy in cross-national perspective, he is the author or coauthor of five books, numerous journal articles, and a wide range of popular writings on American politics and public policy, with a focus on health and economic security. His most recent book is *Winner-Take-All Politics: How Washington Made the Rich Richer and Turned Its Back on the Middle Class* (2011), written with Paul Pierson. With the support of the Rockefeller Foundation, he directs the Economic Security Index, a multiyear project examining economic insecurity in the United States, and he currently serves as a member of the High-Level Expert Group on the Measurement of Economic Performance and Social Progress, housed at the Organisation for Economic Co-operation and Development. He recently won the Heinz Eulau Prize of the American Political Science Association for his 2013 article "The Insecure American," written with Philipp Rehm and Mark Schlesinger.

Stephan Haggard is the Krause Distinguished Professor at the Graduate School of International Relations and Pacific Studies, University of California, San Diego. He is the author of *Pathways from the Periphery: The Political Economy of Growth in the Newly Industrializing Countries* (1990), *The Political Economy of Democratic Transitions* (with Robert Kaufman; 1995), *The Political Economy of the Asian Financial Crisis* (2000), and *Development, Democracy, and Welfare States: Latin America, East Asia, and Eastern Europe* (with Robert Kaufman; 2008). He has also written extensively on North Korea with Marcus Noland, including, among others, *Famine in North Korea: Markets, Aid, and Reform* (2007). He is currently working on a book with Robert Kaufman on inequality, distributive conflict, and regime change during the Third Wave and multimethod approaches to the study of rare events.

Evan S. Lieberman is the Total Professor of Political Science and Contemporary Africa at the Massachusetts Institute of Technology. He conducts research in the field of comparative politics, with a focus on development in sub-Saharan Africa, and he writes and teaches on multimethod research strategies. He is the author of *Boundaries of Contagion: How Ethnic Politics Have Shaped Government Responses to AIDS* (2009), which won the 2010 Giovanni Sartori Book Prize of the Qualitative and Multi-Method Section of the American Political Science Association, and *Race and Regionalism in the Politics of Taxation in Brazil and South Africa* (Cambridge University Press, 2003), which received the 2004 Mattei Dogan Prize for the best book in comparative research. Professor Lieberman is currently working on a book on the politics of democratic governance in Africa.

Steven Levitsky is Professor of Government at Harvard University. His research interests include political parties and party building, authoritarianism and democratization, and weak and informal institutions, with a focus on Latin America. He is author of *Transforming Labor-Based Parties in Latin America: Argentine Peronism in Comparative Perspective* (Cambridge University Press, 2003), coauthor (with Lucan Way) of *Competitive Authoritarianism: Hybrid Regimes After the Cold War* (Cambridge University Press, 2010), and coeditor of *Argentine Democracy: The Politics of Institutional Weakness* (with Maria Victoria Murillo; 2006), *Informal Institutions and Democracy: Lessons from Latin America* (with Gretchen Helmke; 2006), and *The Resurgence of the Left in Latin America* (with Kenneth Roberts; 2013). Professor Levitsky is currently completing an edited volume on the challenges of party building in contemporary Latin America and is writing a book (with Lucan Way) on the durability of revolutionary regimes.

James Mahoney is the Gordon Fulcher Professor in Decision-Making and Professor of Political Science and Sociology at Northwestern University. His substantive work focuses on political and socioeconomic development in Latin America, and his methodological work concerns descriptive and causal inference in case study and small-N analysis. He is the author of *The Legacies of Liberalism: Path Dependence and Political Regimes in Central America* (2001) and coeditor of *Comparative Historical Analysis in the Social Sciences* (with Dietrich Rueschemeyer; Cambridge University Press, 2003). Professor Mahoney's most recent books are *Colonialism and Development: Spanish America in Comparative Perspective* (Cambridge University Press, 2010), *Explaining Institutional Change* (coedited with Kathleen Thelen; 2010), and

A Tale of Two Cultures: Qualitative and Quantitative Research in the Social Sciences (with Gary Goertz; 2012).

Paul Pierson is the John Gross Professor of Political Science at the University of California, Berkeley, and a Senior Fellow at the Canadian Institute for Advanced Research. His research focuses on American national politics and comparative political economy. He is the author of *Politics in Time: History, Institutions, and Social Analysis* (2004), among other books. His most recent book is *Winner-Take-All Politics: How Washington Made the Rich Richer and Turned Its Back on the Middle Class* (with Jacob Hacker; 2011). His article "Path Dependence, Increasing Returns, and the Study of Politics" won the American Political Science Association prize for the best article in the *American Political Science Review* in 2000, and in 2011 it received the Aaron Wildavsky Award of the Public Policy section of APSA for its enduring contribution to the study of public policy.

Wolfgang Streeck is Director emeritus and Professor at the Max Planck Institute for the Study of Societies in Cologne, Germany. He was Theodor Heuss Professor 2013–14 at the New School for Social Research, New York. From 1988 to 1995 he was Professor of Sociology and Industrial Relations at the University of Wisconsin–Madison. His latest publications include *Buying Time: The Delayed Crisis of Democratic Capitalism* (2014), *Re-Forming Capitalism: Institutional Change in the German Political Economy* (2009), and *Beyond Continuity: Institutional Change in Advanced Political Economies* (edited with Kathleen Thelen; 2005). His current research interests are the fiscal crisis of capitalist states, in particular in the context of the global financial crisis of 2008, and institutional change in the political economy of contemporary capitalism.

Kathleen Thelen is Ford Professor of Political Science at the Massachusetts Institute of Technology and a permanent external member of the Max-Planck-Institut für Gesellschaftsforschung in Cologne, Germany. Her latest book is *Varieties of Liberalization and the New Politics of Social Solidarity* (Cambridge University Press, 2014). A previous book, *How Institutions Evolve: The Political Economy of Skills in Germany, Britain, the United States, and Japan* (Cambridge University Press, 2004), received the Woodrow Wilson Foundation Award of the American Political Science Association and the Mattei Dogan Award in Comparative Politics. Other recent works include *Explaining Institutional Change* (edited with James Mahoney;

Cambridge University Press, 2010) and *Beyond Continuity* (edited with Wolfgang Streeck; 2005). Thelen's current work focuses on labor and social policy in the advanced industrial democracies, and on the American political economy in comparative perspective.

Lucan A. Way is Associate Professor of Political Science at the University of Toronto. His research focuses on democratic transitions, postcommunist politics, and the evolution of authoritarian rule in cross-regional perspective. In 2006, his article in *World Politics*, "Authoritarian State Building and the Sources of Regime Competitiveness in the Fourth Wave," received the award for best article from the American Political Science Association's Comparative Democratization Section. His book, *Competitive Authoritarianism: Hybrid Regimes After the Cold War* (with Steven Levitsky), was published in 2010 by Cambridge University Press. Professor Way is completing a new book, *Pluralism by Default: Weak Autocrats and the Rise of Competitive Politics*, in which he argues that democratic politics in the post–Cold War era has often been the product of weak states and underdeveloped ruling parties rather than strong democratic institutions or robust civil societies. Professor Way received a grant from the Social Sciences and Humanities Research Council of Canada to begin a new project with Steven Levitsky on the durability of revolutionary regimes.

Preface

This volume originated in a conversation in 2010 in which Lewis Bateman of Cambridge University Press expressed interest to James Mahoney in a second edition of *Comparative Historical Analysis in the Social Sciences* (coedited by Mahoney and Dietrich Rueschemeyer, 2003). The following year, Kathleen Thelen and Mahoney began discussions about a new project along these lines. Although a fresh programmatic statement about comparative-historical analysis (CHA) seemed appropriate and much needed, it was also apparent that any new undertaking could not replicate – or even simply update – the earlier book. For one thing, Dietrich Rueschemeyer had retired from sociology, making unavailable the senior leader of the earlier project. Moreover, developments in political science and sociology spoke against following the previous book's approach of simultaneously engaging both disciplines. In particular, the rise of new methodologies and approaches in political science seemed to require a new programmatic statement about CHA focused on political science.

Advances in Comparative-Historical Analysis features original contributions that situate CHA within present-day debates in political science. The book retains the earlier volume's threefold structure – exploring the substantive contributions, theoretical accomplishments, and methodological strategies of CHA. It also follows the earlier book in being a collective effort, bringing together leading CHA scholars who otherwise work in diverse empirical areas. However, the essays in this book cover wholly new topics and tools, and they engage recent and ongoing debates and problems in the field.

To us, this project seemed especially important now because of the excitement surrounding the "revolution in causal influence" currently gripping political science. In recent years, the discipline has witnessed an explosion of interest in the experimental method and a smaller but significant movement advocating the use of "big data." In light of the growing interest in new techniques for data collection and theory testing, we felt it important to call to mind the ongoing contributions that CHA has made to theory generation and the explanation of large and complex outcomes at the macro level – outcomes that newer approaches often shy away from as empirically intractable. In our introductory essay we explain the enduring influence of CHA in contemporary political science by highlighting comparative advantages inherent to the approach, and we also consider what is lost in research programs that lack core features of CHA. The epilogue of the book returns to broader themes by examining how CHA rests on a particular ontology of the social world that links it to the classics in political science and that distinguishes it from many prominent contemporary alternative approaches.

After an introduction, the core essays of the volume are organized into three parts. In the first part, "Agenda-Setting Work," authors explore how key works in CHA within specific substantive areas have inspired broad research programs spanning generations of scholars. The essays suggest that orientations inherent to CHA – above all, its concern with deep case-based research and its openness to complex, configurative explanation – enable the tradition to produce agenda-setting works that define the questions and lines of analysis that other scholars of diverse methodologies and orientations subsequently pursue.

The next part of the book, "Tools for Temporal Analysis," consists of essays that explore the theoretical tools and conceptual innovations associated with CHA. These essays focus especially on tools for pursuing temporally oriented analysis within CHA. They include new work on the study of power and path dependence, new guidelines and concepts for the analysis of agency and critical junctures, and new orientations for the study of institutional change, including, especially, change that occurs beneath the veneer of continuity in formal-institutional arrangements.

In the last part of the volume, "Issues of Method," authors focus on some of the methodologies employed in CHA research. These essays summarize the different procedures used in CHA to make inferences about historical causal processes. They also explore how the comparison of historical sequences is central to these procedures, including both cross-case and within-case methods of inference. And they consider how comparative-historical methods can and cannot be combined with other methodologies, such as statistical and experimental methods.

The three main parts are interrelated and connected. Most essays, although centered on one set of issues, in fact reflect on all of the three major themes – agenda-setting work, tools for temporal analysis, and issues of method. In the course of writing the essays, volume contributors were in dialogue with one another at multiple conferences, and they reacted to and commented on each other's chapters, reinforcing connections across the volume. This dialogue and exchange also served to bring us together closely as a group. For us, working with such talented contributors, and witnessing the formation of this wonderfully collaborative group, has been one of the great joys of carrying out this project.

We would first like to thank and acknowledge Dietrich Rueschemeyer, who coedited the earlier book and contributed a career of work that advanced CHA. We also thank Lewis Bateman, whose suggestion to consider a second edition set into motion the events leading to the present volume, as well as Margaret Levi, who enthusiastically supported the earlier project. For this book, it was a great pleasure to work with John Haslam at Cambridge University Press. He was supportive of the volume from the start, arranged reviewer reports from which we benefited, and oversaw the book's production with efficiency and professionalism. Colin Elman and John Gerring, coeditors of the Strategies for Social Inquiry series in which this book appears, were also great supporters of this project.

The first conference at which initial drafts of papers were presented was held at MIT in March 2013. We thank Dick Samuels and the Center for International Studies for sponsoring that event and Kate Searle for managing the logistics with her characteristic care and efficiency. We benefited immensely from the participation and commentary of our colleagues Andrea Campbell, Peter Hall, Ben Schneider, and Lucas Stanczyk.

A follow-up conference was held at Northwestern University in November 2013. We are grateful to Northwestern's Department of Political Science and the Roberta Buffett Center for International and Comparative Studies for supporting this second conference. At the Buffett Center, acting director Brian Hanson encouraged the project from the onset, and Jeff Cernucan and Diana Snyder made sure conference events ran smoothly. Dan Galvin, Edward Gibson, and Rachel Riedl served as excellent discussants and participants at the event. We owe an extra special thanks to Andre Nickow, who not only helped organize conference activities but also assisted in formatting and compiling the volume's chapters for submission to Cambridge University Press.

Many of the chapters were also presented at two panels during the 2013 American Political Science Association meetings, and authors received excellent comments from the discussants of these panels, Nancy Bermeo and Daniel Ziblatt. At these meetings, Theda Skocpol also expressed her encouragement for the project and suggested ideas for framing the introduction. Finally, we would like to extend our thanks to the larger CHA community in political science. This community not only continues to produce some of the best empirical work in the discipline but also sets important theoretical agendas for scholars working from other analytical and methodological orientations.

James Mahoney
Kathleen Thelen

Part I

Introduction

Comparative-historical analysis in contemporary political science

Kathleen Thelen and James Mahoney

Comparative-historical analysis (CHA) has a long and distinguished pedigree in political science. In a discipline in which a succession of different movements has advocated new approaches promising more powerful theory or new methodologies for more rigorously testing theory, or both, CHA has stood the test of time. It remains the approach of choice for many scholars spanning all generations and continues to set agendas – both theoretical and substantive – for many other scholars who use alternative analytical and methodological tools.

In this introductory chapter, we explore the resilience and continuing influence of CHA in contemporary political science. We attribute the enduring impact of CHA to strengths built into its very defining features: its focus on large-scale and often complex outcomes of enduring importance; its emphasis on empirically grounded, deep case-based research; and its attention to process and the temporal dimensions of politics. These features not only distinguish CHA but also endow the approach with comparative advantages not found in other research.

The methodological churning within political science is not new, and yet it seems to have intensified over the past several years. Beginning in the late 1980s, the field underwent important changes as rational choice theory made its way into the mainstream of the discipline. Scholarship using game theory was greeted with considerable fanfare and controversy, celebrated by some for the theoretical elegance of its models, criticized by others for the limited leverage that these models often seemed to offer in explaining real-world outcomes.[1] Even if this line of work did not have the transformative effects that some predicted, clearly it now occupies an important place in the discipline.

We thank the participants in this project for valuable input on previous versions of this chapter. We are grateful as well to Lucio Baccaro, Nancy Bermeo, James Druckman, Daniel Galvin, Anna Grzymala-Busse, Peter Hall, Alan Jacobs, Rachel Riedl, Ben Schneider, Dan Slater, Daniel Ziblatt, and Nick Ziegler for enormously helpful comments.
[1] For a flavor of debates of the day, see Green and Shapiro (1994) and Friedman (1996).

More recently, an empiricist strand of work has emerged with similar energy and force. Billed by its proponents as a "revolution in causal inference," the experimental method has been sweeping through many departments. Today's experimentalists put great emphasis on research design, often recruiting subjects – in the lab, in the field, or online – to participate in experiments that attempt to isolate the effects of variables of concern. This new trend has shifted the terms of debate away from previous disputes about the relative merits of large-N and small-N research. Instead, both traditional regression analysis and qualitative case-based research are increasingly disparaged by those who see all forms of observational research as fatally hobbled in their ability to nail down causation with any reliability (e.g., Gerber, Green, and Kaplan 2014). Strong proponents of the experimental method solemnly advise graduate students to ignore the revolution in causal inference at their peril.

And, finally, even as we write, "big data" is the new watchword on the political science frontier (e.g., King 2014). Although the term is quite loose, what distinguishes big data from more traditional quantitative research is that it involves huge data sets (often more than a million observations) whose analysis requires specialized computer science techniques (e.g., machine learning). Research agendas organized around big data have been driven in part by technological advances and new social science infrastructures that allow researchers to harvest and manipulate large quantities of information. For scholars who are part of this movement, the issue is what questions these new sources of data and these new techniques might be used to address.

In the midst of this maelstrom, CHA remains a prominent and vibrant research tradition. In fact, in the current context characterized by a feverish concern with data collection and theory testing, CHA stands out by remaining resolutely and unapologetically focused on theory generation and on explaining large and complex outcomes at the macro level that other approaches increasingly shy away from as empirically intractable. Complementing but also competing with these other research approaches, CHA continues to find expression in a steady stream of highly celebrated contemporary works that often set theoretical and substantive agendas that are then taken up by scholars deploying other methods, including proponents of the latest "gold standard."[2]

In what follows, we explore the enduring influence of CHA by highlighting the comparative advantages that stem from its three core defining features.

---

[2] Many of the major works in CHA are discussed in Mahoney and Rueschemeyer (2003). Appendix A presents a partial list of prominent, recent works in this tradition that we know won important disciplinary awards since 2000 (inevitably, we will have overlooked some, and we apologize for omissions).

First, CHA's *macroconfigurational orientation* links it to the classics in political science and shares with them an abiding concern to explain large-scale political and political-economic outcomes. Second, its focus on problem-driven *case-based research* has been a key source of agenda-setting insights that have enjoyed broad applicability and resonance. Third, CHA's commitment to *temporally oriented analysis* has allowed it to make distinctive contributions to our understanding of process and time in politics. We elaborate the advantages of CHA by drawing out what is gained from each of these three orientations. More important, we consider what is lost in research programs that lack these characteristics. Along the way, we also consider complementarities between CHA and other approaches. We explore how aspects of alternative approaches have been or might be incorporated into CHA. We look at the ways in which CHA might help compensate for weaknesses associated with alternative approaches.

Macroconfigurational research

As a first distinguishing feature, CHA entails *macroconfigurational research*. This feature breaks out into two separate though related components – the "macro" and the "configurational" – and each may be discussed in turn.

A macroscopic orientation

The macro component entails a concern with large-scale outcomes – state building, democratic transitions, societal patterns of inequality, war and peace, to name a few. Researchers often also focus on large-scale causal factors, including both broad political-economic structures (e.g., colonialism) and complex organizational-institutional arrangements (e.g., social policy regimes). The macroscopic orientation of CHA is also signaled by the analysis of aggregate cases: often nation-states but also including political movements, subnational territories, empires, and, in a few cases, even whole civilizations and world systems. Although macrolevel research is associated with CHA scholarship, it is not unique to that tradition. For example, many statistical researchers also seek to explain macro outcomes and focus on broad structural-institutional causes in their work. This shared concern with macroscopic questions has, in fact, allowed for considerable synergies between CHA and quantitative analysis. Such synergies have sustained highly productive research communities in which competition and collaboration among scholars employing different methods have advanced our understanding of a wide range of outcomes, from revolutions to welfare regimes to democratization (Amenta 2003; Goldstone 2003; Mahoney 2003; Pierson 2000).

In the past, some scholars contrasted CHA's emphasis on macro outcomes and macroscopic causes with alternative approaches committed to "methodological individualism," that is, the idea that political outcomes must be traced back to the actions and motives of individual agents.[3] However, the distinction vanishes in the practice of CHA. In fact, macro theories often direct our attention to which particular microlevel processes or behaviors are likely to be most important and when. For example, Capoccia's analysis of critical junctures turns precisely on identifying moments of structural contingency when actor choice and agency can carry special weight (Capoccia, Chapter 6, this volume). Likewise, macro theories often suggest specific microlevel events and processes that should (or should not) be present within particular cases if the macro theory is correct. As part of testing their theories, CHA scholars who are interested in identifying big patterns over time or across countries often rely on archival and primary sources, zooming in to inspect specific crucial episodes or patterns at closer range, and in some cases delving into the motives and actions of particular historical actors (e.g., Skocpol 1992; Swenson 2002; Ziblatt 2009, forthcoming).

Rather than insist on methodological individualism, CHA takes a position that reflects both pragmatic considerations and a particular ontological commitment. The pragmatic position, well articulated by Daniel Little (2012), is that it is often quite possible to "make careful statements about macro-macro and macro-micro causal relations without proceeding according to the logic of Coleman's boat – up and down the struts" (145).[4] While macrolevel arguments cannot be at odds with micro accounts, their validity does not require that they be broken down into individual-level behaviors; in fact, a requirement to disaggregate all processes into individual-level choices and behaviors would render much macro research infeasible or impossible.

The more foundational point, however, is that where structural features play a key causal role there is nothing to be gained – and much to be

---

[3] Jon Elster (1982), a leading proponent of methodological individualism, defined the term to mean "the doctrine that all social phenomena (their structure and their change) are in principle explicable only in terms of individuals – their properties, goals, and beliefs" (453). For a thoughtful discussion of the origins of the term and the ambiguities in its usage, see Hodgson (2007).

[4] Little refers to Coleman's (1990) macro-micro-macro model of explanation. The example he gives is Bhopal, where he suggests that it is not necessary "to disaggregate every claim like 'organizational deficiencies at the Bhopal chemical plant caused the devastating chemical spill' onto specific individual-level activities" (Little 2012: 8–9).

lost – by insisting that every outcome be traced back to the actions and strategies of individual agents. To adopt an exclusively micro-oriented approach would mean ignoring important causal processes that can only be understood at higher levels of analysis (Gaventa 1980; Lukes 1968). Many of the most influential works in comparative politics point to systemic characteristics in which structural variables, large-scale processes, or organizational features play a crucial causal role by shaping the interests of individual agents. One cannot understand the interests and actions of key actors without appreciating the macrostructural environment in which they are situated. In this volume, Paul Pierson makes the point with a trenchant critique of how much work in political science fundamentally misses the impact of power by reducing politics to the apparently fluid interactions of individuals.

Causal configurations and context

The configurational component of CHA refers to the way in which researchers consider how multiple factors combine to form coherent larger combinations, complexes, and causal packages. One reason this kind of configurational analysis figures so prominently is because the large-scale outcomes investigated in CHA are themselves often aggregated combinations of multiple events and processes. For example, one cannot study revolutions, democratic transitions, and developmental states without analyzing how various events and underlying processes constitute these phenomena.

However, beyond this, configurational analysis also characterizes a specific mode of *explanation* used in CHA. In this field, one frequently explains macro outcomes by examining how variables work together in combinations or "causal packages" (Ragin 1987). This combinatorial approach to causation assumes complexity in the specific sense that interaction effects – including interactions among more than two variables – are presumed to be common, and thus that individual causal factors normally must be analyzed as parts of larger combinations. Even when CHA scholars are interested in studying the effects of a single factor on an outcome, they consider the ways in which the effects of that variable may vary across different settings. In CHA, specifying the effect of X on Y almost always involves taking into account the "context" in which X operates, which means specifying the other variables that interact with X and that shape the nature of its effect (see, especially, Falleti and Lynch 2009).[5]

---

[5] On the potentials and challenges of modeling and interpreting interaction effects in quantitative research, see Kam and Franzese (2007).

To invoke a well-known example, consider how O'Donnell (1973) answered the classic question: does economic development cause democracy? His answer was "it depends," and he then set about specifying upon exactly what it depends. In contrast to the conventional wisdom that economic development contributes positively to democracy, O'Donnell found that in South America in the 1960s and 1970s economic development in fact helped to fuel harsh authoritarianism. He argued it did so because economic growth was unfolding in a context marked by mobilized popular sectors and an increasingly prominent role for technocrats within society. Under these specific conditions, economic development was a motor for the creation of repressive military regimes.

CHA researchers adopt a configurational approach to explanation not because they value causal complexity for its own sake or underappreciate parsimony. Instead, for the macro outcomes under study, CHA researchers believe that there is no alternative to analyzing the effects of causes in light of the context in which they occur. Most scholars in this school thus would emphatically agree with Andrew Abbott (1997) when he points out that abstracting a case from its context in the interest of parsimony can lead to deeply misleading results. As he puts it, if such "decontextualization is merely the removal of excess detail, then it's a fine thing, scientifically." But if it eliminates crucial variables and interactions, "it is a scientific disaster" (1171).

Complementarities and trade-offs

Not all approaches are equally well suited to address the macro phenomena at the center of CHA research. Different approaches are designed to address different kinds of questions, and we should be evaluating the costs and benefits of choosing a given approach for the questions we ask and answer. Arguably, one of the main casualities in the "revolution" in causal inference – increasingly acknowledged as well by otherwise sympathetic observers – is a dramatic narrowing of the type of studies that scholars are likely to undertake (Huber 2013). Many of the questions we want to ask about causes and outcomes at the macro level do not lend themselves to an experimental design. What is the relative impact of coercion and co-optation on the durability of authoritarian regimes? What is the role of organized business in American politics? How do multinational corporations affect development? These questions cannot be answered with an experiment for technical, logistical, ethical, or financial reasons.[6]

---

[6] Lijphart (1971) pointed out long ago that the experimental method "can only rarely be used in political science because of practical and ethical impediments" (684).

The turn to experimental research does not just bias the questions we ask; it often steers the search for answers onto specific paths, toward particular kinds of answers about what factors are seen as causally important.[7] Researchers can almost never manipulate many of the macro factors that we know to be the most important in politics – power, resources, institutions, and ideology – in any meaningful way.[8] Experimental research cannot easily find these factors to be causally consequential, because they simply do not lend themselves to these techniques. By contrast, "information" turns out to be a variable that is especially amenable to treatment, in the lab or in the field.[9] Experiments that vary information (e.g., amount, content, "frame") are relatively easy to design and inexpensive to implement. As a result, a rather large share of experimental work probes the impact of information-based variables, and the findings therefore often report the impact (or not) of treatments that manipulate information in one way or another. Quite apart from the question of whether the resulting experiments are successful on their own terms (for example, avoiding problems of "priming" and other pitfalls), information (or variables that lend themselves to information-based manipulation) may actually be a minor determinant of the outcome of ultimate interest.

From the perspective of the kinds of macrolevel concerns that animate CHA, therefore, one of the more regrettable trends in the discipline is the selection of questions on the basis of methods and data (see also Shapiro 2004, 2014). We all know the story of the drunken man searching for his keys under a lamppost "because this is where the light is best." In the past, this story was invoked as an admonition to pursue the causes of the phenomenon of interest no matter where that search might lead you. Today, however, some scholars suggest that we should seek out questions that lend themselves to "modern" methods and search for answers where the data are most plentiful. They counsel us to leave aside questions – and to bracket possible answers – that, while perhaps important, are empirically intractable. In other words, some scholars are emphatically directing us to look under the lamppost, with the warning that there is no point tapping around in the dark.[10]

---

[7] For assessments of the strengths and weaknesses of experiments in political science, see Morton and Williams (2010) and Druckman *et al.* (2011).

[8] With an experiment, one can manipulate treatments in ways that attempt to simulate macrostructural factors. For example, one study seeking to determine whether a leader's status affects his/her ability to elicit cooperation established participants' "status" through their performance in trivia games (Eckel, Fatas, and Wilson 2010). However, one usually cannot actually manipulate macrostructural factors themselves. For a rare exception, see Beath, Christia, and Enikolopov (2013).

[9] We are indebted to Ben Schneider for this point.

[10] We thank Paul Pierson for this point, based on remarks made by a prominent scholar of American politics who cited the lamppost example in just this way.

However, this intense narrowing of questions comes at a huge cost. We have already seen how the study of economic development in some quarters has been reduced to serial exercises in program evaluation (Deaton 2014) and how the study of American politics has become ever more focused on public opinion and electoral behavior (Pierson 2007). These developments have gone hand in hand with a skepticism toward observational research that has caused some scholars to swear off macrolevel outcomes and complex institutional configurations as hopelessly confounded and instead to zero in on narrower questions for which an experiment can be devised or a large-N data set can be assembled. Yet one cannot help but wonder whether searching for answers where the light is brightest in fact captures the most important explanations. For example, the ready availability of public opinion data (combined increasingly with survey experiments) has driven a significant renaissance in behavioral research centering on what individual citizens say they want. And while we learn a great deal as a result about what people are thinking, citizen preferences are not necessarily the main driver of many of the outcomes we wish to explain. Just as the massive growth of high-end inequality in the United States seems hard to trace back to the preferences of voters, so, too, are outcomes such as the dramatic transformation of the Chinese political economy or the dreary durability of authoritarian regimes throughout much of the world hard to link to the micro attitudes and preferences of ordinary citizens.

Turning now to the configurational aspect of CHA, we noted earlier that CHA research assesses theories that assume complex causal interactions and indeed often puts such configurations at the very heart of the analysis. On the one hand, a concern with configurations rooted in specific cases at least partially differentiates CHA from statistical research, which is often more concerned with estimating the average effects of particular variables or perhaps simple interactions across large populations of cases. On the other hand, however, CHA can and does powerfully team up with statistical analyses that are similarly focused on macrolevel outcomes and variables. As Lieberman points out in this volume, much can be gained by combining traditional regression analysis with a close analysis of systematically selected cases. Statistical studies are often helpful in identifying broad patterns about individual variables, while CHA identifies how these variables work together in configurations to generate outcomes in specific cases. Conversely, CHA findings about causal configurations for particular sets of cases can stimulate statistical hypothesis testing aimed at identifying the more general effects of the variables in these configurations.

By contrast, experimental research cannot as easily join forces with CHA in a collaborative program focused on macro (often macrohistorical) outcomes. Lieberman's chapter shows that the two traditions can certainly inform each other, though he also makes clear that CHA and experimental work occupy opposite ends on key dimensions of empirical social science (see the cube in his Figure 9.1). At a basic level the aim of experimental research – to isolate the impact of individual treatment variables while controlling for other factors – clashes with the more configurational approach of most CHA. By design, experimental research tends to produce discrete findings that cannot simply be "added together" in any straightforward way to illuminate more complex causal interactions.[11] So, although it is possible to apply insights from macro CHA work at the micro level – for example, using experiments to test aspects or modules within a configurative CHA explanation – the discrete micro results of individual experiments cannot be "summed together" to explain the macro outcomes on which CHA scholars typically focus.

These difficulties in aggregating the results of individual experiments are partly related to well-known issues of context and external validity. Although experimental research is designed to control for the effects of various factors via random assignment to treatment, its findings are nonetheless situated in the specific setting where the research is carried out. The question of whether and how these findings might be generalized beyond this context is often quite problematic in contemporary political science. In an era when cross-national regression research is often denigrated, it is important to recognize that regression research usually avoids the problem of generalizing its results to inappropriate contexts or of posing a big question and then – once it has been translated and broken down into a viable experiment or "game" – generating results that apply to a different and often smaller question.

Ultimately, experimental research can complement but it cannot substitute for the kind of macro and configurational research carried out in CHA. Virtually by definition, experimental research is likely to miss many of the broad systemic features that we know to be important components of political life, including the connections across different institutional realms. Such work

---

[11] In a stirring tribute to Albert O. Hirschman, Francis Fukuyama (2013) points to the limitations of experimental work even in the area of developmental economics where it is particularly prevalent. He notes that experiments can be useful for narrow program-evaluation purposes, but not for theory development because the results "don't aggregate upwards into an understanding of the broader phenomenon of development. It is hard to imagine that all the work being done under this approach will leave anything behind of a conceptual nature that people will remember fifty years from now" (93).

will also systematically miss complex reflexive processes and dynamics of reciprocal causation in which "causes" and "effects" are mutually constitutive over time and across different institutional arenas. As Gingrich's chapter shows, the brilliance of Esping-Andersen's research on welfare regimes was precisely how it identified complex causal "syndromes," feedback effects, and coherence across different realms and over time. It is hard to imagine how impoverished welfare state research would be if we reduced everything to simple binary relationships or limited ourselves to looking at specific independent variables one at a time.[12]

Within the experimental tradition, there are more complementarities between CHA and natural experiments.[13] Both employ a similar comparative logic based on carefully matched cases. Moreover, studies based on natural experiments – like much of CHA – typically seek to understand the effect of a variable on a macro outcome in a particular case rather than to generalize about an average effect for a broad population. Yet very few natural experiments in political science meet the demanding criteria for a true natural experiment (Dunning 2012; Sekhon and Titiunik 2012). Instead, scholars examine cases that are matched on key dimensions but that often do not fully meet the assumption of "as-if" random assignment to treatment. For these very reasons, work on natural experiments can benefit enormously from the tools of CHA, which are designed precisely to make inferences about cases that cannot be construed as true natural experiments.

Case-based research

A second defining feature of CHA is *case-based research*. This feature highlights the fact that CHA typically focuses on explaining observed outcomes, often in particular times and places, and it does so by developing explanations that identify the causal mechanisms that enable and generate these outcomes. This orientation again can be unpacked into two separate components: (1) a focus on real-world puzzles, and (2) the use of mechanism-based explanation.

---

[12] Similarly, the Varieties of Capitalism framework (Hall and Soskice 2001), which has inspired such a large and fruitful body of research, is specifically organized around the complex systemic features of political economies (e.g., Iversen and Soskice 2001, 2006).

[13] As Lieberman (Chapter 9, this volume) points out, the same holds true for quasi-experimental designs such as matching techniques and regression discontinuity analysis.

Real-world puzzles

CHA research is *problem driven* in the sense that it is animated by real-world questions, which is why CHA scholars gravitate toward empirical puzzles anchored in particular times and places (Pierson and Skocpol 2002; Shapiro 2004). They may ask why cases that are similar on many key dimensions exhibit quite different outcomes on a dependent variable of interest. This is the approach taken by Maya Tudor (2013) in her analysis of divergent political trajectories in India and Pakistan. Alternatively, CHA scholars may ask why seemingly disparate cases all have the same outcome. This is the main strategy followed by Steven Levitsky and Lucan Way (2010, and Chapter 4, this volume) in their analysis of competitive authoritarianism. Real-world puzzles may also be formulated when particular cases do not conform to expectations from existing theory or large-*N* research. For example, Atul Kohli and collaborators (2001) explore why India is a longstanding democracy despite being poor, ethnically diverse, and regionally divided.

Most CHA research is thus defined by certain scope conditions that delineate the range of cases to which the theory applies. Identifying these scope conditions is part of the process of specifying the context (i.e., the specific configuration of variables) within which the researcher believes his or her argument will be valid. Thus, rather than ask whether wars on average cause state building across all times and places, CHA researchers more typically ask whether wars contributed to state building for a specific set of cases situated in a specific context (e.g., Centeno 2003).

However, regardless of whether scope conditions are defined in narrow or broad terms, high-quality CHA research places great emphasis on *getting its cases right* – that is, developing a deep enough understanding of the case (often on the basis of different types of primary evidence) to adjudicate among competing hypotheses. In contrast to what Lieberman (Chapter 9, this volume) refers to as "mini-cases" invoked for illustrative or heuristic purposes, a good answer in CHA research must be able to withstand scrutiny when one brings more details of the case or cases at hand to bear. Explanations of particular empirical puzzles should not fall apart when these cases are examined again or by other scholars (including specialists) at close range. This requirement demands that CHA researchers become experts on those aspects of their cases relevant to the question under study.

In CHA, getting the cases right is not just essential for valid explanation; a deep understanding of actual – not stylized – cases is also what brings novel explanations to the fore. Working at close range allows scholars to identify new explanatory propositions that will not show up in mini-cases or in research organized around the coding of cases on predetermined independent variables of interest. As an example, consider the impact of Peter Swenson's (1991) research into the origins of democratic corporatism in the advanced industrial world. In the 1970s and 1980s, a large literature documented a strong correlation between the strength of the organized labor movement and the development of tripartite national bargaining associated with wage equality and other outcomes. Leading labor scholars inferred that these outcomes were a matter of labor strength over capital. On the basis of close analysis of two of the most critical cases in these debates, Denmark and Sweden, Swenson upended the conventional wisdom by revealing that specific segments of business were prime movers in the push for centralization. This work sparked a highly fruitful new round of further research – both qualitative and quantitative – that generated key insights into the role employers played in the origins of institutional arrangements that traditionally had been chalked up simply to labor strength. Whether scholars agreed or disagreed with his findings, Swenson's careful case-based research inspired a much broader research program that has taught us a great deal about employer preferences and the politics behind the genesis and reproduction of key political-economic institutions in the developed democracies (e.g., Broockman 2012; Iversen, Pontusson, and Soskice 2000; Mares 2003; Martin and Swank 2004).

Beyond its role in generating novel causal claims, CHA also produces conceptual innovations of broad applicability. Recent research on different modes of institutional change – such as Schickler's (2001) work on layering, Hacker's (2005) study of drift, and Thelen's (2004) analysis of conversion – provides an illustration. The discovery and elaboration of these concepts occurred in the context of detailed analyses of particular empirical puzzles. In the case of drift, for example, Hacker's close analysis of social policy in the United States challenged the conventional wisdom that popular social programs resist retrenchment. In particular, he showed that, in the face of consequential shifts in the social or market context, failing to update a policy can fundamentally alter its impact. In such instances, "doing nothing really means doing something, because stable policy rules produce shifting political outcomes" (Hacker and Pierson 2010, 2). Like conversion and layering, the concept of drift – though rooted and originally observed in a specific case – has in the meantime been adopted and applied much more widely. Work on drift has not just informed a new round of social policy research but also has been applied to explain outcomes ranging from corporate governance reform in Europe (Cioffi 2010) to the reconfiguration of business-state relations in Japan (Vogel 2006).[14]

In short, in addressing real-world puzzles, CHA research often generates new insights and thus creates new theory. These insights can then stimulate broader research agendas as they are taken up by scholars of diverse methodological orientations. Other CHA researchers may seek to assess an initial argument using new historical material or new cases. Statistical researchers may seek to test the generality of the argument – or aspects of the argument – using large-N data sets. Rational choice scholars may seek to specify the micro foundations of the new theory using their analytic and methodological toolkit. And scholars of all methodological orientations working on a wide range of empirical questions may gain new insights into their own cases through the application of the portable concepts and mechanisms that have emerged from CHA studies. The key point to underscore is the power and utility of local explanation in generating new theories that can set the research agenda for a broad range of scholars.

Empirical mechanisms

The quest to explain real-world puzzles in CHA yields explanations in which much attention centers on specifying the *mechanisms* through which causes and causal configurations exert effects within particular cases. In CHA, scholars distinguish incidental correlations from causal associations in part on the basis of whether mechanisms can be identified to explain the associations. When mechanisms cannot be found, researchers may eliminate potential explanations as spurious. Thus, in CHA, it is not sufficient to demonstrate that hypothesized causes covary with outcomes across cases. Rather, the researcher must provide the reasons why this is so by opening up the black box and identifying the steps that connect observed causes to observed outcomes.

In line with case-based research, CHA scholars study mechanisms by observing them at the level of individual cases: mechanisms are identified empirically rather than simply posited as plausible. The researcher may or may not anticipate in advance specific mechanisms and actively look for their presence; in fact some of the theoretical innovations mentioned earlier were uncovered in the process of explaining cases that did not conform to existing theory. The real requirement is that CHA researchers successfully identify linking processes concretely and in sufficient detail to

---

[14] In addition, prominent game theorists have been prompted to formalize Hacker's concept of drift. See Callander and Krehbiel (2013).

persuade others – including case experts – that the initial set of hypothesized causal factors actually contributed to the outcome. This kind of empirically grounded mechanism-based explanation requires delving into the details and thus demands a deep understanding of the cases under analysis.

As an example of this kind of explanation, consider Rueschemeyer, Stephens, and Stephens's (1992) *Capitalist Development and Democracy.* These authors follow a long line of research in noting an association between capitalist development and democracy. However, on the basis of close analysis of individual countries, they find that the effects of development on democracy are contingent on intervening mechanisms. For instance, development contributed to democracy in many cases of historical Europe because it strengthened pro-democratic working classes and weakened anti-democratic landed elites. Yet, in contemporary Latin America, the working class was not always democratically oriented, with the consequence that development often did not yield democracy. Through their empirical analysis of cases, therefore, Rueschemeyer, Stephens, and Stephens not only provide evidence about the mechanisms through which development contributed to democracy in certain historical settings but also arrive at new hypotheses about the specific circumstances under which development contributes to democracy.

A concern with empirical mechanisms within cases is closely associated with the use of process tracing in CHA. Scholars in this field develop and test alternative explanations in part by tracing the processes that link initial events to subsequent outcomes at the level of individual cases (Bennett 2008; Hall 2006; Mahoney 2012). To determine whether factors that covary are actually causally related, CHA scholars carry out process tracing tests, in which specific within-case observations – typically concerning empirical mechanisms – may count heavily for or against causal hypotheses. To identify these within-case observations, a deep knowledge of the history of the case is often essential. Scholars with case expertise have enormous advantages in locating those observations that prove most useful in explaining why an association between two variables is or is not causal in nature.

The discovery via process tracing of within-case observations concerning mechanisms can allow CHA researchers to reach strong conclusions about the validity of hypotheses for particular cases. At the same time, the process tracing of mechanisms within individual cases contributes to the theory-building capacity of CHA. For example, Slater, Smith, and Nair (2014) reject the finding of Acemoglu and Robinson (2006) that economic inequality contributes to military coups (see also Haggard and Kaufman 2012). They do so because, contrary to what Acemoglu and Robinson propose, their process tracing of cases shows that militaries do not act for or with economic elites. Instead, they find that the mechanism at work in their cases is related to weak state institutions: economic inequality and downturns produce coups when they weaken an already fragile state and provoke unhappy military officers. In short, the use of process tracing to assess explanations often goes hand in hand with an empirical analysis of causal mechanisms at the level of individual cases. The analysis of these mechanisms can serve both to test theories about those cases and to build new theories, including theories that often "travel" or generalize well beyond the cases studied.

Complementarities and trade-offs

It is useful to contrast CHA's approach to empirical cases to that of other modes of analysis. In much formal modeling research, empirical cases are invoked to illustrate or demonstrate the plausibility of a deductively derived theory. For example, in Acemoglu and Robinson's (2006) work on democracy, empirical cases serve an illustrative function. They are presented in highly stylized form, as vignettes whose purpose is to provide examples of broader ("general" and therefore often quite abstract) propositions – in this case revolving around the interactions of "elites" and "citizens." Virtually by design, empirical sketches that are meant to illustrate a theory cannot put that theory at risk, nor can they generate additional insights that might be used to refine or improve the theory. Because they do no real "work" in the analysis, stylized cases invoked as illustrations typically do not go deep enough to illuminate the causal mechanisms behind the theory in ways that then yield precise, testable hypotheses for others to pursue.

Contrast this to Swenson's case-based analysis, which offered concrete propositions – for example, the hypothesis that conflicts of interest between employers in sheltered and exposed sectors of the economy, not class conflict, drove the development of corporatism – that clearly invited or provoked others to explore further. The point we are making here might appear counterintuitive. It might seem logical to assume that the more "general" the theory, the more research it would inspire and the more fruitful the resulting research program. But we are suggesting something like the opposite: excellent case-based research in the CHA tradition stimulates further research and applications because it offers especially clear and empirically grounded causal claims. This concreteness (and not the "breadth" of the claims) is what invites other researchers to take up, test, refine, extend, and ultimately confirm or reject the original findings.

The advantages of this orientation for explanation should not to be taken for granted. A significant share of experimental research, for example, adopts a very different approach, reducing the goal of explanation to the identification of average treatment effects. As other observers have also pointed out, although experimental research can be good at measuring the presence or size of a treatment effect, it often fails to open the "black box" and show why the treatment has this effect. However, in an article whose title sums it up, "Enough Already About 'Black Box' Experiments," Donald Green and collaborators reject these criticisms of studies that do not specify the causal mechanisms that link a particular treatment to a particular effect (Green, Ha, and Bullock 2010). For them and others, establishing whether X exerts some influence on Y is the point of the exercise; the question of *why* X affects Y is a second-order concern, to be tackled in due course, but not as a first-order priority.[15]

The model that experimentalists often have in mind is the type of science employed in medical research, where one arguably often does not need to know why X affects Y. For example, if a medicine helps to remove certain symptoms across enough clinical trials, then it may well be a secondary concern why it has this effect. However, in the political world, where we cannot manipulate treatments in the vast majority of cases, it is quite a serious matter if we do not know why a particular cause produces a particular effect.[16] A failure to specify the mechanisms through which X affects Y means that we cannot anticipate how the relationship might be altered by other conditions (i.e., by "context"). Without an understanding of the reasons why X affects Y, we are also then often mystified when, in a different context, X fails to influence Y or perhaps even produces some unanticipated Z instead (see also Woolcock 2013). We therefore agree with Stokes (2014), who argues, "A causal effect that cannot be explained, cannot be identified, in any meaningful sense of that term" (51).[17]

---

[15] On the challenges of studying mediator variables with experiments (and the sometimes herculean assumptions this can entail), see Imai *et al.* (2011).

[16] This is the crux of Deaton's (2010) critique of the use of randomized controlled trial experiments in the study of development (see also Deaton 2014). He argues that, although randomized controlled treatment can help determine whether a particular project has been useful, it cannot say *why*. He thus advocates shifting the focus of research to investigate the (generalizable) mechanisms that explain why and in what contexts projects can be expected to promote development (2010, 6).

[17] Stokes (2014) suggests that in experimental research there are always unobserved interaction effects; average treatment effects mask what is possibly highly relevant variation across subpopulations. From a skeptical standpoint, therefore, "unobservable interactions always threaten the meaningfulness of causal inference based on experimental data" (47).

A striking feature of contemporary political science is the fervor over theory testing. The question of where new insights come from – where the seeds of new theories are cultivated – is often lost in the midst of this fervor. While political scientists are increasingly well equipped to test existing theories with ever more rigorous methods, they are often left adrift when their research turns up anomalies or unexpected null results. At this point, the search for explanations often becomes ad hoc, as researchers cast about to devise some story that is consistent with the data.

The trend toward big data is, if anything, likely to exacerbate the problem of theory generation in contemporary political science. Rational choice analysis was criticized for asking "theory-driven" questions and for posing problems that, as Shapiro (2004) has put it, are often "idiosyncratic artifacts of the researcher's theoretical priors" and whose answers therefore are unconvincing "to everyone except those who are wedded to [these] priors" (22–3). Experimental research has been criticized for asking "methods-driven" questions that generate unremarkable findings (Huber 2013). Although the big data movement may avoid the worst-case scenario of massive fishing expeditions, it is hard to imagine how it will avoid "data-driven" research programs. Having invested heavily in acquiring the skills needed to manipulate big data sets, scholars are understandably likely to gravitate toward questions on which they can bring these hard-won technical skills to bear.

CHA does not define itself primarily in terms of a single metatheory, a specific method, or a particular type of data. Scholars in this camp are typically quite pragmatic, even opportunistic, in these respects. Instead, CHA takes its questions from the empirical puzzles presented by the world around it, and scholars are often especially drawn to cases that do not fit dominant theoretical accounts. This orientation, we think, accounts for the central role that CHA has long played in generating new theoretical insights around which broader research communities form. Stephan Haggard's chapter provides an example. He documents the emergence of a large and fruitful research program on the "developmental state," as scholars grappled with cases that cast doubt on the longstanding orthodoxy that the state was "bad" for development. Drawing on a deep understanding of the operation of specific political economies such as Japan and South Korea, they generated fresh theoretical insights, introduced new concepts, and proposed new theories that then stimulated a vast research agenda spanning generations and methods. Developments such as this demonstrate that sometimes one can fully appreciate the value of CHA only by looking at the research it inspires – including, of course, by scholars who deploy different methods altogether.

Temporally oriented research

The third and final feature of CHA is *temporally oriented research*. CHA researchers assume that the study of temporal processes is essential for the valid understanding and explanation of real-world political outcomes. The reasons for this are several, and they go beyond the obvious point that establishing causality necessarily involves confirming that the hypothesized cause precedes its effect. CHA methods for temporal analysis reflect an ontology in which (1) temporal location shapes the effects of individual variables, and (2) the temporal structure of causes and outcomes matters for explanation and analysis. Let us again examine each of these points in turn.

Temporal location

In CHA, the effect of a variable may depend on its temporal location (e.g., Pierson 2004). The same variable can have different effects depending on *when* it occurs relative to other processes and events. Thus, CHA researchers pay close attention to the sequence in which variables appear and their timing relative to one another. In fact, placing an explanation "in context" often means situating variables in a particular temporal setting. In this sense, explanations in CHA are configurational not only because they consider combinations of causes operating at a given time but also because they consider combinations of causes located at different points in time (see Falleti and Mahoney, Chapter 8, this volume).

This insight about situating causes in time is central to a significant literature on path dependence in politics. Different scholars sometimes embrace somewhat different definitions, but a core claim that runs through virtually all of this work is the idea that early events in a path-dependent sequence exert a stronger causal impact on outcomes than later ones do.[18] With an increasing returns process, options that are available early on, but not chosen, recede as actors organize their strategies around the path "taken" in ways that render a return to the status quo ante more difficult over time (Pierson 2000). Power dynamics can follow a similar logic: early winners may gain resources and other advantages that make it difficult for losers to make a comeback (Mahoney 2000; Pierson, Chapter 5, this volume). These kinds of

---

[18] For a discussion of the different meanings assigned to path dependence as part of a taxonomy of forms of institutional change, see Rixen and Viola (2014).

path-dependent sequences can lock in outcomes over the long run, including suboptimal outcomes that do not serve important human interests or goals. Given the possibility of path dependence, much work in CHA focuses on identifying historical turning points or critical junctures when initial decisions or events occur to launch these sequences. These historical periods hold the selection processes and causes that explain how the long-run pattern was started in the first place.

Other CHA arguments analyze the unfolding of multiple processes in relation to one another. These arguments call attention to the effects of timing and ordering for outcomes of interest (Grzymala-Busse 2011). Consider, for example, Tulia Falleti's (2010) study of decentralization reforms in Latin America. Administrative decentralization reforms can either empower governors and mayors or weaken them depending on their position within an overall sequence of decentralization reforms. Likewise, consider Skowronek's (1982) landmark study of the "patchwork" American state. Skowronek shows that because the United States already had strong democratic politics prior to industrialization and the formation of bureaucracy, political parties were able to exert considerable control over the form of the emergent modern state. The US state developed not as an efficient and rational bureaucracy but instead as a complex amalgam of competing controls that partisans introduced piecemeal over time.

Another variant of sequencing arguments concerns the analysis of conjunctures in which two or more causes come together in time. The precise timing of that intersection may matter a great deal for the effect of the conjuncture. For example, the historical "collision" of the launch of Lyndon B. Johnson's War on Poverty with the urban riots of the mid-1960s powerfully shaped the political fate of social policy in the United States. The redirection of newly introduced social programs to address the problems of African Americans in the country's impoverished urban centers "strengthened the remedial focus of labor market policy and . . . encouraged the creation of separate, racially focused programs" – developments that left such policies politically vulnerable in the long run (Weir 1992, 165–6).

CHA researchers are sensitive to the effects of temporal location because they view their cases historically and situate them in the context of sequences of unfolding events. This orientation is in fact essential for valid explanation in this field. It is thus not incidental that CHA scholars are responsible for developing many of our most powerful analytic tools for the study of temporal location: critical junctures (Capoccia and Keleman 2007; Collier and Collier 1991; Slater and Simmons 2010; Soifer 2012); path dependence

(Alexander 2001; Boas 2007; Mahoney 2000; Pierson 2000); and timing, sequence, and conjuncture (Abbott 2001; Aminzade 1992; Büthe 2002; Grzymala-Busse 2011; Pierson 2004; Rueschemeyer and Stephens 1997). These tools provide concepts for framing and structuring explanations in CHA, and they also provide a basis for comparing CHA works. One can, for example, distinguish CHA studies from one another based on whether they adopt a critical juncture approach or analyze path-dependent processes. Works with quite diverse substantive content can speak to one another because they use the same temporal constructs or adopt the same analytic-temporal framework in formulating their explanations.

Temporal structure

CHA also recognizes explicitly that variables and processes themselves have a temporal structure. A given causal factor or a given process of change may vary in its duration or pace, and these variations may be highly consequential.[19] Thus, one must not only ask whether some process or event occurred at a given intensity but also inquire about the temporal dimensions of its occurrence. How fast or slow does a given process unfold? How long does a given event endure? What is the pace of a causal process? These questions are addressed both because temporal structure can shape the form and nature of causal effects and because the temporal structure of events and processes can be important outcomes worthy of explanation in their own right.

The CHA concern with temporal structure means that works in this tradition take notice of gradual, slow-moving, and hard-to-see causal processes. Pierson's chapter (this volume) provides multiple examples of the operation of power dynamics through which, over time, some options, issues, or viewpoints come to be "organized out of politics" altogether. These "hidden" dimensions of power can be seen only by examining processes as they unfold over time; they remain invisible in studies that adopt a short-run time horizon. The broader temporal range of much of CHA also allows analysts to recover the impact of distal causal processes that alternative approaches are similarly ill suited to capture. For example, in Yashar's (2005) work, the causal process driving indigenous protest in Latin America unfolds over a period of decades. Yashar shows that corporatist structures that were originally created

---

[19] This insight – central to Pierson's (2004) path-breaking work on temporality – has in the meantime been taken up by quantitative researchers who criticize what Pierson called "snapshot" causal inference methods as inappropriate for the analysis of dynamic political processes (e.g., Blackwell 2013).

to turn Indians into national citizens in fact had the opposite effect: they depoliticized ethnic cleavages by sheltering indigenous communities. As a result, when neoliberal reforms slowly eroded those protections, identities were repoliticized, culminating in a wave of indigenous organization and protest. Thus, what might seem like suddenly emerging revolts are in fact better conceived as products of a slow-moving causal process dating to the end of the corporatist period.

Other work in the CHA tradition shows that when a given event or process endures over a long time, it is more likely to trigger a tipping point or set into motion a process of diffusion or accumulation (Grzymala-Busse 2011, 1279). A substantive example is Huber and Stephens's (2001) study of the effect of long-term social democratic control of government for welfare state outcomes. Although a single election result does not shape institutional patterns, electoral success over the long run produces a "ratcheting" effect in which welfare policies that were initially controversial become entrenched and form the point of departure for subsequent debates. To take another example that emphasizes pace: Mark Beissinger (2009) uses event data and case studies to explore the dynamics through which some but not all communist regimes collapsed in the wake of the fall of the Berlin Wall. He draws attention to "streams of activity in which action in one context profoundly affected action in other contexts," producing a tide of changes that unfolded at different paces in different countries (1).

Just as "causes" have temporal dimensions that can affect ultimate outcomes, "effects," too, have temporal structures that are consequential for political analysis. One of the major lessons of the literature on feedback effects is that phenomena of interest to political scientists may emerge only slowly over time (Pierson 2004). For example, the political impact of policies such as the introduction of supplemental (private) retirement accounts manifests only gradually as enrollments increase and growing numbers of citizens become invested – financially and politically – in the fate of these programs (Hacker 2005; Jacobs 2012).

In this volume, Hacker, Pierson, and Thelen examine the key properties of two forms of gradual change that fly under the radar in most political science analyses. They characterize drift and conversion as strategies through which actors can quietly promote significant changes in political outcomes and whose effects emerge only slowly beneath the veneer of apparent institutional stability. Drift occurs when policies or institutions are deliberately held in place even as shifts in the broader political or economic context alter their effects – for example, as demographic or technological changes render existing regulatory regimes ineffective. Virtually by definition, the political consequences of these processes come into view only when one adopts a long-term time horizon. Similarly, the conversion of existing institutions and policies to promote goals that are often radically different from the ones for which they were created often proceeds only very gradually, for example, through the accumulation of new legal interpretations of existing rules or the application of old rules to new problems.

By focusing on the temporal structure of causal processes and effects, CHA scholars have initiated a broad conversation about typical patterns of institutional change. Some writings on path dependence have called attention to a mode of discontinuous change in which a brief episode of rapid transformation is followed by a long period of stability. CHA is well adapted to the study of such developments because of its concern with the analysis of critical junctures and of long-run causal patterns. At the same time, however, other CHA scholarship has emphasized various slow-moving processes that do not evoke this kind of punctuated equilibrium conception of change (e.g., Pierson 2004). These works show how gradual change is a quite common mode of institutional evolution in the political world (Thelen 1999, 2003, 2004), and as a result scholars now often also consider the ways in which long-run processes may be marked by incremental change within the constraints of path dependence.

Recent attention to processes of gradual institutional change has stimulated an important new theoretical and empirical literature (Mahoney and Thelen 2010a; Streeck and Thelen 2005). This literature has evolved from the identification of typical modes of gradual change (e.g., layering, drift, and conversion) to the development of hypotheses about the causes of particular types of change. The new work offers configurational explanations in which both structural contexts and particular kinds of actors combine to produce particular modes of gradual transformation (Hacker, Pierson, and Thelen, Chapter 7, this volume; Mahoney and Thelen 2010b). It is no coincidence that CHA is at the forefront of this exploration of gradual change: even to be able to "see" how incremental changes can cumulate into significant transformations requires one to adopt the long time horizon characteristic of CHA. Approaches that focus only on short-term effects are blind to such gradually unfolding modes of institutional change.

Complementarities and trade-offs

CHA has not been alone in focusing attention on issues of temporality. Beginning in the 1990s, political science as a whole witnessed what might be thought of as a "temporal revolution," a movement in which CHA itself was a central initiator. The temporal revolution in political science reflected a broad chorus reacting to the deficits of viewing politics in cross-sectional, one-off, snapshot ways (see, e.g., Hall 2003; Pierson 2004). The consequence of this movement was unmistakable: it moved temporal analysis into the mainstream of political science, as scholars from a range of methodological approaches brought "time" more centrally into the analysis of politics.[20]

The innovations that grew out of this increased focus on temporality varied across alternative approaches, but they often complemented one another in converging on the idea that time and history are important for the study of politics. In CHA, as we have seen, scholars amplified their focus on long-standing themes and introduced new tools for the study of timing, sequencing, and temporal structure. Statistical researchers contributed to the revolution by developing new longitudinal techniques, making methods such as time-series cross-sectional analysis the norm and advancing new tools rooted in Bayesian statistics (e.g., Beck 2008; Blackwell 2013). Along with these changes, statistical researchers increasingly asked questions about the effects of "historical" causes, such as colonialism, early state formation, and past democratic experience. To carry out tests, these researchers drew on new data sets that often coded cases far into the past. For their part, game theorists formulated new iterative and evolutionary approaches to rigorously consider sequences of strategic choices in which ordering and timing matter (e.g., Smith and Price 1973; Weibull 1997). Some game theorists also became interested in asking historically oriented questions and in using historical sources in their work. Among the results of these developments, the "analytic narrative" approach (Bates *et al.* 2000) and the historical analyses of economists such as Greif (2006) have some parallels with CHA-type work.

Current disciplinary trends, however, threaten to undo the achievements of the temporal revolution. Many of the long-term causal processes that we know to be central to much of politics are not amenable to methods that focus mainly on short-run processes. Unfortunately, most experimental work pulls us back to the analysis of causal processes and outcomes that unfold entirely over short periods of time. In such studies, time stands still because it is possible to isolate the effect of a treatment only where the intervention is

---

[20] Sociologists participated in and contributed to these developments. By contrast, the trend did not extend as deeply into economics, though there are exceptions. Some of the most arresting findings to emerge from Thomas Piketty's (2014) celebrated *Capital in the Twenty-First Century* flow from his having simply situated the current period in a longer time frame. The book thus demonstrates that very different patterns come into view if you pan out from the micro focus that is characteristic of most mainstream economics to track macro processes as they unfold over time.

proximate enough to the effect to rule out other possible intervening variables. The result is again a narrowing of our field of vision, as scholars zero in on the immediate impact of a particular intervention and as large-scale institutional, demographic, and economic trends drop out of view.[21]

Equally important, one-off treatments often generate findings that systematically overlook causal processes that unfold over time and that affect the very outcomes these experiments are designed to explore. This problem is especially easy to spot in experiments that seek to establish the impact of "participation" or "democracy" in contexts that do not feature homegrown participatory or democratic institutions (e.g., Grossman and Baldassarri 2012; Gugerty and Kremer 2008; Khwaga 2009). Many such experiments introduce (through treatment) democratic or participatory practices to test their impact on local political dynamics. The effects sometimes reach statistical significance, but often they are substantively very small and almost always of questionable durability. Even the most serious treatment interventions frequently produce similarly modest and mixed results. Consider, for example, a recent study of democratic participation and gender relations in traditionally religiously conservative settings, conducted in the context of development initiatives in Afghanistan. The treatment was to mandate female participation in village councils to see whether this form of involvement could lead to greater empowerment of women. While these initiatives produced modest improvements in self-reported attitudes toward female participation, they did not produce any change "in more entrenched female roles . . . or in attitudes toward the general role of women in society" (Beath, Christia, and Enikolopov 2013, 540).

Such studies are of value for program evaluation purposes, in this case, for example, underscoring the resilience of local institutions in the face of third-party interventions. However, from a more process-sensitive perspective, the observed outcomes are predictable. When institutions are introduced (treatment style) into a new context, they are unlikely to produce an impact precisely because what also matters is the process through which these institutions themselves emerge. The endogenous political processes through which democratic institutions arrive (historically speaking, often involving prolonged conflict and struggle), as much as the institutions themselves, are what produce the ultimate effects – through the way these processes

---

[21] Although they do not typically concern themselves with possible long-term causes, experimentalists do worry about the duration of their results – for good reason, because it turns out that the effects of many treatments fade away relatively quickly (e.g., Druckman and Leeper 2012). When it comes to much experimental work, therefore, it seems that a few weeks or months constitute the new *longue durée*.

transform citizen expectations and reconfigure social and political dynamics (see, e.g., Baiocchi, Heller, and Silva 2011).

Research organized around understanding short-term processes and outcomes has a place in the discipline. However, the costs to embracing approaches to politics that ignore long-term processes and causal relationships are significant. As Pierson (2004, 81) has pointed out, there is no reason to think that the most important or the most interesting political dynamics can be captured by accounts that are wedded to a short-run temporal structure. The radical renarrowing of our field of vision imposes severe casualties, as causes and outcomes that unfold only gradually and over long periods of time fall from view and as attention comes to be focused more narrowly on variables that, although temporally proximate to the outcome of interest, may actually play a relatively minor role in explaining this outcome (Pierson 2004, 101–2).

Conclusion

This introduction has traced the resiliency and vibrancy of comparative-historical analysis back to the core features that define this approach. Against the backdrop of the ongoing methodological ferment that characterizes political science, one of the strengths of CHA has been its adaptability, born of an openness to engage with scholars from other approaches on substantive issues where complementarities can be leveraged to mutual advantage. CHA and large-N research are in some ways the most natural complements. The strengths of CHA (internal validity) are the mirror image of those of large-N research (external validity), and so these two research streams are especially able to build on each other's findings in productive ways.[22] We see overall fewer complementarities with experimental work, partly because the strengths of that line of scholarship (internal validity) and its weaknesses (external validity) are largely the same as those of CHA. While we worry about the tendencies of experimental research to narrow our research programs and temporal field of vision, we do see potential synergies with quasi-experimental designs (natural experiments, matching, regression discontinuity) and can imagine how experimental work might be useful for testing particular modules in CHA theories. Likewise, big data might also be a useful complement to CHA, for

---

[22] But see Slater and Ziblatt (2013) for a somewhat different view. They see the kind of "controlled case comparisons" that we associate with CHA as strong on both internal and external validity, and they note that in multimethod research, case comparisons are often used to establish external, not internal, validity.

example, as scholars deploy new possibilities to scan and analyze historical and other documents. CHA thrives partly because it is pragmatic, and the field will surely be open to incorporating any insights that might emerge from these other lines of scholarship that are helpful for answering macrolevel questions.

At the same time, however, CHA has been robust because the best work in this tradition remains true to core features that link it to the classics and that continue to define CHA as an approach – its focus on macroconfigurational explanation, its emphasis on deep case-based research, and its attention to process and the temporal dimensions of politics. While we have separated these three dimensions for purposes of exposition, in fact they exhibit strong complementarities and they are thus closely linked in the actual conduct of CHA research. Macroconfigurational explanations often have a strong temporal dimension, because the timing and sequencing of relevant events form part of the context that produces the outcome of interest. Likewise, deep case-based research facilitates the identification of causal mechanisms and interactions among different variables and processes as these unfold in time. We have argued that the core features that define CHA, taken singly and in combination, endow this approach with real advantages relative to other perspectives. The distinctive insights that emerge from this stream of scholarship, we think, contribute mightily to CHA's continuing intellectual attraction and larger disciplinary impact, as others with different tools take up the agendas initiated by CHA scholars.

At the end of the day, our view is that the most productive research communities are not so much those that are defined by a particular technique but instead those in which scholars – possibly armed with quite different methods – are all united by a shared desire to understand substantively big and important problems. Scholars coming out of different research traditions certainly do not have to agree with one another. However, to the extent that they share a common concern with addressing major questions of enduring significance and consider both micro processes and broader structural factors, they can take notice of each other's findings and use and engage them in their own work.

Appendix A
Recent Award-Winning CHA Books in Political Science, 2000–2014

Beissinger, Mark. 2002. *Nationalist Mobilization and the Collapse of the Soviet State.* Cambridge: Cambridge University Press.

Capoccia, Giovanni. 2005. *Defending Democracy: Reactions to Extremism in Interwar Europe*. Baltimore: Johns Hopkins University Press.

Carpenter, Daniel P. 2001. *The Forging of Bureaucratic Autonomy: Reputations, Networks, and Policy Innovation in Executive Agencies, 1862–1928*. Princeton, NJ: Princeton University Press.

2010. *Reputation and Power: Organizational Image and Pharmaceutical Regulation at the FDA*. Princeton, NJ: Princeton University Press.

Christia, Fotini. 2012. *Alliance Formation in Civil Wars*. New York: Cambridge University Press.

Clemens, Elisabeth S., and Doug Guthrie, eds. 2010. *Politics and Partnerships: The Role of Voluntary Associations in America's Political Past and Present*. Chicago: University of Chicago Press.

Culpepper, Pepper D. 2010. *Quiet Politics and Business Power: Corporate Control in Europe and Japan*. New York: Cambridge University Press.

Falleti, Tulia G. 2010. *Decentralization and Subnational Politics in Latin America*. Cambridge: Cambridge University Press.

Gottschalk, Marie. 2006. *The Prison and the Gallows: The Politics of Mass Incarceration in America*. New York: Cambridge University Press.

Grzymala-Busse, Anna Maria. 2007. *Rebuilding Leviathan: Party Competition and State Exploitation in Post-Communist Democracies*. New York: Cambridge University Press.

Herbst, Jeffrey. 2000. *States and Power in Africa: Comparative Lessons in Authority and Control*. Princeton, NJ: Princeton University Press.

Huber, Evelyne, and John D. Stephens. 2001. *Development and Crisis of the Welfare State: Parties and Policies in Global Markets*. Chicago: University of Chicago Press.

Jacobs, Alan M. 2011. *Governing for the Long Term: Democracy and the Politics of Investment*. New York: Cambridge University Press.

Katznelson, Ira. 2013. *Fear Itself: The New Deal and the Origins of Our Time*. New York: W. W. Norton.

Kohli, Atul. 2004. *State-Directed Development: Political Power and Industrialization in the Global Periphery*. New York: Cambridge University Press.

Krippner, Greta R. 2011. *Capitalizing on Crisis: The Political Origins of the Rise of Finance*. Cambridge, MA: Harvard University Press.

Levitsky, Steven, and Lucan A. Way. 2010. *Competitive Authoritarianism: Hybrid Regimes After the Cold War*. Cambridge: Cambridge University Press.

Lieberman, Evan. 2003. *Race and Regionalism in the Politics of Taxation in Brazil and South Africa*. New York: Cambridge University Press.

2009. *Boundaries of Contagion: How Ethnic Politics Have Shaped Government Responses to AIDS*. Princeton, NJ: Princeton University Press.

Lynch, Julia. 2006. *Age in the Welfare State: The Origins of Social Spending on Pensioners, Workers, and Children*. New York: Cambridge University Press.

Mahoney, James. 2001. *The Legacies of Liberalism: Path Dependence and Political Regimes in Central America*. Baltimore: Johns Hopkins University Press.

2010. *Colonialism and Postcolonial Development Spanish America in Comparative Perspective*. New York: Cambridge University Press.

Mann, Michael. 2005. *The Dark Side of Democracy: Explaining Ethnic Cleansing.* New York: Cambridge University Press.

Martin, Cathie Jo, and Duane Swank. 2012. *The Political Construction of Business Interests: Coordination, Growth, and Equality.* New York: Cambridge University Press.

Meierhenrich, Jens. 2008. *The Legacies of Law: Long-Run Consequences of Legal Development in South Africa, 1652–2000.* New York: Cambridge University Press.

Mettler, Suzanne. 2005. *Soldiers to Citizens: The G.I. Bill and the Making of the Greatest Generation.* New York: Oxford University Press.

2011. *The Submerged State: How Invisible Government Policies Undermine American Democracy.* Chicago: University of Chicago Press.

Murillo, Maria Victoria. 2001. *Labor Unions, Partisan Coalitions, and Market Reforms in Latin America.* New York: Cambridge University Press.

Pierson, Paul. 2004. *Politics in Time.* Princeton, NJ: Princeton University Press.

Prasad, Monica. 2006. *Politics of the Free Market: The Rise of Neoliberal Economic Policies in Britain, France, Germany, and the United States.* Chicago: University of Chicago Press.

2013. *The Land of Too Much: American Abundance and the Paradox of Poverty.* Cambridge, MA: Harvard University Press.

Sheingate, Adam. 2001. *The Rise of the Agricultural Welfare State: Institutions and Interest Group Power in the United States, France, and Japan.* Princeton, NJ: Princeton University Press.

Skocpol, Theda. 2003. *Diminished Democracy: From Membership to Management in American Civic Life.* Tulsa: University of Oklahoma Press.

Skocpol, Theda, Ariane Liazos, and Marshall Ganz. 2006. *What a Mighty Power We Can Be: African American Fraternal Groups and the Struggle for Racial Equality.* Princeton, NJ: Princeton University Press.

Slater, Dan. 2010. *Ordering Power: Contentious Politics and Authoritarian Leviathans in Southeast Asia.* New York: Cambridge University Press.

Spruyt, Hendrik. 2005. *Ending Empire: Contested Sovereignty and Territorial Partition.* Ithaca, NY: Cornell University Press.

Steinmo, Sven. 2010. *The Evolution of Modern States: Sweden, Japan, and the United States.* New York: Cambridge University Press.

Streeck, Wolfgang. 2014. *Buying Time: The Delayed Crisis of Democratic Capitalism.* New York: Verso.

Swenson, Peter. 2002. *Capitalists against Markets: The Making of Labor Markets and Welfare States in the United States and Sweden.* New York: Oxford University Press.

Thelen, Kathleen. 2004. *How Institutions Evolve: The Political Economy of Skills in Germany, Britain, the United States, and Japan.* New York: Cambridge University Press.

Tsai, Lily. 2007. *Accountability without Democracy: Solidarity Groups and Public Goods Provision in Rural China.* New York: Cambridge University Press.

van de Walle, Nicolas. 2001. *African Economies and the Politics of Permanent Crisis, 1979–1999.* Cambridge: Cambridge University Press.

Varshney, Ashutosh. 2001. *Ethnic Conflict and Civic Life: Hindus and Muslims in India.* New Haven, CT: Yale University Press.

Winters, Jeffrey A. 2011. *Oligarchy.* New York: Cambridge University Press.

Wood, Elisabeth Jean. 2003. *Insurgent Collective Action and Civil War in El Salvador.* New York: Cambridge University Press.

Yashar, Deborah J. 2005. *Contesting Citizenship in Latin America: The Rise of Indigenous Movements and the Postliberal Challenge.* New York: Cambridge University Press.

Ziblatt, Daniel. 2006. *Structuring the State: The Formation of Italy and Germany and the Puzzle of Federalism.* Princeton, NJ: Princeton University Press.

References

Abbott, Andrew. 1997. "Of Time and Space." *Social Forces* 75 (4): 1149–82.

2001. *Time Matters: On Theory and Method.* Chicago: University of Chicago Press.

Acemoglu, Daron, and James A. Robinson. 2006. *Economic Origins of Dictatorship and Democracy.* New York: Cambridge University Press.

Alexander, Gerard. 2001. "Institutions, Path Dependence, and Democratic Consolidation." *Journal of Theoretical Politics* 13 (3): 249–70.

Amenta, Edwin. 2003. "What We Know about the Development of Social Policy: Comparative and Historical Research in Comparative and Historical Perspective." In *Comparative Historical Analysis in the Social Sciences*, edited by James Mahoney and Dietrich Rueschemeyer, 91–130. New York: Cambridge University Press.

Aminzade, Ronald. 1992. "Historical Sociology and Time." *Sociological Methods and Research* 20:456–80.

Baiocchi, Gianpaolo, Patrick Heller, and Marcelo K. Silva. 2011. *Bootstrapping Democracy: Transforming Local Governance and Civil Society in Brazil.* Stanford, CA: Stanford University Press.

Bates, Robert H., Avner Greif, Margaret Levi, Jean-Laurent Rosenthal, and Barry Weingast. 2000. "The Analytic Narrative Project." *American Political Science Review* 94 (3): 696–702.

Beath, Andrew, Fotini Christia, and Ruben Enikolopov. 2013. "Empowering Women through Development Aid: Evidence from a Field Experiment in Afghanistan." *American Political Science Review* 107 (3): 540–57.

Beck, Nathaniel. 2008. "Time-Series Cross-Sectional Analysis." In *Oxford Handbook of Political Methodology*, edited by Janet Box-Steffensmeier, Henry E. Brady, and David Collier, 475–93. Oxford: Oxford University Press.

Beissinger, Mark R. 2009. "Nationalism and the Collapse of Soviet Communism." *Contemporary European History* 18 (3): 331–47.

Bennett, Andrew. 2008. "Process Tracing: A Bayesian Perspective." In *The Oxford Handbook of Political Methodology*, edited by Janet Box-Steffensmeier, Henry E. Brady, and David Collier, 217–70. Oxford: Oxford University Press.

Blackwell, Matthew. 2013. "A Framework for Dynamic Causal Inference in Political Science." *American Journal of Political Science* 57 (2): 504–20.

Boas, Taylor. 2007. "Conceptualizing Continuity and Change: The Composite-Standard Model of Path Dependence." *Journal of Theoretical Politics* 19 (1): 33–54.

Broockman, David. 2012. "The Problem of Preferences: Medicare and Business Support for the Welfare State." *Studies in American Political Development* 26 (2): 83–106.

Büthe, Tim. 2002. "Taking Temporality Seriously: Modeling History and the Use of Narratives as Evidence." *American Political Science Review* 96 (3): 481–94.

Callander, Steven, and Keith Krehbiel. 2013. "Gridlock and Delegation in a Changing World." Unpublished manuscript, March 1. Stanford Business School.

Capoccia, Giovanni, and Daniel Keleman. 2007. "The Study of Critical Junctures: Theory, Narrative, and Counterfactuals in Historical Institutionalism." *World Politics* 59 (3): 341–69.

Centeno, Miguel Angel. 2003. *Blood and Debt: War and the Nation-State in Latin America.* University Park: Penn State University Press.

Cioffi, John W. 2010. *Public Law and Private Power: The Comparative Political Economy of Corporate Governance Reform in the Age of Finance Capitalism.* Ithaca, NY: Cornell University Press.

Coleman, James S. 1990. *Foundations of Social Theory.* Cambridge, MA: Belknap Press of Harvard University Press.

Collier, Ruth Berins, and David Collier. 1991. *Shaping the Political Arena: Critical Junctures, the Labor Movement, and Regime Dynamics in Latin America.* Princeton, NJ: Princeton University Press.

Deaton, Angus. 2010. "Instruments, Randomization, and Learning about Development." *Journal of Economic Literature* 48 (2): 424–55.

  2014. "Instruments, Randomization, and Learning about Development." In *Field Experiments and Their Critics: Essays on the Uses and Abuses of Experimentation in the Social Sciences,* edited by Dawn Langan Teele, 141–84. New Haven, CT: Yale University Press.

Druckman, James, Donald P. Green, James H. Kuklinski, and Arthur Lupia, eds. 2011. *Cambridge Handbook of Experimental Political Science.* New York: Cambridge University Press.

Druckman, James N., and Thomas Leeper. 2012. "Learning More from Political Communication Experiments: Pretreatment and Its Effects." *American Journal of Political Science* 56 (4): 875–96.

Dunning, Thad. 2012. *Natural Experiments in the Social Sciences.* New York: Cambridge University Press.

Eckel, Catherine D., Enrique Fatas, and Rick Wilson. 2010. "Cooperation and Status in Organizations." *Journal of Public Economic Theory* 12 (4): 737–62.

Elster, Jon. 1982. "The Case for Methodological Individualism." *Theory and Society* 11 (4): 453–82.

Falleti, Tulia G. 2010. *Decentralization and Subnational Politics in Latin America.* New York: Cambridge University Press.

Falleti, Tulia G., and Julia F. Lynch. 2009. "Context and Causal Mechanisms in Political Analysis." *Comparative Political Studies* 42 (9): 1143–66.

Friedman, Jeffrey. 1996. *The Rational Choice Controversy.* New Haven, CT: Yale University Press.

Fukuyama, Francis. 2013. "Albert O. Hirschman, 1915–2012." *The American Interest* (March/April): 93–95.

Gerber, Alan S., Donald P. Green, and Edward H. Kaplan. 2014. "The Illusion of Learning from Observational Research." In *Field Experiments and Their Critics: Essays on the Uses and Abuses of Experimentation in the Social Sciences*, edited by Dawn Langan Teele, 9–32. New Haven, CT: Yale University Press.

Goldstone, Jack A. 2003. "Comparative Historical Analysis and Knowledge Accumulation in the Study of Revolutions." In *Comparative Historical Analysis in the Social Sciences*, edited by James Mahoney and Dietrich Rueschemeyer, 41–90. New York: Cambridge University Press.

Green, Donald P., Shang E. Ha, and John G. Bullock. 2010. "Enough Already about 'Black Box' Experiments: Studying Mediation Is More Difficult Than Most Scholars Suppose." *Annals of the American Academy of Political and Social Science* 628:200–8.

Green, Donald, and Ian Shapiro. 1994. *Pathologies of Rational Choice Theory: A Critique of Applications in Political Science*. New Haven, CT: Yale University Press.

Greif, Avner. 2006. *Institutions and the Path to the Modern Economy: Lessons from Medieval Trade*. New York: Cambridge University Press.

Grossman, Guy, and Delia Baldassarri. 2012. "The Impact of Elections on Cooperation: Evidence from a Lab-in-the-Field Experiment in Uganda." *American Journal of Political Science* 56 (4): 964–85.

Grzymala-Busse, Anna. 2011. "Time Will Tell? Temporality and the Analysis of Causal Mechanisms and Processes." *Comparative Political Studies* 44:1267–97.

Gugerty, M. K., and M. Kremer. 2008. "Outside Funding and the Dynamics of Participation in Community Associations." *American Journal of Political Science* 52:585–602.

Hacker, Jacob. 2005. "Policy Drift: The Hidden Politics of US Welfare State Retrenchment." In *Beyond Continuity: Institutional Change in Advanced Political Economies*, edited by Wolfgang Streeck and Kathleen Thelen, 40–82. Oxford: Oxford University Press.

Hacker, Jacob, and Paul Pierson. 2010. "Drift and Democracy: The Neglected Politics of Policy Inaction." Paper presented at the Annual Meeting of the American Political Science Association, Washington, DC, September 2–5.

Haggard, Stephan, and Robert R. Kaufman. 2012. "Inequality and Regime Change: Democratic Transitions and the Stability of Democratic Rule." *American Political Science Review* 106 (3): 495–516.

Hall, Peter. 2003. "Aligning Ontology and Methodology in Comparative Research." In *Comparative Historical Analysis in the Social Sciences*, edited by James Mahoney and Dietrich Rueschemeyer, 373–404. New York: Cambridge University Press.

    2006. "Systematic Process Analysis: When and How to Use It." *European Management Review* 3:24–31.

Hall, Peter, and David Soskice. 2001. *Varieties of Capitalism: The Institutional Foundations of Comparative Advantage*. Oxford: Oxford University Press.

Hodgson, Geoffrey M. 2007. "Meanings of Methodological Individualism." *Journal of Economic Methodology* 14 (2): 211–26.

Huber, Evelyne, and John D. Stephens. 2001. *Development and Crisis of the Welfare State: Parties and Policies in Global Markets*. Chicago: University of Chicago Press.

Huber, John. 2013. "Is Theory Getting Lost in the 'Identification Revolution?'" *The Political Economist: Newsletter of the Section on Political Economy* 10 (1): 1–3.

Imai, Kosuke, Luke Keele, Dustin Tingley, and Teppei Yamamoto. 2011. "Unpacking the Black Box of Causality: Learning about Causal Mechanisms from Experimental and Observational Studies." *American Political Science Review* 105 (4): 765–89.

Iversen, Torben, Jonas Pontusson, and David Soskice. 2000. *Unions, Employers, and Central Banks: Wage Bargaining and Macroeconomic Regimes in an Integrating Europe*. New York: Cambridge University Press.

Iversen, Torben, and David Soskice. 2001. "An Asset Theory of Social Policy Preferences." *American Political Science Review* 95 (4): 875–93.

2006. "Electoral Institutions and the Politics of Coalitions." *American Political Science Review* 100 (2): 165–81.

Jacobs, Alan M. 2012. *Governing for the Long Term: Democracy and the Politics of Investment*. New York: Cambridge University Press.

Kam, Cindy D., and Robert J. Franzese Jr. 2007. *Modeling and Interpreting Interactive Hypotheses in Regression Analysis*. Ann Arbor: University of Michigan Press.

Khwaga, A. I. 2009. "Can Good Projects Succeed in Bad Communities?" *Journal of Public Economics* 93(7–8): 899–916.

King, Gary. 2014. "Restructuring the Social Sciences: Reflections from Harvard's Institute for Quantitative Social Science." *PS: Political Science and Politics* 47 (1): 165–76.

Kohli, Atul, ed. 2001. *The Success of India's Democracy*. New York: Cambridge University Press.

Levitsky, Steven, and Lucan A. Way. 2010. *Competitive Authoritarianism: Hybrid Regimes After the Cold War*. New York: Cambridge University Press.

Lijphart, Arend. 1971. "Comparative Politics and the Comparative Method." *American Political Science Review* 65 (3): 682–93.

Little, Daniel. 2012. "Explanatory Autonomy and Coleman's Boat." *Theoria* 74:137–51.

Lukes, Steven. 1968. "Methodological Individualism Reconsidered." *British Journal of Sociology* 19 (2): 119–29.

Mahoney, James. 2000. "Path Dependence in Historical Sociology." *Theory and Society* 29:507–48.

2001. *The Legacies of Liberalism: Path Dependence and Political Regimes in Central America*. Baltimore: Johns Hopkins University Press.

2003. "Knowledge Accumulation in Comparative Historical Research: The Case of Democracy and Authoritarianism." In *Comparative Historical Analysis in the Social Sciences*, edited by James Mahoney and Dietrich Rueschemeyer, 131–75. New York: Cambridge University Press.

2012. "The Logic of Process Tracing Tests in the Social Sciences." *Sociological Methods and Research* 41:566–90.

Mahoney, James, and Dietrich Rueschemeyer, eds. 2003. *Comparative Historical Analysis in the Social Sciences*. New York: Cambridge University Press.

Mahoney, James, and Kathleen Thelen, eds. 2010a. *Explaining Institutional Change: Ambiguity, Agency, and Power*. New York: Cambridge University Press.

Mahoney, James, and Kathleen Thelen. 2010b. "A Theory of Gradual Institutional Change." In *Explaining Institutional Change: Ambiguity, Agency, and Power*, edited by James Mahoney and Kathleen Thelen, 1–37. Cambridge: Cambridge University Press.

Mares, Isabela. 2003. *The Politics of Social Risk: Business and Welfare State Development*. New York: Cambridge University Press.

Martin, Cathie Jo, and Duane Swank. 2004. "Does the Organization of Capital Matter? Employers and the Active Labor Market Policy at the National and Firms Levels." *American Political Science Review* 98 (4): 593–611.

Morton, Rebecca B., and Kenneth C. Williams. 2010. *Experimental Political Science and the Study of Causality: From Nature to the Lab.* Cambridge: Cambridge University Press.

O'Donnell, Guillermo. 1973. *Modernization and Bureaucratic-Authoritarianism: Studies in South American Politics.* Berkeley: Institute of International Studies, University of California.

Pierson, Paul. 2000. "Increasing Returns, Path Dependence, and the Study of Politics." *American Political Science Review* 94:251–67.

   2004. *Politics in Time: History, Institutions, and Social Analysis.* Princeton, NJ: Princeton University Press.

   2007. "The Costs of Marginalization: Qualitative Methods in the Study of American Politics." *Comparative Political Studies* 40 (2): 146–69.

Pierson, Paul, and Theda Skocpol. 2002. "Historical Institutionalism in Contemporary Political Science." In *Political Science: The State of the Discipline*, edited by Ira Katznelson and Helen Milner, 693–721. New York: W. W. Norton.

Piketty, Thomas. 2014. *Capital in the Twenty-First Century.* Cambridge, MA: Belknap Press of Harvard University Press.

Ragin, Charles C. 1987. *The Comparative Method: Moving Beyond Qualitative and Quantitative Strategies.* Berkeley: University of California Press.

Rixen, Thomas, and Lora Anne Viola. 2014. "Putting Path Dependence in Its Place: Toward a Taxonomy of Institutional Change." *Journal of Theoretical Politics* 26 (3): 1–23.

Rueschemeyer, Dietrich, and John D. Stephens. 1997. "Comparing Historical Sequences – A Powerful Tool for Causal Analysis." *Comparative Social Research* 17:55–72.

Rueschemeyer, Dietrich, Evelyne H. Stephens, and John D. Stephens. 1992. *Capitalist Development and Democracy.* Chicago: University of Chicago Press.

Schickler, Eric. 2001. *Disjointed Pluralism: Institutional Innovation and the Development of the U.S. Congress.* Princeton, NJ: Princeton University Press.

Sekhon, Jasjeet S., and Rocío Titiunik. 2012. "When Natural Experiments Are Neither Natural Nor Experiments." *American Political Science Review* 106 (1): 35–57.

Shapiro, Ian. 2004. "Problems, Methods, and Theories in the Study of Politics, or: What's Wrong with Political Science and What to Do about It." In *Problems and Methods in the Study of Politics*, edited by Ian Shapiro, Rogers Smith, and Tarek Masoud, 588–611. New York: Cambridge University Press.

   2014. "Methods Are Like People: If You Focus Only on What They Can't Do, You Will Always Be Disappointed." In *Field Experiments and Their Critics: Essays on the Uses and Abuses of Experimentation in the Social Sciences*, edited by Dawn Langan Teele, 228–42. New Haven, CT: Yale University Press.

Skocpol, Theda. 1992. *Protecting Soldiers and Mothers: The Political Origins of Social Policy in the United States.* Cambridge, MA: Harvard University Press.

Skowronek, Stephen. 1982. *Building a New American State: The Expansion of National Administrative Capacities, 1877–1920.* New York: Cambridge University Press.

Slater, Dan, and Erica Simmons. 2010. "Informative Regress: Critical Antecedents in Comparative Politics." *Comparative Political Studies* 43:886–917.

Slater, Dan, Benjamin Smith, and Gautam Nair. 2014. "Economic Origins of Democratic Breakdown? The Redistributive Model and the Postcolonial State." *Perspectives on Politics* 12:353–72.

Slater, Dan, and Daniel Ziblatt. 2013. "The Enduring Indispensability of the Controlled Comparison." *Comparative Political Studies* 46 (10): 1301–27.

Smith, J. Maynard, and G. R. Price. 1973. "The Logic of Animal Conflict." *Nature* 246 (5427): 15–18.

Soifer, Hillel David. 2012. "The Causal Logic of Critical Junctures." *Comparative Political Studies* 45 (12): 1572–97.

Stokes, Susan. 2014. "A Defense of Observational Research." In *Field Experiments and Their Critics: Essays on the Uses and Abuses of Experimentation in the Social Sciences,* edited by Dawn Langan Teele, 33–57. New Haven, CT: Yale University Press.

Streeck, Wolfgang, and Kathleen Thelen. 2005. "Introduction: Institutional Change in Advanced Political Economies." In *Beyond Continuity: Institutional Change in Advanced Political Economies*, edited by Wolfgang Streeck and Kathleen Thelen, 1–39. Oxford: Oxford University Press.

Swenson, Peter. 1991. "Bringing Capital Back In, or Social Democracy Reconsidered: Employer Power, Cross-Class Alliances, and the Centralization of Industrial Relations in Denmark and Sweden." *World Politics* 43 (4): 513–44.

2002. *Capitalists Against Markets.* New York: Oxford University Press.

Thelen, Kathleen. 1999. "Historical Institutionalism in Comparative Politics." *Annual Review of Political Science* 2:369–404.

2003. "How Institutions Evolve: Insights from Comparative-Historical Analysis." In *Comparative-Historical Analysis in the Social Sciences*, edited by James Mahoney and Dietrich Rueschemeyer, 208–40. New York: Cambridge University Press.

2004. *How Institutions Evolve: The Political Economy of Skills in Germany, Britain, the United States, and Japan.* Cambridge: Cambridge University Press.

Tudor, Maya. 2013. *The Promise of Power: The Origins of Democracy in India and Autocracy in Pakistan.* New York: Cambridge University Press.

Vogel, Steven K. 2006. *Japan Remodeled: How Government and Industry Are Reforming Japanese Capitalism.* Ithaca, NY: Cornell University Press.

Weibull, Jörgen W. 1997. *Evolutionary Game Theory.* Cambridge, MA: MIT Press.

Weir, Margaret. 1992. *Politics and Jobs: The Boundaries of Employment Policy in the United States.* Princeton, NJ: Princeton University Press.

Woolcock, Michael. 2013. "Using Case Studies to Explore the External Validity of 'Complex' Development Interventions." *Evaluation* 19 (3): 229–48.

Yashar, Deborah. 2005. *Contesting Citizenship in Latin America: The Rise of Indigenous Movements and the Postliberal Challenge.* New York: Cambridge University Press.

Ziblatt, Daniel. 2009. "Shaping Democratic Practice and the Causes of Electoral Fraud: The Case of Nineteenth Century Germany." *American Political Science Review* 103 (1): 1–21.

Forthcoming. *Conservative Political Parties and the Birth of Democracy in Europe.* New York: Cambridge University Press.

Part II

Agenda-setting work

2 The developmental state is dead: long live the developmental state!

Stephan Haggard

Chalmers Johnson's (1982) *MITI and the Japanese Miracle* rests on a big empirical puzzle – Japan's extraordinarily rapid growth – and two core claims that have driven the surprisingly resilient research program on the developmental state ever since.[1] The first is that Japan's high postwar growth could be traced to industrial policies that differed from both the "plan ideological" systems of state socialism and the "regulatory state" of Anglo-Saxon capitalism. This branch of the research program attracted by far the most attention because it directly challenged liberal orthodoxy in the economics profession and development policy community. Led by outsiders to that community – Johnson, Alice Amsden (1989), Robert Wade (Wade 1990, 2004; White and Wade 1984), and Ha-Joon Chang (1994) – this line of thinking was subsequently brought into the economic mainstream by economists such as Dani Rodrik (1995) and Joseph Stiglitz (2001), who reiterated the microeconomic logic of state intervention.

The second strand of the developmental state approach probed the political foundations of rapid growth. Industrial policy in the developing world was ubiquitous, but not ubiquitously successful. What accounted for successful industrial policies and the institutions capable of conducting them in the first place? The developmental state literature is typically identified with an institutionalist approach to politics, focusing on the autonomy or insulation of the government from rent-seeking private interests, delegation to lead agencies, and coherent bureaucracies. But Johnson was acutely aware of the centrality of business-government relations to the Japanese model, and subsequent contributions by Peter Evans (1989, 1995) refocused debate on the social foundations of rapid growth.

My thanks to Nancy Bermeo, Rick Doner, Dieter Ernst, Jason Kuo, Jim Mahoney, Dan Slater, Kathy Thelen, and the other participants in the project for comments on earlier drafts.

[1] For other reviews of the developmental state approach, see Deyo (1987), Onis (1991), Moon and Prasad (1998), Leftwich (1995), Woo-Cumings (1999), Haggard (2004), and Routley (2012).

This second face of the developmental state research agenda developed a particularly strong comparative-historical component. The literature gradually moved beyond Japan and the paradigmatic Northeast Asian cases of Korea and Taiwan to the rapidly growing countries of Southeast Asia and to comparator cases that were distinctly "nondevelopmental." This comparative-historical research agenda sought to identify the historical sources of development and underdevelopment through close consideration of a small number of cases.

What was theoretically and methodologically distinctive about the developmental state literature? The first point to note is that this literature took an adversarial stance toward orthodox models over an empirical puzzle of pressing practical import: why the East Asian countries had grown so fast. Johnson situated his plan rational model between state socialist and Anglo-Saxon economic models. But the exercise was not simply typological. Johnson, Wade, and Amsden believed that orthodox interpretations of East Asia's rapid growth were deeply flawed, descriptively, theoretically, and methodologically. Neoclassical models were rooted in the claim that rapid growth was caused by the adoption of market-conforming policies, most particularly with respect to the external sector, thus the moniker "export-led growth." But close empirical analyses of cases – what we might now call process tracing or causal process observation – suggested that these policies were not adopted to the extent believed, were combined with other interventions that did not fit prevailing theoretical models, and rested on other causal factors such as institutions and underlying social coalitions. In retrospect, the developmental state literature resembles the Varieties of Capitalism approach to comparative-historical research, in which the identification of types provided the basis for a critique of more generalized models.

The second feature of this work was deep engagement with particular cases and a configurational approach to causal explanation. In her well-known manifesto, Barbara Geddes (2003) challenges one claim of the developmental state literature – that the weakness of labor facilitated export-led growth strategies – by showing that the more general relationship between labor weakness and economic growth does not hold. According to Geddes, the developmental state literature was guilty of selection bias: drawing faulty inferences from cases selected on the dependent variable. And, of course, the small-N comparative-historical work considering whole countries always faced the classic degrees-of-freedom problem, with potentially significant variables far outnumbering the cases under consideration.

But scholars working on the developmental state had relatively modest presumptions about the ability to generate lawlike statements. Johnson (1987) cautiously extended his work on Japan to Taiwan and Korea because he believed the Japanese model diffused organically within the region (see also Cumings 1984). Although he offers a summary statement of the Japanese model in the conclusion to *MITI* (315–24), he explicitly warned that, although "it may be possible for another state to adopt Japan's priorities and its high-growth system without duplicating Japan's history . . . the dangers of institutional abstraction are as great as the potential advantages." Rather than seeking to isolate the influence of discrete causal variables, Johnson and his followers showed how features of these polities and societies combined or were configured in ways that promoted economic growth. Put differently, claims about the effectiveness of any given component of the developmental state – such as the weakness of labor – could not be isolated in the way Geddes sought to do; any given factor was conditional on other features of the model.

A final characteristic of most of the developmental state work was that it took history seriously. A strong theme in Johnson's book is that historical analysis was required because successful strategies emerged only through a process of trial and error and learning by doing. Alice Amsden (Amsden and Chu 2003) and Dani Rodrik (2008) elevated this observation, that governments, societies, and firms need to learn in order to grow, into a virtual dictum about successful development more generally. Historical work on the origins of developmental states often found them in deeply rooted historical factors. These observations raised quite fundamental questions about sequencing (Faletti and Mahoney, Chapter 8, this volume) as well as the replicability of historical findings to other settings.

This chapter is divided into two major sections: the first on the relationship between intervention and growth; the second on the political sources of rapid economic development, including the question of origins of developmental states. In each section, I start with an outline of the theoretical rationale of the developmental state approach followed by a discussion of the evidence and methodological issues of interest to comparative-historical analysis. The conclusion takes note of some of the issues in the current revival of interest in the developmental state and the renewed focus on state capacity, in particular.

The sources of economic growth: policy

The developmental state literature posed itself as an alternative to an emerging neoclassical consensus in development economics. Prior to the appearance of Johnson's book and continuing through the appearance of Wade's, a succession of studies by Anne Krueger (1978), Jagdish Bhagwati (1978), and Bela Balassa (1981), among others, had offered up a neoclassical interpretation of East Asia's rapid growth. This work emphasized stable macroeconomic policies, market-oriented reforms, and trade and exchange rate policy, in particular. The implications of this advocacy of export-led growth were hardly limited to the academy. The neoclassical canon on export-led growth influenced the international financial institutions and provided the key empirical referent for the so-called Washington consensus.[2] Written a decade prior to the collapse of the Soviet Union, Johnson was responding to an earlier variant of this literature on Japan (e.g., Patrick and Rosovsky 1976).[3] Johnson framed *MITI and the Japanese Miracle* in terms of a distinction between the plan-ideological systems of state socialism and two varieties of contemporary capitalism: market-rational and plan-rational systems. The fundamental distinction between the latter two was that market-rational economies took a regulatory approach to economic activity, whereas the plan-rational or developmental state was defined as purposive and goal-directed, seeking to achieve high growth through the allocation of resources to designated economic activities.[4] Johnson is cautious in making causal claims with respect to industrial policy, and he notes the checkered history of state control of industry. Nonetheless, his core theoretical insight is that the process of economic development is characterized by a myriad of market failures that can be solved only by governments that are capable of coordinating private sector activity, intervening in markets, and providing selective and conditional support to firms.

The logic of industrial policy

Robert Wade's (1990, 2004) close study of Taiwan – *Governing the Market: Economic Theory and the Role of Government in East Asian Industrialization*[5] – and the work of Ha-Joong Chang (1994) on Korea sought to give Johnson's

---

[2] When the World Bank (1993) finally did its own review of the East Asian miracle – at Japan's urging – the report downplayed the role of industrial policy, setting off a heated debate over both the substance of the report and the process through which its conclusions were reached (Amsden 1994; Aoki, Kim, and Okuno-Fujiwara 1996; Wade 1996).

[3] The Patrick and Rosovsky book was titled *Asia's New Giant*; Amsden's book on Korea, *Asia's Next Giant*.

[4] Throughout its life, the developmental state literature has been accused of a kind of tautology: that developmental states were little more than those that grew rapidly. But Johnson was rightly cautious on this point, arguing that whether such efforts were successful is not given and requires explanation.

[5] Citations to Wade are to the second edition.

broad approach more structure by outlining the policy elements of the "governed market," or GM, theory in more detail; in doing so, Wade also provided a more expansive definition of the developmental state. The GM approach, Wade (1990, 2004) argued, "emphasizes capital accumulation as the principal general force for growth, and interprets superior East Asian performance as the result of a level and composition of investment different from what FM [free market] . . . policies would have produced, and different, too, from what the 'interventionist' economic policies pursued by many other LDCs would have produced" (29).[6] But sheer accumulation was not the centerpiece of Wade's story, which rested more fundamentally on market failures (11–14, 350–8; see also Chang 1994). In effect, the GM theory interpreted the challenge of growth to reside in coordination problems that private actors cannot resolve efficiently through private contracting and exchange.

Three kinds of coordination problems received particular attention: those that arose in moving from agriculture to industry and within industry; those associated with financial markets; and those that surrounded the transfer and adoption of technology. Wade's dominant line of argument parallels Johnson's and a group of Japanese analysts' (for example, Aoki, Kim, and Okuno-Fujiwara 1996; Rodrik 1995 for a formal model) in focusing on coordination problems in the industrial sector. Efficient investment can be deterred by small market size and the absence of complementary suppliers or customers. Current market prices do not adequately convey information about future growth, and countries thus forgo investments that would lower production costs through larger plant size and learning effects; thus, Alice Amsden's (1989) infamous dictum that the East Asian countries succeeded not by "getting prices right" but by "getting prices wrong." If information is appropriately shared between government and the private sector and firm behavior is appropriately monitored, interventions such as subsidies, protection, and other direct supports to private business could overcome these collective action problems and thus push an economy from a bad to a good equilibrium (see Khan and Sundaram 2000 on the positive role of subsidies or "rents" in this process).

Such coordination problems often are assumed to arise primarily in the heavy and intermediate sectors such as steel and petrochemicals, but coordination problems also emerged in light industries seeking to enter world

---

[6] The GM theory thus anticipated an important set of arguments that emerged in the mid-1990s that capital accumulation – rather than either liberalizing reform or industrial policy – was at the core of the East Asian miracle (Krugman 1994).

markets and in more technology-intensive industries. In a widely read PhD dissertation, sociologist Thomas Gold (1981) documented the role of the government in Taiwan in coordinating complementary investments in the textile industry. Kuo (1995) and Noble (1999) offered comparative-historical analyses of Taiwan and the Philippines and Japan and Taiwan, respectively. Both used detailed industry studies to examine these coordination issues at the sectoral level.

A second theoretical rationale for intervention centered on failures in capital markets and provided one area where heterodox economists – including Nobel Laureate Joseph Stiglitz (Hellman, Murdock, and Stiglitz 1996) – entered the debate. Meredith Woo-Cumings's (Woo 1991) book on Korea is exemplary of comparative-historical work in this vein. Woo-Cumings argued that the financial sector allowed the government to both steer investment and exercise political control over the private sector.

A third rationale for industrial policy centers on technology. Alice Amsden (1989, 1991; Amsden and Chu 2003) and Peter Evans (1995) were most closely associated with this focus, but it is visible in more heterodox economists as well (L. Kim 1997). Explicitly following Gershenkron, Amsden draws a distinction between the early developers, which grew as a result of their own innovation, and latecomers, such as Korea, that grew through technological borrowing and learning. Amsden frontally attacked the idea that latecomers can successfully borrow by focusing on comparative advantage in labor-intensive industries alone. Developing country firms lack full information on technological alternatives, function with imperfect information on the technologies they do acquire, and are subject to variable, unpredictable, and highly path-dependent learning processes. Incomplete appropriability leads to underinvestment in research and development (R&D), forgoing the many externalities that arise around R&D activities.

Method in the analysis of industrial policy: the role of history and counterfactuals

A surprisingly common research design in the literature on industrial policy is to pick a successful (or unsuccessful) industry, demonstrate that policy support existed, and conclude that the case for the significance of industrial policy is made (or rejected). Wade (2004, 29–33, 71–2, 109) recognized this problem explicitly and outlined a counterfactual strategy that other comparative-historical work explicitly or implicitly emulated. First, sector-specific policies must not only be plausibly associated with the success of the industry in question but must yield outcomes equal or superior to a more market-conforming policy counterfactual. Moreover, Wade goes further by arguing that intervention must not have been the result of private sector demands (what Wade calls "followership"); if they were, then the investments in question might have taken place anyway. Rather, intervention must reflect "leadership" by the state that puts the industrial structure or a particular industry on a different path than it would have otherwise taken.

The alternative to this complex counterfactual analysis would appear to be straightforward: to examine industry-level data within a given country to determine whether those that received policy support surpassed those that did not on some metric, such as total factor productivity (TFP), export growth, or profitability. The World Bank (1993) *Miracle* report purports to conduct some tests along these lines, although they are hard to follow (Amsden 1994). Noland and Pack (2003) provide a skeptical overview drawing on the surprisingly small number of econometric studies in this vein.

Rodrik (2007), however, outlines clearly why these efforts do not escape the fundamental dilemmas of the counterfactual analysis undertaken by Wade:

The almost insurmountable flaw in this literature is that the key estimated coefficient [on industrial policy] . . . cannot discriminate between two radically different views of the world: (a) the government uses industrial policy for political or other inappropriate ends, and its support ends up going to losers rather than winners; (b) the government optimally targets the sectors that are the most deserving of support, and does its job as well as it possibly can in a second-best policy environment. Under (a) governments should commit to a hands-off policy. Under (b) a hands-off approach would leave the economy worse off . . . The empirical analysis leaves us no better informed than when we started. (17–18)

These irreducible problems help explain why causal claims about industrial policy in the comparative-historical literature are necessarily posed in a more contingent and contextual way. For Johnson, industrial policy worked because of sequencing (Faletti and Mahoney, Chapter 8, this volume), identifiable path dependencies, and learning. Moreover, growth rested on political relationships and institutions that coordinated, monitored, and disciplined rent-seeking. For example, Haggard (1990) places more emphasis on the effect of neoclassical reforms than others do in the developmental state tradition. However, he argues that these reforms had effect only because prior interventionist policies – some going back to the Japanese era in Korea and Taiwan – had developed firm-level capabilities, a theme in Amsden (1989) and Chang (1994, 2002) as well. Sequencing, in short history, mattered. Moreover, these reforms and successful interventions rested on the political power of the state and its independence from business interests. In short, politics mattered as well.

From policy to politics: institutional, coalitional, and historical foundations of the developmental state

The developmental state literature not only challenged neoclassical economic orthodoxy but also developed a line of reasoning about economic growth that ran counter to prevailing political economy models as well. The dominant political-institutional model of growth in economics and political science focused on property rights, the rule of law, and checks on state power (Barzel 1997; Haggard and Tiede 2011; Weingast 1995, 1997). The growth miracles in East Asia occurred during relatively long periods of political dominance by conservative parties or elites that might have mitigated property rights challenges emanating from the left.[7] But the nature of these political regimes suggests the deeply anomalous quality of Asia's growth: it is hardly a region characterized by strong checks on state power, well-developed rule of law, independent judiciaries, or codified property rights. Either informal institutions protected property rights or altogether different political mechanisms were at work (Chan 2000; Ginsburg 2000).

An integrated statement of the political model undergirding the developmental state is surprisingly hard to find. Nonetheless, the research tradition rested on two, interlinked political observations, one centered on the state, the second on the relationship between the government, the private sector, and other social forces, including labor. On the one hand, developmental states were characterized by substantial delegation to executives and in turn from executives to capable and appropriately incentivized bureaucracies. Johnson's view of the Japanese polity, for example, rested on the controversial assertion – which generated its own revisionist backlash – that politicians reigned but that bureaucrats ultimately ruled through well-developed ministries such as MITI (the Ministry of International Trade and Industry).

On the other hand, the developmental state was politically insulated from social forces that might distract from its accumulationist and industrial policy aims, including not only the Left and working class but also the private sector

---

[7] These include the Liberal Democratic Party (LDP), Kuomintang (KMT), and People's Action Party (PAP) in Japan, Taiwan, and Singapore, respectively; Park Chung Hee, Soeharto, and Mahathir in Korea, Indonesia, and Malaysia; the British colonial administration in Hong Kong; and a surprisingly stable alliance of king, military, and bureaucracy in Thailand.

itself. In Alice Amsden's felicitous phrase, a key feature of the developmental state was its capacity to "discipline" the private sector.

What is the underlying theory that would justify a focus on a state that is centralized, internally coherent, and politically insulated? The answers trace back to the core mechanisms that generate long-run growth. In a simple accounting sense, economic development can result from productive inputs – capital and labor – or from greater efficiency in their use. Early growth accounting suggested that virtually all of Asia's growth could be explained by sheer accumulation (Krugman 1994). This view is still contested, but any model of East Asia's growth must offer an account of the extraordinary level of investment during the high-growth period.

However, accumulation should not yield high growth if allocated inefficiently. Even advocates of industrial policy argued for policies that were in conformity with "dynamic comparative advantage." The second political economy problem is thus one of reform and transition: how to move policy from an economically and politically distorted low-growth equilibrium to a high-growth path. Features of both states and social structures were implicated in achieving these two core objectives of rapid capital accumulation and relatively efficient allocation of resources.

Political institutions, big and small: regime type and bureaucracy

Johnson was clear that Japan's autonomous developmental state was forged under semidemocratic and authoritarian rule, but he was ambivalent about whether authoritarian rule was a necessary condition for rapid growth. After all, Japan was at least nominally democratic in the miracle years of the early postwar period. However, as the developmental state literature migrated away from Japan to the newly industrializing countries – Korea, Taiwan, Hong Kong, and Singapore – the question was quickly joined (Cheng 1990; Haggard 1990).

Several causal arguments linked authoritarian rule to growth. Since capital accumulation demands that resources be diverted from consumption to investment, voters (or citizens, the poor, or labor, depending on the precise specification) are likely to oppose such a reallocation; as Huntington and Nelson (1976) had argued much earlier, participation generates trade-offs. The second route, and the one I took (Haggard 1990), focused on economic reform. Dictators can overcome collective action problems inside and outside the government that hinder the formulation of coherent policy, override rent-seeking and populist pressures, and thus push the economy onto a more efficient growth path. I was particularly interested in underlining the irony that all of the governments that undertook reforms in the region – the darlings of the neoclassical approach – were authoritarian, a finding some intellectuals in the region actually embraced.

The finding of a link between authoritarianism and growth clearly didn't generalize. In 2000, Adam Przeworski and his colleagues found that controlling for income and a number of other variables, regime type had no effect on investment, the growth rate of the capital stock, or overall income growth; this finding also held when limiting the test to a sample of developing countries. But Przeworski *et al.* also found that the standard deviation of growth in the sample of dictatorships was much larger than in the democracies, confirming that autocracies encompassed both high-growth miracles such as those found in East Asia and low-growth debacles. The failure to directly address the puzzle of why some authoritarian regimes grew rapidly while others crashed and burned was a drawback of the method of focusing on a high-growth region; this shortcoming subsequently motivated the cross-regional work by Evans (1995), Kohli (2004), Doner, Ritchie, and Slater (2005), and others on historical origins that I take up in the next section.

The other feature of the developmental state construct – and the one that preoccupied Johnson – was the bureaucracy. Regime type and politicians more generally mattered much less to Johnson than the core bureaucratic agencies, such as MITI, that he believed drove the growth process. Internally, such agencies were motivated by clear missions and were run on meritocratic principles with strong internal systems of both rewards (such as competitive pay and long-term career tracks) and controls (sanctions for corruption). These characteristics also served to insulate the bureaucracy from political or private sector manipulation.

In an innovative study drawing on expert evaluation, Evans and Rauch (1999) found that the "Weberianness" of the bureaucracy was associated with growth in a cross section of thirty-five developing countries. Case study work finds that economic reforms in the region were typically preceded or accompanied by major bureaucratic reorganizations that concentrated economic decision-making authority in one or several lead agencies, strengthened the role of technocrats in formulating policy, and reformed internal bureaucratic routines (Cheng, Haggard, and Kang 1998; Haggard 1990; Kim 1988). Reform of the bureaucracy did not typically reach the entire administrative apparatus. Pockets of bureaucratic efficiency coexisted with ministries that dispensed pork and political favors even in the Northeast Asian developmental states (Kang 2002a, 2002b). Such payoffs may even have been the price for wider reforms. Nonetheless, all of the high-growth Asian countries had at least some core economic ministries and/or specialized agencies with important policy-making powers that looked relatively Weberian in form.

The relationship between politicians and bureaucrats in Japan's economic decision making ended up being one of the most disputed features of Johnson's book. Virtually from the moment it was published, critics pointed out the role that either politicians or private sector actors played in policy formulation (Calder 1993; Krauss and Muramatsu 1984; Noble 1998; Okimoto 1989; Samuels 1987). The most blunt challenge was posed by Ramseyer and Rosenbluth (1993), who argued that Johnson's much-vaunted bureaucrats were little more than agents of the Liberal Democratic Party (LDP).

With the benefit of hindsight, the debate seems somewhat stilted. Johnson was hardly a culturalist and sought to outline the political and administrative rationality of the plan-rational state. And it doesn't take much work to show that asymmetric information and a host of other imperfections can upset the just-so delegation story advanced by rational choice institutionalism. However, the rational choice critique was clearly onto something important. As the developmental state model was extended to authoritarian regimes beyond Japan, it seemed particularly odd to think that bureaucrats enjoyed independence from autocratic political elites. In these cases, bureaucracies were reformed not to ensure their independence but to ensure their loyalty to authoritarian leaderships in the pursuit of some broader political project. This crucial observation led quickly back to state-society relations.

The social foundations of developmental states

From its inception, a central critique of the developmental state approach was its excessive focus on political institutions and its relative neglect of business (Chan, Clark, and Lam 1998; Doner 1991; Evans 1995; Fields 1995; Jayasuriya 2005; E. M. Kim 1997; MacIntyre 1994; Moon and Prasad 1994). Recall that the concept of the plan-rational state assumed a mixed economy and the presence of a private sector that had to be incentivized to invest. Also recall that the property rights model did not appear to comport with the East Asian experience on its face. Authoritarian regimes backed by strong bureaucracies should lack credible checks on executive discretion and therefore suffer from credibility problems in protecting property rights and eliciting investment from the private sector. How could we square a state that was strong, but not predatory, credible to the private sector, but not captured?

Alice Amsden stated the general political problem most clearly. Just as rent-seeking could distort the efficient allocation of resources in neoclassical models, so private sector capture could distort the allocation of subsidies from their developmental purposes. The solution – and for Amsden the defining political feature of the East Asian developmental states – was the ability of strong states to "discipline" business:

In slower-growing late-industrializing regions, subsidies have tended to be allocated according to the principle of giveaway, in what has amounted to a free-for-all. In East Asia, beginning with Japan, there has been a greater tendency for subsidies to be dispensed according to the principle of reciprocity, in exchange for concrete performance standards with respect to output, exports, and eventually, R&D. For example, the government in South Korea disciplined its big business groups by means of price ceilings, controls on capital flight, and incentives that made diversification into new industries contingent on performing well in old ones. (Amsden 1991, 284)

If rents are extended to help solve any of the coordination problems outlined in the previous section, they must be conditional. Governments must define the objectives of the rent in terms of some discernible market failure or externality and monitor rent recipients; clearly, bureaucratic capacity matters in this regard.

But they must also credibly commit to withdraw rents for noncompliance or nonperformance, a politically charged task that goes far beyond bureaucratic monitoring to the nature of business-government relations (Amsden 2001, 8; Aoki, Kim, and Okuno-Fujiwara 1996; World Bank 1993). How could strong governments send credible signals to private actors while simultaneously constraining their rent-seeking behavior? Grabowski (1994, 1997) and Huff, Dewit, and Oughton (2001) formally modeled relations between a developmental state and the private sector as a signaling game in which the government proves its credibility to the private sector by complementary investments that elicit private investment. The point was extended to the distribution of subsidies or rents in an underappreciated study by Khan and Sundaram (2000). Kang (2002a, 2002b) talked about a "mutual hostage" relationship in Korea that bounded both state predation and private corruption. In all of these models, industrial policy is seen not only through the lens of its *economic* effects but as a crucial *political* signal of government intent.

The idea that institutions could help solve these signaling, credible commitment and monitoring problems between the state and the private sector was at the heart of the developmental state approach. At least partly motivated by the East Asian experience, Schleifer and Vishney (1993) provided an influential model of corruption that outlined why centralization increased efficiency; the approach was subsequently picked up by both Kang (2002a, 2002b) and MacIntyre (2003) in their "second-generation" analyses of the Korean case and Southeast Asia's response to the debt crisis, respectively. In Schleifer and Vishney's model, rent-seekers demand a range of complementary government-supplied goods. If the state is highly decentralized, different branches of government, ministries, or bureaus pursue their own interests, pushing the cost of government-supplied goods to a suboptimal level and introducing uncertainty over property rights in those rents. Political centralization does not eliminate corruption but bounds it by solving these collective action problems, pricing rents at an "appropriate" level, and providing security of property rights.

Somewhat similar arguments were made about the internal coherence of the bureaucracy. Meritocratic recruitment and promotion, adequate compensation, and career paths with clear rewards at the top not only were important for performing the tasks outlined in the previous sections but served to control rent-seeking as well. Evans (1995), in particular, argued that the internal coherence of the bureaucracy was the key factor separating efficient "embeddedness" from inefficient rent-seeking. The case study work on industrial policy repeatedly returns to the significance of independent bureaucratic capabilities and information as a condition for effective governance of the private sector.

Yet, this focus on the state still left open the question of how political actors interacted with the private sector and to what effect. A significant strand of research on East Asian development, including Campos and Root (1996), Root (1996), and the World Bank's (1993) own *Miracle* report, developed the argument that "deliberation councils" linking business and government played an important role in resolving credibility problems associated with authoritarian rule and building trust between the public and private sectors. Evans (1995), Maxfield and Schneider (1997), Weiss (1998), and Moon and Prasad (1994) all cast the argument in more general terms, claiming that a complex of both formal and informal networks between the public and private sectors played a role in economic growth. In Evans's (1995) felicitous phrase, the East Asian state was characterized by "embedded autonomy": strong political and bureaucratic institutions that simultaneously maintained dense ties with the private sector but had adequate independence to control the business-state nexus. Root (1996) explains how it worked by reference to an implicit model of costly signaling:

Tying the fortunes of many groups to the continued use of the cooperative decision-making structures raises the cost of altering the system ex post. Once councils permeate an economy, a government that unilaterally imposes its will on an industry or sector will risk undermining the value of councils for other groups, thus subverting the entire system of cooperative decision-making. Government, then, is unlikely to abide only by those decisions it prefers, overturning those it opposes...By institutionalizing deliberative councils, government reduces its discretionary power but gains the confidence of business in the stability of agreed upon policies. (12)

The existence and operation of such councils are thoroughly documented for Japan by Johnson (1982), Okimoto (1989), and others in the developmental state vein. The early Korean experience of export-promotion meetings chaired personally by Park Chung Hee is also a frequently used example. Yet, as we move beyond these two Northeast Asian cases, the evidence thins. The Southeast Asian cases also experienced rapid growth but did not appear to have similar levels or types of state intervention as their Northeast Asian counterparts nor the institutions of coordination (Jomo *et al.* 1997; MacIntyre 1994). Moreover, empirical studies of the region raised serious doubts about the capacity of Southeast Asian states to "discipline" their private sector constituents. In Malaysia, consultative institutions at the federal level did not appear until 1991, when Mahathir's "Look East" campaign sought to emulate the Northeast Asian newly industrializing countries (NICs). Yet, in a succession of outstanding studies, Gomez (1991; Gomez and Jomo 1997) detailed how this period was the high point of corruption, cronyism, and the interpenetration of government, state, and party. In his 1994 study of business-government relations in Asia, MacIntyre (1994) stated the claim more generally: the Southeast Asian countries simply do not fit models of business-government relations derived from the Northeast Asian cases.

In sum, the developmental state literature innovated not only with respect to policy but also in thinking about how politics and institutions might incentivize growth. In contrast to political models that emphasized checks on state power, the rule of law, and property rights, the developmental state model emphasized strong or "insulated" states, coherent bureaucracies, and institutionalized business-government relations that checked rent-seeking and made government support conditional on private sector performance. But as case studies proliferated they revealed tremendous variation across countries, including not only between the Northeast and Southeast Asian cases but also among Japan, Korea, and Taiwan. Was it possible that the taproot of growth did not lie in institutions but in longer-run features of state-society relations? And even if institutions mattered, where did they come from? These questions were raised by an important second generation of work on the origins of developmental states.

Origins: the historical foundations of developmental states

Much of the pioneering work on the developmental state took the form of country case studies. The small-N, cross-regional comparisons that characterized the "origins" literature had a crucial methodological advantage: the studies compared the high-growth East Asian cases to countries that had more mixed records or that had failed to grow over long periods of time (Doner, Ritchie, and Slater 2005; Kang 2002a; Kohli 2004; Vu 2007, 2010; Waldner 1999). The historical literature had broadly the same agenda as the political theories we have outlined in the foregoing sections, looking at the role of strong states and the social foundations of long-run growth. However, the cases raised the crucial question of where these states and social relations came from in the first place. In doing so, the debate on origins raised a number of central questions in comparative-historical analysis: the role of more distal versus proximate causes; questions of sequencing and path dependence; and issues of case selection and causal inference.

Colonialism was a natural place to start. Cumings (1984) had noted the Japanese colonial origins of the developmental states in Taiwan and Korea. Kohli (2004) generalized the argument and tied the literature on the developmental state into the wider debate on state formation. State structures, Kohli argued, were the product of unusual concentrations of power and coercive capability; they did not suddenly appear in response to the functional demands of some development strategy. Once put in place, "core institutional characteristics acquired during colonial rule have also proved difficult to alter. Anti-colonial nationalist movements were one potential organized force capable of altering the basic state forms inherited from colonialism," but for the most part such movements in Asia and Africa "were too superficial and/or fragmented to alter the inherited state forms decisively" (Kohli 2004, 17). Subsequent state forms – what Kohli called cohesive-capitalist states, fragmented-multiclass states, and neopatrimonial states – were thus the products of different types of colonial rule. At least in Korea and Taiwan, the developmental state could be traced to Japanese colonial policies of building coherent bureaucracies, strong ties to private actors, and a massive repressive apparatus for dealing with class challenges from below.

At the other extreme, Nigeria was ruled by the British "on the cheap." Indirect rule resulted in the persistence of personalist and patrimonial relations and weak states that failed to develop even the basic capacity to extract taxes. Kohli's analysis thus stood in stark contrast to Acemoglu, Johnson, and Robinson's (2001) widely cited work on the adverse effects of predatory states. Kohli argued that European colonialism in Africa had adverse long-run effects on growth not because it predated on native populations and failed to protect property rights but because it never developed adequate state capacity or the bureaucratic institutions required for development; this theme has recurred strongly in the recent developmental state revival.[8]

Kohli's story raised classic questions of the nature of historical explanation. How, for example, do we square the disadvantages that Brazil appeared to inherit with its very high growth in the half-century prior to the debt crisis of the 1980s? And how do we square the developmental state institutions implanted by Japan during the colonial period in Korea with the weak performance of the Korean economy in the first postcolonial decade (Haggard, Kang, and Moon 1997)? Were we searching too far back in history to locate sources of economic performance that appeared to be more proximate? The answers go to the configurational nature of causal inference in the developmental state literature. Institutional legacies were a necessary but not sufficient condition for subsequent growth. As with Johnson's account of Japan, the analysis of the "longue durée" must be coupled with an understanding of how inherited institutions are subsequently reoriented or reconfigured to achieve developmental aims that would be impossible to achieve in their absence.

Not all of the literature went back to colonial origins; other cases focused primarily on developments in the postwar period. The literature by economists on the East Asian experience drew a comparison between import-substituting and export-oriented growth paths. As a result, the comparison between the East Asian cases and the middle-income countries of Latin America was a natural focus (Evans 1989; Gereffi and Wyman 1990; Haggard 1990). Why did import substitution persist and "deepen" in Latin America while the East Asian countries shifted course toward greater reliance on exports?[9]

---

[8] As with Evans, Kohli notes intermediate cases, including India and Brazil. The Indian nationalist movement altered British colonial structures to a certain extent. The Estado Novo (1937–45) and period of military rule (1964–84) reflected periods of state "hardening" in Brazil. But Kohli stresses the persistence of inherited political and social structures. In Brazil, for example, the power of landed oligarchs, local authoritarianism, and a weak central government lingered for at least a century after decolonization, and traces of these historical residues can be found to this day.

[9] This comparative work had the advantage of being able to draw on debates in Latin America about similar processes, particularly Guillermo O'Donnell's (1973; Kaufman 1979) model of bureaucratic authoritarianism (BA), which bore a clear family resemblance to developmental state ideas (see, for example, Im 1987 on BA in Korea).

Haggard (1990) looked at the interaction of size, external shocks, and the nature of the state's relationship with key social forces. In the face of external shocks, larger developing countries, and particularly those with a natural resource base, could continue financing import substitution industrialization (ISI) despite the constraints it placed on manufactured exports; they were more likely to move into secondary import substitution ("deepening") than were smaller countries pursuing ISI that lacked natural resources and did not have similar domestic market opportunities. Haggard noted that the shocks of interest in the East Asian cases included a precipitous decline in aid in the canonical cases of Korea and Taiwan, a shock that triggered a scramble for new sources of foreign exchange in exports, foreign investment, and borrowing. Doner, Ritchie, and Slater (2005) similarly noted that foreign exchange and revenue constraints – including those associated with the absence of natural resources – were crucial determinants of efficiency-enhancing institutional developments.

A central issue of interest for Haggard was the interplay between the state and social forces. Labor was weak across the newly industrializing countries but appeared particularly restrained in the anti-Communist authoritarian regimes that were paragons of the export-led growth approach: Korea, Taiwan, Singapore, and colonial Hong Kong. Labor certainly benefited from rapid real wage growth; Campos and Root (1996) went so far as to argue that East Asian growth was "inclusive" and based on an implicit social contract. But, although governments invested in education and real wages rose, labor weakness and even outright repression appeared integral features of an export-oriented model that rested on low-wage labor, labor market flexibility, and managerial autonomy on the shop floor (Deyo 1989).

By contrast, longer periods of import substitution in Latin America had entrenched complex systems of unequal social entitlements that were ultimately rooted in employment in import-substituting activities; Haggard and Kaufman (2008) drew these comparisons in their historical analysis of the origins of welfare states in the two regions. Business interests were wedded to protection in both regions as well, but the sheer duration of import substitution in Latin America entrenched the strategy more deeply. It would have required a particularly powerful and independent state to shift policy in a more outward-oriented direction in the Latin American cases.

Over time, the "origins" literature widened from the East Asia–Latin America comparison to encompass the Middle East, South Asia, and Africa. Waldner (1999) argued that a key difference between Turkey and Syria, on the one hand, and Korea and Taiwan, on the other, was the breadth of the coalitions elites forged at the time states were being formed. In Syria and Turkey, "premature" pressures to widen social coalitions gave rise to what Waldner called "precocious Keynesianism": states that were committed to growth-inhibiting transfers. Kohli (2004) similarly noted that "fragmented multi-class states" – represented in his four-country comparison by Brazil and India – precluded pro-business policies. Evans (1995) similarly described Brazil as an "intermediate" case – between developmental and predatory states – in which clientelistic links to business and labor eroded the capacity to orchestrate a successful entry into global IT markets. By contrast, all four of these cross-regional comparisons emphasized the presence of the features outlined above in the East Asian cases: relatively autonomous states and coherent bureaucracies that were able to impose the short-run costs associated with major policy transitions (Haggard), limit transfers (Waldner), develop a distinctively pro-business environment (Kohli), or coordinate with the private sector to advance international competitiveness (Evans).

The findings of the work on the origins of developmental and other states raised one of the most vexing problems for comparative-historical analysis. The focus on the East Asian cases was driven by pressing pragmatic concerns: an interest in the sources of rapid growth and the concomitant improvement in human welfare. What were we to make of arguments that the success of these cases was rooted in historical factors that could sometimes be traced to the colonial era? Was history fate? Or could it be used to draw meaningful policy lessons?

Conclusion: the developmental state is dead: long live the developmental state!

Although the developmental state literature took off in the 1980s and 1990s, it was largely preoccupied with a much earlier period. Johnson's book built up to the great industrial transformation in Japan in the 1950s. The subsequent literature on the newly industrializing countries of Asia looked back to the "takeoff" of the 1960s and 1970s. As the leading exemplars of the developmental state model gradually liberalized their economies, the concept appeared destined to become a largely historical construct: an explanation for an unusual period of very high growth limited to a small group of Asian countries.

However, the developmental state literature focused on questions that were central to the discipline – the relationship between the state and the market, the political and institutional foundations of economic growth – that were unlikely to fade. More important, ideological winds were about to shift as the market triumphalism of the Washington consensus and early post–Cold War period proved surprisingly short-lived. The financial crisis of 2008 also affected the tenor of the debate, setting in train a quest for a "post-Washington consensus" (Birdsall and Fukuyama 2011). It is worth tracing this intellectual history briefly, because the developmental state has enjoyed a surprising revival in recent years.

The onset of the Asian financial crisis in 1997–8 provided an opportunity for critics to underline the risks associated with industrial policy and restate the case for market-oriented reform. Rather than seeing strong states and well-ordered bureaucracies, critics noted the myriad problems of rent-seeking and moral hazard. Defenders of the developmental state model told a very different story about the crisis, emphasizing the risks of deregulation, and capital account and financial market liberalization, in particular (Stiglitz 2002; Wade and Veneroso 1998). It was only a short step from these observations about policy to the underlying political economy (Haggard 2000; MacIntyre 2003; Mo and Moon 1999). The weakness of regulation was not simply an accident of history, a sin of omission on the road to liberalization. These weaknesses were consistent with growing business influence over regulatory institutions and the declining ability of governments to check rent-seeking, the socialization of risk, and moral hazard. Rather than discrediting the developmental state model, the crisis confirmed some of its central tenets. In the wake of the crisis, reformers such as Kim Dae Jung sought to reverse these trends in business-government relations, in part through liberalization and in part through more robust regulation of the financial sector and corporate governance.

Nor did liberalization spell the end of industrial policy. Rather, empirical work shifted to the question of how to conduct industrial policy in a more open-economy context (Evans 1998; Hayashi 2010; Low 2004; Rodrik 2007; Weiss 1998; Wong 2004; Yusuf 2003). For example, Deyo, Doner, and Hershberg (2001) and Doner (2009) traced the evolution of Asian industrial policy across both natural resource and manufacturing industries over time. Not all of these accounts were success stories. Noble (1998) noted that "coordination" was difficult to distinguish from "collusion," and Wong (2011) offered a cautionary tale on the biotech industry in Asia. Nonetheless, by the end of the 2000s a new round of debate had emerged on the merits of industrial policy based on fears of the so-called middle-income trap (Gill and Kharas 2007). Previously successful economies could not continue to grow through either sheer capital accumulation or further liberalization alone. Rather, the shift to a new development strategy rooted in higher productivity growth required new interventions, business-government relations, and political coalitions (for example, Paus 2012).

For countries at lower levels of development, the great boom of the 2000s saw high growth spread across the developing world and in countries pursuing diverse and heterodox developmental strategies. China was the most obvious example, and it was only a matter of time before efforts were made to explicitly assimilate the country into the broader East Asian model (for example, Baek 2005; Knight 2010). Although not without controversy, no less than the (Chinese) chief economist of the World Bank advanced a model of growth for low-income countries in which the state would "facilitate structural change by aiming to provide information, compensate for externalities, and co-ordinate improvements in the 'hard' and 'soft' infrastructure that are needed for the private sector to grow in a manner consistent with the dynamic change in the economy's comparative advantage" (Lin and Monga 2011, 265; Lin 2009).

The debate over the future of the developmental state was not limited to the role of industrial policy; it addressed the issue of political change as well. The canonical Northeast Asian developmental states – Korea and Taiwan – democratized, followed after a lag by a number of the Southeast Asian countries. These changes raised the empirical issue of how growth might be affected by a more liberal political environment (for example, Rock 2013). In an important and forward-looking collection, a group of British development scholars and practitioners coined the term "the democratic developmental state" (Robinson and White 1998). The collection began by challenging the authoritarian hypothesis, noting the mixed record of authoritarian rule as a whole, and restating the classical liberal argument that democracy and growth were not only compatible but reinforcing over the long run (see also White 2006). The volume raised the issue of how the lessons of the East Asian cases could be adopted to a changed political environment in which the objectives were not simply to grow rapidly but to do so in the context of increased accountability and attentiveness to the provision of social services and the expansion of human capabilities (Evans 2011).[10] Yet the ligaments of earlier argument remained in place. If anything, such a state required even greater

[10] Although it is beyond the scope of our interests here, a new literature emerged on the East Asian welfare state, focusing on its distinctive features during the developmental state era and its transformation following the transition to democratic rule.

capacity than the "classical" developmental state, with its single-minded focus on growth.

Africa became a somewhat surprising theater for this debate (Edigheji 2005, 2010; Meyns and Musamba 2012; Mkandawire 2001). In a scathing indictment, Thandika Mkandawire (2001) challenged "the impossibility theorem": the idea that African states were too dependent, weak, incompetent, and corrupt to emulate the East Asian developmental states. Political scientists working on the region had long focused on the patrimonial nature of African governments, and some of the comparative-historical work cited earlier – including both Evans (1995) and Kohli (2004) – had explicitly drawn comparisons between developmental and predatory African states. From the 1980s, "governance" began to gain attention from the international financial institutions as well.

Mkandawire (2001) argued, however, that "most of the analyses about African states that have led to so much despondency about the prospects of development are based on invidious comparison between African states in crisis and idealised and tendentiously characterised states elsewhere" (290). On the one hand, neoliberal approaches to development in Africa had downplayed the significance of developing state capacity, a core feature of the Asian developmental states. On the other hand, the critics of African governance had overlooked the fact that the East Asian model hardly conformed with the new received wisdom on governance: policy was far from liberal, states intervened pervasively, rents were distributed to chosen firms, and government and business worked hand in hand. Rather than seeking to finesse Africa's governance problems through weakening the state and focusing on liberalization, policy should aim to strengthen state capacity (Fritz and Menocal 2006) and "get interventions right."

Most recently, these arguments have been generalized in an important debate about the role that accountability and capacity should play in the conceptualization and measurement of government performance. In a wide-ranging indictment of contemporary approaches to governance, Francis Fukuyama (2013) argues that both academics and the policy community have placed too much emphasis on the role of regime type, institutions of accountability, the rule of law, and procedural features of the bureaucracy and not enough on state autonomy and capacity. Fukuyama's critique circles back to long-standing themes in the developmental state literature and is tribute to the fact that the questions raised by this research program are alive and well.

Some strands of the new institutionalism in economics (Acemoglu, Johnson, and Robinson 2001) reached implicitly pessimistic conclusions about the capacity to escape poverty traps, noting the heavy weight of the dead hand of history. Yet the developmental state literature was from its inception deeply motivated by an engagement with policy debates; Wade, Amsden, Chang, Rodrik, and others were not simply historians of development but pragmatists wary of cookie-cutter models. Deterministic formulations on the origins of long-run growth – including some of those that lurked in the origins debate – were ultimately of less interest to them than mining history for lessons that could be adapted to different national contexts. Central to these lessons was the observation that growth was not simply the result of market-oriented policy or even appropriate interventions but of underlying state capacity. This observation remains the most simple and enduring of the contributions of the developmental state approach.

References

Acemoglu, Daron, Simon Johnson, and James A. Robinson. 2001. "The Colonial Origins of Comparative Development: An Empirical Investigation." *American Economic Review* 91 (5): 1369–1401.

Amsden, Alice. 1989. *Asia's Next Giant: South Korea and Late Industrialisation.* New York: Oxford University Press.

  1991. "Diffusion of Development: The Late-Industrializing Model and Greater East Asia." *American Economic Review* 81 (2): 282–6.

  1994. "Why Isn't the Whole World Experimenting with the East Asian Model to Develop? Review of *The East Asian Miracle.*" *World Development* 22 (4): 627–33.

  2001. *The Rise of "The Rest": Challenges to the West From Late-Industrializing Economies.* New York: Oxford University Press.

Amsden, Alice, and Wan Wen Chu. 2003. *Beyond Late Development: Taiwan's Upgrading Policies.* Cambridge, MA: MIT Press.

Aoki, Masahiko, Hyung-Ki Kim, and Masahiro Okuno-Fujiwara. 1996. *The Role of Government in East Asian Economic Development: Comparative Institutional Analysis.* New York: Oxford University Press.

Baek, Seung-wook. 2005. "Does China Follow 'the East Asian Development Model'?" *Journal of Contemporary Asia* 35 (4): 485–98.

Balassa, Bela. 1981. *The Newly Industrializing Countries in the World Economy.* New York: Pergamon Press.

Barzel, Yoram. 1997. *Economic Analysis of Property Rights,* 2nd ed. New York: Cambridge University Press.

Bhagwati, Jagdish. 1978. *Anatomy and Consequences of Exchange Control Regimes.* Vol. 11 of *Foreign Trade Regimes and Economic Development.* Cambridge, MA: Ballinger Publishing Co. for the National Bureau of Economic Research.

Birdsall, Nancy, and Francis Fukuyama. 2011. "The Post-Washington Consensus: Development After the Crisis." *Foreign Affairs*, March/April.

Calder, Kent E. 1993. *Strategic Capitalism: Private Business and Public Purpose in Japanese Industrial Finance*. Princeton, NJ: Princeton University Press.

Campos, Edgardo J., and Hilton L. Root. 1996. *The Key to the Asian Miracle: Making Shared Growth Credible*. Washington, DC: The Brookings Institution.

Chan, Steve, Cal Clark, and Danny Lam. 1998. *Beyond the Developmental State: East Asia's Political Economies Reconsidered*. London: St. Martin's.

Chan, Sylvia. 2002. *Liberalism, Democracy, and Development*. New York: Cambridge University Press.

Chang, Ha-Joon. 1994. *The Political Economy of Industrial Policy*. London: Macmillan.

　　2002. *Kicking Away the Ladder: Development Strategy in Historical Perspective*. London: Anthem Press.

Cheng, T. J. 1990. "Political Regimes and Development Strategies: South Korea and Taiwan." In *Manufacturing Miracles: Patterns of Development in Latin American and East Asia*, edited by G. Gereffi and D. Wyman. Princeton, NJ: Princeton University Press.

Cheng, Tun-Jen, Stephan Haggard, and David Kang. 1998. "Institutions and Growth in Korea and Taiwan: The Bureaucracy." *Journal of Development Studies* 34 (6): 87–111.

Cumings, Bruce. 1984. "The Origins and Development of the Northeast Asian Political Economy: Industrial Sectors, Product Cycles, and Political Consequences." *International Organization* 38 (1): 1–40.

Deyo, Frederic C., ed. 1987. *The Political Economy of the New Asian Industrialism*. Ithaca, NY: Cornell University Press.

　　1989. *Beneath the Miracle: Labor Subordination in the New Asian Industrialism*. Berkeley: University of California Press.

Deyo, Frederic C., Richard Doner, and Eric Hershberg. 2001. *Economic Governance and the Challenge of Flexibility in East Asia*. New York: Rowman and Littlefield.

Doner, Richard F. 1991. *Driving a Bargain: Automobile Industrialization and Japanese Firms in Southeast Asia*. Berkeley: University of California Press.

　　2009. *The Politics of Uneven Development: Thailand's Economic Growth in Comparative Perspective*. New York: Cambridge University Press.

Doner, Richard F., Bryan K. Ritchie, and Dan Slater. 2005. "Systemic Vulnerability and the Origins of Developmental States: Northeast and Southeast Asia in Comparative Perspective." *International Organization* 59 (2): 327–61.

Edigheji, Omano. 2005. *A Democratic Developmental State in Africa? A Concept Paper*. Research Report 105. Johannesburg: Centre for Policy Studies.

　　ed. 2010. *Constructing a Democratic Developmental State in South Africa*. Cape Town: HSRC Press.

Evans, Peter. 1989. "Predatory, Developmental and Other Apparatuses: A Comparative Political Economy Perspective on the Third World State." *Sociological Forum* 4 (4): 561–87.

　　1995. *Embedded Autonomy: States and Industrial Transformation*. Princeton, NJ: Princeton University Press.

　　1998. "Transferable Lessons? Re-examining the Institutional Prerequisites of East Asian Economic Policies." *Journal of Developmental Studies* 34 (6): 66–86.

2011. *The Capability Enhancing Developmental State: Concepts and National Trajectories.* Discussion Paper No. 63 (March). Niteroi, Brazil: Centro De Estudos sobre Desiguldade e Desenvolvimento.

Evans, Peter, and James Rauch. 1999. "Bureaucracy and Growth: A Cross-National Analysis of the Effects of 'Weberian' State Structures on Economic Growth." *American Sociological Review* 64 (4): 748–65.

Fields, Karl. 1995. *Enterprise and the State in Korea and Taiwan.* Ithaca, NY: Cornell University Press.

Fritz, V., and A. Rocha Menocal. 2006. *(Re)building Developmental States: From Theory to Practice.* Working Paper No. 274. London: Overseas Development Institute.

Fukuyama, Francis. 2013. "What Is Governance?" *Governance* 26 (3): 347–68.

Geddes, Barbara. 2003. *Paradigms and Sand Castles: Theory Building and Research Design in Comparative Politics.* Ann Arbor: University of Michigan Press.

Gereffi, Gary, and Donald L. Wyman, eds. 1990. *Manufacturing Miracles: Paths of Industrialization in Latin America and East Asia.* Princeton, NJ: Princeton University Press.

Gill, Indermit, and Homi Kharas. 2007. *An East Asia Renaissance: Ideas for Economic Growth.* Washington, DC: World Bank.

Ginsburg, Tom. 2000. "Does Law Matter for Economic Development? Evidence from East Asia." *Law and Society Review* 34 (3): 829–56.

Gold, Thomas. 1980. "Dependent Development in Taiwan." Unpublished PhD diss., Department of Sociology, Harvard University, Cambridge, MA.

Gomez, Edmund. 1991. *Money Politics in the Barisan Socialis.* Kuala Lumpur: Forum Publishers.

Gomez, Edmund, and Jomo K. S. 1997. *Malaysia's Political Economy: Politics, Patronage, and Profits.* Cambridge: Cambridge University Press.

Grabowski, Richard. 1994. "The Successful Developmental State: Where Does It Come From?" *World Development* 22 (3): 413–22.

1997. "Developmental States and Developmental Entrepreneurial Groups: Asian Experiences." *Journal of Asian Business* 13:25–45.

Haggard, Stephan. 1990. *Pathways from the Periphery: The Politics of Growth in the Newly Industrializing Countries.* Ithaca, NY: Cornell University Press.

2000. *The Political Economy of the Asian Financial Crisis.* Washington, DC: Institute for International Economics.

2004. "Institutions and Growth in East Asia." *Studies in Comparative International Development* 138 (4): 53–81.

Haggard, Stephan, David Kang, and Chung-in Moon. 1997. "Japanese Colonialism and Korean Development: A Critique." *World Development* 25 (6): 867–81.

Haggard, Stephan, and Robert R. Kaufman. 2008. *Development, Democracy and Welfare States: Latin America, East Asia and Eastern Europe.* Princeton, NJ: Princeton University Press.

Haggard, Stephan, and Lydia Tiede. 2011. "The Rule of Law and Economic Growth: Where Are We?" *World Development* 39 (5): 673–85.

Hayashi, Shigeko. 2010. "The Developmental State in the Era of Globalization: Beyond the Northeast Asian Model of Political Economy." *Pacific Review* 23 (1): 45–69.

Hellman, Thomas, Kevin Murdock, and Joseph Stiglitz. 1996. "Financial Restraint: Toward a New Paradigm." In *The Role of Government in East Asian Economic Development: Comparative Institutional Analysis*, edited by Masahiko Aoki, Hyung-Ki Kim, and Masahiro Okuno-Fujiwara, 163–207. New York: Oxford University Press.

Huff, W. G., G. Dewit, and C. Oughton. 2001. "Credibility and Reputation Building in the Developmental State: A Model with East Asian Implications." *World Development* 29 (4): 711–24.

Im, Hyug Baeg. 1987. "The Rise of Bureaucratic Authoritarianism in South Korea." *World Politics* 39:231–57.

Jayasuriya, Kanishka. 2005. "Beyond Institutional Fetishism: From the Developmental to the Regulatory State." *New Political Economy* 10 (3): 381–87.

Johnson, Chalmers. 1982. *MITI and the Japanese Miracle: The Growth of Industrial Policy, 1925–1975.* Stanford, CA: Stanford University Press.

1987. "Political Institutions and Economic Performance: The Government-Business Relationship in Japan, Korea, and Taiwan." In *The Political Economy of the New Asian Industrialism*, edited by Frederic Deyo, 136–64. Ithaca, NY: Cornell University Press.

Jomo K. S., with Chen Yun Chubng, Brian C. Folk Irfanul Haque, Pasuk Phongpaichit, Batara Simatupang, and Mayuri Tateishi. 1997. *Southeast Asia's Misunderstood Miracle: Industrial Policy and Economic Development in Thailand, Malaysia, and Indonesia.* Boulder, CO: Westview Press.

Kang, David. 2002a. *Crony Capitalism: Corruption and Development in South Korea and the Philippines.* Cambridge: Cambridge University Press.

2002b. "Money Politics and the Developmental State in Korea." *International Organization* 56 (1): 177–207.

Kaufman, Robert R. 1979. "Industrial Change and Authoritarian Rule in Latin America: A Concrete Review of the Bureaucratic-Authoritarian Model." In *The New Authoritarianism in Latin America*, edited by David Collier, 165–254. Princeton, NJ: Princeton University Press.

Khan, Moishin, and Jomo K. Sundaram, eds. 2000. *Rents, Rent-Seeking and Economic Development: Theory and the Asian Evidence.* Cambridge: Cambridge University Press.

Kim, Byung-kook. 1988. "Bringing and Managing Socioeconomic Change: The State in Korea and Mexico." Unpublished PhD diss., Department of Government, Harvard University, Cambridge, MA.

Kim, Eun Mee. 1997. *Big Business, Strong State: Collusion and Conflict in South Korean Development 1960–1990.* New York: SUNY Press.

Kim, Linsu. 1997. *Imitation to Innovation: The Dynamics of Korea's Technological Learning.* Boston: Harvard Business School Press.

Knight, John. 2010. *China as a Developmental State.* CSAE Working Paper WPS/2012–13. Oxford: Oxford University, Centre for the Study of African Economies.

Kohli, Atul. 2004. *State-Directed Development: Political Power and Industrialization in the Global Periphery.* Cambridge: Cambridge University Press.

Krauss, Ellis, and Michio Muramatsu. 1984. "Bureaucrats and Politicians in Policymaking: The Case of Japan." *American Political Science Review* 78 (1): 126–48.

Krueger, Anne. 1978. *Liberalization Attempts and Consequences.* Vol. 10 of *Foreign Trade Regimes and Economic Development.* Cambridge, MA: Ballinger Publishing Co. for the National Bureau of Economic Research.

Krugman, Paul. 1994. "The Myth of Asia's Miracle." *Foreign Affairs* 73 (6). www .foreignaffairs.com/articles/50550/paul-krugman/the-myth-of-asias-miracle.

Kuo, Chiang-tian. 1995. *Global Competitiveness and Industrial Growth in Taiwan and the Philippines.* Pittsburgh, PA: University of Pittsburgh Press.

Leftwich, Adrian. 1995. "Bringing Politics Back In: Towards a Model of the Developmental State." *Journal of Development Studies* 31 (3): 400–27.

Lin, J. Y. (2009) *Economic Development and Transition: Thought, Strategy, and Viability.* Cambridge: Cambridge University Press.

Lin, Justin, and Célestin Monga. 2011. "Growth Identification and Facilitation: The Role of the State in the Dynamics of Structural Change." *Development Policy Review* 29 (3): 264–90.

Low, Linda, ed. 2004. *Developmental States. Relevancy, Redundancy, or Reconfiguration?* New York: Nova Science Publishers.

MacIntyre, Andrew, ed. 1994. *Business and Government in Industrializing Asia.* Ithaca, NY: Cornell University Press.

2003. *The Power of Institutions: Political Architecture and Governance.* Ithaca, NY: Cornell University Press.

Maxfield, Sylvia, and Ben Ross Schneider. 1997. *Business and the State in Developing Countries.* New York: Cornell University Press.

Meyns, Peter, and Charity Musamba, eds. 2012. *The Developmental State in Africa: Problems and Prospects.* INEF Report 101/2012. Duisburg, Germany: Institute for Development and Peace.

Mkandawire, Thandika. 2001. "Thinking about Developmental States in Africa." *Cambridge Journal of Economics* 25 (3): 289–313.

Mo, Jongryn, and Chung-in Moon. 1999. "Korea After the Crash." *Journal of Democracy* 10 (2): 150–64.

Moon, Chung-in, and Rashemi Prasad. 1994. "Networks, Policies, Institutions." *Governance* 7 (4): 360–86.

Noble, Gregory. 1999. *Collective Action in East Asia: How Ruling Parties Shape Industrial Policy.* Ithaca, NY: Cornell University Press.

Noland, Marcus, and Howard Pack. 2003. *Industrial Policy in an Era of Globalization.* Washington, DC: Institute for International Economics.

O'Donnell, Guillermo. 1973. *Modernization and Bureaucratic-Authoritarianism: Studies in South American Politics.* Berkeley: University of California, Institute of International Studies.

Okimoto, Daniel I. 1989. *Between MITI and the Market: Japanese Industrial Policy for High Technology.* Stanford, CA: Stanford University Press.

Onis, Ziya. 1991. "The Logic of the Developmental State." *Comparative Politics* 24 (1): 109–26.

Patrick, Hugh, and Henry Rosovsky, eds. 1976. *Asia's New Giant: How the Japanese Economy Works.* Washington, DC: The Brookings Institution.

Paus, Eva. 2012. "Confronting the Middle Income Trap: Insights from Small Latecomers." *Studies in Comparative International Development* 47 (2): 155–38.

Przeworski, Adam, Michael E. Alvarez, Jose Antonio Cheibub, and Fernando Lemongi. 2000. *Democracy and Development: Political Institutions and Well-Being in the World, 1950–1990.* New York: Cambridge University Press.

Ramseyer, Frances McCall, and J. Mark Rosenbluth. 1993. *Japan's Political Marketplace.* Cambridge, MA: Harvard University Press.

Robinson, Mark, and Gordon White, eds. 1998. *The Democratic Developmental State.* Oxford: Oxford University Press.

Rock, Michael. 2013. "East Asia's Democratic Developmental States and Economic Growth." *Journal of East Asian Studies* 13 (1): 1–34.

Rodrik, Dani. 1995. "Getting Interventions Right: How South Korea and Taiwan Grew Rich." *Economic Policy* 10 (20): 53–107.

    2007. "Normalizing Industrial Policy." Unpublished manuscript. Kennedy School of Government, Harvard University, Cambridge, MA.

    2008. *One Economics, Many Recipes: Globalization, Institutions, and Economic Growth.* Princeton, NJ: Princeton University Press.

Root, Hilton L. 1996. *Small Countries, Big Lessons: Governance and the Rise of East Asia.* New York: Oxford University Press.

Routley, Laura. 2012. *Developmental States: A Review of the Literature.* Effective States and Inclusive Development Working Paper No. 3. Manchester: ESID.

Samuels, Richard J. 1987. *The Business of the Japanese State: Energy Markets in Comparative and Historical Perspective.* Ithaca, NY: Cornell University Press.

Schleifer, Andrei, and Robert W. Vishney. 1993. "Corruption." *Quarterly Journal of Economics* 108 (3): 599–617.

Stiglitz, Joseph. 2001. *Joseph Stiglitz and the World Bank: The Rebel Within.* Edited with commentary by Ja-joon Chang. London: Anthem Press.

    2002. *Globalization and Its Discontents.* New York: W. W. Norton.

Svolik, Milan. 2012. *The Politics of Authoritarian Rule.* New York: Cambridge University Press.

Vu, Tuong. 2007. "State Formation and the Origins of Developmental States in South Korea and Indonesia." *Studies in Comparative International Development* 41 (4): 27–56.

    2010. *Paths to Development in Asia: South Korea, Vietnam, China and Indonesia.* Cambridge: Cambridge University Press.

Wade, Robert. 1990. *Governing the Market: Economic Theory and the Role of Government in East Asian Industrialization.* Princeton, NJ: Princeton University Press.

    1996. "Japan, the World Bank, and the Art of Paradigm Maintenance: The East Asian Miracle in Political Perspective." *New Left Review* 217:3–36.

    2004. *Governing the Market: Economic Theory and the Role of Government in East Asian Industrialization.* 2nd ed. Princeton, NJ: Princeton University Press.

Wade, Robert, and Frank Veneroso. 1998. 'The Asian Crisis: The High Debt Model Versus the Wall Street–Treasury–IMF Complex." *New Left Review* 228:1–24.

Waldner, David. 1999. *State-Building and Late Development.* Ithaca, NY: Cornell University Press.

Weingast, Barry. 1995. "The Economic Role of Political Institutions." *Journal of Law, Economics, and Organization* 7:1–31.

——— 1997. "The Political Foundations of Democracy and the Rule of Law." *American Political Science Review* 91 (2): 245–63.

Weiss, Linda. 1998. *The Myth of the Powerless State: Governing the Economy in a Global Era.* Cambridge: Polity Press.

White, Gordon, and Robert Wade. 1984. "Developmental States in East Asia." Special issue, *IDS Bulletin* 15 (2): 1–71.

Wong, Joseph. 2004. "The Adaptive Developmental State in East Asia." *Journal of East Asian Studies* 4 (3): 345–62.

——— 2011. *Betting on Biotech: Innovation and the Limits of Asia's Developmental State.* Ithaca, NY: Cornell University Press.

Woo, Jung-en. 1991. *Race to the Swift: State and Finance in Korean Industrialization.* New York: Columbia University Press.

Woo-Cumings, Meredith, ed. 1999. *The Developmental State.* Ithaca, NY: Cornell University Press.

World Bank. 1993. *The East Asian Miracle: Economic Growth and Public Policy.* New York: Oxford University Press for the World Bank.

Yusuf, Shahid. 2003. *Innovative East Asia: The Future of Growth.* Washington, DC: World Bank.

3 Coalitions, policies, and distribution: Esping-Andersen's *Three Worlds of Welfare Capitalism*

Jane Gingrich

The publication of Gøsta Esping-Andersen's foundational work *Three Worlds of Welfare Capitalism* in 1990 marked a decisive moment in the study of cross-national social policy, creating a research legacy enduring over time, across disciplines, and across methodological approaches.[1] What explains this profound influence? This chapter argues that *Three Worlds* was so deeply successful in generating a productive research agenda precisely because of the way that Esping-Andersen grounds his understanding of the welfare state in comparative-historical analysis.

The core argument in *Three Worlds* is that advanced capitalist democracies vary not only in how much they spend on social welfare but also in how they spend on it. Understanding welfare capitalism requires examining how packages of institutions, both in the state and the market, interact to produce particular types of distributive outcomes. It is crucial to emphasize that this insight, which is now widely internalized in the contemporary political economy debate, was extremely novel at the time, challenging previous work presenting welfare development in more or less linear terms. Both the core typology of *Three Worlds* and Esping-Andersen's broader analytic shift in emphasis toward understanding welfare institutions as the product of particular historical struggles opened the space for a vastly productive research agenda.

First, Esping-Andersen's aim is to understand one of the central large-scale shifts in twentieth-century politics: the rise and operation of welfare institutions. To do so, he argues that we cannot hive off a single institution (e.g., gross social spending, labor market policy) from other institutions. Nor can we understand the way institutions operate in an abstract or temporally

In addition to the helpful feedback from the other participants in this project, I thank John Stephens, Nancy Bermeo, and Ben Ansell for comments on a previous draft of this paper.

[1] As of the time of writing, the Google scholar citation count for *Three Worlds* was 21,784.

independent way. Rather, *Three Worlds* argues that the structure of the labor market and the state work in tandem, in configurations, to shape broader power relationships and outcomes.

Second, Esping-Andersen, like many both before and after him, conceptualizes the politics of the welfare state as a product of the tension between the inequality produced by capitalism and the equality of parliamentary democracy. Yet, the resolution of this tension is neither uniform nor linear but a product of particular political struggles. To understand how democratic processes modify markets, he argues, we need to look at how coalitions of actors come together at particular historical moments to construct social policy – not just generic structural determinants. In advancing this claim, Esping-Andersen drew on multiple methods. Indeed, his evidence for variation among welfare states rests as much on a quantitative analysis of policy structures as a direct use of the tools of comparative-historical analysis. This chapter argues, however, that his deep engagement with specific aims of European social democratic movements in key cases provided the conceptual core for his categorization of regimes and understanding of welfare institutions as well as the mechanisms that produced them (see Esping-Andersen 1985; Esping-Andersen and Korpi 1984).

Third, Esping-Andersen argues that, once established, the institutions of the state and market have a crucial structuring power for future political and distributive outcomes. Attention not only to how the politics of welfare states develop in a particular time and place but also to how they then shape politics in systematic ways as they develop over time is crucial to understanding the state itself.

Collectively, these arguments offered a conceptualization of advanced democratic capitalism that moved away from linear and functionalist interpretations of the state, emphasizing instead the structuring power of historically shaped configurations of institutions. This shift rested on both Esping-Andersen's engagement with comparative-historical cases and, fundamentally, his understanding of welfare institutions, and the political dynamics behind their development, as macroconfigurations emerging at particular historical moments with a temporal structure. In so doing, *Three Worlds* offered even its critics new tools for understanding the welfare state.

A first line of research directly engaged the specific claims in *Three Worlds*, interrogating in particular Esping-Andersen's categorization of regimes and their origins. Even as much of this work challenged the precise way that Esping-Andersen defined institutional (and market) variation, it largely reaffirmed the idea that institutions cluster in particular ways with distinct effects.

A second line of research turned to investigating the structuring power of these clusters for contemporary welfare politics. Here, work drawing on *Three Worlds* shows that varying welfare regimes fundamentally shaped both the way advanced welfare states experienced structural economic and demographic shifts and the power of varying political constellations – and the state itself – in addressing these new issues.

A third line of scholarship more fundamentally challenged the underlying claims of *Three Worlds*, moving toward more deductive and less historical arguments about welfare state origins or deemphasizing the role of macroregimes as structuring politics more generally. However, I show that even these critical perspectives often return to aspects of Esping-Andersen's insights when looking to explain distributive politics.

What does this deep legacy tell us? This chapter argues that, although much work casts doubt on components of Esping-Andersen's arguments, attempts to move to either linear or purely deductive understandings of the welfare state, while generating key insights, have rarely eclipsed his core claims: broad macroconfigurations of institutions shape markets and politics in key ways, and these institutions are the product of particular historical moments and distributive struggles. These claims provided a framework for dialogue among researchers from quantitative and qualitative traditions that has been enormously productive in developing knowledge about the welfare state. Both the ongoing relevance of Esping-Andersen's work and his approach to the state suggest that methodological engagement with country cases, attention to the development of institutions over time, and broad comparisons of clusters of institutions remain crucial tools for understanding contemporary political economies.

The following sections examine these arguments in turn, reviewing debates in the field leading up to the publication of *Three Worlds*, the core analytical shifts it made, and responses engaging with the regime typology, the structuring power of institution, and its ontological core. In each case, I show that aspects of Esping-Andersen's work remained deeply influential, an influence drawn from both the power of his original conceptualization of the state and his broader understanding of the political process.

Understanding the welfare state

One of the core questions bedeviling scholars of the welfare state from the nineteenth century to today is how to understand the welfare state as at the intersection of democracy and capitalism (Iversen 2010). Scholars coming from very different analytical traditions asked both how the inequality produced by capitalism could survive the political equality of democracy and how capitalism could survive the demands of democracy. The welfare state was initially an answer to this conundrum, but one that raised new questions.

T. H. Marshall (1964), in his influential theorization of the social rights of citizenship, presents the development of "social rights" as a necessary step following from the earlier expansion of economic and political rights. Modern welfare states are part of the linear, even teleological, logic of development in capitalist democracies, unfolding automatically in response to the earlier expansion of market and democratic rights. So-called logic of industrialism theorists developed this line of thinking. This work argued that capitalist development simultaneously unmoored workers from traditional economic networks and created economic surpluses that allowed states to develop bureaucratic capacity.[2] The development of advanced capitalism, then, created both functional pressures for the welfare state and the resources to expand it, promoting converging developments.

Marxist scholarship, although coming from a highly distinct analytic perspective, also saw the welfare state as an undifferentiated product of capitalism, working to mute class conflict in relatively constant ways. For Claus Offe (1982, 7), the welfare state was the "major peace formula" in advanced capitalist systems. Here, the state served to limit economic or political insurrection rather than transform the capitalist system. While conceptualizing the welfare state as particularly important in the postwar period, this work, too, saw it largely in terms of its functional role in sustaining the market economy.

Whereas both Marxist and modernization approaches occasionally used cross-time quantitative or historical methods, this analysis largely served to provide illustrative examples of the unfolding logic of capitalism rather than to interrogate its comparative-historical development. However, Jill Quadagno (1987), writing about the state of the art in welfare state research in the 1980s, argues that the economic crises across industrial economies in the 1970s constituted a turning point not only in the politics of many advanced welfare states but also in their academic problematization. As states looked to trim entitlements in the face of slowing growth, scholars, too, could no longer take for granted the steady march toward welfare state expansion, raising new questions about its origins and character.

---

[2] This description is stylized; these approaches often admitted more scope for varying historical processes (e.g., Wilensky 1974).

Against this background, two lines of scholarship problematizing linear, structural accounts of welfare development emerged. A first line of work, coming from the "power resources" school, drew on Marxist understandings of conflictual market relations as a defining feature of capitalist systems. However, for these scholars, welfare states did not just arise from the ether of capitalist development; rather, they were the product of "politics against markets" (Esping-Andersen 1985) emerging from political struggles in which the left actors won (Korpi 1983; Stephens 1979). Another line of theorizing, developing particularly in the US context, argued that political institutions and early policy development were crucial to structuring the translation of electoral demands into policies. For instance, Orloff and Skocpol (1984) look at the ways in which the timing of democratization shaped the capacity of the UK and US federal governments, opening, or foreclosing, different political coalitions.

This work suggested that linear or functionalist interpretations of the welfare state missed the conflictual, and at times contextually shaped, nature of its development. In so doing, both power-resource and institutionalist work invoked historical analysis differently from how previous approaches, or historians themselves – who had largely neglected the study of the welfare state – did (Baldwin 1992). This work, however, also raised new questions. If, as power-resource theorists claimed, social policy was fundamentally a product of the political strength of left actors, why did large welfare states also emerge from the actions of the Right (e.g., in Bismarckian Germany)? If politics was institutional, what explained the origins of these institutions? The political struggles within them? These questions called for an explicit theorization of how welfare institutions operated within the broader political economy and democratic process.

Three Worlds of Welfare Capitalism

Three Worlds emerged against this background. The core argument of the book is that welfare states vary not only in how much they spend but in how they spend and that the nature of cross-class coalitions between unions and left parties, and other social groups, explains this variation. The result is three distinct "worlds" of welfare capitalism, which offer different social rights to workers and shape the nature of labor market and social stratification more generally.

To begin, Esping-Andersen conceptualizes welfare variation in simultaneously theoretical and historical terms. He argues that welfare policy and politics are fundamentally multidimensional; although social spending is important, we cannot understand either the nature or origins of welfare states by looking simply at spending levels. To distinguish this dimensionality, Esping-Andersen develops the concepts of decommodification and stratification. The intellectual roots of decommodification are theoretical, lying in both Marx and Polanyi (1944), who look at the ways that market economies, in commodifying labor, force workers into relationships of dependence that curtail their power. However, it is the historical struggles for social rights that "diminish citizens' status as 'commodities'" (3), thus decommodifying them, that lie at the heart of the development of contemporary welfare states and labor markets. Decommodification "occurs when a service is rendered as a matter of right, and when a person can maintain a livelihood without reliance on the market" (22) and thus uphold "their living standards independent of pure market forces" (3). Welfare states and markets are coconstitutive, state-provided social rights change power relationships in labor markets, and power relationships in labor markets, in turn, shape how states can act.

This claim not only is deeply normative – welfare states are potential tools for the emancipation of workers – but also provides a political and sociological foundation for Esping-Andersen's famous distinction among welfare regimes. The Liberal world, which includes the Anglo-Saxon countries, provides meager benefits, producing little decommodification and encouraging citizens' reliance on the market. By contrast, the Social Democratic countries of Scandinavia produce ample decommodification, providing generous benefits extending across classes and crowding out market provision and empowering workers in the broader labor market. The Conservative welfare states of Continental Europe (and Japan), despite high spending, look to preserve the status of privileged groups and thus are less decommodifying. This typology distills many varying institutional features of the welfare state (e.g., unemployment, pension, sickness benefits) into clusters that have a conceptual core based on how they offer social rights to citizens.

These differences in the structure of the state shape not only the distribution of resources in society but also, crucially, the distribution of power. For Esping-Andersen, stratification across classes is neither an inevitable by-product of markets – whether viewed positively or negatively – nor an individual failing but is constructed over time through the political process and its institutionalization in welfare regimes. The Liberal world entrenches market-based stratification along income or class lines. The Conservative world stratifies along traditional status lines, maintaining differences among groups. Finally, Social Democratic welfare states bridge social divisions, promoting a more equal distribution of power and resources in society. Once established, the logic of stratification becomes embedded in the state and market, perpetuating itself over time. The early battles establishing welfare regimes in Continental Europe had lasting effects, as did those fought through the 1930s to the 1950s in Social Democracies, not only for the particular institutions established but also for the power of unions and employers, among other groups, in the political process. Welfare institutions, then, bridge the past to the present, providing (or foreclosing) crucial political resources for actors.

Collectively, these claims profoundly challenged earlier work on welfare state development, offering both a nonlinear conceptualization of the state and market and, more broadly, a nonfunctionalist and historical understanding of political and economic institutions. Both of these moves were possible – and indeed so influential – because of the way Esping-Andersen draws on comparative-historical analysis. In their introductory chapter, Thelen and Mahoney (this volume) argue that the defining features of comparative-historical analysis involve investigations of macroscopic and configural phenomena that draw on contextualized case research of unfolding political or social processes. *Three Worlds* is, in many ways, emblematic of this approach. Esping-Andersen's subject is the development of advanced welfare states, one of the defining political creations of democratic countries in the twentieth century. In examining variation among welfare states, he develops a theoretical edifice that rests on an understanding of welfare regimes as historically shaped products of distributive struggles among representatives of labor, their allies, and other economic elites, which, in turn, have their own temporal structure on future political dynamics.

First, although Esping-Andersen was not the first scholar to suggest variation in welfare states;[3] his typology of the "three worlds" eclipsed more undifferentiated accounts of the state and remains (as I argue below) a remarkably productive framework for analyzing welfare institutions. In developing this typology, he made a key analytic shift from earlier work: explicitly theorizing how social spending could achieve different distributive goals based on its structure. In *Three Worlds,* Esping-Andersen's discussion of policy variation mixes historical analysis of cases with a large amount of cross-national

---

[3] His typology draws on earlier work by Richard Titmuss (1974), who made similar distinctions.

quantitative data linking entitlement structures to distributive outcomes.[4] Indeed, *Three Worlds* draws less explicitly on comparative-historical methods than other contemporaneous work (e.g., Baldwin 1990), and Scruggs and Allan (2008) argue that part of the enduring success of the *Three Worlds* typology lies in how "evidence of regimes was (apparently) confirmed with social data" (642). Yet, these data, and Esping-Andersen's broader break with linear and undifferentiated perspectives on the welfare state through the concepts of decommodification and stratification, were possible precisely because his research puzzle and approach drew on a long-standing engagement with the actual demands of labor and social democratic movements.

Esping-Andersen's earlier work, both in conjunction with Walter Korpi (Esping-Andersen and Korpi 1984) and in his 1985 book *Politics Against Markets*, problematizes the historical trajectory of Northern and Continental European social democratic movements. This examination of the actual political battles at the heart of these nascent welfare institutions provides the grounding for decommodification as a defining concept of variation. He famously states in *Three Worlds* (1990): "it is difficult to imagine that anyone struggled for spending per se" (21). The political actors who created welfare regimes did not think about social and labor market policy in atomized or unrelated terms. Instead, they struggled broadly to redefine – or maintain – particular social and economic power structures. Engaging with the historic goals of labor movements, and their conservative counterparts, for altered power relations – that is, for decommodification and the subsequent stratification among groups – allowed Esping-Andersen to both draw connections among configurations of policy and identify the broad distributive differences across regimes. His break with undifferentiated views of social spending, then, was grounded in a theorization of variation based on the historic experiences of European political movements. This conceptual base allowed him to develop a typology that resonated deeply with the actual practices of welfare states.

Second, *Three Worlds* fundamentally broke with the underpinning assumptions of more functional readings of the development of welfare institutions. If welfare regimes rest on qualitative differences – not just more or less spending – then explaining their development requires a nonlinear theorization of variation. To explain this nonlinearity, Esping-Andersen points to the logic of political coalitions. He rejects the idea that welfare states are an

---

[4] Esping-Andersen draws on data collected as part of the Social Citizenship Indicators Project that quantified aspects of program entitlement, generosity, and conditionality.

automatic by-product of either capitalist needs or economically determined democratic demands, breaking with Marxist and "logic of industrialism" theses. However, welfare states are also not an undifferentiated product of strong labor movements. Rather, he argues, the welfare state follows from the ways in which labor and social democratic movements join (or fail to join) with other social actors. Put differently, it rests on the historic alignment of societal groups.

This claim constituted Esping-Andersen's second key analytic shift from earlier work. The inequality produced by capitalism and the political equality of citizens in a democracy do not create a single set of pressures or resulting outcomes. Instead, to understand the resolution of these generic tensions, Esping-Andersen argues that we need to examine the power of organized groups (most importantly, labor) and the actual historic coalitions they strike. He states, "Whether, and under what conditions, the class divisions and social inequalities produced by capitalism can be undone by parliamentary democracy" (11) is the central question in the study of the welfare state. Social cleavage structures do not automatically produce a given politics (neither do the demands of electoral democracy necessarily foreclose certain possibilities); rather, decommodification emerges from particular class struggles. He writes that there is "no compelling reason to believe that workers will automatically and naturally forge a socialist class identity; nor is it plausible that their mobilization will look especially Swedish" (29). Instead, extensive decommodification occurs in Scandinavia because representatives of the working class formed coalitions first with the agricultural classes and later with the middle classes. Understanding the origins of welfare regimes, then, requires attention to the historic processes of coalition formation: "the comparative and historical method that today underpins almost all good political economy is one that reveals variation and permeability" (12). Engagement with cases provides a way of understanding the mechanisms of welfare state formation, precisely because these processes always emerge in particular contexts.

Finally, Esping-Andersen's third analytic shift, which follows from the previous two, lies in his understanding of institutions themselves. For Esping-Andersen, institutions are political creations that fundamentally shape the distribution of power in society. They do not primarily serve to enhance market efficiency (or inhibit it), and one cannot understand their effects in the abstract, drawing on the particular functional roles they play. Rather, to understand the contemporary state (and market) we need to understand the way early political battles shaped its structure and authority in particular ways that last over time. These claims developed the insights of the institutionalist research agenda, presenting institutions as both a product of particular political coalitions and a structural force in reproducing particular patterns of political life over time.

Three Worlds, then, offers both a methodological and ontological shift from previous research. Not only did it provide a framework for thinking about welfare regime variation that was grounded in real political battles but it also argued that understanding welfare states requires both engaging in case-based comparisons – to map broad macrolevel configurations of relationships between states and markets – and historical analysis – to trace the battles that produce them. In arguing that the logic of capitalism and democracy do not automatically produce a single logic of redistribution or social welfare but instead that coalitions of actors construct state and market institutions to redistribute power, Esping-Andersen opened up an array of new avenues for comparative political research on the origins of the state, the effects of the state of social stratification, and the structuring power of institutions themselves.

Reconceptualizing the origins and character of the welfare state?

In drawing on, and distilling, actual historical demands to define regime variation, Esping-Andersen broke with teleological or functional understandings of democratic capitalism. A first wave of responses to *Three Worlds* directly engaged with Esping-Andersen's understanding of variation and its political origins. Some of Esping-Andersen's claims weathered this critical examination better than others. Ultimately, however, I argue that his basic categorization of welfare regimes has remained quite durable (and, as the next section shows, analytically useful) and that his understanding of institutions as variable, historically shaped forces proved extremely fruitful, with even his critics building on his intellectual break with more linear perspectives on the state.

The most influential strand of *Three Worlds* lies in Esping-Andersen's theorization of the nature and origins of regime variation. Much of the initial scholarship responding to *Three Worlds* directed itself against the concept of decommodification as a conceptual foundation for regime variation. As argued above, decommodification plays a key normative role in Esping-Andersen's work – providing, to some extent, a vindication of social democracy as a political force within capitalism. Yet the concept as he defines and measures it does not always crisply distinguish the institutional configuration in the welfare regimes. Moreover, as Esping-Andersen acknowledges, the most decommodifying welfare regimes, those in Scandinavia, depend on the near full participation of citizens in the labor force to sustain high benefit levels (see Huo, Nelson, and Stephens 2008 on this point).

Early critics jumped on these conceptual concerns, moving to redefine state variation along alternative lines. This work accepted Esping-Andersen's basic break with linear perspectives on the state but emphasized different originative goals – and thus effects – of welfare institutions. For instance, Francis Castles and Deborah Mitchell (1991), writing hot on the heels of *Three Worlds*, suggest the focus on decommodification as a rights-conferring process, rather than on actual redistributive outcomes, is misleading. They move to reconceptualize the state in terms of its redistributive potential. This move breaks Australia and New Zealand out from the other "liberal" welfare states but otherwise confirms the original clusters, but on new grounds. Other work focused on entitlement rules or fiscal redistribution rather than on broad state-market power relations, suggesting yet other ways of understanding the dimensionality of welfare regimes and their historical origins (for a careful review, see Arts and Gelissen 2002). These taxonomical questions spilled into research on particular policy domains, with scholars of health and other services both highlighting within-regime heterogeneity in service provision and questioning the conceptual applicability of the logic of decommodification to services (e.g., Alber 1995; Jensen 2008). Collectively, this work largely confirmed the basic premise of welfare state variation and – despite some recategorization of particular cases – broad qualitative distinctions among Scandinavian, Continental European, and Anglo welfare states. What it challenged, however, was the grounding of these distinctions in analyses of power structures, moving instead toward distinctions drawn primarily on the basis of institutional design.

Feminist scholarship, by contrast, focused directly on analyses of power structures as a way to critique the concept of decommodification. Scholars of gender had long pointed to the critical role that social policies play in structuring gender relations and roles (e.g., Gordon 1990). This work initially seized on these insights to offer a critical perspective on *Three Worlds*. Influentially, Ann Orloff (1993) argues that Esping-Andersen's master concept of decommodification is blind to the historic lack of commodification among women. As such, in theorizing welfare regimes through the lens of decommodification, he fails to elucidate the ways in which policy can affect women by shaping their access to employment and thus their relative independence from men. This critique was a profound one because it challenged the placement of welfare regimes at the intersection of capitalism and democracy, bringing in analyses of power inequalities that are not primarily rooted in market relationships but within families and among families, the market, and the state.

Despite Orloff's critical stance toward Esping-Andersen's work, she builds on aspects of his intellectual project. Orloff (1993) argues that the potential of policy "through the political struggles of citizens and others, to counter domination" (305) is at the heart of the feminist research project. In this regard, Esping-Andersen's analytic perspective, as problematic as it is, provides a bridge linking feminist scholarship to differential regime trajectories and thus the emancipatory potential of politics itself. Indeed, even if decommodification as a concept is gender-blind, the clustering of the *Three Worlds* maps onto quite different gendered outcomes, a finding that prompted an explosion of work linking welfare regimes to women's role in the labor force (Gornick and Meyers 2003), the well-being of lone parents (Lewis 1997), and the power of women more generally (Esping-Andersen 1999; Korpi 2000). This feminist critique, then, confirmed the value of Esping-Andersen's original regime categorization while pushing forward his insights about how configurations of institutions structure power to new nonmarket domains.

In moving away from a focus on decommodification as the defining feature of welfare states and pointing to a broader range of distributive outcomes embedded in welfare institutions, this critical response to Esping-Andersen also ushered in a less labor-focused set of explanations for regime variation. Once again, this work takes Esping-Andersen's break with linear and functionalist understanding of political institutions as a starting point but theorizes a broader range of actors and coalitions at the heart of social policy development.

For instance, a number of scholars have argued that the "religious roots" of welfare states are as important as the class origins of states. Kees van Kersbergen (1995) shows the distinctive ways in which Christian social thinking responded to the tensions created by capitalist development, emphasizing the role of subsidiary organizations (e.g., the family and Church). Philip Manow (2004) develops this analysis, examining the influence of Lutheran and Calvinist Protestant religious actors in distinguishing the trajectories of difficult-to-classify welfare states such as the Netherlands. Other work problematized the relationship between electoral democracy and capitalism more generally (e.g., Lynch 2006). Ferrera (1996), for example, argues that Esping-Andersen's exclusion of the Southern European countries from *Three Worlds* does not just constitute an empirical blind spot but misses how clientelistic party competition (not the power resources of the Left) in these institutionally weak states led to a combination of universal services with highly dualistic income maintenance benefits. Both of these approaches show how the historic interests of nonmarket actors also shaped the distributive functions of the state.

This debate had several important consequences. First, while Esping-Andersen's critics challenged large parts of his conceptual apparatus, his break with linear perspectives and undifferentiated perspectives on the welfare state was nonetheless at the core of their work. If welfare states were not just about "more or less spending" but also about qualitative variation in the structure of spending and entitlement, then the question of what constitutes the core of this qualitative variation becomes important. Those focusing on religious actors, clientalistic parties, and power dynamics in the family, among other facets of political life, debated how to conceptualize the character of policy and its origins. Although some scholars were critical of the "taxonomic slippery slope" around regime categorization (Baldwin 1992), collectively, this work brought a wide range of scholars together into a dialogue, leading to a richer understanding of advanced welfare states.

Second, however, in challenging the logic of decommodification, this work tended toward a more institutional and (with the exception of work on gender) a less sociological definition of the state and less class-based interpretations of its origins. I discuss this point more in the conclusion, but it is worth highlighting here that this move contributed to new avenues of research on the structuring power of institutions while also muting other debates about class power.

Finally, despite hundreds of articles rethinking regime variation and challenging the concept of decommodification, much of this scholarship largely highlighted similar packages of institutions and categorization of cases as those in *Three Worlds*. This latter point is important, not because it suggests that Esping-Andersen was unequivocally right about all aspects of regime variation but, rather, because his typology nonetheless did capture key components of welfare state variation. As discussed below, the deep resonance of the typology provided a framework for those looking to understand the structuring power of institutions in the face of new pressures.

Regimes as a framework for understanding change

For Esping-Andersen, welfare regimes are the product of past political battles and crucially structure future political battles. One cannot understand changes in the welfare state without theorizing the way its existing structure provides key actors – and the state itself – differing capacities and power.

However, even as Esping-Andersen argued that welfare regimes structure both welfare politics and institutional change, others raised questions about their relevance. Just as Quadagno (1987) argues that changes in the global economy in the 1970s ushered in new research questioning Marxist and Liberal linear understandings of welfare development in the 1980s, economic and political developments from the 1990s also raised questions about ongoing diversity among welfare politics and welfare states more generally. As traditional social cleavages and organized labor seemingly waned while the power of business and financial interests grew, and new movements on the Right and Left emerged, many pointed to a growing chasm between the politics of welfare state origins and the configuration of interests battling over economic and social policy. Moreover, in the face of rising income inequalities, cutbacks in pension and unemployment programs, the marketization of public services, a move toward "recommodifying" activation, and some expansion in benefits for families, scholars further asked whether the regime distinctions that defined postwar welfare states remained relevant in structuring political life.

Do welfare regimes continue to structure politics in the way Esping-Andersen suggested? Do they structure the patterns of adjustment to new pressures? Do we even need to understand the historic development of institutions to understand contemporary political economies? In this section I argue that both work adopting aspects of the regime approach and – as I show in the next section – work that ostensibly rejects it demonstrate a deep structuring legacy of welfare regimes on both patterns of change and social and economic outcomes. However, scholarship examining the institutional mechanisms for reproduction hypothesized in *Three Worlds* has yielded more ambiguous evidence. In looking to theorize the way institutions reproduce themselves that extends beyond Esping-Andersen's emphasis on mass attitudes and class power, research on welfare reform has largely developed – not rejected – the claim that attention to the historical structure of institutions, and embedded power dynamics, matters for the contemporary politics of welfare reform. These claims are important because they suggest that changing structural economic forces do not obviate attention to the historical development of institutions; rather, this approach remains crucial to understanding how countries experience new structural economic pressures and the capacities and interests of actors to respond to them.

Table 3.1 Variation in outcomes across welfare regimes

	Welfare generosity		Public social spending as % of GDP		Post-tax/transfers Gini coefficient		Union density	
	1980s	2000s	1980s	2000s	1980s	2000s	1980s	2000s
Australia	21.1	21.2	11.51	17.04	–	0.32	48.5	21.3
Canada	25.9	25.9	16.11	17.21	0.29	0.32	34.71	29.99
Ireland	25.8	34.5	18.42	16.71	–	0.31	55.45	34.5
Japan	24.3	25.3	11.07	18.46	0.30	0.33	28.93	19.36
New Zealand	22.2	21.6	18.14	18.81	0.27	0.33	58.6	21.41
UK	28.9	27.8	18.37	20.45	0.31	0.34	47.59	28.23
United States	21	21.3	13.39	16.24	0.34	0.37	22.1	12.14
Average	**24.2**	**25.4**	**15.29**	**17.85**	**0.30**	**0.33**	**42.79**	**25.49**
Austria	31.8	34	23.05	27.16	–	0.26	52.13	32.8
Belgium	39.3	41.1	25.29	26.56	–	0.27	52.28	51.83
France	37.2	37.8	23.86	29.82	–	0.29	14.39	7.82
Germany	35.8	33	22.53	26.71	0.25	0.28	34.23	21.73
Italy	25.7	29.3	20.35	24.74	0.28	0.32	43.72	33.9
Switzerland	36.3	36.9	14.53	19.10	–	0.30	–	–
Average	**34.4**	**35.4**	**21.60**	**25.68**	**0.27**	**0.29**	**39.35**	**29.62**
Denmark	39.1	34.8	24.37	27.54	0.22	0.24	77.88	71.19
Finland	32.8	34.1	21.19	25.68	0.21	0.25	69.9	71.83
The Netherlands	37.8	38.1	25.37	21.01	0.28	0.29	28.84	21.04
Norway	41.1	42.8	19.38	22.06	0.22	0.26	57.51	54.4
Sweden	45.6	38.4	28.64	28.80	0.20	0.25	81.05	74.59
Average	**39.3**	**37.6**	**23.79**	**25.02**	**0.23**	**0.26**	**63.04**	**58.61**

Sources: Welfare generosity, union density, and spending are decade averages from, respectively: Scruggs *et al.* (2013), Visser *et al.* (2011), and Organisation for Economic Co-operation (2013a). The data on the Gini coefficient are from Organisation for Economic Co-operation (2013b) and represent mid-decade estimates.

Many looking at reforms to advanced welfare states and economic outcomes note ongoing divergence among countries (e.g., Pontusson 2005). Table 3.1 broadly displays this dynamic, showing evidence – albeit not unambiguous evidence – of ongoing variation among regimes on several illustrative indicators of welfare state effort. On average, the Social Democratic regimes continue to spend more and have more generous social programs, stronger unions, and lower inequality, while Liberal regimes tend to spend less publicly and have less generous programs, lower rates of unionization, and more inequality. Continental regimes remain in the middle of these two poles. To be sure, within each group there is much variation (Ahlquist and Breunig 2012); nonetheless, differences across countries remain important.

What explains these ongoing differences in countries in the face of the structural pressures outlined above? In *Three Worlds*, Esping-Andersen postulated that, once established, state-market institutions themselves conditioned their own differential trajectory via two key political mechanisms: they shaped the structure of electoral support for the state, and they shaped the structural power of the Left (organized labor and Social Democratic parties).

In *Three Worlds*, Esping-Andersen's electoral arguments are important but speculative. He argues that the broad encompassing structure of Social Democratic welfare regimes should breed public support for the state and defuse class conflict, thus perpetuating their generous structures, while Liberal welfare states generate lower levels of support and more extensive conflict across groups. However, as researchers turned to examine these claims, they uncovered a more complex pattern of mass attitudes. Stefan Svallfors's (1997) influential study of public opinion in eight nations looks to assess whether differences in public support for the state and differences in the overall salience of class/income in shaping preferences vary across regimes. He finds evidence of the former, but not the latter – a finding itself that spurred a slew of research investigating whether welfare regimes structure typical attitudes, the distribution of attitudes, the salience of class and income, and the use of different moral criteria and, again, produced mixed findings (for a review, see Svallfors 2010). Moreover, other work on the welfare state offered a highly plausible alternative reading, arguing that variation in preferences causes variation in policy structures, not vice versa (Brooks and Manza 2007). Nor did clear evidence emerge for Esping-Andersen's newer hypothesized attitudinal divides in response to postindustrial pressures, for instance, between public and private sector workers in Scandinavia, between insiders and outsiders in Continental Europe, or across classes in the Liberal world (Svallfors 2010). This work raised questions about the nature of political constellations around the state and the sources – if any – of regime reproduction.

For Esping-Andersen, however, regime reproduction did not just work through an electoral mechanism. He emphasizes the crucial institutionalized power of groups, particularly Social Democratic parties and organized labor. Work looking specifically at this dynamic yielded more evidence of direct political feedbacks. Korpi and Palme's (2003) study of retrenchment, for instance, argues that the "power resources" of unions and left parties continue to matter in an era of austerity. They argue that the rise of mass unemployment across advanced welfare states creates pressure for cuts, but in contrast to more "classless" interpretations of the politics of retrenchment (see below), existing institutions shape the constellation of class interests and power in resisting cuts.

However, this work too raised questions. If regimes structure change primarily through their influence on left power, why do countries with a weakening left not more radically alter the state? Why do those with a strong left reform at all? In responding to these questions, Paul Pierson's theorization of welfare state retrenchment (1996, 2001) and the logic of path dependence more generally (2004) emerged as powerful alternative theorizations of institutional reproduction.

Pierson's critical insight is that growing economic and demographic pressures on advanced welfare states do not automatically translate into political demands for welfare cuts; indeed, the outcome is quite the opposite. As welfare states develop, Pierson argues, they create both high direct costs to change and mobilize both interest groups and electoral constituencies looking to preserve them. Understanding the puzzle of retrenchment (or lack thereof) requires historical analysis, but its goal is not to map precisely how broad macroconfigurations of class (or other) interests become institutionalized and self-perpetuating through labor market and political structures but to attend to the ways in which policy creates its own institutional costs (or opportunities) for change and empowers protective interests that may obviate these foundational political struggles. Pierson's work shifts the analytic focus for regime reproduction via left power to the ways in which *all* policies create a distinct political logic through institutional maturation.

Pierson's claims proved to be highly influential in a number of regards, initiating a boom of research looking to conceptualize the nature of change in advanced welfare states (e.g., Green-Pedersen 2004) and examining the relative roles of traditional democratic representatives – namely, unions and parties – and "new" actors in shaping welfare state reform (e.g., Huber and Stephens 2001; Korpi and Palme 2003). However, as influential as this work was (and is), for both Pierson (2001) and scholars drawing on him, the line between "old" and "new" politics quickly blurred.

To explain the dynamics outlined in Table 3.1 – which shows ongoing national and regime trajectories of change – the joint contribution of Pierson and Esping-Andersen proved fruitful. Much work shows that packages of institutions do vary in their logic of reproduction, with regimes following distinct paths (as Esping-Andersen would suggest), but that this reproduction does not occur only through left power but also from "new" political mechanisms (as Pierson would suggest). This work shows how the structure of the state considerably shapes both how countries experience new pressures and the power and capacity of a range of actors in the reform process to address them.

For instance, Iversen and Wren's (1998) classic argument about the "trilemma of the service economy" looks at the puzzle of political responses to new trade-offs in postindustrial economies. Iversen and Wren argue that the rise of the service economy forces a general slowdown in productivity, making it difficult for policymakers to simultaneously maintain high levels of employment, wage equality, and fiscal discipline. Policymakers of different political stripes (which coincide with the three worlds), however, essentially make different trade-offs in the face of these pressures: Social Democrats internalize the costs of adjustment through large budgets to preserve wage equality and employment; Christian Democrats seek to maintain equality and fiscal discipline while allowing growing unemployment; and Liberal politicians allow growing wage inequality while keeping fiscal discipline. The existing institutional structure shapes the way pressures generated by a rising service sector are experienced and conditions the interests and capacities of political actors – here, political parties – in responding to them.

The study of welfare reform in Continental Europe developed these insights. Through the 1990s and early 2000s, the unemployment (and employment) rates of many Continental countries lagged behind other industrial nations, and yet the political response to this unemployment was seemingly anemic. In looking to explain this ostensibly inefficient stasis, Esping-Andersen's understanding of regime variation proved influential. Esping-Andersen (1999) diagnosed the conjunction of "welfare without work" in Continental Europe as a product of its welfare regime, namely, the way its status-preserving benefits raised labor costs and perpetuated chronically low rates of labor force participation. Others developed these claims. David Rueda (2007), for instance, argues that the economic structure in these countries stratifies labor market insiders (with protected jobs) and outsiders (lacking strong protections) in the economy while empowering insiders in the political system. The result is political continuity even in the face of inefficiency.

As scholarship shifted from explaining stasis in Continental Europe to understanding the dynamics of change, particularly changes such as greater labor market activation, pension cutbacks, and expanding family benefits, which appeared to push against the traditional regime structure, this work continued to emphasize the crucial structuring power of the broad welfare regime (e.g., Palier 2010). Silja Häusermann's (2010) analysis of pension reform in Continental Europe, for instance, shows that such reform often combined cutbacks in pensions for traditional workers with an expansion of benefits for "outsiders" (particularly women). Despite this seeming break with the "conservative" welfare logic, Häusermann argues that the existing regime structure created a particular coalition space that shaped the opportunities of political actors (not just labor) to cooperate and shape these multilayered shifts.

Whereas through the 1990s and early 2000s the design of the Continental welfare states seemed to promote the "vices" of high unemployment and low activity rates (Levy 1999), Social Democratic welfare states seemed to offer a powerful vindication of democratic "virtue" in an increasingly globalized economic system. Scholars of Scandinavian welfare states examined how the existing regime structure allowed these countries to eschew the alleged trade-off between unemployment and inequality (Pontusson 2005). Once again, this work highlighted the way packages of Social Democratic institutions shaped the way these countries experienced new pressures. For instance, Iversen and Stephens (2008) argue that institutions promoting general skill acquisition as a means of enhancing labor market equality allowed Social Democratic countries to transition to high-wage, high-employment service economies. At the same time, these regimes empowered both "old" and "new" political actors (including unions and organized labor) that mobilized to defend the state's redistributive capacity (Korpi and Palme 2003).

Collectively, this work provides strong evidence that welfare regimes continue to have a structuring power. This structuring power does not operate precisely through the mechanisms that Esping-Andersen suggested, but it is nonetheless institutional. We see that regimes have shaped the way problems emerge and the political actors' responses. Attention to the way broad configurations of institutions shape reform paths is thus crucial to understanding change.

Politics against markets?

As argued above, Esping-Andersen presents welfare regimes as macroconfigurations of institutions created by coalitions of particular actors, which then institutionalize particular power structures that shape subsequent politics. The preceding two sections of this chapter argue that these claims were powerful in illuminating how welfare institutions work, their origins, and their structuring power on subsequent politics, yet many continued to interrogate the structural relationship between the democratic process more generally, moving away from this approach.

In this final section, I look at two approaches that took up Esping-Andersen's theoretical interest in between distributive institutions, democracy and capitalism, but did so in ways that fundamentally challenged Esping-Andersen's core ontological claims: either rethinking institutions in more functional and less conflictual terms or rethinking economic conflict in less institutional and more structural terms. In this section, I argue that both perspectives, as they have looked to explain variation in actual social policies and economic outcomes, return to aspects (although not the entirety) of Esping-Andersen's insights: emphasizing nonlinear and configural outcomes and the role of historically shaped institutions in shaping these outcomes. These shifts do not suggest Esping-Andersen was unequivocally correct in how he understood contemporary welfare politics, but, rather, they highlight the importance of attention to historical processes, the structuring power of institutions, and the configural nature of the state in understanding contemporary distributional outcomes.

One of the most substantial challenges to *Three Worlds* comes from the Varieties of Capitalism (VoC) approach (Hall and Soskice 2001). Like *Three Worlds*, VoC looks to theorize variation in advanced political economies in macroconfigural terms. However, in contrast to Esping-Andersen's political reading of institutions, VoC draws on institutional theorizing from Oliver Williamson (1985) and Douglass North (1990), who understand institutions in terms of the functional role they play in overcoming various coordination problems among firms. For VoC scholars, institutions, including welfare institutions, serve primarily to solve collective action problems faced by labor *and* employers in the labor market. This emphasis on producer coordination leads VoC work to isolate two (rather than three) types of economies based on the degree of coordination: Liberal Market and Coordinated Market economies. More important, in seeing state institutions in terms of the function they play in shaping firm coordination, work along these lines substantially challenges Esping-Andersen's historical and distributional understanding of the welfare state. Both Isabela Mares (2003) and Peter Swenson (2002), for instance, argue that social policy, in reshaping social risk, serves the needs of firms and thus emerged largely as a response to employers' needs.

As this research agenda developed, however, it raised new questions about the "elective affinity" between the types of productive institutions at the heart of VoC and the redistributive institutions associated with welfare states. In looking to further unpack these connections, VoC research reengaged with two key aspects of Esping-Andersen's work: emphasizing the constitutive role of historically structured distributive conflict and breaking out countries into three groups with similarities to the *Three Worlds*.

Work by Torben Iversen and David Soskice returns to the fundamental question of the relationship among capitalism, democracy, and welfare (the title of Iversen's 2005 book). Iversen (2005) argues that traditional "politics against markets" approaches cannot explain the fundamental compatibility of the welfare state and capitalism. However, the institutional configurations of VoC also require an electoral articulation, as its redistributive aspects lie firmly in the realm of democratic politics. In a series of articles, Iversen and Soskice (2001) first theorize voter preferences for redistribution as function of their skill sets (which follow, in part, from the type of economy they inhabit), turn to the way electoral institutions aggregate these preferences into stable national political coalitions for redistribution (Iversen and Soskice 2006), and, finally, seek to endogenize these institutions in the historical impera- tives of varying forms of capitalism (Iversen and Soskice 2009). This analysis casts itself in contrast to labor-centered interpretations of the state, empha- sizing structural economic (rather than political) forces. Yet, in developing a historically structured framework for understanding varying distributive outcomes, Iversen and Soskice adopt in modified form some aspects of the *Three Worlds* categorization of cases and approach.[5] Understanding today's distributive outcomes requires a historical (albeit structural) articulation.

Work by Kathleen Thelen takes the VoC research in a different direc- tion. Thelen looks to explain diverging outcomes in terms of equality and employment within similar VoC. Thelen (2014) argues that the link between "coordinated" and "egalitarian" capitalism is not automatic; while cross-class coordination has proven tremendously stable over time, the institutions pro- ducing (relative) wage equality have not. To understand why, she examines how some institutions promote broad encompassing coalitions that preserve equality in the face of liberalization while others promote narrower coalitions that preserve coordination and allow its egalitarian effects to wither. Although

---

[5] Martin and Swank's (2012) recent work on the origins of employer coordination further disaggregates the coordinated market economy (CME) model to distinguish between the Scandinavian "macrocorporatist" system and "sectoral" coordination in Germany, as well as the liberal market economies (LMEs).

Thelen's (2014) work emphasizes the role of cross-class coordination among institutionally shaped producer groups in influencing these diverging trajectories, her work breaks out the VoC into three trajectories of adjustment that closely match *Three Worlds* and more generally breaks with functionalist interpretations of economic institutions emphasizing varied historical development (see also Chapter 7, this volume). Thelen's – and to some extent Iversen and Soskice's – work shows that as VoC scholars turned to understanding distributive conflict, they also turned to a more historically variable and political (rather than functional) understanding of institutions.

By contrast, a wave of recent work starting with one core puzzle of distributive conflict – how we should understand both the overall trend toward growing levels of inequality across advanced political economies and variations across economies in the extent of this trend – initially turned toward deductive and formal, rather than historical, reasoning. While the questions raised by growing inequality are ostensibly comparative and temporal, they are made more puzzling because current trends seem to contradict the core claims in key deductive models of the demand for redistribution, particularly that developed by Meltzer and Richard (1981), which suggests that citizens should react to rising inequality by demanding more redistribution.

In order to understand why voters do not seem to demand redistribution when we might expect them to (i.e., when inequality is higher), much recent scholarship has turned to the microlevel, looking to understand how other aspects of individuals' material interests drive demand for social policy. Initially, much of this "microlevel" theorizing did not explicitly examine the role of institutions or temporally bounded processes in shaping conflict. For instance, Rehm, Hacker, and Schleisinger (2012) argue that to understand attitudes toward the state, we need to look at the coincidence of demand for its redistributive and insurance roles. When risk exposure and income levels are cross-cutting (i.e., do not affect the same groups) citizens are more likely to support extensive redistribution than when risk exposure and income levels covary. The theoretical focus of this work is on the link between the economic structure and individual preferences for redistribution (see also Lupu and Pontusson 2011).

While recent microlevel theorizing tends toward a more structural (rather than macrohistorical) understanding of the relationship between inequality and democracy, these arguments are often more historical than they first appear and, indeed, come to familiar conclusions. This work often identifies similar patterns of outcomes as do regime-based studies – with the Scandinavian states redistributing more, the Continental countries less, and the Anglo-Saxon countries becoming even more unequal. Ansell (2008), for instance, argues that higher education spending has different types of redistributive effects based on the level of existing enrollment, thus political parties prioritize it differently across time and space based on their policy context. The result is three patterns of change in higher education, which closely parallel the *Three Worlds*, even though the analysis is not cast in these terms. To explain these configurations in a non-regime-like way, however, this work draws on interactive arguments. The distribution of employment risk, for instance, matters differently conditional on the distribution of income, growing inequality produces different demands conditional on its structure, parties mobilize differently conditional on the logic of the electoral system and rising inequality, and so on. These conditional arguments bring back elements of earlier regime-oriented work even if eschewing this terminology.

The result is a return to engagement in the way institutions structure individual-level demands. First, in moving from preferences to politically salient demands, this work tends to emphasize the structuring role of electoral and other political institutions. Anderson and Beramendi (2012), for instance, argue that rising inequality affects the mobilization of low-income voters differently across electoral systems, shaping turnout levels, with downstream consequences for addressing inequality that vary substantially across types of countries. Second, there has been growing attention to micropreferences themselves as partly endogenous to past economic and welfare institutions, moving back in the causal chain of the production of preferences (e.g., the earlier discussion of Iversen and Soskice 2001, 2006; Lupu and Pontusson 2011).

The preceding discussion is not intended to argue that Esping-Andersen's work presaged the insights advanced by either VoC or recent microlevel theorizing of the demand for redistribution. Nonetheless, the ongoing relevance of the threefold typology, and the more general approach to comparative-historical analysis that it builds on, is telling. Attempts to abstract institutions from conflictual political dynamics, or to abstract conflictual political dynamics from institutions, have both turned back, in part, to more historically grounded understandings of institutions as they look to address a broader range of distributive outcomes. Indeed, far from eclipsing comparative-historical analysis, its methods – and broader ontological commitments to understanding temporally constructed macroconfigurations of institutions – remain foundational to understanding current questions of income distribution, welfare change, and the link between the state and the economy.

Conclusion

This chapter has endeavored to show that Esping-Andersen's original insights have been so profoundly influential because they drew on historical comparisons to provide a deeply resonant conceptualization of politically constructed variation in state institutions. This conceptualization, while hardly beyond criticism, nonetheless continues to capture key features of contemporary social policy. Work on the origins and effects of welfare states builds on Esping-Andersen's basic claim that welfare state structures are variable and multifaceted and often continues to conceptualize welfare states in the ways Esping-Andersen described them. Moreover, while the three worlds have certainly changed, the broad packages of institutions at their core continue to deeply structure the politics of welfare state reform and distributive outcomes, more generally. Table 3.2 summarizes the main claims of the chapter and the research trajectories drawing on Esping-Andersen's work.

What it shows is that neither Esping-Andersen alone nor analysts using comparative-historical analysis exclusively uncovered the dynamics of the historical development of regimes or their structural role. As the discussion here shows, summarized under the research trajectories in Table 3.2, many of the advancements in the field have followed from very different methodological approaches. Nonetheless, what is crucial is that the insights Esping-Andersen developed, drawing on the core features of comparative-historical analysis, opened a research trajectory that promoted synergies across different types of analytic approaches, which ultimately was deeply productive in advancing welfare state research.

What the rise of Esping-Andersen's typology and its ongoing relevance nearly a quarter century later show is not that the configurations that Esping-Andersen theorized in 1990 seamlessly structure politics in 2015. Change has occurred in the state, its role in the economy, and the political coalitions behind it. Rather, what Esping-Andersen's success shows is that comparative-historical research is profoundly important for understanding large-scale political phenomena. Despite many efforts to understand redistribution, the labor market, and the institutions of the welfare state in abstract, deductive, or functional ways – both before and after Esping-Andersen – as these research agendas develop, they often return to an understanding of democratic politics and capitalism that is largely nonlinear, political, and historically created. The intellectual trajectory of Esping-Andersen's research, then, suggests the

Table 3.2 Comparative-historical analysis and *Three Worlds of Welfare Capitalism*

Core claims in *Three Worlds*	Links to CHA	Broader research legacy
There are varying welfare *regimes* that differ in the level and type of spending and links to labor market institutions.	Broad country-based configurations of institutions shape outcomes	Scholarship examining how packages of welfare and other institutions vary in terms of their redistributive capacity, gender relations, age structure, and other features Scholarship examining how packages of institutions shape adjustment patterns, trade-offs, and the capacities of political actors to respond to the new economic and social pressures of deindustrialization, state budgets, globalization, changing skill structures, rising female labor force participation, and family change
Welfare regimes are political creations that follow from political cross-class coalitions.	Engagement with the demands of labor movements and political parties in specific historical cases	Scholarship examining the historic role of nonclass actors, including religious groups, business, mobilized risk groups, women, and patronage-based political parties Scholarship examining the changing political coalitions around the state, in particular, labor market insiders
Welfare regimes are historic products and structure future politics by shaping electoral support and group power in the political process.	Temporal dimension	Scholarship interrogating whether welfare regimes do feed back into mass attitudes and group power Scholarship bridging work on "new" political forces and older class-based actors and parties; more recent scholarship examining how configurations of labor market and other institutions work together to shape change

importance of reengaging with its core ontological and methodological claims in order to address some of the most important questions of the day. I suggest three brief avenues.

First, new data increasingly link rising inequality in liberal countries (and elsewhere) to the dramatic increase in wages at the very top of the income spectrum. While the trends in executive compensation, the rise of the financial sector, and the returns to particular forms of human capital are the proximate causes of this growing inequality, as Hacker, Pierson, and Thelen (Chapter 7, this volume) show, such market changes are hardly prepolitical even if they are not legislated. Whether *Three Worlds* continues to provide intellectual traction in thinking about state-market relationships in this context requires analysis. Many of the downstream implications of deregulation, changes in tax policy and so on, came to fruition only well after the publication of *Three Worlds*. Indeed, as Hacker and Pierson (2011) argue, choices made in the offices of regulators, tax collectors, and boardrooms may be as important (or more) in today's economy as those fought over replacement rates or health spending. Nonetheless, understanding both the causes and consequences of these changes requires articulating the broad links between regulatory, financial, and welfare institutions and the realm of political conflict around them, a task to which comparative-historical analysis is particularly well suited.

Second, much work in recent years has asked whether we are witnessing the "end of class politics," pointing to the reduced salience of class in voting, declining union strength, and new values-oriented voters who cross class lines. Yet, in many countries, social mobility remains low, and socioeconomic background continues to exert a major structuring force on everything from educational attainment to mortality rates. In some places, these issues have become politicized; in others they have not. As argued above, the recent behavioral literature focusing on how economic risk, wealth, and skills shape citizens' preferences, has contributed to our knowledge of the changing structural determinants of citizens' attitudes. However, class as a concept has always encompassed more than a link between economic structures and preferences, drawing on the way groups and other actors shape and politicize economic experiences. One of the core insights of comparative-historical analysis (not just work on the welfare state) is that class relations, coalitions, and power are historically contingent and shaped in multiple ways. I argued earlier that many initial reactions to Esping-Andersen often adopted his institutional framework to the exclusion of its sociological foundation. A return to some of the basic claims of this research tradition, examining how social networks, groups, and parties mobilize class actors and politicize questions of inequalities and social experiences remains important.

Finally, much recent work has looked to trace the link between wealth and power, raising fundamental questions about to whom politicians are responsive, the nature of political accountability for welfare reform, and the theorization of influence in contemporary political economies. Scholarship has split on the question of whether politicians are responsive to broad groups of citizens or primarily to organized – and wealthy – groups (see Pierson, Chapter 5, this volume). Esping-Andersen's work, and the work of those building on it, had a deeply normative claim – to understand how democratic politics offered a route to power for those who lacked it in the economy and, in so doing, a way of reshaping power in the economy itself. The questions of the conditions under which more marginalized groups (whether defined by income, risk, race, migration status, or other features) or citizens more generally can exert influence and when are crucial, and ones that likely require looking at the institutions that promote differential influence and responsiveness.

In answering these questions, contemporary scholars may draw on, or eclipse, the theoretical claims in *Three Worlds*. However, these broad questions point to the ways in which understanding the dynamics of modern welfare states, and their broader role in shaping markets and politics, will very likely require an engagement with case comparison and history.

References

Ahlquist, John, and Christian Breunig. 2012. "Model-Based Clustering and Typologies in the Social Sciences." *Political Analysis* 20 (1): 92–112.

Alber, Jens. 1995. "A Framework for the Comparative Study of Social Services." *Journal of European Social Policy* 5 (2): 131–49.

Anderson, Christopher J., and Pablo Beramendi. 2012. "Left Parties, Poor Voters, and Electoral Participation in Advanced Industrial Societies." *Comparative Political Studies* 45 (6): 714–46.

Ansell, Ben W. 2008. "University Challenges: Explaining Institutional Change in Higher Education." *World Politics* 60 (2): 189–230.

Arts, Wil, and John Gelissen. 2002. "Three Worlds of Welfare Capitalism or More? A State-of-the-Art Report." *Journal of European Social Policy* 12 (2): 137–58.

Baldwin, Peter. 1990. *The Politics of Social Solidarity: Class Bases of the European Welfare State, 1875–1975*. Cambridge: Cambridge University Press.

  1992. "The Welfare State for Historians. A Review Article." *Comparative Studies in Society and History* 34 (4): 695–707.

Brooks, Clem, and Jeff Manza. 2007. *Why Welfare States Persist: The Importance of Public Opinion in Democracies*. Chicago: University of Chicago Press.

Castles, Francis Geoffrey, and Deborah Mitchell. 1991. *Three Worlds of Welfare Capitalism or Four?* Luxembourg Income Study Working Paper Series No. 63. Luxembourg: LIS Cross-National Data Center.

Esping-Andersen, Gøsta. 1985. *Politics Against Markets: The Social Democratic Road to Power*. Princeton, NJ: Princeton University Press.

  1990. *The Three Worlds of Welfare Capitalism*. Princeton, NJ: Princeton University Press.

  1999. *Social Foundations of Postindustrial Economies*. Oxford: Oxford University Press.

Esping-Andersen, Gøsta, and Walter Korpi. 1984. "Social Policy as Class Politics in Post-War Capitalism: Scandinavia, Austria, and Germany." In *Order and Conflict in Contemporary Capitalism*, edited by John Goldthorpe. Oxford: Oxford University Press.

Ferrera, Maurizio. 1996. "The 'Southern Model' of Welfare in Social Europe." *Journal of European Social Policy* 6 (1): 17–37.

Gordon, Linda. 1990. *Women, the State, and Welfare*. Madison: University of Wisconsin Press.

Gornick, Janet C., and Marcia Meyers. 2003. *Families that Work: Policies for Reconciling Parenthood and Employment.* New York: Russell Sage Foundation Publications.

Green-Pedersen, Christoffer. 2004. "The Dependent Variable Problem within the Study of Welfare State Retrenchment: Defining the Problem and Looking for Solutions." *Journal of Comparative Policy Analysis: Research and Practice* 6 (1): 3–14.

Hacker, Jacob, and Paul Pierson. 2011. *Winner-Take-All Politics: How Washington Made the Rich Richer – and Turned Its Back on the Middle Class.* New York: Simon and Schuster.

Hall, Peter A., and David W. Soskice. 2001. *Varieties of Capitalism: The Institutional Foundations of Comparative Advantage.* Oxford: Oxford University Press.

Häusermann, Silja. 2010. *The Politics of Welfare State Reform in Continental Europe: Modernization in Hard Times.* New York: Cambridge University Press.

Huber, Evelyn, and John D. Stephens. 2001. *Development and Crisis of the Welfare State: Parties and Policies in Global Markets.* Chicago: University of Chicago Press.

Huo, Jingjing, Moira Nelson, and John D. Stephens. 2008. "Decommodification and Activation in Social Democratic Policy: Resolving the Paradox." *Journal of European Social Policy* 18 (1): 5–20.

Iversen, Torben. 2005. *Capitalism, Democracy, and Welfare.* New York: Cambridge University Press.

 2010. "Democracy and Capitalism." In *Oxford Handbook of the Welfare State*, edited by Frances Castles, Stephen Liebried, Jane Lewis, Herbert Obinger, and Christopher Pierson, 183–96. Oxford: Oxford University Press.

Iversen, Torben, and David Soskice. 2001. "An Asset Theory of Social Policy Preferences." *American Political Science Review* 95 (4): 875–93.

 2006. "Electoral Institutions and the Politics of Coalitions: Why Some Democracies Redistribute More Than Others." *American Political Science Review* 100 (2): 165–81.

 2009. "Distribution and Redistribution: The Shadow of the Nineteenth Century." *World Politics* 61 (3): 438–86.

Iversen, Torben, and John D. Stephens. 2008. "Partisan Politics, the Welfare State, and Three Worlds of Human Capital Formation." *Comparative Political Studies* 41 (5): 600.

Iversen, Torben, and Anne Wren. 1998. "Equality, Employment, and Budgetary Restraint: The Trilemma of the Service Economy." *World Politics* 50 (4): 507–46.

Jensen, Carsten. 2008. "Worlds of Welfare Services and Transfers." *Journal of European Social Policy* 18 (2): 151–62.

Korpi, Walter. 1983. *The Democratic Class Struggle.* London: Routledge & Kegan Paul.

 2000. "Faces of Inequality: Gender, Class, and Patterns of Inequalities in Different Types of Welfare States." *Social Politics: International Studies in Gender, State & Society* 7(2): 127–91.

Korpi, Walter, and Joakim Palme. 2003. "New Politics and Class Politics in the Context of Austerity and Globalization: Welfare State Regress in 18 Countries, 1975–95." *American Political Science Review* 97 (3): 425–46.

Levy, Jonah. 1999. "Vice into Virtue? Progressive Politics and Welfare Reform in Continental Europe." *Politics and Society* 27 (2): 239–73.

Lewis, Jane, ed. 1997. *Lone Mothers in European Welfare Regimes: Shifting Policy Logics.* London: Jessica Kingsley.

Lupu, Noam, and Jonas Pontusson. 2011. "The Structure of Inequality and the Politics of Redistribution." *American Political Science Review* 105 (2): 316–36.

Lynch, Julia. 2006. *Age in the Welfare State: The Origins Of Social Spending On Pensioners, Workers, And Children.* New York: Cambridge University Press.

Manow, Philip. 2004. *The Good, the Bad, and the Ugly: Esping-Andersen's Regime Typology and the Religious Roots of the Western Welfare State.* MPifG Working Paper. No. 4/3. Cologne: Max Planck Institute for the Study of Societies.

Mares, Isabela. 2003. *The Politics of Social Risk: Business and Welfare State Development.* Cambridge: Cambridge University Press.

Marshall, Thomas H. 1964. *Class, Citizenship and Social Development.* New York: Doubleday.

Martin, Cathie Jo, and Duane Swank. 2012. *The Political Construction of Business Interests: Coordination, Growth, and Equality.* Cambridge: Cambridge University Press.

Meltzer, Allan H., and Scott F. Richard. 1981. "A Rational Theory of the Size of Government." *Journal of Political Economy* 89 (5): 914–27.

North, Douglass C. 1990. *Institutions, Institutional Change and Economic Performance.* Cambridge: Cambridge University Press.

Offe, Claus. 1982. "Some Contradictions of the Modern Welfare State." *Critical Social Policy* 2 (5): 7–16.

Organisation for Economic Co-operation and Development. 2013a. Income Distribution and Poverty Database. Paris: OECD.

   2013b. Social Expenditures Database. Paris: OECD.

Orloff, Ann Shola. 1993. "Gender and the Social Rights of Citizenship: The Comparative Analysis of Gender Relations and Welfare States." *American Sociological Review* 58 (3): 303–28.

Orloff, Ann Shola, and Theda Skocpol. 1984. "Why Not Equal Protection? Explaining the Politics of Public Social Spending in Britain, 1900–1911, and the United States, 1880s–1920." *American Sociological Review* 49 (6): 726–50.

Palier, Bruno, ed. 2010. *A Long Goodbye to Bismarck?: The Politics of Welfare Reform in Continental Europe.* Amsterdam: Amsterdam University Press.

Pierson, Paul. 1996. "The New Politics of the Welfare State." *World Politics* 48 (2): 143–79.

   2001. *The New Politics of the Welfare State.* Oxford: Oxford University Press.

   2004. *Politics in Time: History, Institutions, and Social Analysis.* Princeton, NJ: Princeton University Press.

Polyani, Karl. 1944. *The Great Transformation.* New York: Rinehart.

Pontusson, Jonas. 2005. *Inequality and Prosperity: Social Europe vs. Liberal America.* Ithaca, NY: Century Foundation, Cornell University Press.

Quadagno, Jill. 1987. "Theories of the Welfare State." *Annual Review of Sociology* 13: 109–28.

Rehm, Philipp, Jacob S. Hacker, and Mark Schlesinger. 2012. "Insecure Alliances: Risk, Inequality, and Support for the Welfare State." *American Political Science Review* 106 (2): 386–406.

Rueda, David. 2007. *Social Democracy Inside Out: Partisanship and Labor Market Policy in Industrialized Democracies.* Oxford: Oxford University Press.

Scruggs, Lyle A., and James P. Allan. 2008. "Social Stratification and Welfare Regimes for the Twenty-First Century: Revisiting the Three Worlds of Welfare Capitalism." *World Politics* 60 (4): 642–64.

Scruggs, Lyle, Detlef Jahn, and Kati Kuitto. 2013. *Comparative Welfare Entitlements Dataset 2. Version xx*. University of Connecticut and University of Greifswald. http://cwed2.org/Data/Codebook.pdf

Stephens, John D. 1979. *Transition from Capitalism to Socialism*. Basingstoke: Macmillan.

Svallfors, Stefan. 1997. "Worlds of Welfare and Attitudes to Redistribution: A Comparison of Eight Western Nations." *European Sociological Review* 13 (3): 283–304.

2010. "Public Attitudes." In *Oxford Handbook of the Welfare State*, edited by Frances Castles, Stephen Liebfried, Jane Lewis, Herbert Obinger, and Christopher Pierson, 241–51. Oxford: Oxford University Press.

Swenson, Peter A. 2002. *Capitalists against Markets: The Making of Labor Markets and Welfare States in the United States and Sweden*. Oxford: Oxford University Press.

Thelen, Kathleen. 2014. *Varieties of Liberalization and the New Politics of Social Solidarity*. New York: Cambridge University Press.

Titmuss, Richard Morris. 1974. *Social Policy*. London: Allen & Unwin.

van Kersbergen, Kees. 1995. *Social Capitalism: A Study of Christian Democracy and the Welfare State*. London: Routledge.

Visser, Jelle. 2011. *ICTWSS: Database on Institutional Characteristics of Trade Unions, Wage Setting, State Intervention and Social Pacts in 34 Countries between 1960 and 2007*. Amsterdam Institute for Advanced Labour Studies (AIAS). Amsterdam: University of Amsterdam.

Wilensky, Harold L. 1974. *The Welfare State and Equality: Structural and Ideological Roots of Public Expenditures*. Berkeley: University of California Press.

Williamson, Oliver E. 1985. *The Economic Institutions of Capitalism*. New York: Free Press.

4 Not just what, but when (and how): comparative-historical approaches to authoritarian durability

Steven Levitsky and Lucan A. Way

After a nearly two-decade span in which regime studies focused almost exclusively on democratization, scholarly attention turned back to authoritarianism in the early 2000s.[1] Faced with the persistence of authoritarian rule in the Middle East, China, and elsewhere, as well as its (re)emergence in Russia and other former Soviet states, scholars began to investigate the sources of durable authoritarianism.

Recent research has drawn attention to a range of factors that contribute to authoritarian stability, including natural resource rents,[2] economic performance,[3] and political institutions such as parties, elections, and legislatures.[4] Most of these analyses are based on "constant cause" explanations, in which key causal factors (1) must be present for the predicted outcome to be observed and (2) are treated as having universal, rather than context-dependent, effects.[5] This work has generated important insights. However, an emerging body of research suggests that the effects of standard economic and institutional variables are mediated by historical and contextual factors, such as *when* (relative to the onset of other variables) and *how* authoritarian regimes emerge or consolidate.[6] This growing

---

[1] See, for example, Geddes (1999), Herb (1999), Wintrobe (2000), Brownlee (2002, 2007), Levitsky and Way (2002, 2010, 2012), Schedler (2002, 2006, 2013), Slater (2003, 2010), Bellin (2004), Fish (2005), Smith (2005, 2007), Way (2005, 2015), Magaloni (2006, 2008), Lust-Okar (2007), Greene (2007), Gandhi (2008), Gandhi and Lust-Okar (2009), Pepinsky (2009), Blaydes (2010), Magaloni and Kricheli (2010), Stacher (2012), Svolik (2012), and Dmitrov (2013).

[2] Ross (2001), Morrison (2009).

[3] Przeworski *et al.* (2000), Magaloni (2006), and Reuter and Gandhi (2011).

[4] See Geddes (1999), Magaloni (2006, 2008), Brownlee (2007), Gandhi and Przeworski (2007), Lust-Okar (2007), Gandhi (2008), and Blaydes (2010).

[5] On constant versus historical causes, see Stinchcombe (1968).

[6] On the role of timing, sequence, and historical context, see Mahoney (2001a, 2001b), Pierson (2004), Ziblatt (2006), Falleti and Lynch (2009), Capoccia and Ziblatt (2010), Grzymala-Busse (2011), and Falleti and Mahoney (Chapter 8, this volume).

scholarly attention to timing and context – seen in the recent "historical turn" in regime studies (Capoccia and Ziblatt 2010) – highlights the continued vitality of comparative-historical analysis. Indeed, as we show below, recent comparative-historical research offers powerful tools for understanding the roots of authoritarian durability.

This chapter examines the contributions of comparative-historical analysis to recent research on authoritarianism, highlighting what is gained by paying close attention to regime origins, timing, and sequencing. These factors, we argue, help explain why regimes with similar institutional arrangements vary so widely in their durability and why autocracies respond in diverging ways to similar economic or natural resource "shocks." The chapter then turns to a major challenge facing comparative-historical scholarship: the question of how, and for how long, founding legacies are reproduced. We argue that founding legacies are rarely static, or self-perpetuating, as is sometimes assumed. Rather, many of them are *bounded*, in that their effects weaken and disappear over time, even in the absence of exogenous change. Others are *dynamic*, in that they trigger causally linked sequences that strengthen regimes over time. Finally, the chapter discusses how attention to mechanisms of authoritarian reproduction can help to identify points of regime vulnerability.

Historical causation and authoritarian durability

The recent wave of research on autocracy has generated a range of new theories aimed at explaining authoritarian durability. Most of these new theories are based on constant cause explanations, in which the variables of interest (1) must be present in order for the predicted outcome to be observed and (2) are assumed to have similar effects across time and space (Stinchcombe 1968, 101–3). As such, these studies pay little attention to the ways in which key variables may be mediated by historical context. Such inattention to timing and context, we argue, limits these theories' capacity to variation in regime stability.

For example, recent studies have highlighted the role of institutions in sustaining authoritarian rule.[7] Beginning with Barbara Geddes's (1999) influential finding that single-party regimes are more stable than military or personalistic regimes, scholars have pointed to ways in which ruling parties

---

[7]   See, in particular, Geddes (1999), Magaloni (2006, 2008), Brownlee (2007), Gandhi and Przeworski (2007), Gandhi (2008), and Svolik (2012).

enhance authoritarian durability.[8] Many of these analyses focus on parties' role in sustaining elite cohesion,[9] which is widely viewed as critical to sustaining authoritarian rule.[10] Thus, scholars such as Geddes (1999), Jason Brownlee (2007), and Beatriz Magaloni (2008) argue that ruling parties help limit intra-elite conflict by providing institutional mechanisms to regulate access to the spoils of public office. By offering future opportunities for career advancement, ruling parties lengthen time horizons and encourage elite cooperation over defection (Brownlee 2007, 13; Geddes 1999).[11]

Although institutionalist theories contain important insights, the empirical support for them is mixed. Studies have found, for example, that party-based authoritarian regimes vary widely in their durability (Levitsky and Way 2010, 2012; Smith 2005). Whereas some ruling parties are powerful and cohesive organizations that underlie decades of authoritarian stability, others collapse at the first sign of duress. This variation was especially manifest in the post–Cold War era. Whereas Communist regimes collapsed throughout Eastern Europe in and after 1989, similar party-based regimes in China, Cuba, Laos, North Korea, and Vietnam survived. Likewise, whereas authoritarian ruling parties fell from power in many sub-Saharan African states (e.g., Malawi, Senegal, Zambia), they proved strikingly durable in other cases (e.g., Mozambique, Tanzania, Zimbabwe).

Another line of research focuses on the economic bases of durable authoritarianism. For example, scholars have highlighted the role of economic performance in shaping the fate of authoritarian regimes.[12] Thus, economic crisis is said to undermine ruling parties' capacity to distribute patronage to regime elites and deliver clientelist goods to voters (Magaloni 2006; Reuter and Gandhi 2011). Other work examines the impact of natural resource wealth.[13]

---

[8] See Geddes (1999), Smith (2005), Magaloni (2006, 2008), Brownlee (2007), Gandhi (2008), Levitsky and Way (2010), Reuter and Gandhi (2011), and Svolik (2012). Also see the classic work of Huntington (1968, 1970).

[9] See, for example, Geddes (1999), Brownlee (2007), Magaloni (2008), Levitsky and Way (2010, 2012), and Svolik (2012).

[10] See O'Donnell and Schmitter (1986), Geddes (1999), and Brownlee (2007).

[11] Other scholars identify legislative institutions as essential to authoritarian durability (Gandhi 2008; Gandhi and Przeworski 2007). According to Jennifer Gandhi (2008), for example, legislatures serve as arenas for "controlled bargaining," which help autocrats channel dissent and co-opt opposition (78)

[12] Gasiorowski (1995), Haggard and Kaufman (1995), Przeworski and Limongi (1997), Geddes (1999), Przeworski *et al.* (2000), Magaloni (2006), Reuter and Gandhi (2011), and Tannenberg, Stefes, and Merkel (2013).

[13] See Bellin (2004), Jensen and Wantchekon (2004), Smith (2004, 2007), Herb (2005), Luong and Weinthal (2006, 2010), Ulfelder (2007), Dunning (2008), Morrison (2009), and Haber and Menaldo (2011).

Oil wealth is said to strengthen autocrats by providing them with discretionary income that may be used to pay off loyalists, co-opt opponents, and finance powerful coercive structures. In his seminal article, for example, Michael Ross (2001) theorized a "rentier effect," by which autocrats use oil wealth to co-opt civil society and dampen popular demands for participation, and a "repression effect," by which well-financed security forces help to suppress opposition.[14]

As in the case of institutions, however, there exists considerable variation with respect to how (and to what degree) economic variables shape regime outcomes. Dictatorships vary in their capacity to weather economic crises.[15] For example, whereas economic downturns undermined authoritarian regimes in Albania, Benin, Indonesia, Ukraine, and Zambia during the post–Cold War era, autocracies in Cuba, Malaysia, North Korea, and Zimbabwe proved strikingly robust in the face of economic crises.

Likewise, recent studies reexamining the "resource curse" highlight the limitations of constant cause explanations and suggest a more complex relationship between oil wealth and authoritarianism.[16] Drawing on time series data going back to 1800, for example, Haber and Menaldo (2011) find little evidence that an increase in resource reliance translates into greater autocracy. And as we discuss below, recent comparative-historical studies have shown that the effects of resource wealth are conditional on the character of state, regime, and economic institutions at the moment when resources were discovered and exploited.[17]

In sum, although political institutions, economic performance, and natural resource wealth undoubtedly contribute to regime outcomes, both *how* and *how much* they contribute vary across cases. As recent comparative-historical research shows, the effects of economic and institutional variables are often mediated by historical context.[18] The following section draws on this research to show how both regime origins (*how* authoritarian regimes emerge) and

---

[14] Morrison (2009) makes a similar argument, although he finds that nontax revenue has a "stabilizing" impact on *all* regimes, be they authoritarian or democratic.

[15] See Pepinsky (2009), Levitsky and Way (2010, 2012), Slater (2010), and Tannenberg, Stefes, and Merkel (2013).

[16] See Luong and Weinthal (2006, 2010), Smith (2007), Dunning (2008), and Haber and Menaldo (2011). For example, Dunning (2008) finds that in societies marked by extreme inequality, natural resource wealth may reduce authoritarian pressures by allowing governments to distribute to the poor without taxing the rich.

[17] See Karl (1997), Herb (1999), Smith (2004, 2007), Wiens, Poast, and Clark (2012), and Robinson and Tvorik (2011).

[18] See Mahoney (2001a, 2001b), Ziblatt (2006), Falleti and Lynch (2009), and Capoccia and Ziblatt (2010).

timing and sequencing (*when* regimes emerge, relative to other variables) can play a critical role in shaping long-term authoritarian durability.

Regime origins and founding legacies

A major contribution of comparative-historical analysis has been to highlight the centrality of historical causation. According to Stinchcombe's (1968) original formulation, historical causes are those in which "an effect created by causes at some previous period becomes a cause of that effect in succeeding periods" (103). Comparative-historical analyses have shown how historical causation helps to explain longer-term regime trajectories in Europe and Latin America.[19] Likewise, more recent research on authoritarianism suggests that the *consequences* of developments during a regime's founding period may subsequently become important *causes* of regime durability. Thus, events that occur during a regime's foundation may engender institutional or coalitional configurations that become self-reinforcing or path dependent, or they may trigger sequences that push regimes down paths that prove difficult to reverse (Mahoney 2001a, 2001b).

The importance of historical origins can be seen in recent research on authoritarian institutions. As noted above, party-based authoritarian regimes vary widely in their durability (Levitsky and Way 2010, 2012; Smith 2005). Whereas ruling parties in China, Malaysia, Mexico, and elsewhere proved remarkably robust during the post–Cold War era, others (e.g., UNIP in Zambia, KANU in Kenya, the Socialist Party in Senegal) collapsed in the face of economic crisis or opposition challenges. This variation led scholars to return to a question originally posed by Huntington (1968): "where do strong parties, or single-party regimes, come from?" (Smith 2005, 198). Contemporary institutionalist analyses offer little insight into this question. Many of them ignore or set aside issues of institutional origins.[20] Others fall into what Paul Pierson (2004) calls "actor-centered functionalism," in which institutions are assumed to take the form they do because they are useful for key actors.[21] Such analyses generally focus on the formal structure, or design, of

---

[19] See, for example, Moore (1966), Collier and Collier (1991), Luebbert (1991), Rueschemeyer, Stephens, and Stephens (1992), Yashar (1997), and Mahoney (2001a, 2001b).

[20] Brownlee (2007) is an exception.

[21] For example, Gandhi (2008) treats institutions as a product of the choices of leaders seeking to solve the problems of intra-elite threat and opposition from society (xix, xxii, 164). Likewise, Geddes (2005) claims that autocrats create parties "to solve intra-regime conflicts that might otherwise end their own rule and possibly also destabilize the regime" (2). Such accounts are, in effect,

authoritarian institutions, which can obscure vast differences in how those institutions actually work.[22]

To understand where strong ruling parties come from, it is useful to "go back and look" (Pierson 2004, 47). Indeed, Huntington's own explanation was historical. His seminal analysis (1968, 1970) traced variation in the durability of single-party regimes to their origins and, specifically, to how ruling parties came to power. According to Huntington (1970), the most robust ruling parties are those that come to power as a "product of struggle and violence" (13). Thus, he hypothesized that durable single-party rule was most likely to emerge out of violent social revolutions or "prolonged nationalist movements" against colonial rule (Huntington 1968, 425).

Although Huntington did not elaborate or test this hypothesis, recent research appears to support it.[23] For example, in their comparative analysis of diverging party-based authoritarian regime trajectories, Levitsky and Way (2012) find that origins in revolutionary or armed liberation struggle enhances long-term regime durability in several ways. First, they foster ruling party cohesion. Years of violent struggle, together with the enduring polarization that revolutionary wars engender, strengthen partisan identities and harden partisan boundaries. Polarization and conflict sharpen "us-them" distinctions, strengthening within-group ties and fostering perceptions of a "linked fate" among cadres (LeBas 2011, 44–6). When opponents can be credibly linked to a historic enemy, such that abandoning the ruling party is viewed as disloyalty or even treason, the cost of defection will be high. Elite cohesion is reinforced by militarized party structures produced by years of armed conflict as well as by the existence of a founding revolutionary generation whose legitimacy can help rally the party behind the leadership during crises. Finally, violent origins enhance ruling parties' capacity to repress. Parties that come to power via revolution usually reconstruct the state's coercive apparatus from scratch, creating a party-state in which the army, police, and other security agencies are commanded by cadres from the liberation

---

constant-cause explanations, as the factors that account for institutional creation also explain their persistence (see Thelen 2003, 214).

[22] Huntington (1968) and Levitsky and Murillo (2009). Several scholars have made this point. During the Cold War period, for example, Henry Bienen (1970) criticized analyses of the emergence of a "Soviet model" in Africa for focusing too narrowly on "formal-legal arrangements" rather than on actual practice and power structures (100, 103–4). Also Janos (1970). More recently, Benjamin Smith (2007) warned that scholars must avoid "assuming capacity across similar-looking formal institutions," as "formal similarities in the institutional configurations of states can hide serious substantive differences in the way they work" (55).

[23] See Smith (2005), Levitsky and Way (2010, 2012, 2013), and Slater (2010).

struggle. The result is a highly cohesive coercive apparatus. Security forces created and staffed by veterans of the liberation struggle are less prone to coups and more likely to close ranks behind coercive measures in the face of opposition challenges.

Drawing on a comparative analysis of diverging regime outcomes in post–Cold War Africa, Levitsky and Way (2012) show how regime origins mediated the way authoritarian ruling parties responded to economic crises. Non-revolutionary parties in Kenya and Zambia relied primarily on patronage as a means of ensuring elite cooperation. Although patronage may be an effective source of cohesion during normal times, it often proves insufficient during crises, when the party's capacity to continue delivering the goods becomes uncertain. Thus, whereas violent liberation-based regimes in Mozambique and Zimbabwe remained intact despite severe post–Cold War crises, patronage-based regimes in Kenya and Zambia suffered massive elite defection and collapsed (Levitsky and Way 2012).

According to Levitsky and Way (2012, 2013), then, the roots of robust party-based authoritarianism are historical. Cohesive party and state structures are rarely, if ever, designed by far-sighted autocrats. Rather, they emerge out of particular historical conditions over which leaders exert relatively little control – and which cannot be easily replicated by other autocrats.

Thomas Pepinsky's (2009) analysis of authoritarian responses to economic crisis also highlights the importance of regime origins. Pepinsky observes that economic crises do not affect all authoritarian regimes equally and that some regimes are better equipped to survive them than others. However, he views regime outcome as mediated not by institutions but by coalitions. Pepinsky's study examines the impact of the 1997–8 "twin" (currency and financial) crises on regimes in Indonesia and Malaysia. He argues that the Indonesian regime, which was based on a coalition of holders of mobile capital and domestic holders of fixed capital, was unable to develop an effective policy response to the crisis as a result of the incompatible demands of its constituents (155–91). By contrast, because the Malaysian regime was based on a coalition between lower-income Malays and domestic holders of fixed capital, excluding holders of mobile capital, the Mahathir government was able to adopt a heterodox response to the crisis that facilitated a rapid recovery with a minimum of internal conflict (Pepinsky 2009, 192–224).

Pepinsky (2009) traces these distinct coalitions back to regimes' founding periods. Like Levitsky and Way's analysis of revolutionary parties, he argues that founding regime coalitions are sticky.[24] Coalition formation entails con-siderable "startup costs" (Pepinsky 2009, 16–17). Elites create institutional and policy mechanisms – including patronage networks, mass party organiza-tions, and social and economic policy regimes that privilege and strengthen favored constituencies – that "make defection from the existing political arrangements costly" (17, 41). Due to the cost of reconstructing patronage networks, dismantling or radically transforming ruling parties, and reori-enting policy regimes backed by entrenched constituencies, authoritarian coalitions tend to be stable (17).

Pepinsky's (2009) argument is thus path dependent. The initial coalitions forged under the New Order in Indonesia and in postcolonial Malaysia per-sisted into the 1990s. These coalitions shaped and constrained the ways in which governments responded to the 1997 economic crisis, which, in turn, helps to explain why authoritarian regimes survived or collapsed.

In sum, the analyses by Levitsky and Way and Pepinsky highlight the importance of historical causation in explaining authoritarian durability. Ruling parties and coalitions that emerged during regimes' founding periods are critical to understanding those regimes' subsequent capacity to respond to crises. Thus, although economic crises play a central role in both analyses, their effects are mediated by institutional or coalitional legacies of regimes' founding periods.

Timing and sequencing

Comparative-historical analyses also emphasize the importance of timing and sequencing (Falleti 2010; Falleti and Mahoney, Chapter 8, this volume; Pierson 2004). Indeed, several recent studies in the comparative-historical tradition show how the sequencing of events, and the question of *when* certain variables emerge relative to other ones, is critical to shaping long-term regime outcomes.

For example, Benjamin Smith's (2007) book *Hard Times in the Lands of Plenty* shows how timing and sequencing mediate the impact of oil wealth in late developing states. Smith's core insight is that oil wealth does not have a "single set of effects" (6, 7). Under some conditions, oil wealth weakens states and regimes, as scholars of the "resource curse" argue; in other contexts, however, it may help "bolster regimes and build state capacity" (7). This

---

[24] According to Pepinsky (2009), coalitions are "endogenous in the long run but exogenous in the short run" (16).

variation, Smith argues, is rooted in timing and, specifically, in whether oil wealth "precludes" or "follows" late development (4). Thus, the critical question is "not *whether* countries become oil rich but *when*" (4).

Smith (2007) employs a comparative-historical approach to explaining authoritarian regime trajectories. Regime outcomes, he argues, often have "temporally remote" causes (44). Because the impact of processes such as state and party building "unfolds over time," conditions that are "present only at the outset" may give rise to institutional structures whose persistence "helps to shape actors' choices further along in time" (44). Thus, the "institutional legacies of the early development period . . . constrain and enable state leaders during subsequent economic and political crises" (Smith 2007, 9).

Smith's (2007) analysis centers on the conditions facing regime elites at the initiation of late development. During this critical juncture, two variables are critical in shaping long-run regime trajectories: the availability of oil wealth and the existence of a strong opposition challenge (45). Where regime elites faced strong opposition and resource scarcity at the onset of late development, they had a strong incentive to invest in state and party building, which, over time, resulted in more durable regimes (48–53). In effect, then, early hardship induced elites to invest in institutions that proved to be a foundation for durable authoritarianism. Where robust state and party institutions were created, subsequent access to oil wealth reinforced authoritarian durability. This pattern can be seen in the case of Indonesia, where ruling elites faced both resource scarcity and a powerful communist opposition at the onset of late development (Smith 2007, 79–81). In this context, the regime built up the state's tax and local governing capacity and transformed the ruling Golkar into a well-organized mass party (87–99). The subsequent influx of oil revenue reinforced these state- and party-building processes, resulting in greater regime stability (Smith 2007, 137).

By contrast, favorable initial conditions inhibited authoritarian institution building. Where oil revenue was plentiful early on, rulers were "more likely to choose the option of substituting oil wealth for state and regime building," resulting in the development of oil-dependent states and more fragile regimes (Smith 2007, 53, 198). In Iran, for example, Shah Reza Pahlavi faced little opposition and enjoyed abundant oil revenue at the onset of late development (Smith 2007, 104–5). Consequently, he had little incentive to build a strong party or state. The ruling Novim was born weak and eventually collapsed, and the state's tax capacity eroded significantly over time (Smith 2007, 117–114, 139–46). As a result, the Iranian regime proved strikingly fragile.

Timing and sequencing are also central to Dan Slater's (2010) analysis of the roots of durable authoritarianism in Southeast Asia. A key insight of Slater's work is that durable authoritarianism requires an effective state. Authoritarian state building requires elite collective action: for state officials to develop effective tax and coercive capacity, economic elites must be willing to pay taxes (Slater 2010, 12–13). For Slater, such an outcome was most likely to emerge out of a "protection pact," in which economic elites agree to pay higher taxes and finance ruling party machines in exchange for order and security (13, 16). Thus, in Malaysia and Singapore, postcolonial elites facing powerful class and/or communal threats turned to the state for protection, agreeing to cede authority and tax revenue to emergent autocrats, who then provided order through the construction of authoritarian Leviathans. Greater tax capacity enabled autocrats to finance a powerful coercive apparatus while maintaining long-term fiscal health, and business support facilitated the construction of powerful party machines capable of sustaining hegemonic rule.

Yet protection pacts emerged only under particular historical conditions. First, they required a severe threat, in the form of "endemic" and "unmanageable" contentious politics (Slater 2010, 49). It was only when class and communal conflict threatened to take hold in the cities that economic elites, under "extreme duress," agreed to cede authority and tax revenue to an authoritarian Leviathan (Slater 2010, 13, 16). Second, timing and sequencing are critical. Protection pacts emerged only where class and communal conflict occurred *prior to the consolidation of authoritarian rule*, for it was only when fear struck the elite under pluralistic regimes that emergent rulers could credibly claim that authoritarian state building was necessary to bring order (14).

Variation in the character and timing of mass-based threats pushed states and regimes down distinct paths. Where postcolonial elites faced endemic and unmanageable conflict prior to the installation of an authoritarian regime, they forged protection pacts with emerging autocrats. Protection pacts generated "increasing returns to power," as regimes with large and consistent revenue streams were better positioned to sustain large coercive apparatuses and patronage networks over time (Slater 2010, 18–19). This was the case in Malaysia, where a potent class and communal threat in the 1940s lay the initial bases for a protection pact (Slater 2010, 74–93). The pact was consolidated after the 1969 communal riots, which triggered both an authoritarian turn and the enhancement of the state's coercive and tax capacity (Slater 2010, 120–3, 146–63). The result was a robust regime capable of surviving economic crisis and a strong opposition challenge in the late 1990s (Slater 2010, 211–21).

Where elites did not face a threat of endemic and unmanageable conflict, or where the threat emerged under authoritarian rule, state and regime trajectories were different. In such cases, autocrats tended to forge "provision pacts," in which they maintained support via patronage distribution and public spending (Slater 2010, 19). Provision pacts suffered from "the political equivalent of a 'birth defect'" (19). Lacking tax capacity or elite cohesion, regimes based on provision pacts failed to build strong states or parties and instead grew "increasingly vulnerable to debilitating fiscal crises" (19). An example is the Philippines, where class conflict was less threatening in the preauthoritarian period; elites never acquiesced to a protection pact, and, consequently, authoritarian rule was built upon a weaker state (Slater 2010, 94–105, 163–80). Ferdinand Marcos thus emerged as the "commander of an exceedingly weak authoritarian Leviathan" (Slater 2010, 200), and in the 1980s the regime collapsed in the face of fiscal crisis, elite defection, and mass protest (198–203).

The case of South Vietnam demonstrates the importance of timing and sequencing. Because postwar revolutionary contention was confined to northern rural areas, South Vietnamese elites did not initially acquiesce to a protection pact, and, consequently, the authoritarian regime that emerged under Diem resembled that of the Philippines (Slater 2010, 253–60). The threat posed by the 1968 Tet Offensive unified elites and triggered state-building efforts, but given the weakness of state coercive and tax institutions, these efforts failed (260–3). The South Vietnamese case thus highlights the path-dependent character of Slater's argument: only where an endemic, unmanageable threat led to a protection pact *before* the establishment of postwar authoritarian regimes do we see the development of a robust party-state complex.

In sum, Smith (2007) and Slater (2010) highlight the importance of timing and sequencing in explaining long-term regime outcomes. Their analyses show how particular variables (oil wealth for Smith, waves of contentious politics for Slater) may have substantially different effects on regimes, depending on when they emerge relative to other variables. Such sensitivity to timing and context is missing in much of the contemporary literature on authoritarianism.

Mechanisms of authoritarian reproduction

Comparative-historical analyses thus highlight the role of origins, timing, and sequencing in shaping long-term regime trajectories. Foundational periods set in motion causally linked sequences whose institutional or coalitional legacies may be of great consequence for regime durability (Falleti and Mahoney, Chapter 8, this volume; Mahoney 2001a, 2001b).

No founding legacy is perpetual, however. Indeed, a major challenge for comparative-historical studies of authoritarian durability lies in identifying the mechanisms of reproduction that underlie (and sustain) founding legacies. In other words, scholars must specify how and why ruling parties, protection pacts, or dominant coalitions persist over time as well as when and why these founding legacies end. In this section, we examine three alternative types of founding regime legacy: (1) *static* legacies, which are treated as self-perpetuating and thus stable, absent some exogenous shock; (2) *bounded* legacies, which degrade over time and may thus permit authoritarian breakdown in the absence of exogenous change; and (3) *dynamic* legacies, which trigger chains of events that strengthen regimes over time, potentially allowing them to survive despite exogenous sources of change.

Static legacies

Founding regime legacies are often characterized as static or self-perpetuating. Whether their persistence is explained in functionalist or utilitarian terms,[25] the structures or coalitions that sustain authoritarian rule are, at least implicitly, treated as if they were in an "infinite loop" (Stinchcombe 1968, 103). Thus, they are expected to change or collapse only in the face of exogenous shocks. An example is Jason Brownlee's (2007) analysis of ruling parties and durable authoritarianism. Brownlee explains the emergence of authoritarian ruling parties in historical terms: where would-be rulers decisively defeat their rivals during a regime's founding period, they gain the security to build ruling parties that gradually incorporate a broad stratum of pro-regime politicians (40–5). Once in place, ruling party institutions are self-perpetuating, as politicians develop an interest in sustaining them (13, 39). Because institutionalized ruling parties provide stable opportunities for career advancement, they generate a "sense among power holders that their immediate and long-term interests are best served by remaining within the party organization" (39). These "incentives for long-term loyalty" provide the bases for sustained elite cooperation and regime stability (13).

Another example of self-perpetuating legacies may be found in Michael Herb's (1999) study of Middle Eastern monarchies. Herb argues that dynastic

---

[25] On the distinction among functionalist, utilitarian, and path-dependent approaches, see Mahoney (2001a, 9).

monarchies, in which a single family monopolizes the key offices of the state (e.g., Kuwait, Saudi Arabia), are more durable than nondynastic monarchies, in which rulers partially or fully exclude family members from the government (e.g., Iran, Iraq, Libya) (7–10, 235–6). In dynastic monarchies, the dominant family "forms a ruling institution," distributing access to power and spoils via bargaining, within an elaborate set of informal norms (Herb 1999, 8, 30–6, 45–50). The origins of such arrangements are historical: they emerge where would-be rulers lack the strength to rule alone and are thus forced to build "large family coalitions" via the distribution of state offices (Herb 1999, 11, 155–6). Once in place, dynastic monarchic institutions prove "remarkably stable," as institutionalized mechanisms of bargaining and patronage distribution lengthen ruling family members' time horizons and make cooperation "individually rational" (Herb 1999, 7–8, 47). Where such institutional arrangements were in place prior to the emergence of oil, subsequent oil booms reinforced the family-based spoils system and, consequently, regime stability.

Brownlee (2007) and Herb (1999) thus highlight similar mechanisms of self-perpetuation. In both cases, the resolution of elite conflict during founding periods gives rise to institutional arrangements (ruling parties for Brownlee, dynastic power-sharing arrangements for Herb) that, by regularizing access to power and resources, lengthen elite time horizons and discourage defection. Once in place, then, these institutions are expected to persist. In the absence of exogenous sources of change, they neither weaken nor change.

A problem with arguments based on static legacies is that self-perpetuating dynamics are often asserted rather than demonstrated (see Thelen 2003). Too often, analyses fail to specify how such legacies are reproduced or to consider when and why they might end. Yet, as events such as the collapse of Soviet communism (or, more recently, the fall of Mubarak in Egypt) remind us, there are few infinite loops in politics. Even the most robust authoritarian institutions are not permanent, and those that endure over time often experience important changes in their structure and coalitional bases.[26]

Bounded legacies

Some founding legacies are bounded, in that their effects weaken and expire over time. Although these legacies may be powerful and enduring, they lack endogenous mechanisms of reproduction and thus eventually weaken or

---

[26]   On how communist institutions evolved over time, see Jowitt (1992). Also see Mahoney and Thelen (2010) and Slater (2010).

disappear. Consequently, regimes based on such legacies are vulnerable to collapse even in the absence of exogenous change.

An example of a bounded legacy is found in Guillermo O'Donnell's work on bureaucratic authoritarianism in South America.[27] According to O'Donnell's classic formulation (1973, 1988), bureaucratic authoritarian (or BA) regimes emerged when militaries seized power in a context of a crisis marked by large-scale popular mobilization. The original "coup coalition," which included the domestic and international capital, the middle classes, and an emerging class of technocrats (O'Donnell 1973), united around a "tacit consensus" that highly repressive and exclusionary rule was necessary to restore order, stabilize the economy, and eliminate the popular sector "threat" (O'Donnell 1979, 296–7). Although most BA regimes were initially successful in restoring order and stabilizing economies, O'Donnell argued that their coalitional bases were not sustainable. Over time, as fears of renewed chaos or popular sector "threat" waned, the original BA coalition broke down and the "tacit consensus" that had enabled rule via naked coercion unraveled, generating a legitimacy crisis (O'Donnell 1979). Although O'Donnell (1978) viewed the speed of this unraveling as hinging on the depth of the initial crisis and the level of popular sector "threat," he made it clear that the regime's founding coalitions could not be sustained indefinitely (O'Donnell 1979).

Another example is found in recent work on the durability of revolutionary regimes. As noted above, Levitsky and Way (2012, 2013) argue that regimes that emerge out of violent social revolution tend to be characterized by cohesive ruling parties, a fusion of the ruling party and the coercive apparatus, vast coercive capacity, and a generation of leaders with extraordinary legitimacy and unquestioned authority within the regime. These founding legacies enhance regime durability, and, indeed, revolutionary regimes have been among the most long-lived in the twentieth and early twenty-first centuries (Levitsky and Way 2013). Yet many of these legacies are generated and sustained by the revolutionary generation – the leaders, cadres, and soldiers who participated in the revolutionary struggle and seizure of power. Once the founding generation passes from the scene, the cohesion that characterizes many revolutionary regimes tends to dissipate (Levitsky and Way 2013, 13–14). In such cases, regimes must find alternative bases for stability (e.g., economic growth in China and Vietnam). In revolutionary regimes, then, generational change constitutes a clear endpoint for founding legacies – and an identifiable point of vulnerability for regimes.

---

[27]   See O'Donnell (1973, 1978, 1979, 1988).

Bounded legacies may thus constitute an endogenous source of regime change. As founding legacies weaken, authoritarian regimes may grow more vulnerable to collapse, even in the absence of exogenous sources of change.

Dynamic legacies

Dynamic founding legacies trigger sequences of events that strengthen regimes over time. As the chapter by Falleti and Mahoney (Chapter 8, this volume) shows, such sequences may take various forms. We focus on two of them: self-reinforcing and reactive sequences.

Self-reinforcing sequences

Self-reinforcing sequences are those in which events during a regime's founding period trigger a positive feedback dynamic that strengthens regimes over time (Falleti and Mahoney, Chapter 8, this volume). Thus, early events set in motion processes that enhance authoritarian durability by further empowering regime elites or weakening opponents. Such a dynamic constitutes an example of how "power may beget power" (Pierson, Chapter 5, this volume). As Paul Pierson observes, early political victories may set in motion a self-reinforcing dynamic in which changes in rules, resource flows, or coalitional alignments permanently reshape the balance of power in a polity. Although Pierson focuses on advanced democracies, the dynamics he describes may be even more pronounced in authoritarian settings. Slater's (2010) work on authoritarian Leviathans in Southeast Asia is a clear example. Thus, early "protection pacts," in which elites ceded authority and tax revenue to emergent autocrats in exchange for order, generated "increasing returns to power, as a "consistent flow of resources from society to the state" enabled autocrats to finance increasingly powerful coercive apparatuses and ruling party machines (Slater 2010, 18–19).

Another example of a self-reinforcing legacy is found in David Waldner's (n.d.) work on rural incorporation and regime stability. Waldner argues that rural incorporation, or the mobilization of rural non-elites, empowers emergent regime elites in several ways. For one, land reform expands the government's access to resources and patronage opportunities (chapter 2, 14–15). Moreover, control of the countryside facilitates the construction of robust cross-class coalitions. Mass rural support enhances the government's bargaining position vis-à-vis urban groups, providing the leverage and resources to co-opt organized labor, which, in turn, allows it to negotiate with capitalists from a position of strength (chapter 3, 23). Finally, rural incorporation facilitates the construction of mass integrative parties (chapter 2). For Waldner, then, initial rural incorporation empowers regime elites by facilitating the construction of mass parties and broad cross-class coalitions, both of which are critical to long-term regime stability.

Recent work on dominant party rule in Mexico highlights additional ways in which "power can beget power" under authoritarian rule. These studies have shown that once the ruling Institutional Revolutionary Party (PRI) established itself in power, it used its near-hegemonic status to weaken and discourage opposition, which reinforced authoritarian stability.[28] For example, Alberto Simpser (2013) shows how the PRI's orchestration of overwhelming electoral victories shaped the behavior of a range of actors – including voters, ruling party politicians, opposition parties, donors, business leaders, unions, and bureaucrats – in ways that reinforced regime stability over time. By influencing actors' perceptions about the prospects facing those who challenged the ruling party, massive PRI victories discouraged ruling party politicians from defecting, businesses from financing opposition, and opposition sympathizers from joining opposition parties and turning out to vote (Simpser 2013, 83–8). They also resulted in many opposition politicians "abandoning ship and joining the ruling party" (84). By influencing the "subsequent choices and behavior of a wide range of political actors" (Simpser 2013, 4), then, electoral manipulation enhanced cohesion within the regime and dampened (or preempted) opposition challenges to it.[29]

Kenneth Greene (2007) identifies another way in which the PRI's early dominance proved self-reinforcing. He argues that PRI dominance had a powerful effect on political activism. Ambitious activists who entered politics knew that the only route to career advancement was through the ruling party; given that opposition parties were perceived to have zero chance of success, only committed ideologues joined them. This selection effect reinforced ruling party dominance. Dominated by true believers, opposition parties veered to the ideological extremes, allowing the PRI to maintain a solid hold on the political center into the 1990s (Greene 2007).

Reactive sequences

Reactive sequences are those in which events are linked together via "reaction/counter-reaction" dynamics (Falleti and Mahoney, Chapter 8, this volume; Mahoney 2001a, 2001b). Thus, an initial event triggers a reaction and counterreaction that are "transformative" rather than simply reinforcing

---

[28] See, for example, Magaloni (2006), Greene (2007), and Simpser (2013).
[29] Similarly, Beatriz Magaloni (2006, 58–9) argues that the PRI's overwhelming victories weakened opposition party credibility in the eyes of many voters, thereby reinforcing PRI dominance.

early events (Falleti and Mahoney, Chapter 8, this volume). For example, in his analysis of long-run regime trajectories in Central America, Mahoney (2001a) argues that radical liberal reforms in the late nineteenth century polarized Guatemalan and Salvadoran societies and induced elites to build up the state's coercive apparatus, such that later democratization movements led by disadvantaged groups triggered the installation of harsh military authoritarian rule.

Levitsky and Way's (2013) work on the durability of revolutionary regimes also highlights the role of reactive sequences. Because revolutionary governments threaten powerful interests and, in many cases, the geopolitical status quo, they often trigger violent counterrevolutionary conflict, in the form of civil or external war (or both).[30] Revolutionary regimes are sometimes destroyed by these wars.[31] For surviving regimes, however, postrevolutionary conflict generates two effects that enhance long-term durability. First, war gives rise to a larger and more effective coercive apparatus. Second, wars allow revolutionary governments to eliminate rivals and weaken or destroy independent power centers (e.g., preexisting armies, monarchies, churches, landowning classes) that could serve as a basis for opposition mobilization in the future. Thus, by enhancing the regime's coercive capacity, while at the same time weakening or destroying independent power centers, the military conflicts triggered by revolutionary seizures of power substantially enhance regime durability (Levitsky and Way 2013).

Dynamic founding legacies thus set in motion sequences that reinforce authoritarian durability over time, potentially enhancing regime stability even in the face of exogenous change. By triggering wars that enhance regimes' internal cohesion and coercive capacity, or by empowering regime elites to accumulate resources, broaden their coalitions, or weaken rivals, early victories set in motion chains of events that not only reproduce authoritarian rule but increase the probability that it will endure over time.

Mechanisms of reproduction and points of regime vulnerability

A major challenge facing analyses of dynamic legacies lies in accounting for how and when such legacies end. Many processes that are initially self-reinforcing exhaust themselves over time. Indeed, even highly successful dictatorships may sow the seeds of their eventual demise.[32]

---

[30] See Skocpol (1979, 1988), Gurr (1988), and Walt (1996).

[31] Examples include the Khmer Rouge regime in Cambodia and the Sandinista regime in Nicaragua.

[32] For example, the rapid industrialization fostered under authoritarian rule in South Africa gave rise to a powerful working class–based movement that eventually toppled the regime (Seidman 1994).

A better understanding of the mechanisms of authoritarian reproduction may generate insight into how and why regimes eventually break down. Returning to Slater's study of authoritarian state building in Southeast Asia, for example, if the protection pacts that undergird authoritarian Leviathans are grounded in elite fear, then such pacts unravel if regimes succeed in eliminating the threats that inspired those fears. As Slater (2010, 20) notes, when elites no longer believe that mass unrest will reemerge in the absence of authoritarian controls, they may become "attitudinally available" to the opposition. Thus, developments that substantially reduce elite fears of a communist threat from below – for example, the end of the Cold War – might be expected to pose a particular threat to regimes based on protection pacts.

Pepinsky's (2009) analysis of how authoritarian regime coalitions mediate the impact of economic crisis provides another example. As noted above, Pepinsky argues that regimes based on different coalitions are vulnerable to different kinds of crisis. Whereas regimes based on coalitions of fixed and mobile capital (e.g., Indonesia under Suharto) tend to be especially vulnerable to "twin" banking and currency crises, he suggests that regimes based on coalitions of labor and fixed capital may be more vulnerable to commodity crises (Pepinsky 2009, 273–4).

Simpser's (2013) work on electoral fraud offers a third example. If overwhelming fraud contributes to long-term regime stability by encouraging existing opponents to "hang it up" and by deterring potential opponents from entering the ring, then the Mexican regime's post-1988 strategy of creating credible electoral institutions as a means of securing domestic and international legitimacy (Magaloni 2006) may have been counterproductive. Although credible electoral reform allowed the PRI to simultaneously win elections *and* gain legitimacy in the short run, it eliminated the long-term deterrent effect generated by overwhelming fraud. In adapting to the post–Cold War international environment, then, the PRI may have eliminated a key source of long-term stability.

Finally, variation in sequencing may also provide clues to regime vulnerability. For example, although Bolivia's 1952 revolution is often considered a social revolution (Knight 2003), it did not generate the counterrevolutionary reactive sequence observed in other revolutionary cases. The MNR government was, by revolutionary standards, rather moderate, and at least partly as a result, it failed to trigger either civil or external war. In the absence of counterrevolutionary conflict, Bolivia's revolutionary government lacked the incentive or means to destroy alternative centers of power, including the old army and radical trade unions. These actors played a central role in toppling the new regime in 1964.

Conclusion

The last fifteen years have seen an explosion of studies exploring the sources of authoritarian durability. Most of these studies have neglected historical causes, focusing instead on factors – such as formal institutions, mineral resources, and economic performance – that more closely approximate constant causes. This chapter has argued that such explanations are often insufficient and that to understand why regimes in countries such as Burma, China, Cuba, Iran, Malaysia, Singapore, Vietnam, and Zimbabwe survived well into the post–Cold War era, scholars must turn back to historical explanations. Drawing on both classical studies and recent comparative-historical research, we have argued that the roots of authoritarian durability often lie in timing and historical context. Both *when* regimes emerge – relative to the onset of other variables – and *how* they emerge and consolidate are often critical to explaining their durability. At the same time, comparative-historical analyses of authoritarian durability must move beyond static assumptions about founding legacies and pay closer attention to how those legacies are reproduced.

An important area for future research lies in the question of why and how founding legacies end. Scholars of comparative-historical analysis often assume that such endpoints are exogenously driven, but, as we have argued, this is not necessarily the case. Scholars have been very good at identifying sources of institutional continuity, and in recent years, they have been pushed to examine sources of (gradual) institutional change (Mahoney and Thelen 2010; Streeck and Thelen 2005). It may also be time for scholars of CHA to think more seriously about the endogenous sources of institutional breakdown.

References

Bellin, Eva. 2004. "The Robustness of Authoritarianism in the Middle East: Exceptionalism in Comparative Perspective." *Comparative Politics* 36 (2): 139–57.

Bienen, Henry. 1970. "One-Party Systems in Africa." In *Authoritarian Politics in Modern Society: The Dynamics of Established One-Party Systems*, edited by Samuel Huntington and Clement Moore, 99–127. New York: Basic Books.

Blaydes, Lisa. 2010. *Elections and Distributive Politics in Mubarak's Egypt.* New York: Cambridge University Press.

Brownlee, Jason. 2002. " . . . And Yet They Persist: Explaining Survival and Transition in Neopatrimonial Regimes." *Studies in Comparative International Development* 37 (3): 35–63.

2007. *Durable Authoritarianism in an Age of Democratization.* New York: Cambridge University Press.

Capoccia, Giovanni, and Daniel Ziblatt. 2010. "The Historical Turn in Democratization Studies: A New Research Agenda for Europe and Beyond." *Comparative Political Studies* 43 (8/9): 931–68.

Collier, Ruth Berins, and David Collier. 1991. *Shaping the Political Arena.* Princeton, NJ: Princeton University Press.

Dunning, Thad. 2008. *Crude Democracy: Natural Resource Wealth and Political Regimes.* New York: Cambridge University Press.

Falleti, Tulia. 2010. *Decentralization and Subnational Politics in Latin America.* New York: Cambridge University Press.

Falleti, Tulia G., and Julia F. Lynch. 2009. "Context and Causal Mechanisms in Political Analysis." *Comparative Political Studies* 42 (9): 1143–66.

Fish, M. Steven. 2005. *Democracy Derailed in Russia: The Failure of Open Politics.* New York: Cambridge University Press.

Gandhi, Jennifer. 2008. *Political Institutions under Dictatorship.* New York: Cambridge University Press.

Gandhi, Jennifer, and Ellen Lust-Okar. 2009. "Elections under Authoritarianism." *Annual Review of Political Science* 12:403–22.

Gandhi, Jennifer, and Adam Przeworski. 2007. "Authoritarian Institutions and the Survival of Autocrats." *Comparative Political Studies* 40 (11): 1279–1301.

Gasiorowski, Mark. 1995. "Economic Crisis and Political Regime Change: An Event History Analysis." *American Political Science Review* 89:882–97.

Geddes, Barbara. 1999. "What Do We Know About Democratization After Twenty Years?" *Annual Review of Political Science* 2:115–44.

2005. *Why Parties and Elections in Authoritarian Regimes?* Paper presented at the Annual Meeting of the American Political Science Association, Chicago, IL.

2008. "Party Creation as an Autocratic Survival Strategy." Unpublished manuscript, University of California, Los Angeles.

Greene, Kenneth. 2007. *Why Dominant Parties Lose: Mexico's Democratization in Comparative Perspective.* New York: Cambridge University Press.

Grzymala-Busse, Anna. 2011. "Time Will Tell? Temporality and the Analysis of Causal Mechanisms and Processes." *Comparative Political Studies* 44 (9): 1267–97.

Gurr, Ted R. 1988. "War, Revolution, and the Growth of the Coercive State." *Comparative Political Studies* 21 (1): 45–65.

Haber, Stephen, and Victor Menaldo. 2011. "Do Natural Resources Fuel Authoritarianism? A Reappraisal of the Resource Curse." *American Political Science Review* 105 (1): 1–24.

Haggard, Stephan, and Robert R. Kaufman. 1995. *The Political Economy of Democratic Transitions.* Princeton, NJ: Princeton University Press.

Herb, Michael. 1999. *All in the Family: Absolutism, Revolution, and Democracy in the Middle Eastern Monarchies*. Albany: State University of New York Press.

2005. "No Representation without Taxation? Rents, Development, and Democracy." *Comparative Politics* 37 (3): 297–316.

Huntington, Samuel P. 1968. *Political Order in Changing Societies*. New Haven, CT: Yale University Press.

1970. "Social and Institutional Dynamics of One-Party Systems." In *Authoritarian Politics in Modern Society: The Dynamics of Established One-Party Systems*, edited by Samuel Huntington and Clement Moore, 3–47. New York: Basic Books.

Janos, Andrew C. 1970. "The One-Party State and Social Mobilization: East Europe between the Wars." In *Authoritarian Politics in Modern Society: The Dynamics of Established One-Party Systems*, edited by Samuel Huntington and Clement Moore, 204–38. New York: Basic Books.

Jensen, Nathan, and Leonard Wantchekon. 2004. "Resource Wealth and Political Regimes in Africa." *Comparative Political Studies* 37 (7): 816–41.

Jowitt, Ken. 1992. *New World Disorder: The Leninist Extinction*. Berkeley: University of California Press.

Karl, Terry Lynn. 1997. *The Paradox of Plenty: Oil Booms and Petro-States*. Berkeley: University of California Press.

Knight, Alan. 2003. "The Domestic Dynamics of the Mexican and Bolivian Revolutions." In *Proclaiming Revolution: Bolivia in Comparative Perspective*, edited by Merilee Grindle and Pilar Domingo, 54–90. London: Institute of Latin American Studies and David Rockefeller Center for Latin American Studies.

LeBas, Adrienne. 2011. *From Protest to Parties: Party-Building and Democratization in Africa*. New York: Oxford University Press.

Levitsky, Steven, and María Victoria Murillo. 2009. "Variation in Institutional Strength." *Annual Review of Political Science* 12:115–33.

Levitsky, Steven, and Lucan A. Way. 2002. "The Rise of Competitive Authoritarianism." *Journal of Democracy* 13 (2): 51–65.

2010. *Competitive Authoritarianism: Hybrid Regimes After the Cold War*. New York: Cambridge University Press.

2012. "Beyond Patronage: Violent Struggle, Ruling Party Cohesion, and Authoritarian Durability." *Perspectives on Politics* 10 (4): 869–89.

2013. "The Durability of Revolutionary Regimes." *Journal of Democracy* 24 (3): 5–18.

Luebbert, Gregory. 1991. *Liberalism, Fascism, or Social Democracy*. New York: Oxford University Press.

Luong, Pauline Jones, and Erika Weinthal. 2006. Rethinking the Resource Curse: Ownership Structure, Institutional Capacity, and Domestic Constraints. *Annual Review of Political Science* 9:241–63.

2010. *Oil Is Not a Curse: Ownership Structure and Institutions in the Soviet Successor States*. New York: Cambridge University Press.

Lust-Okar, Ellen. 2007. *Structuring Conflict in the Arab World: Incumbents, Opponents, and Institutions*. New York: Cambridge University Press.

Magaloni, Beatriz. 2006. *Voting for Autocracy: Hegemonic Party Survival and Its Demise in Mexico*. New York: Cambridge University Press.

2008. "Credible Power Sharing and the Longevity of Authoritarian Rule." *Comparative Political Studies* 41 (4–5): 715–41.

Magaloni, Beatriz, and Ruth Kricheli. 2010. "Political Order and One Party Rule." *Annual Review of Political Science* 13:123–43.

Mahoney, James. 2001a. *The Legacies of Liberalism: Path Dependence and Political Regimes in Central America.* Baltimore, MD: Johns Hopkins University Press.

2001b. "Path Dependent Explanations of Regime Change: Central America in Comparative Perspective." *Studies in Comparative International Development* 36 (1): 111–41.

Mahoney, James, and Kathleen Thelen. 2010. "A Theory of Gradual Institutional Change." In *Explaining Institutional Change: Ambiguity, Agency, and Power,* edited by James Mahoney and Kathleen Thelen, 1–37. New York: Cambridge University Press.

Moore, Barrington. 1966. *Social Origins of Dictatorship and Democracy: Lord and Peasant in the Making of the Modern World.* Boston: Beacon Press.

Morrison, Kevin. 2009. "Oil, Non-Tax Revenue, and the Redistributional Foundations of Regime Stability." *International Organization* 63:107–38.

O'Donnell, Guillermo. 1973. *Modernization and Bureaucratic-Authoritarianism: Studies in South American Politics.* Berkeley: Institute of International Studies, University of California.

1978. "Reflections on Patterns of Change in the Bureaucratic Authoritarian State." *Latin American Research Review* 12 (1): 3–38.

1979. "Tensions in the Bureaucratic-Authoritarian State and the Question of Democracy." In *The New Authoritarianism in Latin America,* edited by David Collier, 285–318. Princeton, NJ: Princeton University Press.

1988. *Bureaucratic Authoritarianism: Argentina 1966–1973 in Comparative Perspective.* Berkeley: University of California Press.

O'Donnell, Guillermo, and Philippe C. Schmitter. 1986. *Transitions from Authoritarian Rule: Tentative Conclusions about Uncertain Democracies.* Baltimore: Johns Hopkins University Press.

Pepinsky, Thomas B. 2009. *Economic Crisis and the Breakdown of Authoritarian Regimes: Indonesia and Malaysia in Comparative Perspective.* New York: Cambridge University Press.

Pierson, Paul. 2004. *Politics in Time: History, Institutions, and Social Analysis.* Princeton, NJ: Princeton University Press.

Przeworski, Adam, Michael E. Alvarez, José Antonio Cheibub, and Fernando Limongi. 2000. *Democracy and Development: Political Institutions and Well-Being in the World, 1950–1990.* New York: Cambridge University Press.

Przeworski, Adam, and Fernando Limongi. 1997. "Modernization: Theories and Facts." *World Politics* 49 (2): 155–83.

Reuter, Ora John, and Jennifer Gandhi. 2011. "Economic Performance and Elite Defection from Hegemonic Parties." *British Journal of Political Science* 41 (1): 83–110.

Robinson, James, and Ragnar Torvik. 2011. *Institutional Comparative Statics.* NBER Working Paper No. 17106. Cambridge, MA: National Bureau of Economic Research.

Ross, Michael L. 2001. "Does Oil Hinder Democracy?" *World Politics* 53 (3): 325–61.

Rueschemeyer, Dietrich, Evelyne Huber Stephens, and John D. Stephens. 1992. *Capitalist Development and Democracy.* Chicago: University of Chicago Press.

Schedler, Andreas. 2002. "The Menu of Manipulation." *Journal of Democracy* 13 (2): 36–50.
   ed. 2006. *Electoral Authoritarianism: The Dynamics of Unfree Competition.* Boulder, CO:
      Lynne Rienner.
   2013. *The Politics of Uncertainty: Sustaining and Subverting Electoral Authoritarianism.* New
      York: Oxford University Press.
Seidman, Gay. 1994. *Manufacturing Militance: Workers' Movements in Brazil and South
   Africa.* Berkeley: University of California Press.
Simpser, Alberto. 2013. *Why Governments and Parties Manipulate Elections: Theory, Practice,
   and Implications.* New York: Cambridge University Press.
Skocpol, Theda. 1979. *States and Social Revolutions.* New York: Cambridge University Press.
   1988. "Social Revolutions and Mass Military Mobilization." *World Politics* 40 (2): 147–68.
Slater, Dan. 2003. "Iron Cage in an Iron Fist: Authoritarian Institutions and the
   Personalization of Power in Malaysia." *Comparative Politics* 36 (1): 81–101.
   2010. *Ordering Power: Contentious Politics, State-Building, and Authoritarian Durability in
      Southeast Asia.* New York: Cambridge University Press.
Smith, Benjamin. 2005. "Life of the Party: The Origins of Regime Breakdown and Persistence
   under Single-Party Rule." *World Politics* 57 (3): 421–51.
   2007. *Hard Times in the Lands of Plenty: Oil Politics in Iran and Indonesia.* Ithaca, NY:
      Cornell University Press.
Stacher, Joshua. 2012. *Adaptable Autocrats: Regime Power in Egypt and Syria.* Stanford, CA:
   Stanford University Press.
Stinchcombe, Arthur. 1968. *Constructing Social Theories.* New York: Harcourt, Brace, and
   World.
Streeck, Wolfgang, and Kathleen Thelen. 2005. "Introduction: Institutional Change in
   Advanced Political Economies." In *Beyond Continuity: Institutional Change in Advanced
   Political Economies,* edited by Wolfgang Streeck and Kathleen Thelen. New York: Oxford
   University Press.
Svolik, Milan W. 2012. *The Politics of Authoritarian Rule.* Cambridge: Cambridge University
   Press.
Tannenberg, Dag, Cristoph Stefes, and Wolfgang Merkel. 2013. "Hard Times and Regime
   Failure: Autocratic Responses to Economic Downturns." *Contemporary Politics* 19 (1):
   115–29.
Thelen, Kathleen. 2003. "How Institutions Evolve: Insights from Comparative Historical
   Analysis." In *Comparative Historical Analysis in the Social Sciences,* edited by James
   Mahoney and Dietrich Rueschemeyer, 208–40. New York: Cambridge University Press.
Ulfelder, Jay. 2007. Natural-Resource Wealth and the Survival of Autocracy. *Comparative
   Political Studies* 40 (8): 995–1018.
Waldner, David. n.d. "Democracy and Dictatorship in the Post-Colonial World."
   Unpublished manuscript, Department of Political Science, University of Virginia,
   Charlottesville.
Walt, Stephen. 1996. *Revolution and War.* Ithaca, NY: Cornell University Press.
Way, Lucan. 2005. "Authoritarian State Building and the Sources of Regime Competitiveness
   in the Fourth Wave." *World Politics* 57 (2): 231–61.
   2015. *Pluralism by Default: Weak Autocrats and the Rise of Competitive Politics.* Baltimore:
      Johns Hopkins University Press.

Wiens, David, Paul Poast, and William Roberts Clark. 2012. "Is There a Political Resource Curse? A Theoretical and Empirical Re-Evaluation." Unpublished manuscript.

Wintrobe, Ronald. 2000. *The Political Economy of Dictatorship*. New York: Cambridge University Press.

Yashar, Deborah. 1997. *Demanding Democracy: Reform and Reaction in Costa Rica and Guatemala, 1870's–1950's*. Stanford, CA: Stanford University Press.

Ziblatt, Daniel. 2006. "How Did Europe Democratize?" *World Politics* 58 (22): 311–38.

Part III

Tools for temporal analysis

Power and path dependence

Paul Pierson

A decade after a pointed critique of the discipline's retreat from the study of power (Moe 2005), evidence of a "power-free political science" is more widespread than ever. At least as it is practiced in the field of American politics – which plays a leading role in shaping the contours of the discipline as a whole – power and influence remain elusive, unhelpful, and marginalized concepts. When Americanists have gone looking for "power" – decisive political advantages for those with more resources – they mostly haven't found it. There is very little evidence showing that campaign contributions or lobbying systematically effect roll call votes in Congress (Schlozman, Verba, and Brady 2012). Stephen Ansolabehere, John de Figueiredo, and James Snyder provocatively asked, "Why is there so little money in American politics?" They found that although this was partly because donating raised big collective action problems, it was equally because money seemed to make little difference to electoral outcomes (Ansolabehere, de Figueiredo, and Snyder 2003). A broad and sophisticated study of lobbying from some of the leading scholars of interest groups recently reported that it could "find virtually no linkage between [group] resources and outcomes" (Baumgartner *et al.* 2009). Of course, the inability to find power in empirical research is especially puzzling given the extraordinary increase in economic inequality in the United States over the past generation.

Nor is the elusiveness of power just an empirical matter. More fundamentally, power doesn't really fit in the leading frameworks for studying American politics. These frameworks typically depict politics as fluid or "plastic." Elections follow a Downsian logic; this cycle's loser adjusts and becomes the next cycle's winner. Take out incumbency, David Mayhew observes, and presidential elections over the past century or so have been essentially a coin toss between the two parties (Mayhew 2002). Legislatures are under the sway of

Thanks to James Mahoney, Kathleen Thelen, Jacob Hacker, Terry Moe, Daniel Galvin, Daniel Ziblatt, T. J. Pempel, John Stephens, and the participants in the MIT and Northwestern Conference on Comparative-Historical Analysis for very helpful feedback on an earlier version of this paper.

Arrow's paradox of voting so that losers in any legislative struggle are well positioned to cycle back into the winner's position. The electorate, whose views are usually regarded as a strong constraint on policymakers, fluctuates back and forth over a moderate policy space. Voter preferences operate like a thermostat, bringing the political system back to the middle (Erikson, MacKeun, and Stimson 2002). Whether the focus is on voters, legislatures, or parties, temporary rather than durable advantages appear to be the rule. Jacob Hacker and I have suggested that the dominant frameworks treat politics like the movie *Groundhog Day*. After each day, Bill Murray wakes again to find himself in Punxsutawney, nothing important has really changed, and all the participants just start over (Hacker and Pierson 2014).

If the striking juxtaposition between rapidly growing social inequality and a political science unable to detect inequalities of power is most evident in the study of American politics, it is not limited to that subfield. Recent developments in the field of comparative political economy reveal a similar tendency. In a trend that Hall (2010) describes as "Schumpeterian," comparativists, too, have moved away from more "structured" frameworks toward ones that are more atomized and fluid. Comparative political economy has drifted from exploring systems of organized interest intermediation toward a behaviorist and electoralist focus on the links between voter preferences and policy outcomes. Like their Americanist counterparts, they now see the interface between politicians and voters, mediated by the structure of electoral and legislative institutions, as the heart of politics – indeed, almost its entirety. At the same time, the discipline as a whole has a new infatuation with experimental and quasi-experimental methods that strongly orient research toward the investigation of a restricted set of immediately observable microlevel phenomena.

For the study of power, I will argue, these are unfortunate turns. Power is like an iceberg; at any moment in time most of it lies below the waterline, built into core institutional and organizational structures of societies. This kind of influence can be made visible but only through theoretically grounded analysis and appropriate research designs attuned to what lurks below the immediately observable behavior that preoccupies most contemporary political science.

In fact, to go forward, we first need to go back, to recapture and build upon the insights that emerged from the old community power debate. That debate can remind us why the micro and atemporal orientations of much contemporary scholarship make influence so hard to see. The community power debates ended in a cul de sac, but there are exciting opportunities to build a new generation of systematic studies of influence. These opportunities stem in part from important theoretical developments in rational choice institutionalism. However, they will rely heavily on extensions of core frameworks of comparative-historical analysis. In contrast to work focused relentlessly on microbehavior, CHA has always been extremely well suited to the study of power. This is in part because of its emphasis on analyzing macrolevel outcomes that highlight and seek to explain persistent structural differences in societies. Even more important, I argue, has been the focus on examining historical processes. Going forward, the study of processes unfolding over time, emphasizing critical junctures and path-dependent dynamics, can make a central contribution to a renewed and enhanced examination of power.

Community power revisited

The marginalization of power was not always characteristic of political science. On the contrary, the debate between pluralists and their critics over the nature and distribution of political influence is one of the most famous in the discipline's history. Even after a half century, the community power debate remains the best place to begin a reexamination of the topic of political influence, for it highlights the dimensions of contestation that remain essential to any effort to place power at the heart of political analysis.

The argument over pluralism that came to be known as the "community power" debate remains sufficiently familiar that the broad contours need only to be quickly recapped here. Pluralists such as Dahl and Lindblom maintained that power was widely dispersed in modern polities (Dahl 1961; Dahl and Lindblom 1953). They stressed that the existence of a variety of political resources and the potential access to diverse venues of political activity (especially in the "Madisonian" institutional arrangements of the United States) prevented the concentration of power. Influence was not equally distributed, but it was widely dispersed.

Community power critics countered that this analysis rested on an overly narrow conception of power (Bachrach and Baratz 1962; Crenson 1971; Lukes 1974) – specifically, forms of influence that were visible in open contestation over political alternatives. The anti-pluralists described this open contestation as the "first" dimension or face of power but argued that there were other dimensions that were less visible but more significant. Typically, these are called the second and third dimensions.

The *second dimension* refers to cases where competing interests are recognized (at least by the powerless) but open contestation does not occur because of power asymmetries. This dimension, encapsulated in the overarching term *mobilization of bias*, was more than a bit fuzzy in most formulations. It can usefully be divided into two quite distinct components, which highlight different dimensions of potential influence. The first is what can be termed *nondecisions* and refers to the ways in which formal or informal decision rules may favor some actors' concerns over others. In coining the term, Bachrach and Baratz follow E. E. Schattschneider, whose original formulation remains worth quoting at length:

A conclusive way of checking the rise of conflict is simply to provide no arena for it or to create no public agency with power to do anything about it . . . All legislative procedure is loaded with devices for controlling the flow of explosive materials into the governmental apparatus. All forms of political organization have a bias in favor of the exploitation of some kinds of conflict and the suppression of others because *organization is the mobilization of bias*. Some issues are organized into politics while others are organized out. (Schattschneider 1960, 69)

In contemporary social science we would say that this dimension of influence refers to agenda control. It is now well understood that this is one of the principal ways in which institutions may advantage particular actors. McKelvey's (1976) pathbreaking work demonstrated that, given realistic assumptions about the distribution of preferences, the structure of agenda control could determine the final outcome. McKelvey's work catalyzed a rich literature. The allocation of agenda control can indeed effectively organize some issues (or groups) into politics while others are organized out.

The other central mechanism in the second dimension is that of anticipated reactions. Here, too, potential issues are "organized out" of politics, but the way in which this happens is fundamentally different. Sometimes open contestation does not occur because the weaker actor rationally chooses not to engage in light of their weak position. Contestation is costly, both because of the need to expend resources and, if you are weak, because of the prospect that the powerful will retaliate. To underscore what we are talking about, *retaliation* can mean the loss of a job, social ostracism, or physical violence against you, your family, or friends. Given these costs, choosing not to act may be completely reasonable if defeat seems likely. The crucial point is that the decision not to contest takes place in the shadow of power relationships. If a slave chooses not to rebel, we should not take the absence of open contestation as a sign that there is no power involved. Again, this dynamic is widely appreciated in some modern contexts – anticipated reactions feature prominently in standard game theoretic analyses – but it is not well integrated into core understandings of political influence in democratic polities.[1]

What is typically termed the third dimension concerns ideational elements of power. Powerful actors can gain advantage by inculcating views in others that are to their advantage. In essence, this involves what Marx termed false consciousness. Those controlling the media, schools, churches, or other key cultural institutions may foster beliefs in others (about what is desirable or possible) that serve the interests of the powerful. Again, what looks like consensus on the surface may reflect underlying inequalities of influence.

Pluralists had insisted that the focus should be on open conflict. As the pluralist Nelson Polsby (1980) argued, looking at who prevailed in decision making "seems the best way to determine which individuals and groups have 'more' power in social life, because direct conflict between actors presents a situation most closely approximating an experimental test of their capacities to affect outcomes" (4). Articulation of the three dimensions of power represented a powerful assault on this conception of influence. The core theme of the anti-pluralists was that surface appearances were just that – appearances. If taken at face value, they were likely to be highly misleading guides to the structure of power in a society.

The force of the anti-pluralist critique rested on a critical insight: the exercise of power will often *not* take the form of open contestation. Indeed, the point can be put more strongly: where the distribution of power is quite unequal we should expect to see *little or no open contestation*. Instead, some combination of agenda control, anticipated reactions, and cultural manipulation mutes conflict and restricts it to a much narrower and less fundamental subset of potential issues. Most of the time clashes occur only on those matters, and between those political actors, where the balance of power is (believed to be) relatively even. It is thus unsurprising that on this skewed subset of possible conflicts empirical research reveals no clear pattern of outcomes. Pluralists were, and still are, looking for power in all the wrong places. Their methodological insistence on studying open conflict – which most Americanist studies of influence have followed – systematically biased their results. As Walter Korpi (1985) summarizes, "since the probability of manifest conflicts decreases with increasing differences in power resources between actors, to focus the study of power on situations involving manifest conflicts

---

[1]   For instance, in most contexts it seems of limited relevance to the act of voting, often treated in mainstream political science as the supreme exercise of influence.

considerably increases the likelihood of discovering 'pluralist' power structures" (36).

The critics' insight, however, proved to be a double-edged sword. The pluralist counterattack, launched through a series of influential rebuttals, boiled down to a single formidable response: you can't study what you can't see (Polsby 1980; Wolfinger 1971). Because anti-pluralists seemed to focus on what didn't happen, they could not systematically observe the mechanisms they asserted were operating. To the pluralists, assertions that the strong were silently dominating the weak were little more than ideological conceits masquerading as social science – a series of claims about all the (progressive or radical) things that mass publics would implement in the absence of hidden structures of power.

By the late 1970s, the debate seemed to have reached an impasse, and most political scientists were ready to move on.[2] As Moe (2005) notes, "The community power debates of the 1960s, combined with the large and contentious philosophical literature on power, seem to have convinced much of the discipline that power cannot be defined or studied rigorously" (226). Equally important, the behaviorist and rational choice revolutions were shifting the discipline's focus to a much more atomized vision of politics, emphasizing individual choice as well as cooperation around mutually beneficial institutional arrangements.

Bringing power back in

Ironically, even as power has receded as a concern within the discipline we are actually in a much stronger position today to identify the kinds of influence explored by pluralism's original critics. Theoretical progress has made some of the claims of the anti-pluralists more tractable. Social scientists now have the capacity to see much more of what lurks below the waterline. Yet much of the discipline has failed to exploit these opportunities – precisely because the atomized and micro orientations of contemporary research undercut social scientists' emerging capacity to study influence systematically.

The new opportunities to study power systematically are most likely to be seized if they draw heavily on insights derived from comparative-historical

---

[2]   Virtually ignored in the shift to a different set of intellectual concerns was the striking change in position of the two most prominent pluralists, Robert Dahl and Charles Lindblom, who effectively defected to the anti-pluralist camp in their later work (Dahl 1982; Lindblom 1977).

analysis. Indeed, during the discipline's long retreat from the study of power comparative-historical analysis has stood out as a crucial exception. Its defining features – an interest in substantive, high-stakes outcomes, its design of inquiry around the careful comparison of large-scale cases, and its concentration on historical process – have always been distinctly well suited to the examination of deeply rooted and highly consequential structures of power. Today, there are exciting opportunities to expand on its distinctive capacities to study power by combining it with increasingly sophisticated tools for investigating subterranean politics.

Why has influence become a more tractable problem? Some of the credit should go to rational choice institutionalism, which has succeeded in unpacking and investigating the two distinct dimensions of the second face of power (agenda control and anticipated reactions) discussed above. As already noted, it has given us a much richer appreciation for the importance of agenda control and how particular rule structures allocate authority over agendas.

We now know that particular institutional arrangements will systematically favor the representation of certain views and interests. Consider two fundamental and well-researched examples:

- The construction of independent central banks is likely to durably shift monetary policy in predictable ways, by empowering particular sets of actors and reducing their vulnerability to particular kinds of political pressure (e.g., Franzese 1999).
- Legislative leaders can use their power of "negative agenda control" to keep items off the agenda that would divide their coalitions, obtaining outcomes that would not be sustainable otherwise (Cox and McCubbins 1993).

The same holds true for the idea of anticipated reactions. Recognition of the phenomenon obviously predates the rise of rational choice institutionalism (Friedrich 1963). Still, game theory has given social scientists a more sophisticated understanding of the role of anticipated reactions in politics. This in turn has encouraged the development of techniques for studying bargaining power that treat "nondecisions" as a completely expected and researchable aspect of politics (Cameron 2000). In practice, systematic attentiveness to anticipated reactions can provide political scientists with a powerful means of identifying shifts in the distribution of influence in important settings (Broockman 2012; Hacker and Pierson 2002).

For the most part, however, these theoretical developments have failed to reinvigorate the study of power. Instead, they have uneasily coexisted with the broader turn toward an atomized, micro-oriented and power-free political science. They have been applied in a limited way to a limited set of problems, operating more or less at the margins of discussions emphasizing cooperation, responsiveness to citizen preferences, and the general fluidity of political arrangements (Hacker and Pierson 2014).

Rather than shoved to the margins, power should be at political science's core. This was the thrust of Terry Moe's (2005) broad critique of how the variant of institutionalism rational choice scholars imported from economics subordinated questions of power. Moe noted that the central arguments of rational choice institutionalism, which stressed how institutions facilitated coordination, enforced commitments, and facilitated gains from trade, rested on an assumption of *voluntary* exchanges. Although some might gain more than others, everyone was made better off as a result of these arrangements. If individuals weren't better off, they would simply choose not to participate. Moe countered that while these frameworks generated crucial insights about how institutions helped particular political coalitions, they ignored a crucial feature of politics. Unlike the case of market exchanges, in politics a winning coalition gets to use political authority, and it can use it to impose outcomes on losers. These losers often have no viable exit option. Ignoring (or downplaying) this crucial difference misses much that is at the heart of politics and makes contestation look far more benign than it typically is.

 The implications of Moe's insistence that in politics winners can exercise authority over losers run deep (Gruber 2000). Most fundamentally, this premise suggests the need to recognize that political contestation is *both* a battle to gain control over political authority *and* a struggle to use political authority to institutionalize advantage – that is, to lay the groundwork for future victories. In short, it calls for an appreciation of how political influence is often invested. The exercise of authority is not just an exercise of power; it is potentially a way of generating power. What I wish to suggest is that Moe's analysis points the study of influence in a promising direction. It also suggests that carrying that agenda forward requires further development of the intellectual agenda that has long characterized comparative-historical analysis.

The most fundamental point is that power is something that develops over time and simultaneously becomes less visible as it does so. To see this, we can combine Moe's argument about winners exercising authority over losers with John Gaventa's (1982) analysis of power. In *Power and Powerlessness: Quiescence and Rebellion in an Appalachian Valley*, Gaventa develops an astute defense of the anti-pluralist position, countering the pluralists' objection that you could not study what you could not see. He presents a careful empirical study of political conflict in a setting – a poor mining community simultaneously marked by ostensibly pluralist political institutions and vast economic inequalities – conducive to identifying how influence is deployed.

Power and Powerlessness is a sustained methodological answer to the pluralists. Gaventa argues that one *could* study what wasn't happening if one clearly explicated the mechanisms through which these dimensions of power should operate and specified what the observable implications of power's exercise might be. Crucially, Gaventa highlights that those implications had a pronounced temporal dimension. We could uncover the "hidden" dimensions of power through historical analysis. Over time, open rebellion would give way to quiescence in predictable ways, and we could study that historical process systematically.

Unfortunately, Gaventa's incisive argument came too late to exert much influence among political scientists. The conversation had already shifted away from issues of power to the study of institutions. Yet Gaventa's analysis provides the essential bridge between the community power debate – where critics of pluralism rightly insist that political power is akin to an iceberg, with most of its mass lying under the waterline – and contemporary efforts to build theories more attentive to inequalities of influence. Gaventa's turn to historical analysis was not just a methodological move. True, he persuasively argues that we could *detect* political influence through historical process tracing. Gaventa's analysis was also a theoretical move, because it stressed that important forms of influence often became amplified over time. In the terminology of comparative-historical analysis, power was potentially subject to positive feedback or self-reinforcement. It is in making these dynamics more explicit that we possess the best opportunities for extending Gaventa's and Moe's insights.

Path dependence and power

Consider the following very brief historical sketches:

- The battle over post–Civil War Reconstruction reached a critical stage with the compromise over the contested presidential election of 1876. In return for conceding the White House to Republicans, Democrats won a major policy victory. Republicans agreed to withdraw federal troops from the

South, where they had provided protections for the civil and voting rights of African Americans. The result was not an immediate end to Reconstruction. Instead, it ushered in a "period of limbo and contestation, of participation coexisting with efforts at exclusion." Until the 1890s the "Republican Party hung on, and large, if declining numbers of blacks continued to exercise the franchise." The 1877 compromise initiated a brutal fifteen-year war of attrition in which segregationists slowly but surely gained what eventually became an overwhelming advantage (Keyssar 2000, 107–8).

- In 1954, a savvy (and personally popular) President Eisenhower privately ridiculed the desire of conservatives to roll back the New Deal:

> Should any political party attempt to abolish social security, unemployment insurance, and eliminate labor laws and farm programs, you would not hear of that party again in our political history. There is a tiny splinter group, of course, that believes you can do these things. Among them are H.L. Hunt (you possibly know his background), a few other Texas oil millionaires, and an occasional politician or business man from other areas. Their number is negligible and they are stupid. (Eisenhower 1970 [1954])

Eisenhower's point was that the New Deal had achieved durable victories. Despite his own electoral success, he and other Republicans now operated within a policy space that the consolidation of prior Democratic successes had fundamentally altered. There was no going back.

- Dismayed by political setbacks in the early 1970s, the American business community mobilized on an unprecedented scale to increase its influence in Washington (Edsall 1984; Hacker and Pierson 2010; Vogel 1989). In a series of pitched battles with organized labor and public interest groups in 1978 and 1979, the newly energized business groups won striking victories. The initial triumphs were defensive ones, blocking long-anticipated liberal initiatives. These early wins, however, laid the foundation for more aggressive and broadly successful efforts to remake the contours of the American political economy through deregulation and lower taxes on the richest Americans.

These examples are taken from American history, but similar dynamics can be found in any polity. Similar themes emerge in the journalist David Remnick's recent interview with Dani Dayan, chairman of the Yesha Council, the main political organization of Israeli settlers:

Dayan . . . is embarrassed by the thugs among the settlers who carry out "price tag" reprisals: torching mosques, cutting down olive trees, harassing and beating up Arabs.

But, ideologically, he is a clarion voice in the increasingly assured right-wing Israeli chorus that tells the Palestinians and the world that the settlers have achieved their goal, that they are the "facts on the ground" that will rule out the establishment of a Palestinian state. "We're a key player – maybe *the* key player," he said. "We are the focus. Everything is a response to what we do. The fact that we are here and develop here is the ultimate political maneuver that sets the reality. Why do we prevail? We've reached the point of irreversibility." (Remnick 2013)

All these vignettes share two key characteristics. First, they stress (often brutal) political contests between competing forces, in which one side wins and the other loses. Second, they emphasize that the victorious side does not win in a single encounter – even though a single encounter or a cluster of encounters may be "critical." Decisive victory comes through a more complex and extended process unfolding over time. Of course, this "juncture plus feedback" template is a very familiar one for comparative-historical analysis (Capoccia and Keleman 2007). What I wish to focus on here is exactly how this critical juncture/path dependence apparatus can be connected to the daunting question of studying power.

The idea that power distributions themselves may be path dependent is not a new one. My own work on the subject makes frequent reference to winners and losers and suggests that path dependence arguments link up to concerns about power. Yet, as Mahoney (2000) rightly points out, Pierson (2000) primarily examines processes of self-reinforcement that involve "utilitarian" dynamics such as network externalities and adaptive expectations. Pierson 2004 (36–7, 47–8, 71–4) is a little better in this respect but fails to develop arguments about power dynamics systematically.

Does it make sense to think about power relationships as path dependent, as involving dynamics where power can beget power? Mahoney (2000) suggests the answer is yes, and I concur. This section attempts to pursue that claim in a more sustained way, highlighting the particular mechanisms that might be involved in such a dynamic, their connection to relevant existing work, and the kinds of empirical and theoretical questions that they suggest merit our attention.

I anchor this discussion (as the broader literature on critical junctures would expect) around the notion of political victories – moments of open contestation in which one faction or another achieves some substantial advantage. In many cases, of course, this is the same moment that Moe's analysis highlights from a different angle – the moment when one set of actors (the "winners") gets to exercise political authority over another set (the "losers").

The question is whether we can say anything about what may happen next and the ways in which that initial result may influence disputes yet to come. In fact, we can usefully distinguish five ways in which power may beget power: (1) the transfer of resource *stocks*, (2) the transfer of resource *flows*, (3) *signals* about the relative strength of political competitors, (4) *alterations* to political and social *discourse*, and (5) the inducement of preference-changing *investments*. Distinguishing and specifying these possibilities not only facilitates careful empirical work but also makes it possible to highlight the connections between arguments about path-dependent power dynamics, prominent arguments in the old debate over pluralist conceptions of power relationships, and the more recent advances in the analysis of power outlined above.

The transfer of resource stocks

The most obvious mechanism through which an initial victory might beget additional power is the direct impact on the distribution of political resources. As they say, "to the victor go the spoils." Winners gain resources, which they can deploy in future rounds of contestation; losers, of course, see their resources diminish. In some contexts – particularly those involving the direct deployment of coercion – this transfer of stocks by itself may be sufficient to produce a gradually increasing inequality of resources as a result of future rounds of contestation. One might be able to analyze wars, civil wars, and various forms of insurrection in this way. Decisive victories in and of themselves shift the distribution of resources in ways that increase the likelihood of additional victories in the future.

The alteration of resource flows

That spoils from victory can induce positive feedback is especially likely if the initial triumph confers not just a one-time transfer but a stream of resources extending over multiple rounds. Many political victories shift control not just of a fixed stock of resources but of a flow of resources.[3] This, indeed, has always been a central preoccupation of comparative-historical analysis. Victory over core institutional arrangements or a critical policy outcome tilts the playing field for future rounds of contestation, increasing the probability

---

[3] As many long-suffering parents can tell you, the game of *Monopoly* has this quality. One player gains a decisive structural advantage at some juncture, leading to a steady flow of ever-greater resources over time. There follows an interminable endgame in which the advantaged party slowly but inevitably grinds the other players down under the heel of his eight-year-old boot.

of victory (or the likely scale of victories) for one of the contending parties. The bargain of 1877 was critical in bringing Reconstruction to an end because it ensured that future conflicts over the Southern political economy would occur in a different arena (the states), freed from federal intervention. This new venue was heavily slanted in favor of segregationists. Although they did not achieve instantaneous victory, they steadily gained the upper hand.

Here the analysis of self-reinforcing power links up to the anti-pluralist idea of a "mobilization of bias" and the more recent interest of social scientists in agenda control. New institutions or policy regimes are often the main prizes awarded to the victors during critical junctures (Hacker and Pierson 2014). These new arrangements create advantages for certain actors over others, organizing some issues in and other issues out. In the field of comparative politics, the most famous of these institutional arrangements dictated by victors is democracy itself – a new configuration of authority that durably altered the rules for allocating political authority. New decision rules diminished the value of political resources based on the possession of property or coercive capacity and increased the value of resources based on sheer numbers (Acemoglu and Robinson 2012; Rueschemeyer, Stephens, and Stephens 1992). Specific constitutional arrangements can have similar effects of durably advantaging particular actors, for instance, by creating super-majority requirements for revision (Starr 2014).

On a somewhat less grand scale, "tilting the playing field" operates through the establishment of new policy arrangements, which may constitute a kind of miniconstitution in a particular domain of social life. Eskridge and Ferejohn (2001) coined the term "super statutes" to distinguish extraordinary laws that exert a strong gravitational pull on jurisprudence and norms, but when one looks more broadly at the capacity of policies to remake political circumstances the ranks of miniconstitutions expand dramatically (Pierson 2006). In Eric Patashnik's (2008) *After Reform*, for instance, airline deregulation was cemented in part by eliminating the Civil Aeronautics Board, the regulatory venue where the old-line airlines had their greatest leverage. At the same time, the new legislation unleashed market forces that induced a war of attrition, steadily removing the high-cost airlines (which were deregulation's strongest opponents) from the playing field. This is just one example of a ubiquitous feature of modern polities. In comparative political economy, comparative-historical analysts have emphasized the profound structuring role of such miniconstitutions – systems of rules grounded in policy. These include social programs (Esping-Andersen 1990), the regulation of industrial relations (Thelen 2004), and structures of corporate governance (Gourevitch and Shinn 2007). All are understood to deeply shape domestic life, with powerful effects not only on how ostensibly neutral and apolitical markets distribute rewards and risks but on the future political prospects of competing interests.

Victory as signal

A distinct feedback dynamic is related to the signaling effects of outcomes at critical junctures. Success in a highly visible conflict doesn't simply transfer a stock or flow of tangible resources; it can send a powerful signal about the relative capabilities of the contestants. In such instances, strategic accommodation to the new signal may be extremely important, and it is worth distinguishing the forms that it may take:

- Actors may defect from the losing side to the winning side.
- Actors who had previously stayed on the sideline (perhaps out of indifference or out of fear of betting on the wrong horse) may now enlist with the winning side.
- Actors on the losing side may choose to become "quiescent" (Gaventa) in light of the growing likelihood of future defeat, the increasing risks associated with continued mobilization, or both.[4]

The argument Jacob Hacker and I have made about the shifting balance of "organized combat" in the United States in the late 1970s stresses these signaling dynamics (Hacker and Pierson 2010). The years 1977 and 1978 featured a series of pitched battles in which newly emboldened Democrats – whose large majorities in Congress were paired with control of the White House for the first time in eight years – squared off against a business community that had gone through an aggressive five-year project to ramp up its organizational capabilities. Many observers viewed the political outcome of this contest as highly uncertain. Business groups vigorously lobbied the most conservative or electorally vulnerable Democrats. In the end, they won a string of stunning victories on issues from consumer protection to industrial relations reform to taxes (in the latter case, the Carter administration's mildly progressive proposal was hijacked and replaced by a sharp cut in capital gains taxes). We suggest that these unexpected events sent a strong signal to political participants, producing the kinds of adjustments described above. Most

---

[4] Of course, a major loss may also trigger countermobilization and a politics of backlash. Although the issue cannot be explored here, analyzing the conditions under which political loss is likely to produce quiescence or backlash should be an important part of the research agenda for those studying power.

notably, both major political parties reoriented their policy stances to be more responsive to business demands.

Altering discourse

What has traditionally been termed the "third" dimension of power occurs when actors deploy social resources to shift others' views of what is desirable or possible, to the benefit of those who generated these ideational shifts. These social resources may shape the dissemination of information and argumentation in diverse arenas, including schools, the media, and religious organizations. Wuthnow (1989) argues that "communities of discourse" emerging during brief periods come to share, institutionalize, and reproduce ideologies. Berman (2003) has made a similar argument about the spread of radical Islam. Extremists gained control over key institutions of cultural production; they then used that control to foment a revolutionary transformation in citizens' worldviews. A recent report on new textbooks introduced in Hamas-controlled Gaza provides a contemporary example (Akram and Rudoren 2013). These textbooks describe Jerusalem's Western Wall as "Islamic property," do not recognize modern Israel, and fail to mention the Oslo Peace Accords.

These transformations are closely related to the arguments about signaling and anticipated reactions discussed above, but here the focus is on changes in beliefs about what is possible or about what is desirable. In democratic polities, one important mechanism for generating these changes is what Noelle-Neumann (1984) termed "spirals of silence." As actors see a particular viewpoint becoming marginalized, they are less willing to articulate that view. Noelle-Neumann's social psychological analysis emphasized the individual's desire for social conformity. However, there may be other incentive structures involving unequal power. Expression of particular views may become more costly as they become less prevalent. Such tendencies can "spiral" or become self-reinforcing as actors conclude that few people hold a particular view, and the spreading silence generates a false consensus that potentially can become "real" as particular arguments and viewpoints become increasingly rare in public discourse. Microlevel evidence for this argument is sketchy (Lang and Lang 2012), but one can imagine it working in important domains. This dynamic is especially likely in contexts where participants in discourse make strategic decisions in the context of power relations. For instance, politicians who see a particular argument become a political loser face strong incentives to drop that argument and join (or at least fail to challenge) the emerging consensus. If elite discourse is a major source of mass opinion (Zaller 1992), these processes may in turn have a major impact on mass culture.

A striking recent example in the United States of such a self-reinforcing process of ideational change is the evolving discussion of the Second Amendment (Siegel 2008). Beginning in the 1970s, gun rights activists sought to overturn the long-standing consensus in American law that the Second Amendment provided no protections for individual gun ownership. They launched a multipronged and well-financed effort to establish the doctrinal credibility of a contrary position and then spread support for that stance among conservatives. This effort eventually yielded the 5–4 *Heller* decision of 2008, in which five conservative justices overturned seventy years of legal precedent. As the meme of "Second Amendment rights" gained force, politicians (including those who supported gun control) found it increasingly prudent to adopt the ascendant rhetoric.[5] Their behavior reinforced a rapid shift in discourse. Following sustained and substantial exertions of organized pressure, consensus understandings of a core constitutional issue had flipped completely.[6]

It is perhaps not surprising that the very concept of ideology has lost ground in the empirical study of politics with the rise of behaviorism and experimentalism. Ideologies generally develop gradually and require broad and durable mobilization. Behaviorists typically focus on observed individual attitudes. By the time changes in attitudes are widespread the impact of resource mobilization is likely to be obscured – either lying in the past or deeply embedded in seemingly neutral or relatively apolitical structures. As Korpi (1985) notes, "The analysis of the role of ideologies and beliefs in the context of power cannot be easily incorporated into the behavioral approach to the study of power" (39). Any successful approach to the "third face" of power is likely to require attentiveness to the generation and reproduction of cultural power over extended time periods.

Inducing new investments

Establishing how power leads to the manipulation of preferences through cultural structures is extremely tricky. A distinct mechanism of power-induced

[5] A Google Ngram search reveals the phrase "Second Amendment rights" was virtually unheard of until the late 1970s. Its emergence between 1978 and 1982 coincides with the takeover of the National Rifle Association by extreme conservatives. Then, between 1982 and 2000, frequency of use of "Second Amendment rights" grows 500 percent.

[6] Again, this case highlights the importance of considering the dynamics of backlash and countermobilization. For present purposes, the key point is that sustained deployment of social resources appears to have had a considerable impact on the ways in which both elites and ordinary citizens think and act on matters related to gun ownership.

preference change may be more tractable. Indeed, this mechanism has been central to the way path-dependent arguments have been deployed in the social sciences. Outcomes at critical junctures, such as new policy structures, induce patterns of individual investment in such disparate social arrangements as particular asset classes and organizations. Once these investments are made, they will shift the relevant actors' calculations about what states of the world are desirable – in short, they will change preferences.

These arguments (including in my own formulations) have drawn heavily on work in institutional economics. They have been generally framed as involving shifts in material incentives. Yet the potential linkage to arguments about power balances is straightforward and deep. Coalitions competing for power may recognize that political authority can be used to induce investments. Typically, this is done through new policy arrangements. Like the Israeli settler leader, political actors seek to create new "facts on the ground." They recognize that once established these commitments will shift the distribution of preferences to the advantage of one political coalition over another. This is not just a matter of shifting the numerical balance of adherents but of shifting the balance of *intensity*. Those with big investments are likely to be politically determined. Here is Remnick's (2013) settler leader again: "Dayan is confident that the settlers' level of commitment dwarfs that of any other faction. The Left shows its commitment, he says, 'by pushing the "like" button on the last editorial in *Haaretz*.'"

Much of my own thinking about path dependence stemmed from my efforts to understand the political implications of a single policy initiative, the Social Security Act. The SSA was the cornerstone of the American welfare state. It is still going strong as it approaches its eightieth birthday. There is no doubt that the earnings-related, pay-as-you-go structure of Social Security generated deep commitments among program participants in ways that produced substantial changes in political behavior and preferences (Campbell 2003). Is it right to see this policy initiative as, in part, an effort by one political coalition to durably alter the balance of power around a set of key social issues? The answer is a pretty clear yes. As Martha Derthick (1979) recounts, FDR personally made the call on crucial components of this policy design, overturning his own committee's initial plan. In responding to a visitor who later complained that the financing system was regressive, FDR emphasized the *political* benefits of a contributory pension system:

I guess you're right on the economics, but those taxes were never a problem of economics. They are politics all the way through. We put those payroll contributions there so as to give the contributors a legal, moral, and political right to collect their pensions . . . With those taxes in there, no damn politician can ever scrap my social security program. (quoted in Derthick 1979, 230)[7]

Huber and Stephens (2001) make this dynamic central to their analysis of comparative welfare state development. Policy development was not like Groundhog Day, where after each round everyone starts over in their original spot. Instead, Huber and Stephens describe a "policy ratchet" in which policy enactments produce mass attachments to public benefits, engineering a shift in the distribution of political preferences. All social actors had to take this shift into account and adapt their behaviors accordingly. This is precisely what President Eisenhower was trying to get his (more right-wing) brother to understand in 1954. Huber and Stephens leave little doubt that this dynamic should be viewed as involving a conscious political project in which control over policy is used to strengthen political support down the road.

Much more could be said about each of these five mechanisms. My goal here has been simply to distinguish important ways in which power can beget more power over time and to show that there is good reason to think each of these mechanisms operates in significant social processes. Of course, it is worth stressing that these mechanisms (following Gaventa) can help to flesh out (and render empirically tractable) the nonpluralist dimensions of power. Thus, the second dimension's focus on anticipated reactions often plays out through signaling dynamics that mobilize the strong and demobilize the weak. Critical junctures are often "critical" because the "mobilization of bias" they generate operates through new institutions that alter agenda control (the other aspect of power's second dimension). The third dimension of power's focus on preference formation may operate through self-reinforcing processes of ideological mobilization, spirals of silence, and preference-shifting investments of resources following the establishment of new institutions. Taken together, these mechanisms show how power inequalities generated over time diminish the degree to which divisions between the weak and the powerful will generate open conflict.

The methodological implications are clear. Open conflict is not the best place to look for evidence about the distribution of power, unless those conflicts are treated as a subset of the observable implications of theories attentive to more subterranean processes as well. The operation of anticipated reactions and agenda control can be studied systematically. The tools of comparative-historical analysis – sensitive to historical process and focused on large-stakes

---

[7] FDR does not mention the pay-as-you-go structure of Social Security, which was also critical to shifting the distribution of preferences. That design feature was not added until 1939.

outcomes – are well designed for this research agenda. They can fruitfully be combined with well-developed aspects of game theory and institutional analysis, and there are exciting new opportunities related to the emergence of new techniques such as "big data" analysis that could revolutionize efforts to study the evolution of mass and elite discourse. Power is a tractable topic, but only if you know where to look for it.

Political science and the problem of power

It is an odd situation. Scholars of American politics observe an increasingly unequal distribution of resources (Schlozman, Verba, and Brady 2012), but when they go looking to see how that translates into unequal power they have a hard time finding it.[8] Mark Smith's (2000) careful study found that when the reputedly powerful business community was highly unified on a major policy issue, it had a very anemic record in achieving its preferred outcome. Similarly, a team of leading interest group scholars (Baumgartner *et al.* 2009) could find no evidence that the side with greater resources had any discernible advantage in policy fights.

This is because the original critics of pluralism were right on a crucial point: most of the iceberg of power hides below the waterline. Smith is not examining *all* issues where other social actors might oppose the interests of a unified business community. He is looking only at the much more restricted set of issues on which (once anticipated reactions, tilted playing fields, and other obstacles are taken into account) other political actors believe they have a reasonable prospect for success and in fact manage to push their concerns onto the political agenda. In the absence of a big shock, which alters the balance of power in fundamental ways, we should expect high-visibility political conflict to emerge *only* where the power resources of contending forces are relatively even. Thus, when examining the smallish visible tip of the iceberg, we should *expect* to see no clear pattern.

Much to their credit, Baumgartner and colleagues recognize this limitation to their analysis. Just as economists say that the stock price of a company may embody all the information there is about the company's value, they suggest

---

[8] I exaggerate. One place where Americanists are beginning to find some evidence is in research on legislators' responsiveness to public opinion (Bartels 2010; Gilens 2012; Gilens and Page 2014). But even here the research is better at revealing a disconnect between attitudes and outcomes than it is at explaining where the disconnect comes from. In other words, if voters don't govern, who does, and how?

that the policy status quo may be said to embody the inherited distribution of power. If some groups have had greater influence over time, we should expect that the status quo *already reflects* this. Unless their relative power is continuing to grow (perhaps through one or more of the feedback mechanisms identified here), we shouldn't expect that they will win additional open conflicts going forward. Existing policy is an equilibrium. They argue, in short, that their findings of little advantage stemming from the open deployment of greater political resources are consistent with a view of politics that sees underlying power resources as very unequally distributed.

The implication, though, is that to get a handle on these power inequalities we need a different strategy: we need to look at processes unfolding over time. This was Gaventa's position. Not coincidentally, it is the strategy invoked by some of the most effective recent works seeking to revise our understandings of power relationships in modern societies (Broockman 2012; Carpenter 2001). To say that power often is not expressed in visible conflict does not mean we cannot study it. On the contrary, we have made progress on multiple fronts over the past few decades that make exploration of what is under the waterline more feasible than it was for community power theorists. Some of that progress has come from game theorists and rational choice institutionalists, but arguments about critical junctures and path dependence have been and will be central to this effort.[9]

Consider one brief closing illustration from the field of comparative political economy. A central expectation of those studying the topic of inequality from a perspective that emphasizes the preferences and behavior of atomized voters is that of Meltzer and Richard (1981). Rising inequality skewed to the highest income groups should produce more egalitarian policies, as the median voter faces growing incentives to vote for redistribution. As Huber and Stephens (2012) have recently noted, the logic may be elegant, but the empirics are "plain wrong" (11). It is the *most egalitarian* societies that make the greatest efforts to equalize income. Moreover, as societies become more unequal they often decrease, rather than increase, their redistributive efforts. The reason, as Huber and Stephens emphasize, is that "a greater distance between the median and the mean income tends to be accompanied by a more skewed distribution of political power and thus lower responsiveness to demands for redistribution."

---

[9] Like Moe (2005, 229), I believe that if social analysis focuses on power, "rational choice theorists and historical institutionalists will have more in common than ever before, and the theoretical and the empirical are likely to come together in far more productive ways."

Here Huber and Stephens draw on the central ideas of power resources theory, with its emphasis on what Korpi (1985) calls "'the Matthew effect' in exchange: to him that hath, shall be given" (36). All of the mechanisms of power reinforcement discussed here can help to account for this striking result. The example clarifies why comparative-historical analysis has typically emphasized the importance of distinctive policy regimes, which either enhance or discourage pressures for egalitarianism. More fundamentally, it points to the need to focus on how power is built into durable social structures rather than operating exclusively at the level of open conflict. Only by explaining how outcomes at key junctures produce durable (but not permanent or unchanging) shifts in social arrangements can we make inequalities of influence visible. Indeed, arguably the most important contribution of comparative-historical analysis to social science is its commitment to understanding the ways in which inequalities of power are built deeply into the subterranean structures of modern societies.

References

Acemoglu, Daron, and James Robinson. 2012. *Why Nations Fail.* New York: Crown Books.

Akram, Fares, and Jodi Rudoren. 2013. "To Shape Young Palestinians, Hamas Creates Its Own Textbooks." *New York Times*, November 4, p. A1.

Ansolabehere, Stephen, John de Figueiredo, and James Snyder. 2003. "Why Is There So Little Money in American Politics?" *Journal of Economic Perspectives* 17:105–30.

Bachrach, Peter, and Morton S. Baratz. 1962. "The Two Faces of Power." *American Political Science Review* 56:947–52.

Bartels, Larry. 2010. *Unequal Democracy.* Princeton, NJ: Princeton University Press.

Baumgartner, Frank R., Jeffrey M. Berry, Marie Hojnacki, David C. Kimball, and Beth L. Leech. 2009. *Lobbying and Policy Change: Who Wins, Who Loses, and Why.* Chicago: University of Chicago Press.

Berman, Sheri. 2003. "Islamism, Revolution, and Civil Society." *Perspectives on Politics* 1:257–72.

Broockman, David. 2012. "The 'Problem of Preferences': Medicare and Business Support for the Welfare State." *Studies in American Political Development* 26 (2): 83–106.

Cameron, Charles. 2000. *Veto Bargaining.* Cambridge: Cambridge University Press.

Campbell, Andrea. 2003. *How Policies Make Citizens.* Princeton, NJ: Princeton University Press.

Capoccia, Giovanni, and Daniel Keleman. 2007. "The Study of Critical Junctures: Theory, Narrative, and Counterfactuals in Historical Institutionalism." *World Politics* 59:341–69.

Carpenter, Daniel. 2001. *The Forging of Bureaucratic Autonomy.* Princeton, NJ: Princeton University Press.

Cox, Gary, and Matthew McCubbins. 1993. *Legislative Leviathan: Party Government in the House*. Berkeley: University of California Press.

Crenson, Matthew A. 1971. *The Un-Politics of Air Pollution: A Study of Non-Decision-Making in the Cities*. Baltimore: Johns Hopkins University Press.

Dahl, Robert A. 1961. *Who Governs? Democracy and Power in an American City*. New Haven, CT: Yale University Press.

   1982. *Dilemmas of Pluralist Democracy*. New Haven, CT: Yale University Press.

Dahl, Robert A., and Charles E. Lindblom. 1953. *Politics, Economics and Welfare: Planning and Politico-Economic Systems Resolved into Basic Social Processes*. Chicago: University of Chicago Press.

Derthick, Martha. 1979. *Policymaking for Social Security*. Washington, DC: The Brookings Institution.

Edsall, Thomas. 1984. *The New Politics of Inequality*. New York: W. W. Norton.

Eisenhower, Dwight D. (1954) 1970. "Letter to Edgar Newton Eisenhower." Document #1147, November 8. In *The Papers of Dwight David Eisenhower*, Vol. XV, edited by Louis Galambos. Baltimore: Johns Hopkins University Press.

Erickson, Robert, Michael MacKuen, and James Stimson. 2002. *The Macro Polity*. Cambridge: Cambridge University Press.

Eskridge, William, and John Ferejohn. 2001. "Super Statutes." *Duke Law Journal* 50:1215.

Esping-Andersen, Gøsta. 1990. *Three Worlds of Welfare Capitalism*. Princeton, NJ: Princeton University Press.

Franzese, Robert. 1999. "Partially Independent Central Banks, Politically Responsive Governments, and Inflation." *American Journal of Political Science* 43:681–76.

Friedrich, Carl J. 1963. *Man and His Government*. New York: McGraw-Hill.

Gaventa, John. 1982. *Power and Powerlessness*. Champaign-Urbana: University of Illinois Press.

Gilens, Martin. 2012. *Affluence and Influence*. Princeton, NJ: Princeton University Press.

Gilens, Martin, and Benjamin I. Page. 2014. "Testing Theories of American Politics: Elites, Interest Groups, and Average Citizens." *Perspectives on Politics* 12 (3): 564–81.

Gourevitch, Peter A., and James Shinn. 2007. *Political Power and Corporate Control: The New Global Politics of Corporate Governance*. Princeton, NJ: Princeton University Press.

Gruber, Lloyd. 2000. *Ruling the World: Power Politics and the Rise of Supranational Institutions*. Princeton, NJ: Princeton University Press.

Hacker, Jacob, and Paul Pierson. 2002. "Business Power and Social Policy: Employers and the Formation of the American Welfare State." *Politics and Society* 30:277–325.

   2010. *Winner-Take-All Politics: How Washington Made the Rich Richer – and Turned Its Back on the Middle Class*. New York: Simon and Schuster.

   2014. "After the 'Master Theory': Downs, Schattschneider, and the Rebirth of Policy-Focused Analysis." *Perspectives on Politics* 12 (3): 643–62.

Hall, Peter A. 2010. "Politics as a Process Structured in Space and Time." Paper presented at the Annual Meeting of the American Political Science Association, Washington, DC, September 2–5.

Huber, Evelyn, and John Stephens. 2001. *Development and Crisis of the Welfare State*. Chicago: University of Chicago Press.

2012. *Democracy and the Left: Social Policy and Inequality in Latin America.* Chicago: University of Chicago Press.

Keyssar, Alex. 2000. *The Right to Vote.* New York: Basic Books.

Korpi, Walter. 1985. "Power Resources Approach vs. Action and Conflict: On Causal and Intentional Explanations in the Study of Power." *Sociological Theory* 3 (2): 31–45.

Lang, Kurt, and Gladys Engel Lang. 2012. "What Is This Thing We Call Public Opinion? Reflections on the Spiral of Silence." *International Journal of Public Opinion Research* 24 (3): 368–86.

Lindblom, Charles E. 1977. *Politics and Markets.* New York: Basic Books.

Lukes, Stephen. 1974. *Power: A Radical View.* London: Macmillan.

Mahoney, James. 2000. "Path Dependence in Historical Sociology." *Theory and Society* 29 (4): 507–48.

Mayhew, David. 2002. *Electoral Realignments: A Critique of an American Genre.* New Haven, CT: Yale University Press.

McKelvey, Richard. 1976. Intransitivities in Multidimensional Voting Models and Some Implications for Agenda Control." *Journal of Economic Theory* 12 (3): 472–82.

Meltzer, Alan H., and Scott F. Richard. 1981. "A Rational Theory of the Size of Government." *Journal of Political Economy* 89 (5): 914–27.

Moe, Terry M. 2005. "Power and Political Institutions." *Perspectives on Politics* 3:215–33.

Noelle-Neuman, Elisabeth. 1974. "The Spiral of Silence: A Theory of Public Opinion." *Journal of Communication* 24:43–51.

Patashnik, Eric. 2008. *After Reform.* Princeton, NJ: Princeton University Press.

Pierson, Paul. 2000. "Increasing Returns, Path Dependence, and the Study of Politics." *American Political Science Review* 94:251–67.

2004. *Politics in Time: History, Institutions and Social Analysis.* Princeton, NJ: Princeton University Press.

2006. "Public Policies as Institutions." In *Rethinking Institutions: The Art of the State*, edited by Stephen Skowronek, Ian Shapiro, and Daniel Galvin, 114–34. New York: New York University Press.

Polsby, Nelson. 1980. *Community Power and Political Theory: A Further Look at Problems of Evidence and Inference.* 2nd ed. New Haven, CT: Yale University Press.

Remnick, David. 2013. "The Party Faithful: The Settlers Move to Annex the West Bank – and Israeli Politics." *The New Yorker*, January 21.

Rueschemeyer, Dietrich, Evelyn Stephens, and John Stephens. 1992. *Capitalist Development and Democracy.* Princeton, NJ: Princeton University Press.

Schattschneider, E. E. 1960. *The Semi-Sovereign People.* New York: Holt, Rinehart and Winston.

Schlozman, Kay Leyman, Sidney Verba, and Henry E. Brady. 2012. *The Unheavenly Chorus: Unequal Political Voice and the Broken Promise of American Democracy.* Princeton, NJ: Princeton University Press.

Siegel, Reva B. 2008. "Dead or Alive: Originalism as Popular Constitutionalism in Heller." *Harvard Law Review* 122:191–245.

Smith, Mark. 2000. *American Business and Political Power.* Chicago: University of Chicago Press.

Starr, Paul. 2014. "Three Degrees of Entrenchment: Power, Policy, Structure." Unpublished manuscript, Princeton University Department of Sociology.

Thelen, Kathleen. 2004. *How Institutions Evolve*. Cambridge: Cambridge University Press.

Vogel, David. 1989. *Fluctuating Fortunes*. New York: Basic Books.

Wolfinger, Raymond E. 1971. "Nondecisions and the Study of Local Politics." *American Political Science Review* 65:1063–80.

Wuthnow, Robert. 1989. *Communities of Discourse*. Cambridge, MA: Harvard University Press.

Zaller, John R. 1992. *The Nature and Origins of Mass Opinion*. New York: Cambridge University Press.

6 Critical junctures and institutional change

Giovanni Capoccia

Critical juncture analysis is popular in comparative-historical analysis (CHA) since it provides tools for studying the political origins and reform of important institutional arrangements that exert a long-lasting influence on their social and political environment. This chapter clarifies a number of theoretical and conceptual issues, explores the strengths and weaknesses of the critical juncture approach, and proposes a methodological strategy for studying critical junctures in comparative perspective.

It is necessary to define the scope of the discussion by making two preliminary observations. First, the "dual" model of historical development intrinsic to critical juncture analysis – shorter phases of fluidity and change alternating with longer periods of stability and adaptation – has been applied to a wide range of outcomes and entities, from individual life histories to the development of groups and organizations and the evolution of entire societies (e.g., Swidler 1986, 280).[1] In this chapter, I focus on the use of the concept of critical junctures in the context of the development of *institutions*, broadly defined as organizations, formal rules, public policies, political regimes, and political economies. These have generally been the object of critical juncture analysis in CHA in both political science and sociology.

Second, within CHA, the concept of critical juncture applies only to the analysis of *path-dependent* institutions and not to all forms of institutional development. The analysis of critical junctures is a part of path dependence arguments, according to which institutional arrangements put in place at a certain point in time become entrenched because of their ability to shape the incentives, worldviews, and resources of the actors and groups affected by the

---

For comments I thank Jacob Hacker, Jim Mahoney, Craig Parsons, Paul Pierson, Kathy Thelen, Daniel Ziblatt, the participants of the workshops "Comparative-Historical Analysis in the Social Sciences" at MIT and Northwestern University, as well as the participants and the audience of the APSA panel "Comparative-Historical Analysis: Tools for Analysis," Chicago, August 30, 2013. The usual disclaimer applies.

[1] At times, synonyms such as *crisis, turning point*, and *unsettled times* are used. I refer to critical junctures throughout this chapter.

institution. In this analytical context, critical junctures are cast as moments in which uncertainty as to the future of an institutional arrangement allows for political agency and choice to play a decisive causal role in setting an institution on a certain path of development, a path that then persists over a long period of time.[2]

The chapter begins by identifying the components of critical juncture analysis, presenting important examples of the approach from the literature, clarifying its advantages vis-à-vis ahistorical approaches, and linking those advantages to the key characteristics of CHA. In the central section, the chapter proposes a theoretical framework for making the agency and contingency at the core of critical junctures analytically tractable and discusses the resulting theoretical and methodological payoffs of the framework. In essence, the conceptualization developed here alerts scholars to several features of the *politics of institution making* during critical junctures that are causally important for the creation or reform of path-dependent institutions. First, by underscoring the importance of political entrepreneurs in assembling coalitions for institutional change during critical junctures, the approach draws attention to the constraints and inducements derived from the organizational landscape of politics in driving many institutional innovations. Furthermore, by pointing to the possible disconnect between the institutional outcome and the initial preferences of the most powerful actors on the scene, critical juncture analysis avoids the pitfall of attributing institutional outcomes to such preferences, and it uncovers the political dynamics that often guide the strategies of political actors in situations of uncertainty. Finally, by focusing on situations in which influential actors exploit situations of uncertainty to manipulate the preferences of important social groups through the strategic promotion of change in the relevant social norms, critical juncture analysis calls attention to the potentially important role that the cultural construction of the institutional preferences of social actors may play in institution making. In all these cases, a close analysis of political agency and decision making during critical junctures yields fresh empirical findings and furthers the scholarly conversation on institutional change. Methodologically, the concept of "near-miss" reform provides scholars with the theoretical lens for

---

[2] I refer to path dependence arguments that are based on logics of increasing returns. For a broader view of path dependence, see Mahoney (2000). The theoretical literature on path dependence is extensive and its discussion goes beyond the scope of this chapter. A small selection of important contributions includes, in economics, North (1990), Arthur (1994), and David (1985, 2000); in sociology, Goldstone (1998) and Mahoney (2000); in political science, Pierson (2000 and Chapter 5, this volume) and Page (2006). For a review of the use of the concept in the field of international relations, see Fioretos (2011).

unearthing negative cases of institutional change that enhance the leverage of comparative research designs.

The chapter is organized as follows. In the next section, I illustrate the main characteristics of the critical juncture approach with reference to important comparative work in the field. In the section that follows, I clarify some theoretical issues and discuss the theoretical and methodological payoffs of the approach. I then offer methodological advice for the comparative study of critical junctures. In the conclusion, I summarize the main points of the chapter and discuss the limitations of the critical juncture approach in CHA, pointing to avenues of further theorization.

Critical junctures and historical explanation

The critical juncture approach gained the important place that it currently occupies in CHA with Berins Collier and Collier's (1991) influential volume on modes of labor incorporation in Latin America. Their crucial theoretical move was to see explicitly their analysis as a specific case of a *more general approach* to the study of institutional development, in which critical junctures give rise to *path-dependent* processes, a conceptual apparatus imported into political science from institutional economics (e.g., Arthur 1994; David 1985; North 1990). In these and later works, the analysis of critical junctures and institutional development is explicitly linked to economic research on path dependence (e.g., Berins Collier and Collier 1991, 27; Lieberman 2003, 23; Mahoney 2001, 7; Yashar 1997, 3). This was an important change from the first use of the concept by Lipset and Rokkan: they traced the origins of Western European party systems to three "crucial junctures" located much earlier in the history of each nation, during which "decisions and developments" shaped mass politics in the region for decades to come (Lipset and Rokkan 1967, 37–8). Their analysis, however, was largely couched in macrostructuralist language that left little space for the analysis of decisions and developments and reconstructed, instead, the roots of historical variation *ex post*, starting from variation in the outcome of interest and looking backward in time (Berntzen and Selle 1990).

The reference to the theory of path dependence, with its emphasis on the mechanisms (increasing returns, network effects, lock-in, and others) through which institutional arrangements become entrenched by shaping their social underlay, not only gave critical juncture scholars a powerful language to support the claim of *distal causation* – the thesis that decisions and developments in the distant past can have a long-lasting effect on institutional arrangements, which constitutes the essence of the approach – but also entailed a fundamental shift of analytical perspective from *ex post* to *ex ante*. The theorization by institutional economists that "small and contingent events," although generally of insignificant influence during periods of institutional reproduction, could instead play a crucial role at the beginning of an institutional path (e.g., David 1985, 2000) induced political scientists and sociologists to theorize explicitly that different possibilities were open during critical junctures, and that initial conditions did not determine the type and direction of subsequent institutional developments (e.g., Goldstone 1998; Mahoney 2000). This analytical perspective induced scholars –albeit sometimes only implicitly – to consider not only the institutional path selected during the critical juncture but also the paths that plausibly could have been, but were not, taken.

Another building block of the critical juncture approach was added by Capoccia and Kelemen (2007), who pointed out that the economists' model of "small and contingent events" as unconnected microdecisions that cumulate to create a state of institutional "lock-in" is ill suited to capture the *political* dynamics of institutional path selection during critical junctures (see discussion in Capoccia and Kelemen 2007, 354). They note that during moments of social and political fluidity such as critical junctures, the *decisions and choices of key actors* are freer and more influential in steering institutional development than during "settled" times (Swidler 1986). In other words, by analytically linking the concept of contingency to the choices, strategies, and decisions of political decision makers rather than to a series of bottom-up microdecisions by individuals, the researcher is more likely to capture the dynamics that in most cases influence the selection of one institutional solution over others that were available during the critical juncture.[3] This offers the theoretical basis for a definition of critical junctures as relatively short periods of time during which there is a substantially heightened probability that agents' choices will affect the outcome of interest. By "relatively

---

[3] Contingency is at times linked to *events* happening during periods of uncertainty as well as to decisions. However, as discussed below, connecting contingency to decisions not only makes the concept analytically more tractable but also underscores that what is often decisive in critical junctures is how key actors *react* to unexpected events, provided that, in line with the definition of critical junctures set forth in the text, actors have different options to choose from. If an event forecloses all but one option and therefore leaves the actors with no choice, then the situation is better conceptualized as a *sequence* rather than a critical juncture (see, for related discussions, Falleti and Mahoney, Chapter 8, this volume; Mahoney 2000).

short periods of time," Capoccia and Kelemen mean that the duration of the juncture must be brief relative to the duration of the path-dependent process it instigates (which leads eventually to the outcome of interest). By "substantially heightened probability," they mean that the probability that agents' choices will affect the outcome of interest must be high relative to that probability before and after the juncture. This definition captures both the notion that, for a brief phase, agents face a broader than typical range of feasible options and the notion that their choices from among these options are likely to have a significant impact on subsequent outcomes (Capoccia and Kelemen 2007, 348).

This theoretical work combines to create the following explanatory approach: an event or a series of events, typically exogenous to the institution of interest,[4] lead to a phase of political uncertainty in which different options for radical institutional change are viable; antecedent conditions define the range of institutional alternatives available to decision makers but do not determine the alternative chosen; one of these options is selected; and its selection generates a long-lasting institutional legacy.

Some examples of recent comparative work in this vein illustrate the power of the approach. In her *Demanding Democracy: Reform and Reaction in Costa Rica and Guatemala*, Yashar compares the different political trajectories of authoritarian Guatemala and democratic Costa Rica to explore the question of why democracies are founded and endure. Her argument is that enduring democracy depends on whether emerging democratic forces seize the opportunity to forge cross-class coalitions during a democratic transition (the critical juncture in her framework; Yashar 1997, 3, 235) and pass bounded redistributive reforms that weaken the power of rural elites while at the same time allowing for the possibility that traditional social forces will continue to play a role in politics. The uncertainty typical of democratic transitions, triggered by a split among authoritarian elites (O'Donnell and Schmitter 1986), makes it impossible for traditional elites to confidently oppose such reforms, since they do not have a sufficiently clear view of the future and cannot count on reliable political allies. The implementation of such reforms during the transition, therefore, reduces the power of traditional elites and empowers other social groups, making democracy more likely to endure well

---

[4] For simplicity's sake, the discussion in this chapter refers only to exogenous shocks as triggers of critical junctures. However, it is possible that a critical juncture in the development of a given institution is generated endogenously by power holders that may disrupt existing institutional equilibria to achieve political objectives. Kohli, for example, discusses how Indira Gandhi intentionally deinstitutionalized the institutions of the Indian federal state in pursuit of her political agenda (Kohli 1997, 331).

after the critical juncture. If the attempt to pass democratic reforms is instead delayed, established forces will generally have the power and the resources to oppose them and restore authoritarian rule. A high level of development of civil society constitutes a necessary condition for democratizing elites to form cross-class coalitions during the critical juncture since these coalitions draw their power from the politically mobilizable masses (Yashar 1997, 22–3). At the same time, however, Yashar makes clear that this favorable antecedent condition makes pro-democratic coalitions possible, but "agency can prove paramount precisely at the political moment offered with a transition to democracy . . . in the event that actors do not act at the moment of democratic transition, they will lose a historic opportunity to reshape institutions in an enduring way" (Yashar 1997, 22).

The study of regime change in Central America is also at the core of Mahoney's *The Legacies of Liberalism: Path Dependence and Political Regimes in Central America*. In his analysis, the period of liberal oligarchic regimes at the turn of the twentieth century constitutes the critical juncture during which political developments shaped the variation of regimes across Central America during the subsequent decades (traditional dictatorship developed in Honduras and Nicaragua, military authoritarianism in Guatemala and El Salvador, and democracy in Costa Rica). In Mahoney's account, the increased world demand for indigenous Central American agricultural products as well as the technological advances that allowed long-distance shipping of perishables opened up new possibilities for agricultural development in these countries. The choices that liberal presidents and their political allies made in relation to agricultural development during the critical juncture were crucial in setting the political institutions of these countries on different paths of development. Importantly, Mahoney shows that these initial choices, some of which failed to promote agricultural development because of foreign intervention, and others of which succeeded but varied according to whether they sought rapid or gradual development, put into place institutions and policies that affected class relations in the countryside. These class relations, in turn, created the social constituencies that underpinned the persistence of the original institutional choices, structured political dynamics in predictable ways, and encouraged the development of the type of state that sustained the different models of agricultural development. As in Yashar's account, antecedent conditions were an important backdrop during the critical juncture but did not determine the decisions of political actors (Mahoney 2001, 14). Mahoney emphasizes the "historical contingency" of the choices made by liberal presidents, arguing that their decisions were directly influenced by the immediate political imperative to maintain or expand power rather than by the desire to forge social coalitions that would persist over the long term (Mahoney 2001, 42).

Lieberman's *Race and Regionalism in the Politics of Taxation in Brazil and South Africa* addresses the question of why states vary in their capability to extract tax from the more affluent social strata. His argument is that different types of "tax state" (important tax policies and their implementation) emerge as legacies of critical junctures in the development of constitutional orders, in particular the formal rules of citizenship. Lieberman defines such junctures as foundational moments in which the boundaries of the National Political Community (NPC) are set, namely, when notions of "us" and "them" identifying who has the rights and duties of a citizen and who does not, are socially constructed and entrenched in constitutions and formal rules. The entrenchment of such categories in formal institutions, as well as in important carriers of symbolic meaning such as maps, museums, census rules, and media discourse, "cast[s] a long shadow on the future, even once the initial conditions have changed" (Lieberman 2003, 14) and sets in motion path-dependent processes of development of fiscal institutions, giving rise to nationally distinctive patterns of tax policy that are resistant to significant change (Lieberman 2003, 19). The choices that Brazilian and South African elites made during brief periods of constitution making around the turn of the century led to different definitions of NPC: racial categories prevailed in South Africa, leading to the exclusion of blacks from citizenship, whereas in Brazil racial categories were deemphasized, and regional categories prevailed and were entrenched in a strongly federalized polity (Lieberman 2003, 80–4). Lieberman makes clear that alternative choices on both dimensions were not only possible but seriously considered in both cases: "Comparative historical analysis reveals that there was nothing pre-ordained about how the NPC would be defined in either country . . . Legacies of immigration from Europe, Asia and Africa; slavery; miscegenation; and centuries of internal conflict created important political cleavages that obscured any obvious basis for nationhood in Brazil and South Africa" (Lieberman 2003, 70–1). In South Africa, a race-based definition of citizenship created interclass solidarity among whites so that the more affluent groups in society (who are white) felt an obligation to pay taxes out of solidarity with poorer whites. In Brazil, racial criteria were not made salient for the definition of citizenship, official discrimination was banned, and an official policy of miscegenation was promoted, but de facto racial discrimination remained in society; as a result, poor whites were more likely to be perceived as poor, not as whites, by the members of the (white) affluent groups. Moreover, the combination of highly salient regional identities, strong federal institutions, and income differences among regions made affluent groups likely to perceive taxes as drawing resources from "us" (defined regionally) to "them" (people in other regions). By the same token, the salience of regional differences made it more difficult for the poor majority to make unitary demands for more progressive taxation. These patterns shaped the organizational landscape of politics and had a strong impact on tax policy, leading to long-lasting legacies of more fiscal progressivism in South Africa and less fiscal progressivism in Brazil.

These and other works show how a rigorous application of the critical juncture approach can have important advantages over ahistorical approaches, which typically focus on contemporaneous social (or international) correlates of the institutional outcome of interest. In general terms, critical juncture analysis tests the hypothesis that the domestic social factors that correlate with the institutional outcome of interest may be *endogenous* to political decisions made much earlier in time and for reasons unrelated to such factors. Mahoney, for example, shows that patterns of agrarian class relations, which many consider key determinants of political regimes in Central America during the twentieth century, were largely the consequence of the previous choice of a particular model of agricultural development on the part of liberal leaders. These choices were in turn not endogenous to dominant class interests of the time, nor were they simply a response to the "objective" needs of an incipient agrarian capitalist mode of production. Central American liberal states were generally headed by personalistic dictators who were capable of making decisions without negotiation or consultation with classes and groups from civil society and who were mainly interested in maintaining and expanding their own personal power (Mahoney 2001, 19). Apart from demonstrating that "purely structural explanations...are clearly incomplete" (Lieberman 2003, 2–3),[5] Lieberman's focus on critical junctures and their institutional legacies allows him to show that macrosocial and cultural factors at the core of alternative explanations of taxation capability, such as the "trustworthiness of the state" (Levi 1988, 1997), the diffusion of social capital (Putnam 1993), and the strength and preferences of the groups which strike different "tax bargains" with the state (Levi 1988), are largely endogenous to the earlier

---

[5] Through the application of a nested analysis (Lieberman, Chapter 9, this volume), Lieberman shows how levels of economic development, although correlated cross-nationally with taxation capability, heavily underpredict South Africa's taxation capability and overpredict Brazil's, and therefore not only fail to provide a satisfactory explanation for these important cases but also leave significant room for theory building (Lieberman 2003, 10–12).

definition of the NPC (Lieberman 2003, 22–32). In sum, a focus on critical junctures and their legacies shows that what might be at play in shaping important institutional arrangements is not correlational causation but *distal causation*: decisions and events happening much earlier in time give rise to path-dependent institutions that *shape their social underlay* and thereby persist over time.

The power of the critical juncture approach to provide important correctives to ahistorical explanations turns on its reliance on some key tools of CHA (Thelen and Mahoney, Chapter 1, this volume). First-hand *knowledge of the cases* studied is essential to critical juncture analysis not only to rule out alternative explanations for specific cases[6] but also, importantly, to identify the key critical juncture(s) in the development of the institution of interest and to provide a compelling account of the exact mechanisms that give rise to the path-dependent legacy. Furthermore, the analysis of critical junctures and their legacies represents a form of *temporal analysis*, and similar to all such analyses in CHA, it compels scholars to focus on *when* something happens in order to establish whether and how much causal force it exercises over their *explanandum*. In the context of the critical juncture/path dependence approach, this has three main consequences. First and foremost, the approach exemplifies Polanyi's dictum that in some moments in history "time expands . . . and so must our analyses" (Polanyi 1944, 4). This expansion of time underscores the fact that an event that occurs during a critical juncture may have a large effect on the outcome even though the same event may not have important consequences in later phases of institutional development, when the costs of change are higher (David 2000; North 1990), and encourages scholars to perform detailed historical analysis of the decisions and developments that happen during critical junctures. Second, the approach points to the possibility that transformative institutional change (although not a necessary characteristic of critical junctures, as explained below) may be abrupt and concentrated in relatively short periods of time rather than be gradual and protracted. Third, as discussed above, by enlarging the temporal horizon of the analysis (Pierson 2004) the approach may reveal that what may seem to be causing the institutional outcome at a certain moment may in fact be the effect of decisions made much earlier in time that became entrenched in institutional arrangements.

---

[6] For example, Yashar's (1997, 12) analysis enables her to criticize accounts that consider the US involvement in the 1954 coup an important cause of the failure of democracy in Guatemala and to show that the United States "was not the only or even the most important actor" in those events.

Theoretical and methodological payoffs

But is this real progress? Can a focus on agency and contingency as key causal factors of institutional path selection during critical junctures offer the foundations for theoretical advances and knowledge accumulation on why certain institutions are selected over others? This concern drives a number of recent theoretical contributions that, while not denying the causal importance of agency and contingency during critical junctures, nevertheless take the view that a focus on the *antecedent conditions* of critical junctures is analytically more useful than a focus on political agency and contingency. According to this scholarship, the defining feature of critical junctures is not contingency but *divergence*: critical juncture analysis is appropriate in situations in which a "common exogenous shock" affects a set of cases (typically countries), causing them to "diverge" as a result of the combination of the common shock and their different antecedent conditions, which therefore exert a significant causal force on the outcome (Acemoglu and Robinson 2012, 106; Slater and Simmons 2010, 888; Soifer 2012, 1593).

Since, as clarified in more detail below, agency-based conceptualizations of critical junctures *do* take the structural context of decision making into account insofar as it constrains or enables[7] a certain range of choices on the part of key actors and do *not* equate agency with the free-floating determinations of politically disembedded actors (e.g., Capoccia and Kelemen 2007; Katznelson 2003), the disagreement would appear at first glance to be one of emphasis. However, insofar as these critics promote a research program based on the causal predominance of *structural* antecedent conditions in the selection of path-dependent institutions, the disagreement is substantial.[8] To be sure, *structure* is one of the most contested and ambiguous terms in comparative politics. A comprehensive theoretical discussion of the concept, however, is unnecessary here,[9] since the term as used by these critics refers

[7] In many cases, structural antecedent conditions may restrict the range of choices available to actors; in other cases, structural conditions may provide the necessary conditions for certain developments during critical junctures, thus making certain choices possible (e.g., Yashar 1997, 22; see also Soifer 2012).

[8] Falleti and Lynch (2009, 1155) interpret the conception of agency put forward by Capoccia and Kelemen (2007) as "de-linked from context" and bemoan it as unproductive. Soifer (2012, 1593) argues that he is "agnostic" about the relative importance of agency and contingency vis-à-vis structural factors during critical junctures. Even though not all the examples of "critical antecedents" that Slater and Simmons discuss can be considered structural according to the definition adopted here, they explicitly mention their intent to uncover the role of "deeper structural forces" and "long-term causal factors" (Slater and Simmons 2010, 887) and various synonyms (892–3, 895, 905).

[9] For an insightful discussion, see Sewell (1992).

broadly to the distribution of material resources and technology exogenous to human agency (e.g., Parsons 2007, 49–51),[10] which is the same general definition typically adopted in agency-focused critical juncture analyses. These, however, circumscribe or even deny the decisive causal force of such structural antecedent conditions (e.g., Lieberman 2003, 30; Mahoney 2001, 7).

In general terms, views that emphasize the importance of structural antecedents offer a welcome reminder that scholars should not assume too easily that the background conditions of the cases that they compare are similar. Cases may differ in significant ways prior to the critical juncture and those differences may be important causally. However, an analytical focus that emphasizes the causal significance of structural antecedents also raises several concerns. To begin with, scholars in this line of analysis do not deny that agency (Slater and Simmons 2010, 890) and contingency (Acemoglu and Robinson 2012, 110; Soifer 2012, 1573) play a potentially important causal role during critical junctures. Such a role, however, is logically inconsistent with a *definition* of critical junctures in terms of divergence. Divergence is a *consequence* of critical junctures in which agency and contingency are causal, and as such it cannot be used to define them.[11] Furthermore, as explained above, the critical juncture/path dependence approach postulates that institutions exert causal force on their social underlay, a claim that would need to be nuanced if the selection of the institutions in question were endogenous to "long-term structural forces," which in many cases would be likely to continue to influence the institutions after these had been put in place. Finally, structuralist explanations picture "people reacting in regular, direct ways to their 'material' surroundings" (Parsons 2007, 51): all aspects of political life, including institutional ones, once stripped of unimportant detail, are unequivocally shaped by the underlying structural landscape. To be sure, this does not mean that structuralist explanations are necessarily deterministic: it is perfectly possible to build probabilistic arguments showing a robust correlation between structural conditions and institutional outcomes in a sufficiently large number of cases, where deviations from the regularities dictated by structural conditions are relegated to the error term of a regression

---

[10] Or that can be considered exogenous to human agency for the temporal scope of the analysis (see discussion in Parsons 2007, 49–65).

[11] Furthermore, whether divergence between cases is observable depends on which cases are selected for comparison. Some authors talk about "divergence" also in the context of a single case, with reference to situations in which radical institutional change happens (Slater and Simmons 2010, 888; Soifer 2012, 1593; see also Acemoglu and Robinson 2012, 106). However, a causal role of agency and contingency is incompatible with considering change as a *defining* element of a critical juncture (see Capoccia and Kelemen 2007, 352, and the discussion on "near misses" below).

model. However, as discussed above, it is precisely these arguments that, drawing on the strengths of CHA, critical juncture analysis demonstrates can be insufficient or problematic.

More generally, though, as Greif (2006, 33) rightly puts it, "Institutional analysis is about situations in which more than one behavior is physically and technologically possible." There may be significant organizational and ideational gaps between "physical and technological" conditions and institutional outcomes, which point to a potentially substantial *causal ambiguity* between the two. On the one hand, the organizational landscape of politics does not necessarily map onto the social cleavages defined by the distribution of material resources (e.g., Capoccia and Ziblatt 2010, 949–52). On the other hand, "different agents can hold different mental models regardless of the similarities of their structural positions" (Blyth 2003, 697). During critical junctures, the uncertainty created by the disruption of the institutional status quo and the ensuing demand for radical institutional change, this causal gap is likely to be even *wider*. This raises the risk that "portable" causal arguments based on the analysis of long-term structural forces preceding the critical juncture will be quite vague and at times possibly misleading.

Decision making under uncertainty: the politics of institutional formation during critical junctures

Theoretical and methodological progress in critical juncture analysis depends largely on how contingency is defined. Indeed, if theorists of an agency-based view of critical junctures equated contingency with randomness and conceived of critical junctures as characterized by "complete contingency" and "blank slates" (Slater and Simmons 2010, 890), the criticism of theoretical sterility would be justified. However, my contention, discussed in previous work (Capoccia 2004, Capoccia and Kelemen 2007, 355–7; see also Katznelson 2003, 277), is that Isaiah Berlin's definition of historical contingency provides the most useful starting point for the study of critical junctures. Berlin defines the analysis of contingency as "the study of what happened in the context of *what could have happened*" (Berlin 1974, 176, emphasis added).[12] Hence, in the context of the critical juncture approach, contingency has two key characteristics. First, as discussed above, to account for the political dynamics leading to institutional path selection, it should be linked to the analysis of

---

[12] For different definitions of contingency, see Mahoney (2000, 514) and the discussions in Bennett and Elman (2006) and Shapiro and Bedi (2006).

political choice and decision making, and in this respect it simply points to the intrinsic *plausibility of the twofold counterfactual argument* that, first, actors could have plausibly made different decisions, and second, had they done so, this would have had led to the selection of a different path of institutional development. The second characteristic of this definition of contingency points to the fact that the range of plausible options during critical junctures – in Berlin's words, "what could have happened" – is not infinite: its boundaries are defined by prior conditions even though, within the limits of those conditions, actors have real choices. It is the analyst's task to reconstruct the context of the critical juncture and, through the study of historical sources, establish who were the key decision makers, what choices were available to them – *historically* available, not simply *hypothetically* possible – how close actors came to selecting an alternative option, and what likely consequences the choice of an alternative option would have had for the institutional outcome of interest (Capoccia and Kelemen 2007, 355; see also Gourevitch 1992, 67; Katznelson 2003, 282).

Against the background of this conceptualization, the study of agency during critical junctures does not refer to the idiosyncratic creation of institutions by fiat through the unbridled action of free-floating demiurges but to "the choice (within given constraints) of *triggering a specific process among many possible, rather than ensuring a particular outcome*" (Kalyvas 1996, 262–3, emphasis added). As mentioned above, the uncertainty typical of critical junctures widens the organizational and ideational gap that often exists between structural preconditions and institutional outcomes. Hence, during critical junctures, political decision making, initiatives for political mobilization and coalition formation, and strategic interactions between key actors are likely to be directly influenced by multiple and contradictory *political pressures* of varying strength, which, given the generalized uncertainty, are likely to be ambiguous and to change rapidly. Political actors, therefore, typically have substantial leeway to choose which pressures to yield to, and which instead to resist, in deciding their best course of action. In their choices and interactions, there is significant scope for intentionality, interpretation, and unintended consequences. The different forms of political pressure on agents are inseparable from the study of political agency – what political actors want, think, prefer, and actually do to transform their surrounding social relations – indeed, they constitute the very *substance* of it. At the same time, such political pressure is not random: it is often possible to identify commonalities across cases involving struggles on similar institutional choices. Indeed, by analyzing these political pressures and actor responses during critical junctures, scholars have built compelling midrange theoretical arguments (the typical scope of most arguments in CHA) on the origins and reform of important institutional arrangements. These arguments have often led to fresh insights into their specific object of study as well as theoretical payoffs capable of informing research on other cases and methodological advances in the design of comparative research. The next section discusses and illustrates three typical patterns of the politics of institutional formation during critical junctures and shows their achievements and potential in advancing the scholarly conversation on the origins and change of important political institutions.

Pathways to institutional change: coalitional engineering, out-of-winset outcomes, and the politics of ideas

Political entrepreneurs and coalitional engineering

The insight that structural conditions may not map unequivocally onto the organizational landscape of politics creates space for the analysis of political entrepreneurship: in times of uncertainty, when multiple institutional options are available, political agents may play a crucial role in determining which coalition forms in support of what type of institutional change and when. More broadly, focusing on the gap between structural constellations and institutional arrangements brings to the fore the possibly decisive role of the *organizational landscape of politics* in generating constraints and inducements that condition political entrepreneurs seeking institutional reform during critical junctures (Capoccia and Ziblatt 2010). While unconsolidated political organizations may enable actors to exploit their internal divisions and fluidity to obtain political realignment in favor of their preferred institutional reform, organizational loyalties may at times constrain innovative coalition making, and interests vested in political organizations may constitute powerful obstacles to reform. Even in those cases, however, a fragmented organizational landscape does not necessarily stand in the way of institutional reform via creative coalitional engineering. In some circumstances, situations of uncertainty coupled with a fragmented organizational landscape offer opportunities for "herestetic" political entrepreneurship (Riker 1986) in forging coalitions in support of specific reforms (Häusermann 2010).[13]

---

[13] Häusermann (2010) shows how government can exploit the multidimensional nature of pension policies – in which benefit levels, type of financing, and eligibility criteria vary largely independently from each other – and take advantage from the overall level of fragmentation of social and political organizations to "package" proposals for reform that attract the support of a certain social coalition.

An illustration of these dynamics is Ertman's (2010) recent analysis of the 1832 Reform Act in Great Britain, which he explains as the outcome of a critical juncture in which a "fundamental, unforeseen transformation of a political regime occur[red] over a relatively short period of time as a result of decisions of a small number of actors" (1001). In his careful reconstruction of the tumultuous political interactions of the years 1827–35, Ertman underscores the importance of political choices, in particular those made by important leaders such as Peel and Wellington in forming a coalition for electoral reform that cut across party lines (1009); at the same time, he embeds his detailed analysis of political agency in the key cleavages that characterized British politics in that period, in particular the emancipation of religious minorities and the fight against "Old Corruption." Ertman makes clear that these cleavages had been prominent in British politics for several decades, that "demand for parliamentary reform were present at both the popular and elite level since the mid-18th century," and that "the intensity of such demands fluctuated substantially, rising during periods of economic distress and/or budget crisis, but falling during times of national emergency or prosperity" (1008). Ertman's analysis has important implications for the scholarly debate on British democratization. Among other things, he shows that the reforms of 1827–35, and in particular the 1832 Reform Act, were not the result of a "long and continuous build-up pressure," as others have argued (e.g., Morrison 2011), but rather were a series of decisions and political interactions through which powerful political leaders assembled a coalition for reform that cut across traditional party lines.

Out-of-winset outcomes and strategic interaction

Focusing on political interactions and decision making during critical junctures may uncover situations in which the institutional outcome does not reflect the preferences of any of the key actors on the political scene or even a compromise between them – in the language of formal analysis, the outcome falls outside the "winset" defined by actor preferences (Tsebelis 2002). In these situations, objective sociostructural conditions may empower specific social groups, which interact to push for their preferred institutional solution. However, as a result of both the high political uncertainty of the situation and the nature of the interaction itself, the outcome does not reflect the preferences of any of the key actors involved in the institution-making process. Making sense of these situations requires at least two analytical steps: first, carefully unpacking the actual impact that objective macrostructural conditions have on the influence of political actors and organizations; second, focusing at close range on political agency and interactions (the *politics* of institution making) and the institutional outcome of the process. By avoiding placing agency and interactions in a "black box," this second, and potentially causally decisive, step in the process may produce results that would be inexplicable from a structuralist perspective.

An important illustration of this type of analysis, which shows how smaller-scale and more proximate determinants of political strategies and interactions can be decisive in forming new institutional arrangements, comes from Kalyvas's comparative analysis of the emergence of confessional parties in Western Europe.[14] Even though he does not explicitly use the language of critical junctures, Kalyvas analyzes in comparative perspective a situation in which the demand for institutional innovation was present and several options were possible during a relatively brief window of opportunity. In his analysis Kalyvas shows how the choices and strategies of the conservative elites and the Catholic Church were decisive for the formation of confessional parties. At the same time, Kalyvas leverages a large amount of historical evidence to show that both the Catholic Church and conservative politicians, on the basis of a rational assessment of costs and benefits, *opposed* the formation of confessional parties. Confessional party formation was thus the unintended outcome of the strategic moves made by both actors in response to the liberal anticlericalism of the late nineteenth century (Kalyvas 1996, 262). Kalyvas devotes an extensive part of his discussion to showing that the structural antecedent conditions that several leading theories in comparative politics and history (e.g., Lipset and Rokkan 1967) consider causally decisive for the emergence of confessional parties had at best an indirect impact on this outcome. In Kalyvas's account, variation in outcomes, namely nonformation of a confessional party in France and formation in all other cases, was not driven by structural conditions. Rather, the variation was the product of the circumstance that for some years after the establishment of the Third Republic the French Catholic Church (whose preferences were similar to those of the Church in other Western European countries) believed that the Monarchy would soon be restored, and the Church's privileges with it. This belief derived from the postrevolutionary history of rapid regime change in France and influenced the Church's risk calculations and therefore the payoffs that it attached to different strategies, inducing it to decide – contrary to the Church's actions in other Western European countries – against supporting the creation of

---

[14] A further example is the comparative analysis of self-abdication by democratic parliaments developed by Ermakoff (2008).

Catholic mass organizations in response to anti-clerical attacks. This initial move made it more difficult (although not impossible; Kalyvas 1996, 151, 160) for the Church to sponsor the creation of successful Catholic mass organizations in France at a later stage, even after its beliefs changed and it had come to believe in the stability of the Republic.

The Church's initial belief in the transitory nature of the French Third Republic should be considered as one of the several proximate and changing (it waned after some years) political factors that influenced decision making.[15] Kalyvas is very explicit on the point: the Church could have created Catholic mass organizations and was subject to important pressures to do so by Catholic forces in French society (e.g., Kalyvas 1996, 124, 131, 134): "the absence of mass Catholic organizations was mostly a result of factors not independent on [the Church's] will ... the potential was there. The French Church could have created mass organization but *chose not to do so*" (Kalyvas 1996, 137, emphasis added). Kalyvas's analysis points to the plausibility of the double counterfactual at the basis of the Berlinian conception of contingency discussed above: the Church could have made different choices at key moments, and had it done so, France would have had a confessional party like other Western European countries.

The most important theoretical insights to be drawn from Kalyvas's analysis come from his unpacking of the processes of cleavage formation, identity formation, and party formation through "a close focus on agency" (Kalyvas 1996, 262). Once created, confessional parties moved away from the Church and embraced democratic politics, redefining their identity in order to protect their autonomy. They reinterpreted Catholicism in an increasingly general, vague, and secular way, which allowed them to integrate masses of previously disenfranchised voters into democracy, thereby becoming able to form coalitions and access power more easily. This means that secularization, integration, and acceptance of democracy were not the outcome of the "adaptation" of these parties to a secular and secularizing environment but were the by-product of the choices made by the new parties in response to endogenous

---

[15] For this reason, the view that arguments that assume instrumental rationality and interest- or power-maximizing preferences on the part of the actors have an essentially structuralist logic, since variation in outcomes can only be given by variation in external conditions and not by agency (e.g., Parsons 2007, 55; see also Blyth 2003), does not apply to Kalyvas's analysis, where variation in outcome is driven by a nonstructural factor. More generally, whether rational choice arguments respond to a structuralist logic – and therefore whether assuming rationality in modeling interactions during critical junctures validates the causal power of structural antecedent conditions – depends on whether the factors driving strategic interactions are structural or (like in Kalyvas's case) of a different nature.

constraints that were built into the process of their formation (Kalyvas 1996, 261). In dealing with these constraints, confessional parties contributed to the secularization and democratization of their political and societal environment. Kalyvas himself extends these insights to guide his own research on the conditions under which religious movements become democratic in other contexts (Kalyvas 1998, 2003).

The politics of ideas and the promotion of normative change

Extant normative understandings and value systems supporting institutional arrangements may be difficult to dislodge (e.g., Steensland 2006). The disruption of the institutional status quo and the ensuing uncertainty that characterizes critical junctures can create the possibility for otherwise unlikely normative change. Strategically placed actors may use their position of influence to diffuse ideas that legitimize particular institutional innovations and through this process prevail over others affected by the institutional change at stake, including social groups that may be substantially larger. This operation of social construction can be decisive in the selection of path-dependent institutions that do not reflect the "objective" (i.e., structurally given) interests of the social actors affected by the institutions in question.

To illustrate, Blyth analyzes the critical junctures of the Great Depression and the economic downturn of the 1970s in Western democracies with the aim of explaining why new macroeconomic policies emerge after economic crises. He argues that crises are not simply a reflection of the "objective" fact of economic dislocation (e.g., deflation or negative growth) but also socially constructed by powerful actors to be *crises of a certain type* – the same actors that then promote new institutions to "solve" the so-defined crisis (Blyth 2002). In Blyth's account, collective actors such as the state (in the 1930s) or business (in the 1970s) act politically to promote, diffuse, and entrench certain ideas in the public sphere, ideas which both define the crisis and provide an institutional recipe to "solve" it, and in so doing they seek to bring around social groups with different "objective" interests.[16] When this ideational

---

[16] It is worth underscoring that, although his analysis focuses on the interaction of collective actors, Blyth does not attribute agency to abstract entities. For example, his account of how American and Swedish business promoted neoliberal ideas to both define the 1970s economic crisis and provide an institutional "solution" to it is extremely precise in detailing the internal dynamics within the business world, showing how important donors, organizations, foundations, conservative media, and other actors acted in a concerted fashion to promote pro-business ideas. His historical analysis shows empirically that in the critical juncture of the 1970s, business "acted as a class" (Blyth 2002).

battle is won, collective action to build new institutions is undertaken, which can count on a broader range of supporters than would be predicted by a focus on structural antecedent conditions (Blyth 2002, esp. 152–66 and 209–19). Referring to the economic crisis of the 1970s, during which business success-fully promoted anti-inflationary and monetarist policies, Blyth argues: "other agents' interests had to be reinterpreted so that they became homologous with business', a homology that was neither obvious *nor structurally determined*" (Blyth 2007, 86, emphasis added; see also Blyth 2003).

The insight that the *politics of ideas* is what ultimately determines the institutional outcome of a critical juncture points to the possibility that during situations of institutional uncertainty, powerful actors strategically promoting new social norms to manipulate the preferences of social groups may have more chances of success than during periods of stability. This insight has been applied in other contexts besides Blyth's macroeconomic policy making. Krebs, for example, applies a similar framework in his analysis of the domestic institutional consequences of "limited wars," which may constitute critical junctures for the reform of executive powers. In his account, reform of the executive branch is decisively shaped by the normative positions promoted by political leaders in the public debate on the purpose and outcome of such wars (Krebs 2010; Kier and Krebs 2010, 15; see also the discussion in Capoccia forthcoming).

Methodological payoffs: near misses and negative cases

The analysis of agency and contingency in critical junctures not only yields innovative theoretical payoffs that can guide comparative research on the origins and reforms of important institutions but also has important method-ological advantages. A logical consequence of stressing the importance of contingency as a defining element of critical junctures is that, as counterintu-itive as it may seem, change is not a necessary element of a critical juncture. If change is possible, considered, sought after, and narrowly fails to materi-alize, there is no reason not to consider this situation as a critical juncture (Capoccia and Kelemen 2007, 350–1). Such "near-miss" critical junctures may arise from two main sets of circumstances.

First, near-miss critical junctures may arise from the dynamics of political entrepreneurship and coalition formation discussed above: the social and political bases for reform may exist, but political entrepreneurs may *fail to mobilize the necessary coalition* to achieve reform (Ertman 2010, 1008; see also Yashar 1997, 22).[17] One illustration of this pattern can be found in Nichols and Myers's (2010) recent work revisiting Skowronek's (1993) theory of "reconstructive presidency" in the United States. Nichols and Myers argue that not all presidents who are "unaffiliated with a vulnerable regime" have seized the opportunity to "reconstruct" the political order – that is, shift the main axis of partisan cleavage and assemble a new majority coalition. Presidents may fail to do so, in which case reconstruction may still happen but only in a much more protracted way.

A second source of near-miss critical junctures is one in which the political forces in favor of institutional change *narrowly lose their struggle* to forces favoring stability – in other words, cases in which the political struggle over the choice of different institutional options during a phase of uncertainty and institutional fluidity results in *reequilibration* rather than change. Capoccia (2005), for example, in a study of democratic crises in the interwar years, compares cases of democratic breakdown with cases of democracies that survived despite the severe challenge posed by totalitarian parties to their persistence. Through the close analysis of the political process, he identifies the key political actors whose decisions and actions at crucial moments were decisive in steering the outcome of political crises toward democratic survival or breakdown.

The concept of near-miss critical junctures adds an important methodological tool to the toolbox of CHA scholars, giving them the possibility to make space, in their comparative research designs, for what the British historian Hugh Trevor-Roper (1988) calls "the lost moments of history": potentially important "negative cases" in which institutional change was possible but did not happen, which can improve analytical leverage. In the examples above, by bringing the concept of near-miss critical junctures to bear on their objects of analysis, both Nichols and Myers (2010) and Capoccia (2005) unearth previously invisible negative cases of change, thus proposing a fresh analytical perspective and attaining new empirical results on scholarly terrains that seemed well trodden.

---

[17] Soifer (2012) considers such situations as "crises without change" (i.e., not critical junctures), thus addressing a similar theoretical problem in the context of a partially different framework. The approach proposed here entails stricter theoretical conditions to consider such cases as "negative cases" that can be most usefully compared to "positive" cases of change: social forces for change need to be present *and* their activation through mobilization, coalition building, or decision making should fail narrowly.

Building a critical juncture argument: logical steps and comparative design

To sum up at this point, critical juncture analysis can provide important integrations and correctives to ahistorical approaches and can yield innovative theoretical insights and methodological progress. This section outlines the methodology of critical juncture analysis, illustrating its logical steps and including a discussion of problems of cross-sectional and longitudinal comparisons. The overall goal is to build and test midrange theoretical arguments that address the question of the origin or the reform of important political institutions.

Clarify the unit of analysis

The first step in the study of critical junctures is the *identification of a unit of analysis*, which in CHA is typically some institutional setting: an organization, a public policy, a set of formal rules, a political regime (Capoccia and Kelemen 2007, 349–50). When considering whether a series of events and decisions constitute a critical juncture, the preliminary question to be asked is "a critical juncture in the development of what?" At times, scholars identify relatively brief periods of momentous political, social, or economic upheaval and assert that these are critical junctures in a general sense (e.g., Dion 2010, 34). This, however, can be misleading since different kinds of external shocks may affect some decision-making arenas and not others (e.g., Cortell and Peterson 1999, 187). Similarly, even when political systems as a whole face "unsettled times," many institutions within the system may remain unaffected (Streeck and Thelen 2005, 8–9). Indeed, if one concurs with Skowronek's (1995) view that "in a historical/institutional view, politics is structured by persistent incongruities and frictions among institutional orderings" (95), this should not come as a surprise. While events at one level of analysis may also have an impact on other levels of analysis, it is important to keep them separate and to be careful to define the critical juncture in light of the specific unit of interest (Shermer 1995, 71; Thelen 1999, 213).

Identify "candidate" critical junctures

Once the unit of analysis is identified, scholars should study the history of that institution to identify "candidate" critical junctures – moments in which the institutional status quo was challenged and in which demands for radical institutional change emerged. The triggers (generally labeled "shocks") are often exogenous to the institution and can take various forms depending on the institution analyzed (e.g., Cortell and Petersen 1999). Moments already identified in the literature as critical junctures for related institutions can be counted as candidate critical junctures, keeping in mind, however, that their destabilizing effect on the institution of interest should be shown empirically and not assumed a priori. For example, in Lieberman's (2003, 79–105) work discussed earlier he considers (and discounts) the potential impact of democratic transition and labor incorporation on the emergence of different "tax states" in Brazil and South Africa. These are critical junctures for the political regime and the system of industrial relations that in some accounts are considered to have implications for the tax state.

Test for structural effects

Once such moments of challenge and radical institutional change are identified, the hypothesis that structural antecedents, not agency, drive institutional change should be tested. Are the institutional outcomes driven by political choices between available alternatives, as might appear prima facie – or as Berins Collier and Collier (1991, 27) put it, are the choices in question only "presumed," but not real? Logically, the potential irrelevance of agency and choice during critical junctures can take two forms, which in turn give rise to testable hypotheses. First, structural and impersonal conditions may *close off choice* by excluding all options but one from the range of conceivable alternatives in a given situation. Apart from being the hallmark of conventional structuralist logic, as discussed above, this possibility is also underscored in some versions of social constructivism, which argue that diffuse cultural norms provide cognitive and moral scripts for decision makers in specific circumstances (e.g., March and Olsen 1989). For example, Katzenstein's comparative analysis of security policy in Germany and Japan after 9/11 points to the importance of deeply embedded and radically different scripts in explaining the different ways in which the two countries reacted to a similar exogenous shock (Katzenstein 2003). Second, antecedent structural conditions may *trump* choice: the actors that rise to prominence and the options that are available during a critical juncture may be fully endogenous to structural conditions operating in the long run. This points to situations in which the availability of significant alternative options is only illusory: a choice is made during the critical juncture but is immediately reversed as a result of underlying structural conditions. An example is Luebbert's (1991) classic structuralist analysis of Western European political development. Talking about the selection of working-class leaders in countries with lib-lab arrangements, he writes: "It is always possible to speculate that a different set of leaders would have produced different policies with different outcomes. But it must be borne in mind that their ascensions to party leadership were not simply random outcomes" (230). In addition to observing that the selection of political decision makers may be endogenous to structural conditions and therefore have no independent effect on the institutional outcome of interest, Luebbert also remarks, talking about liberal political office holders in aliberal societies such as for example Giolitti in Italy, that at times leaders could in principle have made different choices but that these choices were in any case bound to fail as a result of the prevailing force of structural conditions. Whether structural antecedent conditions close off or trump choice in moments in which agency prima facie appears to expand is fully amenable to empirical testing. If positive, such tests would falsify the hypothesized causal role of agency and validate the decisive causal force of structural antecedents in those moments, also clarifying *which* impersonal antecedent factors matter for the outcome and *how* they generate the outcome of interest. Generally speaking, this research task should not be too onerous, since the in-depth analysis of political choices can be concentrated on the relatively short period of the (candidate) critical junctures.

Compare candidate critical junctures longitudinally and select for analysis the most "critical" one(s)

The tests outlined above should rule out some candidate critical junctures and help focus attention on those moments in which agency and political dynamics play an important role in selecting a path of institutional development. Even though it is possible to employ a research design that includes more than one critical juncture in the same spatial unit(s) (e.g., Lynch 2006, Nichols and Myers 2010), the researcher may ask, once different potential critical junctures have been identified, which one had the greatest influence in shaping the key durable characteristics of the institution of interest. Capoccia and Kelemen (2007) operationalize the "criticalness" of candidate critical junctures by focusing on two components: the probability that at the end of the critical juncture the institution acquires its durable path-dependent characteristics observable for the duration of the legacy of the critical juncture, and the duration of the critical juncture relative to its legacy. They recommend that the analysis begin with those critical junctures that had the largest impact on the outcome and that occurred earlier in time (see Capoccia and Kelemen 2007, 360–3, for a formalization of this operationalization). Although she does not use the language of critical junctures, one example is Grzymala-Busse's (2002) analysis of the development of successor Communist parties in post-Communist democracies. She shows that parties that had chosen to allow the intelligentsia and nonparty members to fill high positions in the administration in response to political crises that affected the Communist regime were much better placed to remake themselves after the transition as compared to those parties that had instead reacted to prior crises with closure and repression. The earlier critical juncture of the regime crisis (e.g., 1956 in Hungary, 1968 in Czechoslovakia), which provoked markedly different reactions from Communist parties, was therefore *more critical* for the shape of party organization and ideology in the new democratic regime than the (candidate) critical juncture of the transition itself, in which the choices of party elites were constrained by the consequences of their earlier decisions.[18] More broadly, this strategy of starting the analysis at the "most critical" critical juncture also offers a handle on the oft-mentioned problem of *infinite regress* – namely, the arbitrariness of beginning the analysis at a certain point in time (the critical juncture) and not exploring the importance of prior events and developments. Such longitudinal comparisons of the "critical-ness" of candidate critical junctures are not infrequent (even though at times implicit), and scholars can and do build arguments as to which candidate critical juncture was more "critical" for their outcome of interest (see, e.g., Lynch 2006, 59–63; Mahoney 2001, 26–7). In the example mentioned above, Lieberman (2003, 105) shows that the later junctures of democratic transition and labor incorporation are in fact *much less critical* for the emergence and persistence of different "tax states" in Brazil and South Africa than the *earlier* constitutional moments in which the National Political Community was defined.

[18] This example is often quoted as an illustration of the decisive causal importance of antecedent conditions during critical junctures (e.g., Slater and Simmons 2010). In this view, only the regime transition of 1989 is considered as a critical juncture. However, once it is made clear that critical junctures should be related to a precise unit of analysis, and that such unit in this case is the party organization, there is no reason not to conceptualize the earlier regime crises during the Communist era as critical junctures. These regime crises caused disruption in the ruling Communist parties and faced party elites with important choices. This conceptualization allows then to compare the critical-ness for the outcome of interest of the two critical junctures and to focus (as Grzymala-Busse correctly does) on the more critical one.

Reconstruct the political process in the selected critical juncture(s)

Once they identify the critical juncture(s) for analysis, scholars should "read history forward" (Capoccia and Ziblatt 2010), identify the main decision makers and the dynamic of their interaction, and reconstruct which institutional alternatives were politically viable at the time. Actors can be individual or collective. In the latter case, scholars should not attribute agency unproblematically to corporations or social groups but problematize the connection between the leadership of collective actors and their social and political base and reconstruct the dynamics that led collective actors to pursue a coherent line of action (Sewell 1992, 145).[19] Scholars should further clarify which social and political forces stood behind each option and identify which decisions were most influential in shaping the outcome. Consistently with the Berlinian conception of contingency discussed above, researchers should also analyze the "paths not taken" (and that could plausibly have been taken) in the selection of the institutional outcome as well as the path that was in fact taken.[20]

Perform counterfactual analysis

The latter move takes us into the realm of counterfactual analysis, which, after several decades of considerable skepticism (e.g., Carr 1961), has been restored to its rightful place in history and historiography (e.g., Bulhof 1999; Bunzl 2004) as well as in historically oriented social sciences (e.g., Fearon 1991; Lebow 2000a, 2000b, 2010; Tetlock and Belkin 1996). In the context of the critical juncture approach, the purpose of counterfactual analysis is to establish the *plausibility* of the twofold counterfactual argument that, first, a different institutional arrangement could have been selected and, second, that had such been the case, the institutional arrangement in question would also have had a long-lasting legacy. The literature has elaborated a whole roster of logical and methodological criteria for building plausible counterfactual scenarios, differentiating counterfactuals with good heuristic value from those belonging to the thought-provoking but insufficiently rigorous realm of "virtual history" (e.g., Lebow 2010, 52–7; Tetlock and Belkin 1996, 23–4). The

---

[19] The works, discussed above, of Kalyvas (1996) on the Catholic Church and of Blyth (2002) on economic collective actors offer excellent examples on how to do so.

[20] Several methods are apt for the task at hand: process tracing (e.g., Bennett and Checkel forthcoming), "analytic narratives," (Bates *et al.* 1998), and in general any form of structured, theory-guided narrative.

most relevant criteria for critical juncture analysis, apart from the general ones of clarity and logical consistency, are theoretical consistency and historical consistency. Regarding *theoretical consistency,* Mahoney (2000) explains that analysts should focus on "a counterfactual antecedent that was actually available during a critical juncture period, and that, according to theory, should have been adopted" (513; see also Mahoney and Goertz 2004). *Historical consistency* is also known as the "minimal-rewrite rule" and constrains counterfactual speculations in several ways: only include policy options that were available, considered, and either not pursued by the relevant actors or narrowly defeated; only entertain decisions that could plausibly have been made but for some reason were not; exclude counterfactuals in which the antecedent and the consequent are so distant in time that it is implausible that all other things would remain equal. As several authors have underscored, there may be as much historical evidence on plausible counterfactual arguments as on factual arguments (e.g., Lebow 2000b, 559; 2010; Turner 1999). Similarly, enough evidence may be available to produce informed speculation at least on the immediate institutional consequences of the other decisions that could realistically have been made (Lebow 2000a).

Show that the institution selected had a long-lasting legacy

Critical juncture analysis is a component of the study of path-dependent institutions. As demonstrated by the examples of critical juncture research discussed earlier, scholars go to great length to substantiate empirically the mechanisms supporting the long-lasting institutional legacy of the critical juncture.

Cross-sectional comparison of critical junctures

All of the above can – and, whenever possible and appropriate, should – be done in the context of comparative analysis. As the examples discussed earlier show, such comparative analyses are most commonly based on a design that identifies similar historical processes in different institutional units in which the same kind of actors act against the background of broadly similar background conditions and face similar challenges, and in which eventual variation is the product of the decisions and strategic interactions that occur during a critical juncture. Analyzing critical junctures in comparative perspective presents several important advantages. First, a counterfactual argument in one unit may actually be a factual argument in another. In other words, if critical junctures occur in similar units and under similar conditions, then different decisions of the same actors can give rise to different outcomes, allowing variation and increasing the overall leverage of the analysis. Second, comparison facilitates the identification of negative cases, that is, junctures that present the same characteristics of structural fluidity and actor prominence but that do not actually give rise to sweeping change. Third, comparing similar junctures (possibly with different outcomes) sheds light on which actors, moments, and choices are important and which contextual detail is less relevant. If the study involves similar junctures in different spatial units and at different points in time, political learning and diffusion can have an impact on the independence of the cases being compared (Weyland 2010), since actors involved in the later cases may know of the outcomes of earlier cases and adjust their behavior accordingly (Büthe 2002). In such circumstances researchers must account for the potential influence of such earlier junctures on the outcome of later ones.

Conclusion: situating critical juncture analysis in the comparative study of institutional development

In a recent essay on theoretical innovations in American political development, Skowronek and Glassmann (2008) write: "There is little patience in any quarter today with explanations that invoke disembodied historical forces or political processes... How to put the actor center stage and still keep open a view to the larger whole, how to assess changes effected in the moment against the standards of the *longue durée* – these are outstanding challenges" (2). The critical juncture approach is one way in which these challenges can be tackled in CHA, in particular in the context of the analysis of path-dependent institutions. In synthesis, the approach offers a framework for studying relatively *rare* moments of political openness in the history of a given institution, during which agency and choice are decisive in putting into place institutional arrangements that have a long-lasting legacy. The chapter has outlined the basic characteristics of the approach, discussed its strengths vis-à-vis alternative approaches to the analysis of institutional variation, and has offered methodological indications on how to apply the approach in comparative analysis. The main thesis of the chapter is that the approach, by adopting an appropriate theorization of contingency as referred to individual and collective agency and by focusing on their causal power in the uncertainty typical of critical junctures, can yield significant theoretical pay-offs for the comparative-historical analysis of the creation and reform of important institutional arrangements.

In this concluding section, I briefly situate this form of analysis in the context of other approaches to institutional development in CHA. In essence, the key strength of the critical juncture approach – path dependence – is also its main limitation. On the one hand, the theory of institutional path dependence provides scholars with a powerful language for substantiating claims of distal causation. On the other hand, recent scholarship on "weak institutions" and on models of endogenous institutional change has highlighted that the conceptual apparatus of path dependence may not always offer a realistic image of institutional development. Given the close connection between critical junctures and path dependence, these strands of theorization on institutional development also indirectly call into question the analytical leverage of the critical junctures approach and suggest key priorities for future theoretical work.

In their theoretical work on "weak institutions," Levitsky and Murillo note that path dependence assumes "institutional strength," namely, the consistent enforcement and high degree of persistence of formal rules in a polity, which engenders expectations in actors that the investment in skills, tech-nologies, and organizations that is necessary for successful engagement with institutions will not go to waste (Levitsky and Murillo 2009, 123). In the developing world, where the "politics of institutional weakness" is the typical pattern (Levitsky and Murillo 2005), institutional path dependence is inhib-ited, and institutional change is most likely to take the form of "breakdown and replacement" (Levitsky and Murillo 2009, 128). In this context, critical juncture analysis offers little leverage: the institutional arrangements result-ing from the political struggle over institutional design are unlikely to last (or if lasting, are likely to remain unenforced), and new contestation over institutional design, reversing the existing rules and establishing new formal rules, is likely to ensue in short order.

Theories of endogenous institutional change (Streeck and Thelen 2005; Thelen 2004) criticize theories of path dependence as displaying a "stability bias," which relegates change to exogenous shocks. In the effort to incorpo-rate change in a theoretical account of institutional development, scholars in this tradition have conceptualized institutions as "arenas of conflict" rather than as equilibria. Institutions are constantly reshaped by groups that try to bend them to their priorities and preferences and that resort to an iden-tifiable repertoire of strategies, including piecemeal reform (layering) and reinterpretation (conversion), to achieve this goal. These endogenous processes of institutional change, for which these scholars have provided broad empirical support, are not deployed in short periods but take place gradually, radically transforming institutions over the long run (Hacker, Pierson, and Thelen, Chapter 7, this volume). Critical junctures are virtually absent in this theoretical literature, and *pour cause*: if institutions are constantly vulnerable to piecemeal modification and reinterpretation and their shape changes continuously in accordance with shifts in power and influence among the relevant actors (Mahoney and Thelen 2010), then there is little reason to study in detail the politics of their origins.

Despite these important alternative approaches to the conceptualization of institutions and institutional change, both the theory of path dependence and the concept of critical junctures continue to be popular in CHA. To be sure, these alternative approaches are not mutually exclusive and may be applicable in different circumstances. At the same time, however, these approaches are now simply *juxtaposed* in the theoretical toolbox of CHA scholars (Capoccia 2012). More robust theorization is needed on the *conditions* under which each of them applies – in particular on the conditions that encourage the path dependence logic of adaptive expectations and specific investments, thus raising the cost of institutional reversal, and the conditions that, instead, produce incremental but transformative institutional change by virtue of continuous strategic action over time on the part of actors vying for power. Advances on this front would go a long way to clarifying the scope, potential, and limitations of the concept of critical juncture, along with alternative approaches to the analysis of institutional change, in CHA.

References

Acemoglu, Daron, and James A. Robinson. 2012. *Why Nations Fail. The Origins of Power, Prosperity and Poverty*. London: Crown Business.

Arthur, Brian. 1994. *Increasing Returns and Path Dependence in the Economy*. Ann Arbor: University of Michigan Press.

Bates, Robert H., Avner Greif, Margaret Levi, Jean-Laurent Rosenthal, and Barry R. Weingast 1998. *Analytic Narratives*. Princeton, NJ: Princeton University Press.

Bennett, Andrew, and Jeffrey Checkel. Forthcoming. *Process Tracing: From Metaphor to Analytic Tool*. Cambridge: Cambridge University Press.

Bennett, Andrew, and Colin Elman. 2006. "Complex Causal Relations and Case Study Methods: The Example of Path Dependence." *Political Analysis* 14 (3): 250–67.

Berins Collier, Ruth, and David Collier. 1991. *Shaping the Political Arena: Critical Junctures, the Labor Movement, and Regime Dynamics in Latin America*. Princeton, NJ: Princeton University Press.

Berlin, Isaiah. 1974. "Historical Inevitability." In *The Philosophy of History*, edited by P. Gardiner, 161–86. London: Oxford University Press.

Berntzen, E., and P. Selle. 1990. "Structure and Social Action in Stein Rokkan's Work." *Journal of Theoretical Politics* 2 (2): 131–50.

Blyth, M. 2002. *Great Transformations: Economic Ideas and Institutional Change in the Twentieth Century*. Cambridge: Cambridge University Press.

2003. "Structures Do Not Come with an Instruction Sheet: Interests, Ideas and Progress in Political Science." *Perspectives on Politics* 1 (4): 695–706.

2007. "When Liberalisms Change: Comparing the Politics of Inflations and Deflations." In *Neoliberalism: National and Regional Experiments with Global Ideas*, edited by R. Roy, A. Denzau, and T. Willet, 71–96. London: Routledge.

Bulhof, J. 1999. "What If? Modality and History." *History and Theory* 38 (2): 145–68.

Bunzl, M. 2004. "Counterfactual History: A User's Guide." *American Historical Review* 109 (3): 845–58.

Büthe, T. 2002. "Taking Temporality Seriously: Modeling History and the Use of Narratives as Evidence." *American Political Science Review* 96 (3): 481–93.

Capoccia, G. 2004. "Structuralism, Contingency and Regime Survival: Evidence from Interwar Europe." Paper presented at the Conference of Europeanists, Chicago, March.

2005. *Defending Democracy: Reactions to Extremism in Interwar Europe*. Baltimore: Johns Hopkins University Press.

2012. "Historical Institutionalism and the Politics of Institutional Change." Manuscript, University of Oxford.

Forthcoming. "Critical Junctures." In *The Oxford Handbook of Historical Institutionalism*, edited by T. Falleti, O. Fioretos, and A. Sheingate. Oxford: Oxford University Press.

Capoccia, G., and R. D. Kelemen. 2007. "The Study of Critical Junctures: Theory, Narrative, and Counterfactuals in Institutional Analysis." *World Politics* 59 (3): 341–69.

Capoccia, G., and D. Ziblatt. 2010. "The Historical Turn in Democratization Studies: A Research Agenda for Europe and Beyond." *Comparative Political Studies* 43 (8/9): 931–68.

Carr, E. H. 1961. *What Is History?* New York: Random House.

Cortell, A., and S. Peterson. 1999. "Altered States: Explaining Domestic Institutional Change." *British Journal of Political Science* 29 (1): 177–203.

David, P. 1985. "Clio and the Economics of QWERTY." *American Economic Review* 75 (2): 332–7.

2000. "Path Dependence, Its Critics, and the Quest for 'Historical Economics.'" In *Evolution and Path Dependence in Economic Ideas: Past and Present*, edited by P. Garrouste and S. Ioannides, 15–40. Cheltenham, UK: Elgar.

Dion, M. L. 2010. *Workers and Welfare: Comparative Institutional Change in Twentieth-Century Mexico*. Pittsburgh: University of Pittsburgh Press.

Ermakoff, I. 2008. *Ruling Oneself Out: A Theory of Collective Abdications*. Durham, NC: Duke University Press.

Ertman, T. 2010. "The Great Reform Act of 1832 and British Democratization." *Comparative Political Studies* 43 (8/9): 1000–22.

Falleti, T. G., and J. F. Lynch. 2009. "Context and Causal Mechanisms in Political Analysis." *Comparative Political Studies* 42 (9): 1143–66.

Fearon, J. 1991. "Counterfactuals and Hypothesis Testing in Political Science." *World Politics* 43 (2): 169–95.

Fioretos, O. 2011. "Historical Institutionalism in International Relations." *International Organization* 65 (2): 367–99.

Goldstone, J. A. 1998. "Initial Conditions, General Laws, Path Dependence, and Explanation in Historical Sociology." *American Journal of Sociology* 104 (3): 829–45.

Gourevitch, P. 1992. *Politics in Hard Times: Comparative Responses to International Economic Crises.* Ithaca, NY: Cornell University Press.

Greif, A. 2006. *Institutions and the Path to the Modern Economy: Lessons from Medieval Trade.* Cambridge: Cambridge University Press.

Grzymala-Busse, Anna. 2002. *Redeeming the Communist Past: The Regeneration of Communist Parties in East-Central Europe.* Cambridge: Cambridge University Press.

Häusermann, S. 2010. *The Politics of Welfare State Reform in Continental Europe: Modernization in Hard Times.* Cambridge: Cambridge University Press.

Kalyvas, S. N. 1996. *The Rise of Christian Democracy in Europe.* Ithaca, NY: Cornell University Press.

  1998. "From Pulpit to Party: Party Formation and the Christian Democratic Phenomenon." *Comparative Politics* 31 (2): 293–312.

  2003. "Unsecular Politics and Religious Mobilization." In *European Christian Democracy: Historical Legacies and Comparative Perspectives*, edited by T. A. Kselman and J. Buttigieg, 293–320. Notre Dame, IN: Notre Dame University Press.

Katzenstein, P. 2003. "Same War, Different Views: Germany, Japan, and Counter-Terrorism." *International Organization* 57 (4): 731–60.

Katznelson, I. 2003. "Periodization and Preferences: Reflections on Purposive Action in Comparative Historical Social Science." In *Comparative Historical Analysis in the Social Sciences*, edited by J. Mahoney and D. Rueschemeyer, 270–303. Cambridge: Cambridge University Press.

Kier, E., and R. Krebs. 2010. "Introduction: War and Democracy in Comparative Perspective." In *In War's Wake: International Conflict and the Fate of Liberal Democracy*, edited by E. Kier and R. Krebs, 1–21. Cambridge: Cambridge University Press.

Kohli, Atul. 1997. "Can Democracies Accommodate Ethnic Nationalism? The Rise and Decline of Self-Determination Movements in India." *Journal of Asian Studies* 56 (2): 325–44.

Krebs, R. 2010. "International Conflict and the Constitutional Balance: Executive Authority After War." In *In War's Wake: International Conflict and the Fate of Liberal Democracy*, edited by E. Kier and R. Krebs, 187–210. Cambridge: Cambridge University Press.

Lebow, R. N. 2000a. "Contingency, Catalysts, and International System Change." *Political Science Quarterly* 115 (4): 591–616.

  2000b. "What's So Different about a Counterfactual?" *World Politics* 52 (4): 550–85.

2010. *Forbidden Fruit: Counterfactuals and International Relations*. Princeton, NJ: Princeton University Press.

Levi, M. 1988. *Of Rule and Revenue*. Berkeley: University of California Press.

1997. *Consent, Dissent, and Patriotism*. Cambridge: Cambridge University Press.

Levitsky, S., and M. V. Murillo. 2005. *Argentine Democracy: The Politics of Institutional Weakness*. University Park: Pennsylvania State University Press.

2009. "Variations in Institutional Strength. *Annual Review of Political Science* 12 (1): 115–33.

Lieberman, E. 2003. *Race and Regionalism in the Politics of Taxation in Brazil and South Africa*. Cambridge: Cambridge University Press.

Lipset, S. M., and S. Rokkan. 1967. "Cleavage Structures, Party Systems, and Voter Alignments." In *Party Systems and Voter Alignments: Cross-National Perspectives*, edited by S. M. Lipset and S. Rokkan, 1–64. New York: Free Press.

Luebbert, G. M. 1991. *Fascism, Liberalism, and Social Democracy: Social Classes and the Political Origins of Regimes in Interwar Europe*. Oxford: Oxford University Press.

Lynch, J. 2006. *Age in the Welfare State: The Origins of Social Spending on Pensioners, Workers, and Children*. Cambridge: Cambridge University Press.

Mahoney, J. 2000. "Path Dependence in Historical Sociology." *Theory and Society* 29 (4): 507–48.

2001. *Legacies of Liberalism: Path Dependence and Political Regimes in Central America*. Baltimore: Johns Hopkins University Press.

Mahoney, J., and G. Goertz. 2004. "The Possibility Principle: Choosing Negative Cases in Comparative Research." *American Political Science Review* 98 (4): 653–69.

Mahoney, J., and K. Thelen. 2010. *Explaining Institutional Change: Ambiguity, Agency, and Power*. Cambridge: Cambridge University Press.

March, J. G., and J. P. Olsen. 1989. *Rediscovering Institutions: The Organizational Basis of Politics*. New York: Free Press.

Morrison, B. 2011. "Channeling the Restless Spirit of Innovation: Elite Concessions and Institutional Change in the British Reform Act of 1832." *World Politics* 63 (4): 678–710.

Nichols, C., and A. Myers. 2010. "Exploiting the Opportunity for Reconstructive Leadership: Presidential Responses to Enervated Political Regimes." *American Politics Research* 38 (5): 806–41.

North, D. C. 1990. *Institutions, Institutional Change, and Economic Performance*. Cambridge: Cambridge University Press.

O'Donnell, G. A., and P. C. Schmitter. 1986. *Transitions from Authoritarian Rule: Tentative Conclusions about Uncertain Democracies*. Baltimore: Johns Hopkins University Press.

Page, S. 2006. "Path Dependence." *Quarterly Journal of Political Science* 1 (1): 87–115.

Parsons, C. 2007. *How to Map Arguments in Political Science*. Oxford: Oxford University Press.

Pierson, P. 2000. "Increasing Returns, Path Dependence, and the Study of Politics." *American Political Science Review* 94 (2): 251–68.

2004. *Politics in Time: History, Institutions, and Social Analysis*. Princeton, NJ: Princeton University Press.

Polanyi, K. 1944. *The Great Transformation: The Political and Economic Origins of Our Time*. Boston: Beacon Press.

Putnam, R. D. 1993. *Making Democracy Work: Civic Traditions in Modern Italy.* Princeton, NJ: Princeton University Press.

Riker, W. 1986. *The Art of Political Manipulation.* New Haven, CT: Yale University Press.

Sewell, W. H. 1992. "A Theory of Structure. Duality, Agency, and Transformation." *American Journal of Sociology* 98 (1): 1–29.

Shapiro, I., and S. Bedi. 2006. *Political Contingency: Studying the Unexpected, the Accidental, and the Unforeseen.* New York: New York University Press.

Shermer, M. 1995. "Exorcising Laplace's Demon: Chaos and Antichaos, History and Metahistory." *History and Theory* 34 (1): 59–83.

Skowronek, Stephen. 1993. *The Politics Presidents Make: Leadership from John Adams to George Bush.* Cambridge, MA: Belknap Press of Harvard University Press.

  1995. Order and Change. *Polity* 28 (1): 91–6.

Skowronek, Stephen, and Matthew Glassman. 2008. "Formative Acts." In *Formative Acts: American Politics in the Making*, edited by Stephen Skowronek and Matthew Glassman, 1–9. Philadelphia: University of Pennsylvania Press.

Slater, D., and E. Simmons. 2010. "Informative Regress: Critical Antecedents in Comparative Politics." *Comparative Political Studies* 43 (7): 886–917.

Soifer, H. 2012. "The Causal Logic of Critical Junctures." *Comparative Political Studies* 45 (12): 1572–97.

Steensland, B. 2006. "Cultural Categories and the American Welfare State: The Case of Guaranteed Income Policy." *American Journal of Sociology* 111 (5): 1273–1326.

Streeck, W., and K. Thelen. 2005. "Introduction: Institutional Change in Advanced Political Economies." In *Beyond Continuity: Institutional Change in Advanced Political Economies*, edited by W. Streeck and K. Thelen, 1–39. Oxford: Oxford University Press.

Swidler, A. 1986. "Culture in Action: Symbols and Strategies." *American Sociological Review* 51 (2): 273–86.

Tetlock, P., and A. Belkin. 1996. *Counterfactual Thought Experiments in World Politics.* Princeton, NJ: Princeton University Press.

Thelen, K. 1999. "Historical Institutionalism in Comparative Politics." *Annual Review Political Science* 2:369–404.

  2004. *How Institutions Evolve: The Political Economy of Skills in Germany, Britain, the United States, and Japan.* Cambridge: Cambridge University Press.

Trevor-Roper, H. 1988. "The Lost Moments of History" [Romanes lecture]. *New York Review of Books*, 35 (16), October 27.

Tsebelis, G. 2002. *Veto Players: How Political Institutions Work.* Princeton, NJ: Princeton University Press.

Turner, H. A. 1999. "Human Agency and Impersonal Determinants in Historical Causation." *History and Theory* 38 (3): 300–6.

Weyland, K. 2010. "The Diffusion of Regime Contention in European Democratization, 1830–1940." *Comparative Political Studies* 43 (8/9): 1148–76.

Yashar, D. J. 1997. *Demanding Democracy: Reform and Reaction in Costa Rica and Guatemala, 1870s–1950s.* Stanford, CA: Stanford University Press.

7 Drift and conversion: hidden faces of institutional change

Jacob S. Hacker, Paul Pierson, and Kathleen Thelen

Until recently, institutionally minded scholars in the social sciences generally treated institutions as fixed. Whether defined as the rules of the political game, the standard operating procedures of bureaucracies, or the regularized norms guiding organizational behavior, institutions were associated with stability and were invoked as independent or intervening variables to explain persistent cross-national differences in outcomes. More recent work in the field, however, has attempted to provide greater insight into how institutions evolve and how institutional effects can change over time. Instead of seeing institutions as largely unchanging features of the political environment, these arguments seek to specify *what kinds* of institutional changes propelled by *what kinds* of social processes are most likely under *what kinds* of political configurations.

This chapter advances this more recent agenda, examining two important, common, and theoretically explicable processes through which institutional effects change over time, which we call "drift" and "conversion." Drift occurs when institutions or policies are deliberately held in place while their context shifts in ways that alter their effects. A simple example is the US minimum wage, which is not indexed to inflation and thus declines in value as prices rise unless new federal legislation is enacted. Those wishing to effect change through drift need only prevent the updating of existing rules. Drift thus depends on how sensitive the effects of an institution are to its context, whether policies are designed in ways that foster updating in the face of changing circumstances, and whether it is easy or difficult to block such updating.

Conversion, by contrast, occurs when political actors are able to redirect institutions or policies toward purposes beyond their original intent. An

For helpful comments, we thank Karen Alter, Mareike Kleine, Ben Schneider, John Stephens, Daniel Ziblatt, all the participants in the MIT and Northwestern conferences on comparative-historical analysis in the social sciences, and the anonymous reviewers for Cambridge University Press. James Mahoney deserves special thanks for his continuing thoughtful reactions.

example is the ability of corporations to use the Sherman Antitrust Act of 1890 to hinder labor unions. Passed amid widespread concern about corporate collusion, the legislation was meant to break up business trusts that were "in restraint of trade." Yet corporations managed to convince federal courts that *union organizing* was "in restraint of trade." In cases like these, actors who are not part of the coalition that created formal rules redeploy these rules to achieve their own (sometimes very different) goals. Conversion thus feeds off rule ambiguity and the multiplicity of political arenas in which ambiguous rules can be reinterpreted.

In advanced industrial societies, drift and conversion are both very common and very consequential. Yet scholars have only started to pay attention to these two "hidden" forms of institutional change, when and why they happen, and how they are related to each other. In prior writings, we have explored drift (Hacker 2005; Hacker and Pierson 2010, 2011) and conversion (Streeck and Thelen 2005; Thelen 2004) largely as separate processes. In our collaboration here, we present a unified perspective that shows how drift and conversion, seen alongside each other, enhance our understanding of institutional change and challenge some of our most common conceptions of democratic politics. To begin with, these two neglected modes of change alter our conception of who is playing offense and defense in ongoing struggles over governance. When institutions are subject to drift or conversion, political actors wishing to preserve those institutions as is – who usually have the upper hand in status-quo-biased political systems – suddenly look much more vulnerable to challenge.

Drift and conversion also change our view of the political venues in which such contestation occurs and the types of actors advantaged in these struggles. Because they happen through the transformation of existing institutions, rather than wholesale institutional replacement, drift and conversion often occur beyond the bright glare of legislative politics. Not only that, the processes themselves are generally difficult for all but the most attentive political actors to anticipate, monitor, and influence. These features advantage organized interests with long time horizons and the resources to play the long game – the political actors who are most likely to be aware of opportunities inherent in existing formal rules and best positioned to act on this awareness as well as most capable of protecting their gains once drift or conversion has altered institutional operations or effects.

In stark contrast, the actors who are the main focus of contemporary theorizing about democratic politics – voters – are unlikely to be the prime movers in a wide range of critical cases of institutional evolution involving drift and conversion. Of course, voters may play an important constraining role, and their importance rises as institutional changes become more salient. Nonetheless, voters typically enter the picture late, and then only under circumstances already heavily conditioned by processes of drift and conversion. Thus, a research program that takes drift and conversion seriously requires returning to fundamental questions about who has the power to shape outcomes over the long term in capitalist democracies. Very often, we argue, the answer to this question will be at odds with dominant perspectives in American and comparative politics that emphasize changes in voting and public opinion as the wellspring of major reform (Hacker and Pierson 2014).

Finally, this research program has important methodological implications as well. The mainstream focus on voters and public opinion – on the behavior of discrete individuals – is closely associated with statistical and experimental methods. Yet processes of drift and conversion can be observed only in analyses that are at once configurational and attentive to changes unfolding over significant periods of time. Identifying drift and conversion usually requires close examination of the interaction among multiple sites of social activity. Moreover, these interactions usually take considerable time to play out. Theoretically, this focus justifies a shift in emphasis from voters to the organized actors most likely to engage in politics across sites and over time. Methodologically, it encourages a shift toward case-based analyses of configurations and historical process. Though this chapter emphasizes the theoretical implications, the concepts of drift and conversion reinforce the larger conclusion of this volume that there is a close alignment between theories of institutional change and comparative-historical analysis.

Drift, conversion, and institutional change

The new wave of research on institutional change is concerned with two questions: first, how do institutions change, and second, what is the relationship between institutional change and political outcomes? In recent scholarship, some analysts of developing nations have documented and explained a surprising *lack* of change in political outcomes despite significant formal-institutional change.[1] In this chapter, we focus on highly developed

---

[1]   The work of Levitsky and his colleagues, for example, has shown that in developing countries characterized by "weak" institutions, changes in formal ("parchment") rules often do not produce the expected, or indeed *any*, change at all in established political dynamics (Levitsky and Slater 2011, 1; see also Helmke and Levitsky 2006; Levitsky and Murillo 2009). Levitsky and Murillo (e.g., 2009) have

democracies where formal-institutional rules are typically observed and enforced, and look at the other side of the picture: significant changes in political outcomes despite formal-institutional stability. In other words, we examine cases where the formal rules embodied in institutions remain constant but either the outcomes of these rules (drift) or the ways in which they are interpreted and used (conversion) change in politically consequential ways.

By "formal-institutional rules," we mean rules that are in principle obligatory and subject to third-party enforcement.[2] Furthermore, we believe it makes sense to think of public policies as constituting formal institutions insofar as they embody legally enforceable rules, create new organizations with state-backed decision-making or enforcement power, or both (Pierson 2006).[3] This conceptual expansion makes clear that some policies constitute enduring features of the political landscape that should be studied in similar fashion to traditional state institutions. It also connects theories of legislative politics (which typically focus on the production of authoritative public laws) and theories of institutional design (which are typically concerned with more encompassing political institutions).

The fundamental source of both drift and conversion is the strong status quo bias of many aspects of democratic politics. In established democracies with extensive existing policies and programs, a range of factors militate against the easy creation of new institutions. These include partisan polarization, institutional rules requiring high levels of agreement or empowering specific veto players, the presence of vested defenders of existing arrangements, and collective action and coordination problems facing those who favor reform. These and other factors make authoritatively replacing existing institutions difficult – and thus make drift or conversion relatively attractive as a pathway to institutional change. In the case of drift, the trigger for change is *context discontinuity*, the occurrence of environmental shifts that existing

---

explored important sources of variation in the "strength" of formal institutions in various settings relating to the interaction of formal and informal rules.

[2] Many institutionalists follow North (1990) in adopting a broad definition of institutions that includes both formal and informal arrangements, but the work of Levitsky and Murillo shows that we are far better off if we do not conflate the two under the same heading. Only by distinguishing formal (obligatory) institutions from informal norms (based on shared understandings and conventions) can we explore the connections and relationship between the two. Thus, without denying the importance of informal conventions, the arguments we elaborate are subject to specific scope conditions; they assume institutional "strength" in Levitsky and Murillo's (2009) sense, including the rule of law and state capacity to enforce formal rules.

[3] Such policies include those that set rules for social interaction that are enforced through the exercise of public authority as well as those that establish organizations or agencies (for example, central banks in most countries) whose existence is publicly guaranteed and whose actions are backed up by state authority.

institutions are poorly adapted to handle. In the case of conversion, the trigger is *actor discontinuity*, as actors not involved in (in some cases not even around for) those rules' creation seek to redirect them toward new ends. We consider each in turn.

Drift

Drift is defined as the failure of relevant decision makers to update formal rules when shifting circumstances change the social effects of those rules in ways that are recognized by at least some political actors (Hacker 2004, 2005; Hacker and Pierson 2010, 2011; for extensions, see Béland 2007; Falleti and Lynch 2009; Lynch 2006; Mahoney and Thelen 2010; Streeck and Thelen 2005). By formal rules, we mean the specific operating language created by authoritative public decisions. By changing social circumstances, we mean the shifting context of those rules. Drift occurs when such shifts alter rules' outcomes without a change in the rules themselves.

Drift is therefore more than just political inaction. It requires that (1) the circumstances around policies or institutions change in ways that alter the effects of those policies or institutions on the ground, (2) this change in outcomes is recognized, (3) there are alternative rules that would reduce the degree to which these shifts in outcomes occur (in other words, that the shifts are *potentially* remediable), and (4) efforts to update these rules are not undertaken or are blocked.[4]

To offer just one telling example, drift was integral to the process of financial deregulation that preceded the 2008 economic crisis in the United States. In 1997, the chair of the US Federal Reserve, Alan Greenspan, observed a growing mismatch between a dynamic financial economy and sclerotic regulatory policymaking – and applauded:

With technological change clearly accelerating, existing regulatory structures are being bypassed, freeing market forces to enhance wealth creation and economic growth . . . As we move into a new century, the market-stabilizing private regulatory forces should gradually displace many cumbersome, increasingly ineffective

---

[4] This definition recognizes that democratic majorities may support the inaction that causes drift. However, in many cases the failure to update formal rules is not explained by the preferences of democratic majorities but instead by the blocking activities of intense minorities or actors possessing veto powers. In a prior formulation (Hacker and Pierson 2011), we made this second possibility part of the definition of drift. Though we offer a more expansive definition here, we continue to believe that one of the most interesting features of drift is that it provides a particularly potent way for political actors to pursue change that would likely not command majority support if carried out in more overt ways.

government structures. This is a likely outcome since governments, by their nature, cannot adjust sufficiently quickly to a changing environment, which too often veers in unforeseen directions. (Quoted in Johnson and Kwak 2010, 101)

Greenspan's faith in "market-stabilizing private regulatory forces" proved badly misplaced, of course. Yet his pronouncement accurately captured the degree to which federal financial policies – failing to "adjust sufficiently quickly to a changing environment" – were simply being outflanked by shifting market realities. It is true that new laws that deregulated the financial sector played an important role in encouraging these changes. At least as important, however, was policy drift: the failure of policymakers to respond to these developments, in part because of intense lobbying by the financial industry to head off such responses.[5]

Conversion

By conversion we mean the transformation of an already-existing institution or policy through its authoritative redirection, reinterpretation, or reappropriation. Thus conversion, like drift, combines elements of constancy in institutional *form* with changes in institutional *impact*. Also like drift, conversion allows reformers to pursue important substantive changes even in the face of formidable obstacles to more direct forms of institutional reengineering. Yet, in contrast to drift, conversion requires active reinterpretation of existing formal rules to serve new ends. Conversion occurs when (1) institutions or rules are sufficiently malleable that they can serve multiple ends; (2) those ends are politically contested; and (3) political actors are able to redirect an institution or policy to serve new functions while (4) leaving its formal rules in place.

Conversion reminds us that institutions are "multipurpose tools" that can be used to different ends – and whose goals and functions are therefore contested by groups both outside and within them (Perrow 1986, 11–12).[6] Moreover, not only do institutions have multiple possible effects, these effects are frequently unanticipated, especially if an institution endures for a long

---

[5] In fact, the growing gap between regulation and reality led to pressures for post hoc adjustments to the law to accommodate these behaviors and practices (Johnson and Kwak 2010). This points to a complex but important dynamic, which we cannot explore here, in which drift can create pressures that result in further formal-institutional change. In the case of finance, rather than drift serving as a catalyst to "update" rules to restore the eroding regulatory regime, it became a justification for further deregulation of those still covered by the old rules. The result was a "deregulatory ratchet" that included elements of drift, conversion (the interpretive loosening of existing rules), and new statutes.

[6] The reference in Perrow is to what he calls "complex organizations," but the insights apply much more generally, as we argue below.

time. This is in part because these effects often unfold only slowly in frequently dense institutional environments, and in part because the actors charged with shaping and operating institutions are often distinct from those who create them (Pierson 2004, esp. chapter 4). Indeed, if drift requires environmental shifts, changes in the key actors who are directing an institution represent the critical trigger for conversion.

In some cases, conversion is a matter of political expediency. For example, when the Labour government came to power in Britain in 1945, it redeployed economic instruments and institutions that had been developed to wage war to pursue growth and redistributive goals in peacetime.[7]

Often, however, conversion is pursued by actors who are seeking to directly alter or even subvert an institution's original purposes or functions. The development of the European Union provides a telling example. When the member states of the (then) EEC adopted Article 234, it included a "preliminary ruling mechanism" that would allow them to use the European Court of Justice to "hold EU legislative and executive bodies in check" (Alter 2000, 491). Clearly designed as a mechanism to allow member states to resist excessive encroachments by EU bodies, domestic groups within these countries seized on this provision to challenge national policies they opposed. Their successes before the European Court of Justice transformed the preliminary ruling mechanism from a tool for reaffirming member sovereignty into one for powerfully increasing the obligations of the member states under EU law (Abbott *et al.* 2000, 438; Alter 2000).[8] As this example suggests, conversion often involves a shift in the arena of contestation – away from more visible venues (in this case, domestic legislatures) to less visible ones (the European Court), and away from high-profile clashes of parliamentarians and parties toward low-profile struggles among groups with sufficient organization, resources, and durability to win in nonlegislative arenas.

Explaining drift and conversion

The analytic benefits of identifying drift and conversion increase if we can specify the conditions under which they are likely to take place. The focus

---

[7] As Kenneth Harris, the biographer of Clement Attlee, Britain's postwar Labour leader, would later remark, many of the policies that "seemed the result of a Labour government putting socialist principles into effect, were to a great degree the legacy of a state which had been organized to fight a total war" (quoted in Judt 2008, 68–9).

[8] Conversion strategies of this sort need not be attempts at wholesale reversals, of course. They can also take the form of changes that bend or stretch rules beyond their original intent.

on clearly defined processes of institutional change in recent scholarship has encouraged cumulative research and conceptual refinement that have greatly advanced our understanding of the institutional settings, political circumstances, and social contexts in which drift and conversion are most likely to emerge. In this section, we build on recent scholarship to develop more specific claims about what makes drift and conversion more or less probable.

What drift and conversion share: the significance of status quo bias

As already noted, drift and conversion are united by a common source – the difficulty of directly changing formal rules. A first simple proposition, therefore, is that the prevalence of drift and conversion increases with the strength of a political system's status quo bias. But what explains variation in status quo bias? A large institutional and choice-theoretic literature speaks to this question, delineating the institutional arrangements, procedural rules, and distribution of political preferences that foster stasis in authoritative decision making. All of this work suggests that status quo bias results from the interaction of basic decision-making institutions and the distribution of preferences. Tsebelis's work on veto players, for example, associates heightened policy stability with contexts in which more actors must accede to change, when the ideological distance between them is greater, and when they are more internally cohesive (Tsebelis 1995; see also Immergut 1992). Keith Krehbiel (1998) similarly argues that legislative politics are more likely to be stalemated when legislators are more polarized and the status quo is relatively close to the position of the "pivotal" legislators whose votes determine whether a bill becomes law.

Crucially, who is pivotal depends on institutional structures and rules – and is rarely the vaunted "median voter" within national decision-making systems. In the United States, political institutions create especially high barriers to the enactment of new legislation (Stepan and Linz 2011). The separation of powers gives rise to the possibility of divided government, and the different electoral calendars (two- versus six-year terms) and constituencies (more or less equally populated House districts and states whose populations differ by a factor of 65) foster preference divergence between the House and Senate. Add to the mix such supermajority hurdles as the Senate filibuster and presidential veto, as well as increasing levels of ideological polarization within government, and the tendencies toward political stalemate are strong. Nonetheless, the United States is not alone; the political systems of many democracies contain multiple veto points, supermajority requirements, or both.[9]

Moreover, beyond formal governance structures democratic polities often provide opportunities for intense minorities to block change even if that change has the actual or potential support of popular majorities. Well-organized interests often enjoy blocking power through their influence on individual legislators on key committees, through their importance to pivotal political parties in proportional representation systems, or through their participation in "expert commissions" charged with developing legislative proposals. In such cases, there is no guarantee that alternatives to the status quo that would garner the support of popular or legislative majorities will be put in place.

Decision-making rules and points of access are just two crucial factors affecting the intensity of status quo bias. In addition, as the literature on institutional stability has shown, replacing institutions or policies outright often involves significant costs and risks even when the political landscape is more forgiving. Among these barriers are uncertainty about the effects of institutional changes (Shepsle 1986), the vested interests created by the feedback effects of existing policies (Pierson 2000), the efforts of the original creators of the institutions or policies to "hardwire" them to reduce the chance they will be unraveled by present and future opponents (Moe 1989), the crowding of agendas that makes it difficult to revisit past decisions (Baumgartner and Jones 1993; Kingdon 1984), the collective action barriers and transaction costs of creating new coalitions and coordinating on a single reform proposal (Hardin 1989), and the ever-present danger of "collateral damage" when institutions or policies are tightly intercoupled. All of these considerations suggest that changing formal institutions or policies is a difficult task in established democracies, and thus that drift and conversion are likely to be common processes within such settings.

What distinguishes drift and conversion: rule design and strategies of influence

If the crucial similarity between drift and conversion is that they are encouraged by status quo bias, the crucial difference concerns the opening that an

---

[9] Other federal systems often have such characteristics (as, for example, Fritz Scharpf's [2009] work on *Politikverflectung* in Germany demonstrates), as do some parliamentary systems that feature dual executives and/or dual chambers with overlapping jurisdictions.

institution or policy creates for altering the interpretation or application of existing formal rules. Borrowing the language of legal scholars, we call this variable the "precision" of an institution or policy.[10] While considerations of status quo bias call attention to the political context of formal rules, the issue of precision draws attention to the character of the rules themselves – whether, in the words of Kenneth Abbott and his coauthors, they specify "clearly and unambiguously what is expected of a state or other actor (in terms of both the intended objective and the means of achieving it) in a particular set of circumstances" (Abbott *et al.* 2000, 412). To return to our earlier examples, the rule that stipulates that employers must pay a minimum wage of at least $7.25 per hour is precise; the rule that renders actions "in restraint of trade" illegal, much less so.

Imprecision and precision create distinctive opportunities. Policies whose provisions are ambiguous and whose effects depend on interpretation and discretion offer fertile terrain for strategies of conversion. Moreover, such strategies thrive within venues – courts, bureaucracies, "parapublic" governing bodies – where the meaning of ambiguous rules is worked out. By contrast, policies whose rules are unambiguous are far less hospitable to conversion, though potentially more vulnerable to drift. This is because what is not *in* the rule is also not covered *by* the rule. For example, treaties with the USSR about arms control were very precise; yet for this very reason, they also left unregulated all sorts of behaviors that were outside their specific provisions.

We can sum up the combined effects of status quo bias and the tradeoffs involved in rule design. Status quo bias protects policies from direct revision but makes strategies of change through drift and conversion both more attractive and more difficult to reverse. Greater precision reduces ambiguity and facilitates enforcement, but it also reduces the adaptability of rules to new circumstances, rendering them more vulnerable to drift. In contrast, less precise rules are more flexible but also more susceptible to conversion, because they require working out what the rule calls for in a specific situation. In choosing the level of precision to adopt, policy designers often find themselves caught between the Scylla of drift and the Charybdis of conversion.

We can begin to grapple with the interaction between drift and conversion by considering the limits of two archetypal political responses to the trade-offs that they pose: automaticity and delegation.

---

[10] In previous work we have called this "barriers to internal change." Here we adopt the concept of precision as defined by legal scholars such as Kenneth Abbott, Anne-Marie Slaughter, and Thomas Franck.

Potential remedies and their limits: automaticity and delegation

One response to the risk of unanticipated changes in the environment and the threat of future actors seeking to exploit rule ambiguity is to design policies so they feature *automaticity* – in effect hard-wiring them to change in response to specified environmental shifts.[11] As R. Kent Weaver (1986) argues, one of the purest cases of automaticity is indexation – the explicit tying of policies to quantifiable changes in environmental conditions relevant to policy performance, such as wage growth, inflation, and demographic change. Our earlier minimum wage example would not exist if the US minimum wage were automatically updated to reflect consumer prices. Cost-of-living adjustments are the most familiar form of automaticity, but recent pension reforms in Europe have sometimes incorporated automatic adjustments for demographic variables (such as increasing life expectancy) into calculations of future benefits. Such automatic provisions all pose the same basic trade-off: in return for giving up some measure of control over policy, legislators free themselves from the need to enact periodic updates. For this reason, automaticity generally reduces the chance of drift. When policies are hardwired to reflect shifts in the external environment, there is much less likely to be a departure from the policy's original aims as a result of contextual changes.

But automaticity is not a panacea. In many areas, it will be difficult for elected officials to anticipate all the contextual conditions that might affect the policy, let alone to secure agreement on all contingencies. Moreover, automaticity may itself generate outcomes not foreseen or desired, as when tax breaks mushroom as individuals or organizations restructure their activities to exploit them. In such instances, policymakers may wish to write into the legislation some imprecision, which brings us to the second topic: delegation.

If policymakers are not willing to hardwire policies, they may be willing to cede power to frontline officials who are charged with implementing imprecise rules in a changing environment. As the vast literature on delegation suggests

---

[11] We will put to the side one feature of policy that can obviously lead to a shift in the status quo without new legislation – namely, explicit limits on the duration of policies. A law may create new benefits for only ten years or require reauthorization after five. In such cases, policymakers need to pass new legislation if they wish to continue a policy. Such "temporal bounding," however, is not equivalent to drift. Drift occurs when policy outcomes change as a result of environmental shifts. The process may be gradual and not immediately perceptible. A pure time limit is more like an on-off switch: one day the policy is in place, the next it is not. Moreover, such temporal limits are explicitly written into law and thus relatively easy to see and mobilize around. The same is generally not true of drift, which results from the over-time interaction of environmental change and often complex features of policies – including features that are *not* written into law, such as the absence of automatic inflation updates.

(for a good review, see Bendor, Glazer, and Hammond 2001), it is difficult for policymakers to specify *ex ante* what particular steps need to be taken to achieve their goals, especially when the context of policymaking is unpredictable and frontline decisions require specialized information.[12] In such circumstances, elected officials (the "principals" in the familiar principal-agent model) may wish to delegate power to bureaucratic "agents," who can use their greater information to respond to changes in the environment. In essence, delegation involves crafting rules that give frontline agents the flexibility to adapt those rules to changing circumstances.

But what prevents these agents from deviating from the principal's intent? The thrust of most of the literature on delegation is that the principals can handle the problem (Callender and Krehbiel 2012; McCubbins, Noll, and Weingast 1987). Using both formal legislative language and formal and informal *ex post* controls, they are able to ensure outcomes consistent with original goals. For example, lawmakers can empower affected interest groups to shape agency decisions on an ongoing basis. Or they can adopt recruitment or oversight processes that keep bureaucrats in line even as the environment shifts. In essence, the delegation literature implies that policymakers can navigate between the twin perils of drift and conversion through *ex ante* and *ex post* controls. Even without new rules or automatic provisions, legislators can get frontline actors to do what they want in the face of changing external circumstances.

Yet the solution is not that simple. To accommodate the kinds of major demographic or technological changes we have discussed, discretion would need to be exceptionally wide and flexible. Constraining frontline agents with this much latitude – agents who essentially have rule-making power – would be difficult, if not impossible. More likely, it would create an enormous amount of imprecision that frontline agents could exploit, opening the door to conversion. In other words, the level of discretion required to keep a policy on track would effectively transfer policymaking authority to bureaucrats. Policymakers avoid drift only by facilitating conversion; they avoid conversion only by risking drift.

The politics after politics

The problem is not just technical. It is deeply political. The delegation literature presents a view of policymaking in which coherent coalitions craft clear

---

[12] See also the vast literature on "incomplete contracting" that deals with these problems.

legislation, the effects of those policies are easily traceable, and the players in the political game are more or less constant and equally powerful across time and venue. In the real world, however, policies and institutions are frequently messy compromises abounding with inconsistencies and contradictions based on coalitions of convenience and "ambiguous alliances" (Palier 2005). Sometimes, for example, policymakers will intentionally leave aspects of a policy vague to make it easier for competing interests to "sign off" on a measure or to enhance the durability of the rule by leaving room for it to be extended and applied to new situations. Such ambiguity may facilitate agreement in the short run and often renders the formal rule less brittle, but it also provides a strategic opening for interested parties to attempt to steer substantive outcomes in their preferred direction in the implementation and enforcement phases.

More important, the political forces that shape the implementation of legislation are generally very different from those that craft the laws to begin with. For starters, public salience is almost always vastly lower, both because of the passage of time and because of the complexity and opacity of administrative and judicial processes. In addition, organized interests are usually much more active and influential (Culpepper 2011; Moe 1990). To be sure, policymakers are well aware of this reality. Still, there may be real limits to their ability to foresee or forestall future challenges, especially when these processes play out over long periods of time.

When new rules clash with the interests of powerful groups, they invite challenge, and the more ambiguous the rules, the greater the scope for influencing their interpretation. Questions of interpretation are inherently political, and actors with intense interests can be counted on to weigh in on such questions, seeking at all turns to invoke – and impose on others – their preferred interpretation. In many countries, the courts play the crucial function of providing the authoritative interpretation, but other venues – from expert commissions to quasi-public organizations with implementing power – are part of the mix, too. In these respects, as well, delegation as a "solution" to drift often opens up opportunities for conversion by moving the politics of institutional change into less visible venues where challengers with advantages in these domains seek outcomes quite distant from original intentions.

In short, neither automaticity nor delegation offers a magic bullet to policymakers seeking to retain control over institutional outcomes. To understand when and how drift and conversion occur and interact, we need to extend our gaze outward to the social context of institutions and to the organized political actors most advantaged in these hidden processes of change. In the next section, we carry out this investigation and, in doing so, underscore just what is lost in analyses that neglect such processes and the social forces and political organizations that bring them about.

Drift and conversion in the real world

The politics after politics is characterized by two realities often missed by contemporary theories of lawmaking. The first, most relevant to drift, is that policies enter dense social environments that pervasively condition their effects, sometimes in unexpected ways. The second, most relevant to conversion, is that once a policy is established an important set of political actors enter the scene – actors who feature much less or play very different roles prior to enactment. Let us consider the social environment first.

Drift: political stalemate, social flux

Developed democracies face dramatic economic and social changes. Yet, as public programs have matured, these polities have also experienced growing tendencies toward gridlock, making it harder to update policies. Loss of adaptability is particularly notable in the United States, where the growing polarization of American legislators and increasing use of the Senate filibuster have made legislative stalemate ever more the norm (McCarty, Poole, and Rosenthal 2006; Wawro and Schickler 2010). However, it is also a problem in other advanced democracies where polarization manifests in increasing fragmentation and sprawling coalition governments with weak mandates. Within the scholarship on American politics, gridlock is typically characterized as a source of stability, reinforcing the status quo. Yet drift suggests a large exception to this assumption: when the effects of formal rules are heavily dependent on their environment, gridlock can produce major changes in the status quo, as failure to adapt rules to their changing context produces substantial shifts in policy outcomes. In other words, doing nothing in the legislature often means doing something quite big in the world.

In their introduction to this volume, Thelen and Mahoney emphasize that a strength of comparative-historical analysis is its focus on configurations that are only visible at the meso or macro level. Indeed, one of the exciting features of drift as a concept is its potential for linking fairly circumscribed arguments about legislatures and other decision-making institutions to substantively interesting social phenomena by systematically incorporating aspects of the broader social context. As Falleti and Lynch (2009) argue, "Drift is a mechanism that can operate *only* in a system characterized by multiple layers of relevant context" (1157, emphasis added). We can say more than "drift happens." We can also explicate the major environmental dynamics and characteristics of formal rules that are likely to give rise to this kind of mismatch.

Drift is often difficult to anticipate and prepare for precisely because some of the major sources of drift are substantially external to politics. Consider technological change. Rapid technological change introduces new possibilities for social organization or interaction that can radically alter the functioning of existing policies. For example, trade unions and left-leaning politicians in many European countries are now watching with consternation and concern as new technologies and patterns of social interaction have facilitated the emergence of a "gray labor market" in a growing range of services. "Digital capitalism" has encouraged actors to aggressively probe the bounds of the existing rules as they create wholly new markets beyond the reach of current policies and collective bargaining institutions (e.g., "Minister gegen Über" 2014). Similar to the example of financial deregulation, such developments have fundamentally changed the effects (and effectiveness) of existing arrangements by creating a parallel market whose existence outside the formal regulatory framework puts new pressures on actors inside that framework.

As with technology, so too with demography. Many policies are implicitly designed around particular distributions of actors or activities within a population. Over time, however, these distributions can undergo dramatic changes. In many democratizing nations a century ago, for example, property and income thresholds for voting were fixed only in nominal terms and assumed a small pool of wage laborers. As inflation and wage growth effectively lowered these standards and the working class grew, workers were gradually brought into the electorate without explicit expansion of the franchise.

A final powerful source of drift is differential growth rates across different parts of the affected policy landscape. Many policies fail to cover all activity in a particular issue area or cover different aspects in different ways. When these differences in coverage are associated with differential growth rates, the result can be substantial drift. In Germany, for example, so-called mini-jobs have expanded massively since 1980, contributing to the spectacular growth of low-wage employment in that country. This form of employment, characterized by low hours and low pay and without the usual social benefits, was conceived in the 1950s as a way for students, housewives, and pensioners – groups that already enjoyed benefits either as a result of previous employment or through their connection to male breadwinners – to supplement family income or earn a little pocket money. In the 1980s, however, employers in the rapidly growing service sector eagerly seized on this form of employment as a way to reduce costs. As a result, mini-jobs have grown exponentially and at the expense of regular part- or full-time employment, diminishing the effective reach of important public policies.

Similarly, across advanced industrial economies, unionization rates have fallen steadily. The main cause in many nations is not explicit anti-union legislation. Instead, unionization (and collective bargaining coverage) have shrunk "naturally" as employment has shifted away from organized labor's traditional strongholds in manufacturing toward services, where union presence is much weaker, especially among higher-skilled salaried employees. Much the same process has played out in the American pension system. Traditional rules grew gradually outmoded as more and more employers shifted from highly regulated defined-benefit plans offering a fixed benefit in retirement to lightly regulated defined-contribution retirement accounts like 401(k)s (Hacker 2004). In this case as in the others, the source of change was differential growth rates, and the political struggle was over whether and how to respond. Revealingly, those who wanted to update pension policies to reflect the new realities – now swimming against the tide of status quo bias – lost.

Again, comparative-historical analysis is particularly well equipped to consider these kinds of institutional changes. A shared and distinctive feature of many of these contextual shifts is that they involve "big, slow-moving processes" (Pierson 2004) that most political analyses downplay or ignore. Bringing these processes into view helps us better understand drift. It also encourages us to see political struggles within their evolving social contexts, laying bare deeper transformations of society that condition political outcomes (Hacker and Pierson 2014).

Conversion: interpretation and its venues

Drift is a strategy of holding firm while the world changes. Conversion is a strategy for actively altering what institutions do. If the possibility of drift arises when contexts change, opportunities for conversion typically arise when the players change – when political actors inherit institutions not of their own making and inconsistent with their ends.

Like drift, strategies of conversion respond to the considerable barriers to dismantling existing institutions. Yet they also reflect the distinctive challenges of constructing *new* institutions. Even when vested interests can be conquered, the prospect of institutional innovation can galvanize opposition from previously neutral groups who begin to contemplate how their interests might be jeopardized by new institutional arrangements or by "collateral damage" to adjacent institutions. Previously neutral parties often emerge in defense of existing institutions or policies even if the impact of the proposed change on their own interests is indirect or unknown (Mahoney and Thelen 2010, chapter 1). For all these reasons, reformers may have strong incentives to avoid frontal assaults on existing institutions, and conversion may allow a flanking maneuver toward the goal of institutional change.

But the possibilities for conversion are not constant. Beyond the issues of rule ambiguity already discussed, they hinge on the opportunities for opponents of existing rules to pursue hidden change through authoritative reinterpretation. Democratic political systems vary greatly in the number and authority of the venues they provide for such reinterpretation. More important, political actors vary greatly in their capacity to use these venues to achieve their ends.

Like moths to a flame, political scientists are drawn to the highly visible political theater within legislatures and parliaments. Yet, as the work of Aaron Wildavsky, R. Shep Melnick, and Eric Patashnik (among others) has reminded us, "The passage of a reform law is only the beginning of a political struggle" (Patashnik 2008, 3).[13] Conflicts over the enactment, implementation, and interpretation of the Affordable Care Act in the United States provide a particularly vivid example of the more general point. No sooner had the law passed than it was fiercely challenged in the courts and in state legislatures across the country. Where legislative "redos" are not possible, political actors may shift their attention to other venues, including government agencies and the courts – settings in which contestation over implementation and interpretation then continue. Ironically, the multiple veto points that many institutional analyses treat as obstacles to change may become *vehicles* for change in the politics of conversion.

Bureaucratic agencies are the first crucial arena. Judith Layzer's (2012) *Open for Business*, for example, explains how conservative interests have advanced policy change in the area of environmental regulation through "low-profile policy challenges" at the agency level. "Although conservatives have failed to repeal or revamp any of the nation's environmental statutes," she argues, "they have influenced the implementation of those laws in ways that increased the risks we face, prevented or delayed action on newly recognized problems, and

---

[13] This point is echoed, from an international relations perspective, by Jönsson and Tallberg (1998), who note that "agreements – whether in political or legal garb, whether on national or international levels – do not put an end to political processes" (373).

altered the way Americans think about environmental problems and their solutions." Of course, environmental groups have not idly accepted these developments; instead, they have pressured President Obama to reinterpret the powers of the Environmental Protection Agency and use those powers to fight climate change.

The courts are a second crucial arena of conversion in many countries. Saying what a law or policy calls for is precisely what courts do, and judicial rulings on such matters often have an enormous impact on substantive outcomes (Melnick 1994). A large literature on political jurisprudence has convincingly shown how statutory interpretation and judicial influence shape important areas of public policy. In the case of civil rights in the United States, for example, court decisions famously pushed public policy beyond where legislative majorities were prepared to go. The 1964 Civil Rights Act – a deeply controversial piece of legislation that outlawed various forms of discrimination – was hotly contested and very nearly failed in Congress. The compromises that had been required to get the bill passed had weakened many of its key provisions (Frymer 2003; Lieberman 2007). Once enacted into law, however, civil rights lawyers aggressively probed the bounds of the legislation by bringing a steady stream of cases before the courts. The result was to establish a "robust private enforcement regime" that transformed initially weak formal rules into one of the strongest affirmative action regimes in the world (Frymer 2007, 84).

As in this case, conversion is often a strategy employed by those on the losing end of some previous conflict. Yet the civil rights example should not be read to suggest that conversion is primarily a strategy for weak interests. To the contrary, well-organized groups and those with substantial resources and lobbying and legal capacities – such as employers and their associations – generally loom largest in the politics of conversion. For example, for decades now, Mexican entrepreneurs like the telecommunications tycoon Carlos Slim have been able to shield their companies from unwelcome intrusions by government regulatory agencies by invoking a writ of amparo, a legal provision originally designed to protect human rights (Schneider 2013, 145). Just to the north in the United States, according to a study of the politics of the Federal Communications Commission, firms have been able to change the regulatory environment in which they operate through the strategic use of litigation to "overturn potentially harmful regulations passed by federal administrative agencies" (de Figueiredo 2000, A1). Business interests in the United States have proved unusually successful under the Roberts Court in securing favorable interpretations of legislation of importance to them (Epstein *et al.* 2013,

1471 and *passim*). Sometimes David wins, but he had better be able to hire a good team of lawyers. In the politics of conversion, Goliath has the upper hand.

In sum, the concept of conversion highlights a major avenue of political influence: shifting substantive issues into arenas (or keeping them out of arenas) so as to marginalize or exclude opponents and magnify particular resource endowments. The balkanization of much contemporary political science, focusing special attention on legislatures and elections and featuring less prominent and separate literatures on "bureaucracy" and "the courts," obscures the reality that these are not separate arenas animated by fundamentally different political forces. Instead, each is deeply imbricated in a large network of political institutions (and, often, coordinated political activity) that jointly shape substantive outcomes (Barnes 2007; Burke and Scherer 2012; Carpenter 2001; Kagan 2003; Melnick 1994).

The politics of hidden change

What are the payoffs of recognizing drift and conversion? The first, just discussed, is greater awareness and understanding of political struggles that occur outside legislatures. These crucial conflicts frequently escape not just the notice of political scientists but also the control of voters, who face acute disadvantages when policymaking moves from legislatures into less visible political arenas. Indeed, a second major payoff is a deeper appreciation of the role of organized interests – marginalized by much contemporary scholarship – in institutional and policy change. Finally, once we appreciate the politics of drift and conversion, we gain a very different picture of who is playing "offense" and "defense" in democratic politics. Conversion and drift effectively turn the tables, transforming status quo bias from an enemy of reform into its friend. When opponents of existing rules are able to block updating or to successfully convert institutions, it is the supporters of the status quo ante (the winners in the last round) who face the difficult challenge of returning those institutions to their prior state.

Looking beyond big legislative changes

When studying institutional change, it is tempting to focus on high-profile episodes of reform when formal rules are rewritten. Yet such breakthroughs are not the only way institutions evolve, nor do such reforms always endure after the fanfare has ended. As Patashnik (2008) emphasizes in his study of major US policy reforms, "The losers from reform cannot be counted on to vanish without another fight, and new actors may arrive on the scene who seek to undo a reform to further their own agendas" (3). Well-organized and well-resourced groups that lack a large social base may in fact *wish* to avoid frontal assaults on popular institutions, preferring to seek change in "quieter" places (Culpepper 2011): the bureaucracies charged with implementing rules and the institutions (including courts) charged with interpreting them.

Venue shopping of this sort is about more than finding sympathetic ears. Post-enactment fights are typically low-salience, high-information affairs. They reward actors who can monitor implementers and interpreters across multiple venues. They reward a capacity for patience, favoring contestants willing to play the long game to prevent the updating of existing rules or shape the way those rules are carried out on the ground. In short, they favor a certain breed of political animal – ones who have the "span" to pursue their ends across venues and over time. To see these actors and understand their influence, analysts have to take the long view and pay close attention to configurative and temporal processes that are usually most visible when looking across polities. This is why, we have argued, there is such a close fit between comparative-historical analysis and the kind of theorizing about institutional evolution offered in this chapter.

The role of organized interests

Who are the political actors most likely to possess the attributes just discussed? The short answer is organized interests. They, as Terry Moe (1989) puts it, "are normally the only source of political pressure when structural issues are at stake" (269). When issues are low profile and the link between legislative action (or *inaction*) and outcomes is opaque, organized interests, not voters, hold the strongest hand. Of course, these are precisely the main attributes of drift and conversion that we have charted. Evolving often slowly, rising to voters' attention only episodically, if at all, and devilishly difficult to trace back to particular leaders, drift and conversion are processes that advantage those most capable of long-term monitoring, foresight, and coordination.

This observation carries substantial implications for how we understand democratic politics. Much contemporary research adopts a perspective that is at once fixated on voters and sanguine about the responsiveness of politicians to the electorate. Even scholars who are doubtful about political responsiveness (e.g., Bartels 2008) tend to root their explanations for nonresponsiveness in the voter-politician nexus, focusing more on what is *not* driving political outcomes (voter preferences) than on what is (e.g., the activities of groups).

The ubiquity of drift and conversion creates serious challenges for this dominant perspective. In the politics of hidden change, the sway of organized groups will typically be greater than the pull of atomized voters. With their notoriously short attention spans and limited appetite and aptitude for technical and legal detail, voters are simply outclassed in the long-term political battles associated with conversion and drift. Indeed, because it is so hard to link the resulting changes in outcomes back to particular elected officials, drift and conversion are perhaps the least risky ways for politicians in democratic polities to cater to organized interests.[14] Drift and conversion are not just mechanisms of change, in other words; they are means by which politicians can cater to such groups with limited electoral risk.

So, organized groups are likely to loom large, but which groups and why? To guide our thinking, we can draw on insights from a growing literature on policy reform and public law. In different ways, Patashnik (2008) and Stuart Scheingold (2004) have noted that even big victories are rarely sufficient to alter political outcomes. Both note the possibility of considerable slippage after legislation is passed or rulings handed down. Scheingold emphasizes the important role of social mobilization as a necessary complement to legal activism (see also Barnes and Burke 2006, 497; also Epp 1998, 2009). Without high levels of mobilization to ensure consistent and vigorous implementation and enforcement, even big legal victories may prove Pyrrhic. Patashnik (2008) draws the same conclusion in his study of legislative reforms, arguing that "even the most solid reform ideas require ongoing collective support to endure" (xi).

More important, these analyses stress that concentrated groups enjoy distinct advantages over diffuse interests in post-enactment politics. A classic article by Marc Galanter (1974) makes this point powerfully in the legal realm, drawing a broad distinction between "one shotters" and "repeat players." Galanter argues not only that repeat players enjoy myriad advantages over one shotters but also that these advantages *cumulate over time,* resulting in a gradual shift of law in favor of repeat players. Repeat players enjoy economies of scale in terms of developing in-house legal expertise. And because they

---

[14] The legislative politics literature ignores this conditional nature of group influence in part because it assumes that both groups and voters factor into legislators' ideal points in a more or less stable fashion. But, as a result, this work misses how legislators can shift their focus (groups versus voters) and thus their positions relatively quickly in those rare cases when voters gain the upper hand vis-à-vis groups.

have numerous cases under their belts, they are in a better position both to anticipate and head off problems (for example, avoiding lawsuits through particular contractual language) and to prevail in the cases that do arise. With this experience in turn come many opportunities to develop relationships with institutional incumbents and build a reputation that becomes an asset in itself.

As the label implies, moreover, repeat players play for the long term. This involves a cluster of strategies and accompanying advantages. They can play the odds and aim to maximize gains over a series of cases rather than go for a big victory on a single case. Crucially, they can play for rules instead of playing for immediate gains. In other words, they can settle – in poker terms, "fold" – when victory seems out of reach and the danger exists that a loss will result in unwelcome precedents. Conversely, they can accept a loss if it comes bundled with a more favorable interpretation of the rule of which they have run afoul.[15]

One shotters are disadvantaged on both counts. First, by definition, they lack equivalent experience. Even if they happen to command a superior grasp of the substantive issue at stake, they lack equivalent legal experience (and associated reputational effects). Second, one shotters have shorter time horizons and thus more limited strategic options. Actors who are engaged in a one-off contest obviously cannot play the odds strategically across a number of cases. Moreover, in one-shot contests the cost of defeat is likely large given the sunk investment in a single battle. Just as poker amateurs can have a good night but over the long run will lose to professionals, one shotters may win particular cases, but over time the table favors repeat players.

These insights extend beyond the realm of the courts. Elections are blunt instruments and voters are classic one shotters whose influence is felt only sporadically and in ways far removed from actual outcomes. Organized interests are repeat players par excellence. Their presence is virtually permanent, their influence is targeted at specific legislative and policy outcomes, and they are in it for the long run and well positioned to follow legislation into the implementation and enforcement stages. One shotters, even if backed up by strong social mobilization, are like the amateur poker player mentioned above. They may be able to score a victory in a particular case, but they are unlikely to have ongoing durable success unless they develop the kind of

---

[15]   An example is a Supreme Court decision on sexual harassment in which the victim won the case but the majority opinion (written by Justice Scalia) makes harassment very hard to demonstrate in subsequent rounds.

organizational capacity that could turn them into repeat players (Barnes and Burke 2006, 497).

Reconceiving defense and offense

As this discussion suggests, drift and conversion force us to reconceive who is playing offense and defense. Repeat players are advantaged not because they always win but because they have a special capacity to overcome momentary defeats. In their arsenal lies the ability to block updates to policies that are drifting in their direction or to pursue authoritative reinterpretations of existing formal rules. When successfully deployed, these distinctive strategic capacities change their political situation fundamentally. What had been a status quo they wished to change is now, through drift or conversion, a status quo they wish to preserve.

This matters a great deal, since one of the clearest findings of institutional scholarship is that there are very large differences between attacking and defending in politics. As strategies, drift and conversion capitalize on this inherent asymmetry. When policies are vulnerable to drift, the coalition that was previously seen as playing offense (attacking the status quo) finds itself in the easier stance of playing defense (blocking the updating of a drifting policy). Once the minimum wage has begun to erode, for example, workers will progressively lose ground unless their political allies can successfully remobilize to update formal rules. By the same token, once a new interpretation is in place due to conversion through agencies or courts, proponents of the original rule must remobilize to restore the prior status quo. To return to the example with which we began, the Sherman Antitrust Act, it took nearly a quarter of a century before a new law (the Clayton Act) finally protected unions from some of the specific types of judicial injunctions that had been visited upon them under the Sherman Act.

Put more broadly, a focus on drift and conversion forces us to reconsider the concept of multiple veto points – a staple of modern institutionalism. Typically, veto points are seen as strengthening the status quo by blocking change. It would be more accurate to say that multiple veto points alter, rather than simply impede, the politics of institutional change. They force politics onto alternative tracks. In doing so, they also empower those actors – typically the most organized ones – who thrive on a politics of complexity that privileges a capacity for sustained rather than intermittent activity. The effect of veto points, in other words, is conditional. They shift the balance of power among competing political actors and the mix of institutional changes, as well as the capacity to create new formal rules.

Probing a bit more deeply, many organized interests can exert substantial influence on the social environment as well as on politics. Large employers, for instance, are not simply collective actors in the political realm; they are also capable of extensive, politically consequential action in the economic realm (Lindblom 1982; Offe and Wiesenthal 1980). For these actors, it may be possible to achieve their goals not by changing rules but by "breaking out" from them: altering their behavior while preventing the updating of law. In the late 1970s and early 1980s, for example, American employers adopted a more aggressive stance toward unions in the private sector. They backed up their private actions with a strong political push, blocking union efforts to update industrial relations law. With a crucial boost from the Senate's filibuster rules, business successfully engineered a major episode of policy drift. Thinking systematically about these forms of private power and how they play into policymaking could give more specific content to arguments about the "structural" influence of political actors that once featured prominently in political and social analysis (Hacker and Pierson 2002).

Conclusion and implications

Until recently, institutionalism was dominated by the analysis of "comparative statics." Stable institutional differences explained cross-national divergence. The burst of interest in institutional change usefully challenges this older tradition. Yet it has proved less successful at producing clear and systematic explanations of when, why, and how institutions change. The concepts of drift and conversion seek to provide such explanations. By focusing on one important variety of bounded innovation – strategies pursued in contexts in which a more direct and overt institutional overhaul is excessively costly or difficult – we have sought to show *what specific sorts of institutional changes* pursued by *what kinds of actors* are likely under *what kinds of conditions*.

Drift and conversion also provide a crucial link between processes of institutional change and institutional reproduction, often treated as distinct. Particularly in punctuated equilibrium models of change, scholars are prone to separate the analysis of innovation (where agency often looms large) from the analysis of subsequent institutional reproduction (where the emphasis is on structural constraints). Yet the arguments in this chapter suggest that reproduction and change are two sides of the same coin (for a more extended argument, see Thelen 1999, 2004). Institutions do not survive long stretches of time by standing still: as the world around them changes, their survival often requires ongoing active adaptation to their political and economic environment. Drift reminds us that institutional reproduction is not a simple matter of stasis but depends upon active interventions to adapt these institutions and rules to changes in context. Conversion reminds us that institutional evolution is shaped by the adaptation of institutions inherited from the past to new purposes. These forms of change have enormous implications for how institutions evolve – and who benefits from their evolution.

Finally, drift and conversion expand our range of vision by prompting us to adjust not just what kind of change we are looking for but where we are looking for it and whom we expect to produce it. Drift, for example, can only be seen once we are attentive to the structure of policies and how those structures interact with a particular environment (Hacker and Pierson 2014) as well as the blocking strategies of political actors. By problematizing issues of interpretation and enforcement, conversion draws our attention to frequently neglected political arenas where ongoing struggles over imprecise rules often end up, especially the courts and bureaucracies. In this way, the concept offers the opportunity to tap into well-developed traditions of research on bureaucracy and jurisprudence while inviting a more sustained dialogue with scholars in public law, public administration, and public policy whose work sometimes seems disconnected from the rest of political science.

Above all, drift and conversion bring us back to fundamental questions of political economy. In a world marked by stark information and power asymmetries and vast differences in resources and organizational capacities, who actually governs (Dahl 1961)? Political contestation often pits the organized and information-rich – the political actors most able to block the updating of policies, the actors most capable of changing institutions from within – against the disorganized and information-poor (Arnold 1990; Bawn *et al.* 2012; Cohen *et al.* 2008; Hacker and Pierson 2005, 2010, 2014). By opening our eyes to drift and conversion, we can better understand not just the sources of institutional change but also the structure of power in advanced societies.

References

Abbott, Kenneth W., Robert O. Keohane, Andrew Moravcsik, Anne-Marie Slaughter, and Duncan Snidal. 2000. "The Concept of Legalization." *International Organization* 54 (3): 401–419.

Alter, Karen J. 2000. "The European Union's Legal System and Domestic Policy: Spillover or Backlash?" *International Organization* 54 (3): 489–518.

Arnold, R. Douglas. 1990. *The Logic of Congressional Action*. New Haven, CT: Yale University Press.

Barnes, Jeb. 2007. "Bringing the Courts Back In: Interbranch Perspectives on the Role of Courts in American Politics and Policy Making." *Annual Review of Political Science* 10:25–43.

Barnes, Jeb, and Thomas Burke. 2006. "The Diffusion of Rights: From Rights on the Books to Organizational Rights Practices." *Law and Society Review* 40 (3): 493–524.

Bartels, Larry M. 2008. *Unequal Democracy: The Political Economy of the New Gilded Age*. Princeton, NJ: Princeton University Press.

Baumgartner, Frank R., and Bryan D. Jones. 1993. *Agendas and Instability in American Politics*. Chicago: University of Chicago Press.

Bawn, Kathleen, Martin Cohena, David Karola, Seth Masketa, Hans Noela, and John Zaller. 2012. "A Theory of Political Parties: Groups, Policy Demands, and Nominations in American Politics." *Perspectives on Politics* 10 (3): 571–97.

Béland, Daniel. 2007. "Ideas and Institutional Change in Social Security: Conversion, Layering, and Policy Drift." *Social Science Quarterly* 88 (1): 20–38.

Bendor, Jonathan, A. Glazer, and T. Hammond. 2001. "Theories of Delegation." *Annual Review of Political Science* 4:235–69.

Burke, Thomas, and Nancy Scherer. 2012. "The Bush Administration and the Uses of Judicial Politics." In *Building Coalitions: Making Policy: The Politics of the Clinton, Bush, and Obama Presidencies*, edited by M. Levin, D. DiSalvo, and M. Shapiro, 215–46. Baltimore: Johns Hopkins University Press.

Callander, Steven, and Keith Krehbiel. 2012. *Gridlock and Delegation in a Changing World*. Working Paper No. 2100, Stanford Graduate School of Business. www.gsb.stanford.edu/faculty-research/working-papers/gridlock-delegation-changing-world.

Carpenter, Daniel. 2001. *The Forging of Bureaucratic Autonomy: Networks, Reputations, and Policy Innovation in Executive Agencies*. Princeton, NJ: Princeton University Press.

Cohen, Marty, David Karol, Hans Noel, and John Zaller. 2008. *The Party Decides*. Chicago: University of Chicago Press.

Culpepper, Pepper. 2011. *Quiet Politics and Business Power*. New York: Cambridge University Press.

Dahl, Robert. 1961. *Who Governs: Democracy and Power in an American City*. New Haven, CT: Yale University Press.

de Figueiredo, John M. 2000. Litigating Regulation: Corporate Strategy in Telecommunications. *Academy of Management Proceedings*, A1–A6. web.mit.edu/jdefig/www/papers/litigation_regulation.pdf.

Epp, Charles. 1998. *The Rights Revolution: Lawyers, Activists, and Supreme Courts in Comparative Perspective*. Chicago: University of Chicago Press.

2009. *Making Rights Real: Activists, Bureaucrats, and the Creation of the Legalistic State*. Chicago: University of Chicago Press.

Epstein, Lee, William M. Landes, and Richard A. Posner. 2013. "How Business Fares in the Supreme Court." *Minnesota Law Review* 97:1431–72.

Falleti, Tulia, and Julia Lynch. 2009. "Context and Causal Mechanisms in Political Analysis." *Comparative Political Studies* 42 (9): 1143–66.

Frymer, Paul. 2003. "Acting When Elected Officials Won't: Federal Courts and Civil Rights Enforcement in US Labor Unions, 1935–85." *American Political Science Review* 97:483–99.

2007. *Black and Blue: African Americans, the Labor Movement, and the Decline of the Democratic Party.* Princeton, NJ: Princeton University Press.

Galanter, Marc. 1974. "Why the 'Haves' Come Out Ahead: Speculations on the Limits of Legal Change." *Law and Society Review* 9 (1): 165–230.

Hacker, Jacob S. 2004. "Privatizing Risk without Privatizing the Welfare State: The Hidden Politics of Social Policy Retrenchment in the United States." *American Political Science Review* 98 (2): 243–60.

2005. "Policy Drift: The Hidden Politics of US Welfare State Retrenchment." In *Beyond Continuity: Institutional Change in Advanced Political Economies*, edited by W. Streeck and K. Thelen, 40–82. Oxford: Oxford University Press.

Hacker, Jacob S., and Paul Pierson. 2002. "Business Power and Social Policy: Employers and the Formation of the American Welfare State." *Politics & Society* 30 (2): 277–325.

2005. "Abandoning the Middle: The Bush Tax Cuts and the Limits of Democratic Control." *Perspectives on Politics* 3 (1): 33–55.

2010. *Winner-Take-All Politics.* New York: Simon and Schuster.

2011. *Drift and Democracy: The Neglected Politics of Policy Inaction.* Paper prepared for the Working Group on Institutional Change, Cambridge, MA, February.

2014. "After the 'Master Theory': Downs, Schattschneider, and the Rebirth of Policy-Focused Analysis." *Perspectives on Politics* 12(3): 643–62.

Hardin, Russell. 1989. "Why a Constitution?" In *The Federalist Papers and the New Institutionalism*, edited by Bernard Grofman and Donald Wittman, 100–19. New York: Agathon.

Helmke, Gretchen, and Steven Levitsky, eds. 2006. *Informal Institutions and Democracy: Lessons from Latin America.* Baltimore: Johns Hopkins University Press.

Immergut, Ellen. 1992. *Health Politics: Interests and Institutions in Western Europe.* New York: Cambridge University Press.

Johnson, Simon, and James Kwak. 2010. *13 Bankers: The Wall Street Takeover and the Next Financial Meltdown.* New York: Pantheon.

Jönsson, Christer, and Jonas Tallberg. 1998. Compliance and Post-Agreement Bargaining. *European Journal of International Relations* 4 (4): 371–408.

Judt, Tony. 2008. *Postwar: A History of Europe Since 1945.* New York: Penguin.

Kagan, Robert A. 2003. *Adversarial Legalism and American Government.* Cambridge, MA: Harvard University Press.

Kingdon, John W. 1984. *Agendas, Alternatives, and Public Policies.* New York: HarperCollins.

Krehbiel, Keith. 1998. *Pivotal Politics: A Theory of U.S. Lawmaking.* Chicago: University of Chicago Press.

Layzer, Judith. 2012. *Open for Business: Conservatives' Opposition to Environmental Regulation.* Cambridge, MA: MIT Press.

Levitsky, Steven, and Maria Victoria Murillo. 2009. "Variation in Institutional Strength." *Annual Review of Political Science* 12:115–33.

Levitsky, Steven, and Dan Slater. 2011. "Ruling Politics: The Formal and Informal Foundations of Institutional Reform." In *Ruling Politics*, edited by S. Levitsky and D. Slater. Cambridge, MA: Harvard University Press.

Lieberman, Robert C. 2007. *Private Power and American Bureaucracy: The EEOC and Civil Rights Enforcement*. Columbia University. http://web1.millercenter.org/apd/colloquia/pdf/col_2005_0318_lieberman.pdf.

Lindblom, Charles E. 1982. "The Market as Prison." *Journal of Politics* 44 (2): 324–36.

Lynch, Julia. 2006. *Age in the Welfare State: The Origins of Social Spending on Pensioners, Workers, and Children*. Cambridge: Cambridge University Press.

Mahoney, James, and Kathleen Thelen, eds. 2010. *Explaining Institutional Change: Ambiguity, Agency, and Power*. Cambridge: Cambridge University Press.

McCarty, Nolan, Keith T. Poole, and Howard Rosenthal. 2006. *Polarized America*. Cambridge, MA: MIT Press.

McCubbins, Mathew D., Roger G. Noll, and Barry R. Weingast. 1987. "Administrative Procedures as Instruments of Political Control." *Journal of Law, Economics, and Organization* 3:243–77.

Melnick, R. Shep. 1994. *Between the Lines: Interpreting Welfare Rights*. Washington, DC: The Brookings Institution.

"Minister gegen Über." 2014. *Der Spiegel*, September 15, 71.

Moe, Terry M. 1989. "The Politics of Bureaucratic Structure." In *Can the Government Govern?*, edited by J. Chubb and P. Peterson, 267–329. Washington, DC: The Brookings Institution.

1990. "The Politics of Structural Choice: Toward a Theory of Public Bureaucracy." In *Organization Theory: From Chester Barnard to the Present and Beyond*, edited by O. E. Williamson, 116–53. New York: Oxford University Press.

North, Douglass C. 1990. *Institutions, Institutional Change, and Economic Performance*. New York: Cambridge University Press.

Offe, Claus, and Helmut Wiesenthal. 1980. "Two Logics of Collective Action: Theoretical Notes on Social Class and Organizational Form." *Political Power and Social Theory* 1:67–115.

Palier, Bruno. 2005. "Ambiguous Agreement, Cumulative Change: French Social Policy in the 1990s." In *Beyond Continuity: Institutional Change in Advanced Political Economies*, edited by Wolfgang Streeck and Kathleen Thelen, 127–44. Oxford: Oxford University Press.

Patashnik, Eric M. 2008. *Reforms at Risk: What Happens After Major Policy Changes Are Enacted*. Princeton, NJ: Princeton University Press.

Perrow, Charles. 1986. *Complex Organizations: A Critical Essay*. 3rd ed. New York: McGraw-Hill.

Pierson, Paul. 2000. "Path Dependence, Increasing Returns, and Political Science." *American Political Science Review* 94 (2): 251–67.

2004. *Politics in Time: History, Institutions, and Social Analysis*. Princeton, NJ: Princeton University Press.

2006. "Public Policies as Institutions." In *Rethinking Political Institutions: The Art of the State*, edited by Ian Shapiro, Stephen Skowronek, and Daniel Galvin, 114–31. New York: New York University Press.

Scharpf, Fritz. 2009. *Föderalismusreform: Kein Ausweg aus der Politikverflectungsfalle?* Frankfurt: Campus Verlag.

Scheingold, Stuart. 2004. *The Politics of Rights: Lawyers, Public Policy, and Political Change.* Ann Arbor: University of Michigan Press.

Schneider, Ben Ross. 2013. *Hierarchical Capitalism in Latin America: Business, Labor and the Challenges of Equitable Development.* New York: Cambridge University Press.

Shepsle, Kenneth A. 1986. "Institutional Equilibrium and Equilibrium Institutions." In *Political Science: The Science of Politics*, edited by H. Weisberg. New York: Agathon.

Stepan, Alfred, and Juan J. Linz. 2011. "Comparative Perspectives on Inequality and the Quality of Democracy in the United States." *Perspectives on Politics* 9 (4): 841–56.

Streeck, Wolfgang, and Kathleen Thelen. 2005. *Beyond Continuity: Institutional Change in Advanced Political Economies.* Oxford: Oxford University Press.

Thelen, Kathleen. 1999. "Historical Institutionalism in Comparative Politics." *Annual Review of Political Science* 2:369–404.

    2004. *How Institutions Evolve: The Political Economy of Skills in Comparative-Historical Perspective.* New York: Cambridge University Press.

Tsebelis, George. 1995. "Decision Making in Political Systems: Veto Players in Presidentialism, Parliamentarism, Multicameralism, and Multipartyism." *British Journal of Political Science* 25 (3): 289–325.

Wawro, Gregory J., and Eric Schickler. 2007. *Filibuster: Obstruction and Lawmaking in the U.S. Senate.* Princeton, NJ: Princeton University Press.

Weaver, R. Kent. 1986. "The Politics of Blame Avoidance." *Journal of Public Policy* 6 (4): 371–98.

Part IV

Issues of method

8 The comparative sequential method

Tulia G. Falleti and James Mahoney

Although comparative-historical analysis (CHA) is often understood to entail the comparison of a small to medium number of cases (usually countries or other macro units), we argue in this chapter that it may be more informative to say that this field involves the systematic comparison of sequences (Rueschemeyer and Stephens 1997). We suggest that a principal overarching methodology of comparative-historical analysis is the *comparative sequential method* (see Falleti 2010, 20–4). This method is defined by the systematic comparison of two or more historical sequences. In CHA, the "cases" studied nearly always are decomposed into sequences of events, and CHA causal claims rest upon the inferences derived from the analysis and comparison of those sequences. To take a classic example, Barrington Moore's (1966) main cases in *Social Origins of Dictatorship and Democracy* include countries such as England, France, the United States, and Germany. But these cases are studied as types of sequences of events that unfold over time. These sequences are the central units of comparison, and they provide the main basis for Moore's inferences about the causes of dictatorship and democracy.

The comparative sequential method is an overarching methodology in the sense that it can and must encompass more specific methods of cross-case analysis and within-case analysis. The main cross-case methods include simple matching tools such as J. S. Mill's methods of agreement and difference as well as more complex tools such as statistical analysis and qualitative comparative analysis (QCA). The within-case methods include inductive process tracing and modes of hypothesis testing such as hoop tests and counterfactual analysis. In this chapter, we show how cross-case (in particular, Millian) methods and within-case (specifically, process tracing) are put to use to analyze and compare sequences of events in CHA. We argue that, depending on the *kind* of sequential argument, contrasting sets of methods are more or less

We thank Jacob Hacker, Verónica Herrera, Alan Jacobs, Rudra Sil, Hillel Soifer, Kathleen Thelen, and an anonymous reviewer for helpful comments on earlier versions of this chapter.

appropriate – and more or less useful – as tools for analyzing sequences and carrying out causal assessment.

To briefly foreshadow our arguments, we contend that process tracing is especially valuable for establishing the features of the events that compose individual sequences (e.g., their duration, order, and pace) as well as the causal mechanisms that link them together. There is no substitute for process tracing when analyzing the events that make up the sequences and processes that are studied in comparative-historical research. For their part, cross-case methods are the basis through which CHA scholars compare and contrast sequences and processes. These methods are used to evaluate whether the specific features of a sequence (e.g., the ordering of events) affect outcomes of interest in previously hypothesized ways. As we highlight, the comparative sequential method brings together the literature on temporality with the literature on case-study methods of causal inference.

Conceptual building blocks

We begin our explication of the comparative sequential method by introducing and defining the concepts that form the building blocks of this approach, emphasizing the distinctions between event and occurrence, and between sequence and process.

Events, occurrences, sequences, and processes

Events are spatially and temporally bounded happenings that can be compared across cases (cf. Abbott 2001; Griffin 1992; Sewell 1996). They are defined by general characteristics specified by the investigator, such that all instances of a given event have certain features in common. Different events are marked by different characteristics, which can vary significantly, depending on their level of analysis (e.g., an assassination versus an international systemic change), their duration (e.g., an economic shock versus an economic depression), their scope of change (a coup versus a revolution), and so on. Events have a fractal character, such that more micro events are always embedded within any given event (e.g., Grzymala-Busse 2011, 1281; Sewell 1996). By our definition, however, events are always happenings that have *general characteristics* that allow for them to apply to multiple cases. With an event, one can inquire meaningfully whether or the extent to which two or more cases experience the same event. Although some historical events may occur only once, if they are events, they could *in principle* have occurred multiple times.

By contrast, we reserve the term *occurrence* for a noncomparable happening that is, by definition, distinctive to a single case. The assassination of Martin Luther King Jr., the Great Depression, World War I, and the 1973 military coup in Chile are examples of occurrences. An occurrence can be recast as an event by viewing it at a more general level of analysis. Thus, these occurrences could be viewed as events if recast as an assassination, a depression, a war, and a military coup. Comparative-historical researchers often discuss occurrences in their historical narratives, but, when these occurrences are given analytic weight in explanation, they are treated as events – that is, as instances of more general phenomena that can be compared across units (Gerring 2007).

Both events and occurrences take place against the backdrop of – and interact with – temporal and spatial *contexts*. The contexts in which events and occurrences occur provide them with meaning and shape their causal effects. A given occurrence or event may trigger a certain reaction or series of events and ultimately an outcome in a given context but a different sequence and outcome in an alternative context (Falleti and Lynch 2009). For example, the bipolar international context of the post–World War II period made the rise of leftist ideologies and governments in the 1960s and 1970s in Latin America a serious political threat in the eyes of large portions of the population. Within that international context, many saw the military coups of that time as a remedy to or a lesser evil than the threat of communism. However, since the inception of the new century, and in a unipolar international context, the rise of the Left in Latin America does not invoke the same ideas of political threat that could explain or justify military intervention.

A *sequence* is a temporally ordered set of events that takes place in a given context (cf. Abbott 2001; Aminzade 1992; Pierson 2004). For example, and to oversimplify, Moore constructs the following sequence for England in the context of early modern Europe: royal peace (event *A*) → commercialization of agriculture (event *B*) → destruction of traditional peasantry (event *C*) and emergence of a strong bourgeoisie (event *D*) → parliamentary democracy (outcome). The "case" of England is decomposed into events like these that unfold over time in the narrative. Likewise, to use the example of Elizabeth Wood's (2000) insurgent path to democracy, the following sequence of events led to pacted transitions to democracy in El Salvador and South Africa in the specific context of oligarchic societies with extra-economic coercion of labor: sustained mobilization from below (event *A*) → decline of profits in the traditional economic sectors (event B) → change of elite's economic interests (event C) → negotiated transition to democracy (outcome).

In the narratives by Moore and Wood, events are presented as occurrences distinctive to particular cases. For instance, the development of capitalist agriculture in England is discussed by Moore as the Enclosure Movement, which was a singular occurrence. However, he makes it clear that the Enclosure Movement was a transition to capitalist agriculture. Likewise, in Wood's narrative, events such as sustained mobilization from below took different specific forms in El Salvador and South Africa. In El Salvador, sustained mobilization entailed a civil war led by the FMLN (Farabundo Martí Front for National Liberation), whereas in South Africa labor militancy – not guerilla actions – constituted the ANC (African National Congress) as an insurgent counterelite (Wood 2000, 132). While the occurrences are distinctive in each case, they constitute the same event: sustained mobilization from below. When comparative-historical analysts assert that their arguments are consistent with nuanced historical evidence, they often mean that the events in their sequences encompass key occurrences from the societies under study.

Last, a *process* is a particular type of sequence in which the temporally ordered events belong to a single coherent mode of activity. Processes often describe transitions between states, including movement toward a new state or movement away from a prior state. Examples of social, political, and economic processes are democratization, social mobilization, privatization, flexibilization of labor, regulation, and decentralization (examples of natural processes are aging, photosynthesis, evaporation, and combustion). Like events, processes have a fractal character in that smaller, partial, or more restricted processes may be part of larger and more encompassing ones. For example, the process of suffrage expansion is part of a larger process of democratization.

Within a process, the researcher can identify the component events that unfold over time from the start to the end of the theoretically relevant period of analysis. The researcher can identify such events because they belong to a single coherent pattern of reproductive or transformative activity. Thus, the researcher can establish whether the temporal succession of events tends to reproduce the initial conditions and early characteristics of the unit of analysis or whether the events trigger reaction/counterreaction dynamics that considerably change the unit of analysis. In her study of postdevelopmental decentralization in four Latin American countries, Falleti (2010) identifies the specific policies and legal and constitutional changes of administrative, fiscal, and political decentralization, which are the three main component events of the process of postdevelopmental decentralization. She also explains why the process of decentralization had reproducing features in the cases of Argentina, Brazil, and Colombia but entailed a reactive logic in Mexico.

We contend that CHA is often fundamentally concerned with the comparison of sequences operating in particular contexts, whether these are composed of events that are part of a single underlying process or events that refer to multiple processes. For instance, and to oversimplify again, part of Moore's narrative sequence for China is maintenance of traditional agriculture (event A) → lack of empowerment of the bourgeoisie (event B) and empowerment of the peasantry (event C) → revolution from below (event D) → communist dictatorship (outcome).[1] When one compares this sequence with the earlier sequence for England, one can start to see how Moore arrived at his central insights, such as the necessary role of the commercialization of agriculture (an event that refers to a process of economic transformation) and a strong bourgeoisie (which refers to a process of social class formation) for democracy as well as the importance of a strong traditional peasantry (class formation) and revolution (social mobilization) for communist dictatorship. In Wood's case, the comparison of two dissimilar cases allows her to isolate the common contextual factors (oligarchical societies with extra-economic coercion of labor) that triggered the common sequence of events (protracted mobilization from below and change in elites' interests) and that resulted in negotiated democratic transitions.

Elucidating the concepts of event, sequence, and process allows us to understand the basic units of comparison in much CHA. While CHA scholars do make comparative statements about "whole cases" (e.g., England versus China), these comparative statements are grounded in more disaggregated comparisons of events, sequences, and processes. These disaggregated comparisons are the basis through which CHA researchers make generalizations about the macro units under study.

Types of sequences and processes

Works of CHA vary in the kinds of sequences they construct and compare. In classifying and analyzing ideal-typical sequential arguments, we proceed

---

[1] As this example suggests, causal sequences may be composed of "nonevents" in which the absence of a happening during a specific temporal period is causally consequential. The outcomes of sequences may also be nonevents. A good example is Tannenwald's (2008) explanation of the "nonuse" of nuclear weapons in the United States since World War II.

in four stages.[2] First, we classify sequences according to whether their constitutive events are causally connected and distinguish between *causal sequences* and *strictly temporal sequences*. Second, we argue that the order and pace of events can be causally consequential for the outcome of interest. We thus also identify *ordered* and *paced* sequences to describe those sequences (whether causal or strictly temporal) in which event ordering and pace matter.

Third, we distinguish process-type sequences depending on whether the direction of initial steps helps establish the direction of the entire sequence. Do initial steps in a particular direction (e.g., toward a particular outcome) induce further movement in that same direction? We specifically distinguish between *self-reproducing processes* (the direction of early steps is followed) and *reactive processes* (the direction of early steps is not followed).

Finally, we distinguish three kinds of self-reproducing processes by taking into account the specific nature of reproduction. In particular, we consider whether the reproductive pattern involves a process of continuity, expansion, or diminishment. On this basis, we identify: *continuous, self-amplifying*, and *self-eroding processes*.

These distinctions are analytically and methodologically important because different sequences and processes must be analyzed in different ways, including often with distinct methods. For example, the ways in which process tracing can be most productively applied varies depending on the *kind* of sequence under analysis. Thus, we return to these distinctions in the next sections when we explore cross-case and within-case methods.

Causal and strictly temporal sequences

Most CHA studies formulate *causal sequential arguments* in which the events in a sequence are understood to be causally connected to one another. These causal chains start with an antecedent cause or condition (X) and, through a series of causally connected events (events A, B, C, and so on), culminate in a final outcome of interest (Y), as illustrated in the top left quadrant of Table 8.1. These types of sequential arguments can be thought of as pathway explanations. The nature of the causal linkages among events can vary: each event may be understood as necessary for each subsequent event, as

---

[2] It is worth emphasizing this is an ideal-typical classification of sequences, which for the most part thinks of sequences as self-contained units. In reality, however, sequences are often multilayered or interact and intersect with other sequences in complex ways. Some of these nuances will come to the fore in the analysis of Goldstone's (1998) work below.

Table 8.1 Types of sequential arguments in CHA

According to type of linkage between events	According to temporal effects of events	
	Ordered	Paced
Causal	*Causally ordered sequences*	*Causally paced sequences*
$X \to A \to B \to C \to Y$	$X \to A \to B \to C \to D \to E \to Y$	Fast $A \to B \to Y$
$\sim X \to \sim A \to \sim B \to \sim C \to$	$X \to A \to C \to D \to E \to B \to \sim Y$	Slow $A \to B \to \sim Y$
$\sim Y$		
(Ex.: Rustow 1970)	(Ex.: Rueschemeyer, Stephens, and Stephens 1992)	(Ex.: Collier and Collier 1991; Ahmed 2013)
Strictly temporal	*Temporally ordered sequences*	*Temporally paced sequences*
$A - B \to Y$	$A - B - C \to Y$	Fast $A - B \to Y$
$B - A \to \sim Y$	$C - B - A \to \sim Y$	Slow $A - B \to \sim Y$
(Ex.: Dahl 1971)	(Ex.: Falleti 2010; Smith 2007)	(Ex.: Skocpol 1979)

Notes: $\to$ indicates causal relationship; $-$ indicates lack of causal relationship.

probabilistically increasing the likelihood of each subsequent event, or as a part of conditions that are sufficient for each subsequent event.

Rustow's (1970) theory of the origins of democracy provides a good example of a causal sequential argument, in which the earlier events are necessary conditions for later ones.[3] Rustow starts his model with national unity, which he considers a necessary background condition (X) (we can also call it context) before the process of democracy can take off. The timing of this event in relation to the first stage of democratization is irrelevant; it may have happened in the recent or in the distant past (Rustow 1970, 351). The process of democratization itself starts with the preparatory phase (event A), a period of prolonged and inconclusive political struggle among social classes. Next is the decision phase (event B), when the political leadership accepts the existence of diversity and institutionalizes some crucial aspects of democratic procedure (355). This second phase leads to the final habituational phase (event C), when the population at large accepts the leadership agreement. In Rustow's model, each event (using our terminology, or phase, using his) is a necessary cause for the event that follows, and the end result is democracy. In this type of causal sequential argument with necessary conditions, the absence of any event entails the absence of outcome.

[3] In an excellent analysis of the comparative politics literature on democratization in relation to temporal and institutional arguments, Barrenechea, Gibson, and Terrie (forthcoming) cite the works of Rustow and Dahl as examples of sequential arguments. We draw from their article to further explore these early works of democratization as examples of *causal* and *strictly temporal* types of sequential arguments.

CHA works also often encompass the analysis of sequences in which the events are not causally connected to each other, but the temporality of these events (their duration, order, pace, or timing) is causally consequential for the outcome of interest (see second row in Table 8.1). We call these *strictly temporal sequential arguments.*

Dahl (1971) provides excellent examples of strictly temporal sequences in his analysis of the historical events leading to democratization. Dahl asks: "Does sequence matter? Are some sequences more likely than others to lead to mutual security and thus to facilitate the shift toward a more polyarchal regime?" (31). His answer is a resounding yes. When the process of liberalization (or increased public contestation, event *A*) precedes the process of inclusiveness (or increased popular participation, event *B*), the resulting polyarchal regime is more stable (*Y*), as was the case in England and Sweden. On the contrary, "when the suffrage is extended *before* the arts of competitive politics have been mastered" [event *B* before *A*], the resulting political regimes are unstable and could easily reverse to authoritarianism, as was the case in Weimar Germany (Dahl 1971, 38 and following). But contestation does not cause participation, or vice versa (see also Grzymala-Busse 2011, 1275). Instead, Dahl argues that the order of these events is causally consequential for democratic stability as a result of an exogenous factor: the process of political socialization of the excluded social strata, which takes place between the time of increased elite competition and the time of increased popular participation (Dahl 1971, 36). In other words, Dahl suggests that elite competition causes political socialization and the moderation of the masses, a phenomenon that in turn facilitates political regime stability provided it happens before increased participation. Hence, the order in which participation and competition occur is consequential to the political regime's stability, but competition does not cause participation (or vice versa).

Ordered and paced sequences

In both the causal and strictly temporal types of sequential arguments in CHA, the order and pace of the events may be causally relevant. Thus, we distinguish between *ordered sequential arguments* and *paced sequential arguments.* With ordered sequential arguments, the temporal order of the events in a sequence is causally consequential for the outcome of interest (Abbott 2001; Aminzade 1992; Falleti 2010; Jacobs 2008; Pierson 2004). *Timing matters* in the sense that the temporal relationship among events is consequential. For example, Smith (2007) makes an ordered sequential argument: the timing of oil wealth exploitation in relation to economic development and state institutional building is consequential to regime stability. As he writes, "The effect of oil wealth on politics and institutions is not a question of *whether* oil but *when*" in relation to economic development and state institutional building (193). Falleti (2010) makes a similar ordered sequential claim. She argues that if political decentralization precedes administrative decentralization in the sequence of decentralization reforms, subnational governments are likely to end up with higher levels of political and fiscal autonomy than if the order of events is the reverse.

The events in an ordered sequential argument may or may not be causally connected. Rueschemeyer, Stephens, and Stephens's (1992) classic work on capitalist development and democracy provides a good example of a causal and ordered sequential argument. In this pathway explanation, the earlier events are (for the most part) sufficient for each subsequent event. Schematically, the authors argue that capitalism, with its consequent process of industrialization (event *A*) weakens the landed upper class (event *B*) and strengthens the working and other subordinate classes (event *C*), who are brought together in factories and cities, where they associate and organize (event *D*). Capitalism, moreover, improves the means of communication and transportation, facilitating nationwide organization (reinforcing event *D*). Thus, the working class can successfully demand its own political incorporation (event *E*), which results in successful democratization (outcome *Y*) (Rueschemeyer, Stephens, and Stephens 1992, 271–2).[4] If the sequence was different, such that the weakening of the landed upper class happened after labor class incorporation (i.e., event *E* preceded event *B*), the result would be a highly unstable regime or a reversal to authoritarianism (as was the case in Argentina after working class incorporation with Peronism).

Paced sequential arguments are similar to ordered sequences except that the speed or duration of events – not their timing relative to one another – is causally consequential (Abbott 2001; Aminzade 1992; Grzymala-Busse 2011; Pierson 2004).[5] For example, in Collier and Collier's (1991) causal sequential argument of regime type, the unusually extended duration of labor incorporation in Mexico (slow event *A*) meant that this episode lasted until the

---

[4] Rueschemeyer, Stephens, and Stephens (1992) also analyze transnational and state-centered processes in their explanation of democracy.

[5] Our general category of paced sequential argument encompasses more fine-grained distinctions found in other work on temporality (e.g., Aminzade 1992; Grzymala-Busse 2011). For our purposes here, the general category of paced sequential argument is useful, though we recognize that it includes considerations about duration, speed, and pace that others may want to keep distinct.

Great Depression (event B), which in turn helps explain the radical form of party incorporation in Mexico (outcome $\sim Y$). That is, if the labor incorporation period had been shorter in Mexico (as in most of Latin America), it may well have been less radical in content. In her study of electoral system choice in the USA and Europe, Ahmed (2013) provides another example of a causal and paced argument. She argues that the time elapsed between industrialization and the electoral incorporation of the adult male population was consequential to the relative strength of labor organizations. Where suffrage was extended soon after industrialization (event B quickly follows event A), unions remained weak. The longer suffrage expansion (event B) was delayed after industrialization (event A), the more likely that workers would organize to achieve their political and economic goals (49). Skocpol's (1979) classic work on the outcomes of social revolutions contains a strictly temporal *and* a paced type of argument. She argues that the pace at which revolutionaries consolidated state power affected the extent to which they transformed state, class, and societal structures. In Russia, revolutionaries were forced by circumstances to rapidly consolidate power, which implied a more thoroughgoing transformation than in France, where the revolutionary reconstruction of state power unfolded more gradually.

Self-reproducing and reactive processes

Whether causal or strictly temporal, ordered or paced, sequential arguments can be further differentiated depending on whether their events follow a self-reproducing or reactive logic. On the one hand, sequences may embody events that move consistently in a particular direction and that track an outcome over time. Adapting Stinchcombe's (1968) terminology, we call these sequences *self-reproducing processes.* On the other hand, early events in a sequence may produce a series of reactions and counteractions that do not move the process in a consistent direction. With a *reactive process*, early events are followed by backlashes and reversals of direction, which in turn may trigger further backlashes and reversals, such that the final outcome of the sequence may appear unrelated to early events in the sequence (Mahoney 2000).

If a sequence of events is characterized by a *self-reproducing process*, the movement of initial events in a particular direction induces subsequent events that move the process in the same direction. Over time, it becomes more and more difficult to reverse direction or return to the original starting point (Hacker 1998, 2002; Pierson 2000; see also Thelen 1999, 2003). Although the events are linked by self-reproduction mechanisms, the underlying process may (1) remain unchanged (e.g., a background constant condition); (2)

Table 8.2 Types of processes in CHA

Type of process	Definition	Diagram of process	Examples
Self-reproducing	Initial events in a particular direction induce subsequent events to move the process in the same direction.	*Continuous process* A → A → A → A → A *Self-amplifying process* A → A → A → A → A *Self-eroding process* A → A → A → A → A	Jacobs (2010); Skocpol (1999) Arthur (1994); David (1985); Spruyt (1994) Onoma (2010); Rosenblatt (2013)
Reactive	Events are linked via reaction/counterreaction dynamics.	A → ~A → B → ~B → Y	Collier and Collier (1991); Riofrancos (2014)

amplify (e.g., the concentration of elite power over time); or (3) erode (e.g., institutional decay dynamics). These differences in reproductive logic permit us to distinguish three types of self-reproducing processes: *continuous, self-amplifying,* and *self-eroding processes,* represented graphically in Table 8.2.

In a *continuous process,* an early event is stably reproduced over time or leads to other events that maintain the underlying process in (approximately) a continuously stable form. Scholars often formulate continuous sequential arguments to characterize the perpetuation of longstanding policies, such as social security in the United States (Jacobs 2010). Organizational continuity often can also be described as a continuous process (e.g., Skocpol 1999).[6] Other phenomena that are often analyzed as continuous processes include cultural characteristics, institutional outcomes, and geographic features.

With a *self-amplifying process,* the initial events move the sequence in a particular direction, such that it becomes more and more likely that the process will be expanded, increased, strengthened, or otherwise enhanced. Over time, the process (or its outcome) does not remain stable but increases, grows, or becomes more prominent as a result of self-amplifying mechanisms. Famous examples of self-amplifying processes come from economic history, where technologies capitalize on small initial advantages and experience rapid proliferation via increasing returns (e.g., Arthur 1994; David 1985). Likewise, evolutionary processes are often subject to self-amplification as an innovation and adaptation spreads within a population. The proliferation of the modern state has been explained in these terms (Spruyt 1994). Economists characterize self-amplifying processes with the expression *increasing returns.*

---

[6] At times, a continuous background process may become, in the words of Soifer (2012), a permissive condition for change, combining with an intersecting sequence of events, at which juncture the process's logic of reproduction may change to a self-amplifying or self-eroding one.

In such processes, the probability of further steps along a given path increases with each move down that path (Arthur 1994; David 1985). Each individual step may be only a small change, but each step reinforces the direction of the prior one, and together the steps add up to a large cumulative effect.

With a *self-eroding process*, the logic of transformation is self-reproducing, but each event in the sequence serves to weaken, diminish, or undermine the configuration found in the early stages of the sequence. Each step down the path moves away from the established outcome associated with the early process and makes it increasingly less likely that the outcome or the process itself will be sustained. The status quo becomes harder and harder to maintain. Gradual processes of decay, drift, and exhaustion may be examples of self-eroding processes: in these sequences each event can feed into the next and diminish a prior pattern or process. For instance, the institutionalization of private property rights in Kenya was marked by a sequence in which the land titling process was rigged with fraud. Each fraudulent move triggered another fraudulent move and made the preservation of legal practices less and less likely over time, eroding the institutionalization of private property rights (Onoma 2010). Likewise, in Rosenblatt's (2013) comparative study of political party vibrancy, the phenomenon of trauma – the shared experience of a revolution or a civil war – activates retrospective loyalty and enhances party vibrancy. However, trauma is marked by decreasing returns: as time goes by, the generation that suffered political trauma ages out and the new generation does not forge the strong bonds that previously kept the party vibrant.

Finally, sequences may also unleash *reactive processes* in which events are linked together via reaction/counterreaction dynamics (Mahoney 2000). Each event is a cause of each subsequent event because it triggers a reaction or a response to the prior event. The events in these sequences are *transformative* in the sense that they change and perhaps reverse prior events (Sewell 1996). Often, reactive processes entail causal chains in which the initial event and the final event seemingly bear little relationship to one another, yet they are connected by virtue of the reaction/counterreaction dynamics that compose the overall causal chain. For example, in Collier and Collier's (1991) argument, the reactive sequences marking populist/postpopulist dynamics in Latin America moved countries from labor incorporation periods to party system regimes through a complex set of intermediary steps marked by reversals and backlashes. Riofrancos (2014) also makes a reaction/counterreaction sequential argument when analyzing the political interactions between indigenous movements and the state in Ecuador from the early 1990s to the present. In her explanation of the institutionalization of an extractivist discourse, Riofrancos traces the succession of political events that confront indigenous movements with the state and through which the discourse of *extractivismo* evolves.[7] In both examples, the basic mechanism of change is reaction/counterreaction.

Sequences and processes applied to the CHA of industrialization

Examples of several of the sequences and processes described above are found in Jack Goldstone's (1998) work on the origins of the Industrial Revolution (see Figure 8.1). In this work, the environmental sequence (events *A–E* in Figure 8.1) is a causal sequence in which each event is a logical response to each prior event; at certain points (e.g., *C* → *D*), the sequence moves along via reaction/counterreaction dynamics, such that it has components of a reactive sequence. By contrast, the industrialization sequence (events *M–R*) is a self-amplifying process and exhibits positive feedback. Each step in the causal chain serves to expand a process of industrialization that was launched with the invention of the steam engine. By the end of the sequence, industrialization has amplified to the point that a return to a preindustrial past is impossible. The example also contains a continuous process represented by the stable reproduction of a liberalizing culture open to technological experimentation. The endurance of this background event is important because it influences the industrialization sequence at various points. Most important, this continuous sequence intersects with the environmental sequence to produce the first steam engine (event *M*), which in turn launches the industrialization sequence. This "coming together" or collision of separately determined sequences is common in comparative-historical research, and it is sometimes described as a *conjuncture* (e.g., Mahoney 2000).

The Goldstone example is an illustration of a sequential argument in which the timing and duration of earlier events matters for subsequent events. For example, the long duration of context condition *A* (limited forest area, abundant coal, and cold climate) was essential for the environmental sequence to continue along its path. This event had to endure for England to become dependent on coal (event *B*), itself a long-run event, and eventually exhaust much of the coal supply (event *C*). Issues of duration, speed, and order can also affect the dynamics of self-reproducing sequences. For example, the ordering of events is consequential in the self-amplifying industrialization sequence of

---

[7] At times, counterreactions may seek to preempt more radical change. Other examples of preemptive counterreactions can be found in the literature on the origins of social welfare provision. In her analysis of social policy creation in Uruguay at the beginning of the twentieth century, for instance, Castiglioni (2014) argues that the Uruguayan state sought to preempt or anticipate the otherwise likely mobilization of the working class.

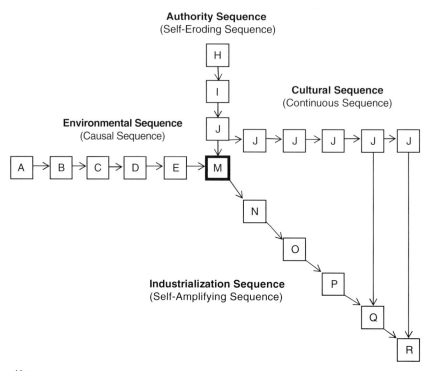

Authority Sequence
(Self-Eroding Sequence)

Cultural Sequence
(Continuous Sequence)

Environmental Sequence
(Causal Sequence)

Industrialization Sequence
(Self-Amplifying Sequence)

Key:
A: Limited forest area, abundant coal near sea, and cold climate.
B: Long-term heavy reliance on coal for heat.
C: Surface coal is exhausted.
D: Effort to dig for deeper coal.
E: Ground water fills mine shafts.

H: Limited monarchy.
I: Limited Anglican authority and toleration.
J: Liberalizing culture open to technological experimentation.

M: Development of first steam engine.
N: Improvement of steam engine.
O: Reduction in coal prices.
P: Reduction in price of iron and steel.
Q: Development of railways and ships.
R: Mass distribution of industrial production and goods.

Note: Adapted from Mahoney (2000).

Figure 8.1   Goldstone's explanation of English industrialization

the Goldstone example. A reduction in the price of iron and steel (event *P*) would not have spurred the development of railways and ships (event *Q*) if it had occurred substantially earlier. With many chains of events, in fact, it is difficult to imagine a different ordering. For instance, it seems inconceivable that the development of railways and ships (event Q) could occur before the development of the first steam engine (event M). The more basic point is simply that issues of order and pace frequently are important to the logic of all kinds of sequences in CHA work.

Finally, the Goldstone example illustrates how a single-country study may embody multiple sequences and processes. It has long been noted that multiple observations may be contained within a single case, such that a small-N study actually entails a large number of observations (Campbell 1975; Collier 1993; George and Bennett 2005; Rueschemeyer 2003). Our point here, however, is that one can view the main "cases" of a comparative-historical study in terms of sequences. This is certainly true for any historical work that systematically compares two or more sequences within a given case. With these studies, the sequences are central units of analysis, not only the national or other spatial unit in which they are located. In turn, when one treats sequences as central units of analysis, it is possible to revisit traditional CHA methods, which are often understood to apply mainly or exclusively to the macrospatial unit under analysis. A new vantage point for thinking about CHA methods comes into being by treating sequences and processes as core units of analysis and comparison.

Cross-case methods

In this section, we consider how the kinds of sequences and processes under analysis can shape the kinds of methods (or specific applications of a given method) that are most appropriate for assessing causal hypotheses. Perhaps the most basic comparative techniques are J. S. Mill's method of agreement and method of difference. As conventionally employed, the method of agreement matches cases that share a given outcome, and it eliminates any potential causal factor that is not shared by these cases. The rationale of this eliminative procedure is that the factor is not *necessary* for the outcome. By contrast, as conventionally used, the method of difference compares a case in which the outcome is present to a case in which it is absent. If these cases share a given causal factor, that factor is eliminated as a potential explanation. The logic of this eliminative procedure is that the factor is not *sufficient* for the outcome (Mahoney 1999).

When used in isolation, the methods of agreement and difference are weak instruments for small-N causal inference. Most simply, while these methods may be able to discover that an individual factor is *not* necessary/sufficient for an outcome, they cannot establish that a given condition *is* necessary/sufficient. Small-*N* researchers thus normally must combine Millian methods with process tracing or other within-case methods to make a positive case for causality. Alternatively, they can attempt to use stronger variants of cross-case methods, such as QCA and statistical analysis (Lieberman, Chapter 9, this volume; Ragin 2000, 2008). However, these methods may require the analysis of a medium number of cases, such that the design is no longer a small-*N* analysis.

The application of Millian methods for sequential arguments has not been systematically explored, although we believe it is commonly used in practice. With ordered sequential arguments, one evaluates hypotheses about the relative timing of events by comparing two or more sequences. Normally, the design entails the use of the method of difference, but it can also be combined with the method of agreement. For example, Ertman (1997) hypothesizes that the early timing (before 1450) of sustained geopolitical competition for Latin Europe led these countries to develop patrimonial states (rather than bureaucratic states). If Ertman had only analyzed the Latin European countries, the resulting method of agreement design would have led him to depend on counterfactual reasoning to support his argument about the importance of timing. However, Ertman also carried out a method of difference design by comparing Latin Europe to the German countries, cases where bureaucratic states were created. In the German states, Ertman shows how the late timing (after 1450) of sustained geopolitical competition allowed leaders to take advantage of the latest techniques of administration and finance and thereby develop more coherent bureaucracies. While this method of difference comparison does not clinch Ertman's ordered sequential argument, it does make it more plausible and allows him to avoid a purely counterfactual argument.

The joint application of the methods of agreement and difference also can be used with paced sequential arguments. One compares cases that are matched on a number of dimensions but that experienced a causal process at a different speed or with events of varying durations. For example, Prasad (2012) uses the method of difference in conjunction with a paced sequential argument to explain why the United States did not develop a robust public welfare state whereas European cases did. She argues that the stunning endurance of US economic prosperity during the late nineteenth and early twentieth centuries, itself rooted in the vast material resources of the country, set the United States down a path that allowed the government to avoid building a welfare state to reconcile citizens to capitalism. At the same time, Prasad applies a method of agreement design to account for the similar outcomes among the European cases, where sporadic and unreliable growth consistently encouraged welfare state formation.

The matching logic of Millian-type methods furthermore is often implicitly used for the study of self-reproducing sequences. For instance, with a self-amplifying logic, scholars may employ time periods as their cases and treat each increase in the magnitude of the phenomenon of interest as an outcome that repeats across multiple periods. The method of agreement can then be used in the search for a common source of the repeating outcome; factors that are not shared across each time period can be eliminated as nonessential. This logic applies well to famous examples of path dependence and technological standards, such as the QWERTY keyboard (David 1985). In the explanation of QWERTY, technological efficiency is eliminated as a possible explanation, given that efficiency was present only in the initial time periods when QWERTY was first adopted. Thereafter, QWERTY was inferior to available alternative options, such that technological efficiency was not necessary for QWERTY's reproduction over time.[8]

When temporal sequences are analyzed as particular types of processes, it is natural to treat those processes as the centerpiece of the comparative analysis. One compares and contrasts the nature of democratization, bureaucratization, colonization, and so on. With such comparisons, however, *events* are the basis for the similarities and differences that exist across sequences. For example, consider Kohli's (2004) argument about the colonial origins of types of states in the developing world. In Korea, the sequence of events is approximately as follows: Japanese colonial strategy of economic transformation and political control (event A) → introduction of new state personnel, bureaucratic techniques, and well-organized police force (event B) and modernization of agriculture and promotion of exports (event C) and control of peasants and workers (event D) → cohesive-capitalist postcolonial state (event E). In Nigeria, by contrast, indirect British colonial rule followed a

---

[8] Recent work on critical junctures also suggests new ways in which Millian methods may be used for sequential analysis. For example, Soifer (2012) recommends that scholars first select potential critical juncture cases by matching them on the outcome of interest (i.e., applying the method of agreement). If these cases are marked by critical junctures, he argues, they all must feature a "permissive condition" – that is, an underlying context in which the causal power of agency is increased (see also Capoccia, Chapter 6, this volume). The permissive condition must be present because, in Soifer's (2012) framework, permissive conditions are *necessary* but not sufficient for a critical juncture. As he puts it, "Cases where the permissive condition is absent are not relevant for testing" (1590). The eliminative logic of Millian methods thus serves as a first cut for testing potential critical junctures.

quite different sequence: British colonial strategy of rule "on the cheap" (event *A*) → empowerment of traditional chiefs and hands-off administration (event *B*) and maintenance of traditional agriculture (event *C*) and manipulation of ethnic divisions (event *D*) → patrimonial postcolonial state (event *E*). While Kohli certainly compares Korea and Nigeria, he does so by assessing the sequences of events in their colonial and postcolonial histories. The macro units differ because of the contrasting sets of events that constitute colonial and other processes in their histories.

CHA scholars employ different strategies when analyzing and aggregating events to compare sequences and processes. For example, Kohli's (2004) approach is to examine how similar processes are constituted by contrasting forms of events across different countries. Thus, Kohli studies events across countries that are part of the same kinds of colonial processes: colonial state building, colonial agricultural policy, and colonial political governance. These two countries differ because they sharply contrast in the events that constituted these processes, which also allows Kohli to generalize broadly about differences in processes of colonialism itself (e.g., intensive and transformative colonialism in Korea versus indirect and laissez-faire colonialism in Nigeria). Other scholars aggregate events based on their intensity or their temporal properties. For example, Skocpol's (1979) comparative study of social revolutions compares processes such as international pressure across cases by exploring how events endowed those processes with different intensities and durations. The differences at the level of events allow her to generalize across cases about differences in the nature of the process of international pressure.

Finally, it bears emphasis that, even with Millian methods, the analysis of sequences usually demands a focus on *combinations of factors*, not individual factors. These combinations are often temporal configurations. For example, with ordered sequences, the analyst explores combinations of temporally ordered causal factors, such as *AB* versus *BA*, treating each combination as an individual factor for the purposes of using Millian methods. Likewise, analysts may distinguish two sequences with the same basic events (e.g., *ABC*) on the basis of the duration of those events (e.g., whether event *B* was long or short in duration). This kind of comparative analysis is like QCA in that it puts the emphasis on the effects of packages of variables or configurations, not the effects of discrete individual variables. However, unlike atemporal versions of QCA, it assumes that the causal contribution of each event within a combination depends on its temporal characteristics and its temporal position within the configuration.

Process tracing

Process tracing is the foundational method of within-case analysis in CHA. Yet, the literature on process tracing has generally not explicitly engaged the literature on temporal analysis. Here we try to begin to correct that omission by linking process tracing to the analysis of sequences and the temporal effects of events as they unfold over time.

From the rapidly growing literature on process tracing (Beach and Pedersen 2013; Bennett and Checkel 2015; Kittel and Kuehn 2013), two basic logics of inquiry may be distinguished. The first mode of process tracing is an inductive approach in which the analyst derives propositions and formulates sequences from empirical observations (Hall 2013, 27). This mode of process tracing is often used for the purpose of *theory development* through the identification of key events and through the specification of hypotheses about how these events connect together to form sequences and processes. The second mode of process tracing embodies a deductive logic of inquiry, in which scholars deduce propositions from more basic premises and carry out (implicitly or explicitly) *process tracing tests*. This mode is often used to test specific causal claims that were initially formulated from inductive process tracing or derived theoretically. We discuss each logic in turn.

Inductive process tracing

Inductive process tracing is perhaps the most powerful method in CHA for formulating new theory. It is commonly used to identify the events that comprise the core sequences and processes at the center of most CHA works. Inductive process tracing plays a large role in the construction of any complex, conjunctural, and multilayered historical narrative, including – we presume – the Goldstone (1998) example summarized above. Inductive process tracing is essential to the enterprise because the analyst cannot anticipate in advance many of the key events that comprise sequences and processes of central analytic importance. As a result, inductive analysis must be used to formulate historical-sequential arguments in most CHA studies (Bennett and Elman 2006, 263).

Inductive process tracing operates on two levels. At one level, it allows for the discovery of specific events in a sequence that were not anticipated (i.e., novel theory generation). These discoveries may then lead the scholar to reformulate key aspects of the originating theory. At another level, the inductive approach is particularly useful for pulling out and assembling events into coherent and connected sequences. Inductive process tracing allows the CHA researcher to go back and forth between theory and events to build a coherent sequential argument that can then be evaluated further using other within-case tests or comparisons to other cases.

Inductive process tracing furthermore works well for identifying the events that comprise specific kinds of processes. With self-reproducing sequences, an inductive process tracing approach can help the analyst assess the amplitude of change (or lack of change) between events. In these sequences, the order of events might be theoretically deduced in advance, but the understanding of the extent to which the unfolding of events leads to a continuous reproduction of the underlying process of interest, the amplification of that process, or to its self-erosion will most likely require an in-depth analysis of the events and direction (or trajectory) of the sequence. At least to some degree, the process tracing researcher must let the events and their effects "speak for themselves" when establishing the specific logic of self-reproduction. The occurrences and events themselves – as found in the established historical evidence – can make it clear to the researcher whether a reactive or reproductive logic is at work, and, if the latter, whether that logic involves continuity, amplification, or erosion. When formulating theory and building sequential hypotheses, therefore, the process tracing researcher might be best served by not deploying too-strict theoretical expectations that could act as blinders and straightjacket the interpretation of the process under study.

Strictly temporal sequences also lend themselves naturally to the application of this kind of inductive process tracing. With these sequences, researchers do not propose or presume causal connections among the events of interest. Nor do they explore the historical material to determine whether a specific piece of evidence is present in order to carry out a process tracing test. Instead, they situate events from the historical record into a larger (temporal or spatial) context and analyze whether the order in which they unfold is consequential for the outcome of interest. For example, Caraway's (2004) recommendation of "episodic analysis" for single-country studies of democratization presupposes this approach. For Caraway, each episode corresponds to the inclusion of previously excluded groups based on class, gender, or race. Inductive process tracing allows the researcher to "consider the *sequencing* of the extension of democratic citizenship, the *extent to which previous expansions of the franchise affected the next round of democratization*, and the extent to which transnational factors altered domestic debates" (455, emphasis added). This approach to temporal sequences facilitates an in-depth analysis of the unfolding of events and their cumulative or interactive effects on the outcome of interest.

While inductive process tracing is significantly a tool for theory formulation, it has substantial implications for theory testing. In CHA, as in other modes of research, the omission of essential variables or the misspecification of relationships among variables can cause serious problems for causal analysis. Inductive process tracing is a key instrument for avoiding omitted variable bias and for formulating theories that are correctly specified. Both the capacity of CHA to generate new theory and the capacity of CHA to build theories that can withstand intense empirical scrutiny depend on sound inductive process tracing.

Process tracing tests

Process tracing tests – such as hoop tests and smoking gun tests – are also a central mode of within-case analysis used with the comparative sequential method (Bennett 2008; Collier 2011; Mahoney 2012; 4 Rohlfing 2013; Van Evera 1997). These tests have a deductive logic in which an analyst combines specific insights from a case with established principles and general knowledge to make a logical (deductive) inference about that case. When compared to inductive process tracing, deductive process tracing tests usually have a more focused purpose. They are often applied to specific links within inductively or deductively derived causal chains. They can be used to help show that controversial links in a sequence are in fact causal. Process tracing tests can also be used to determine whether specific hypotheses about ordering and pace are correct.

All process tracing tests leverage specific pieces of evidence, typically events from within a case. Scholars use the existence of certain events (or the absence of certain events) as their evidence for making inferences (Bennett 2008; Collier, Brady, and Seawright 2010; Mahoney 2010; McKeown 1999).[9] CHA researchers often actively search for specific revealing pieces of evidence in much the same way as a detective looks for key clues to solve a case.

For some hypotheses, a specific piece of evidence from within a case (e.g., the presence of some specific event) in effect *must* be present for the hypothesis to be true. This kind of evidence allows for a *hoop test*: the hypothesis must

---

[9] As Bennett (2008; Bennett and Colin 2006) points out, process tracing is closely analogous to Bayesian inference in the sense that the discovery of evidence can lead us to update our subjective beliefs about the validity of particular explanations (see also Humphreys and Jacobs 2013).

"jump through the hoop" (e.g., the event must be present) to warrant further consideration. Failing a hoop test in effect *eliminates* a hypothesis, but passing a hoop test does not confirm a hypothesis (though it can lend support for the hypothesis).

In other cases, the existence of a given event can strongly suggest the validity of a hypothesis. This kind of evidence allows for a *smoking gun test*: the evidence (e.g., the existence of the event) is strong proof that the hypothesis is correct. Passing a smoking gun test in effect *confirms* a hypothesis, though failing a smoking gun test does not disconfirm a hypothesis (but it can count against a hypothesis).

As an example of a hoop test, consider Luebbert's (1991, 308–9) critique of Gerschenkron's (1943) sequential argument about the origins of fascism in Germany. Gerschenkron links powerful landed elites to fascism via an electoral mechanism, arguing that landed elites are able to deliver rural electoral support to fascist parties by ensuring subordinate peasants support their candidates. Thus, the basic sequence is landed elites exercise control over peasantry (event *A*) → peasants vote for fascism (event *B*) → fascist electoral victory (outcome *Y*). Luebbert suggests that if Gerschenkron is correct, one should expect to observe rural electoral support for fascism in areas where landed elites predominate. In fact, however, Luebbert's historical research shows that rural support emanated from the family peasantry, not peasants controlled by labor-repressive landed elites. He therefore concludes that Gerschenkron's proposed causal sequence and event chronology cannot possibly be right: subordinate peasants did not deliver large number of votes for fascists in Germany.

A standard way of conducting hoop tests and smoking gun tests involves examining the intervening steps between *X* and *Y*. One can look for specific intervening events that should be present (or should be absent) to make the case that *X* causes *Y*. For example, in his comparative-historical explanation of failed industrialization in India, Chibber (2003) hypothesizes that the direct opposition of domestic capitalists blocked state managers from building the institutions that could sustain successful industrialization during the critical juncture of 1947–51. To test this hypothesis, he suggests that one should be able to find evidence that efforts by big industry (e.g., lobbying, personal pleas, slowing down investment) actually influenced state managers and changed the direction of state policy and institution building. The discovery of this evidence by Chibber amounts to passing a difficult hoop test, which lends support for his overall argument about the role of domestic capitalists as key cause of failed industrialization.

Process tracing tests often leverage the fact that it is easier to establish causal connections between temporally proximate events than between temporally distant events. For example, imagine that one seeks to show that X is necessary for Y. The challenge is often to find a well-established causal connection in which a more proximate event E is necessary for Y. If one can then show that X is necessary for E, one can make the logical inference that X must also be necessary for Y (this inference takes the form of a smoking gun test). Likewise, if one knows that the proximate E is sufficient for Y, and one can show that a more remote X is sufficient for E, then one can reason logically that X must also be sufficient for Y. This is the kind of reasoning that animates Rueschemeyer, Stephens, and Stephens's (1992) sequential argument about capitalist development and democracy, discussed above. They connect together temporally proximate sufficient links to make a long but compelling causal chain; the overall claim that capitalist development is approximately sufficient for democracy is built from the sufficiency links in the chain.

To illustrate how this kind of sequence elaboration can work with a smoking gun test, it is helpful to return to the environmental causal sequence in the Goldstone example above (see Figure 8.1). How do we know the contextual feature A (i.e., limited forest area, abundant coal near sea, and cold climate) is causally connected to the outcome M (i.e., the development of the first steam engine)? Goldstone persuades readers by appealing to the tightly coupled events that compose the middle of the sequence (i.e., B, C, D, and E). In effect, he makes a logical inference about the connection between A and M on the basis of his confidence in the validity of these intervening steps. His narrative suggests that the connection for each small step is highly plausible, intuitive, or even obvious. On this basis, he can deduce that it is extremely likely that A is also connected to M.

Process tracing tests can also be used for hypotheses concerning temporal ordering or pace. One possibility is to carry out a test with counterfactual analysis: one imagines a different ordering or a different pace. If the counterfactual thought experiment makes it clear that a different outcome would have followed, one has, in effect, carried out a smoking gun test. In some cases, an alternative order seems almost inconceivable. For example, in Goldstone's narrative one cannot imagine the improvement of the steam engine without first allowing for the invention of the steam engine. Likewise, Falleti (2010, 57–8) counterfactually argues that if after an initial political decentralization reform a reactive (instead of self-reinforcing) type of mechanism were to ensue, the second type of decentralization reform to be adopted likely would be administrative (instead of fiscal) decentralization, leading to a lower degree of power for subnational officials.

Finally, process tracing tests are often used implicitly when scholars construct arguments about the mechanisms driving self-reproducing sequences. The processes underlying these sequences consist of causally connected events; in turn, the connections among these events can be evaluated with process tracing tests. Consider, for example, the self-eroding process that Onoma (2010) documents for property rights in Kenya. The erosion of property rights begins in the early postcolonial period with small-scale fraud carried out by conmen posing as real estate agents. These fraudsters are successful precisely because the colonial period left behind a relatively functional land rights system that established trust among individuals buying and selling property. In time, however, the process of fraud spreads as more and more conmen became active; it reaches a culmination point when high-level politicians themselves become key agents of land fraud. To establish that early episodes of fraud generated later ones, Onoma searches for and finds much evidence that criminals and, later, politicians learned from prior examples. In effect, Onoma shows that his hypothesis can pass a hoop test: if events did not show a process of copying and learning by example, the hypothesis about a self-reproducing cycle of fraud likely would be wrong. But the evidence is present, which, while not fully confirming his argument, adds support in its favor.

To conclude this section, process tracing – inductive and deductive – is an indispensable component of CHA work. It is a central tool that CHA researchers use for establishing causal linkages between events when constructing sequences. In conjunction with cross-case comparison, it is essential to the family of methods that compose the comparative sequential method.

Conclusion

The comparative sequential method is the basic overarching approach used by CHA researchers to formulate arguments and make inferences. On the one hand, this method is a set of tools and concepts for constructing different types of sequences and processes. On the other hand, it encompasses a set of cross-case and within-case methodologies for making causal inferences. Thus, the comparative sequential method brings together two literatures that rarely are connected explicitly: the literature on temporality and the literature on case-study methods of causal inference. Elucidating the comparative sequential method invites a conversation among these literatures.

First, concerning the temporal components of the comparative sequential method, specific historical occurrences within cases are the starting point of the method. These occurrences are typically cast as more general events, which in turn form the building blocks of sequences. Sequences, as they unfold within certain contexts, then are at the very heart of much CHA work. They are often the central units of analysis and the main components of comparison. Comparative-historical work, including work focused on a single national unit, is comparative in part because different sequences of events are systematically juxtaposed. Sequences themselves may be causal or strictly temporal; they may be temporally ordered or temporally paced. Processes, a subset of temporal sequences, may also be differentiated according to whether they follow a self-reproducing or reactive logic. Among self-reproducing processes, further important distinctions concern whether their logic is continuous, self-amplifying, or self-eroding.

Second, concerning its methodological tools, the comparative sequential method often involves the use of variants of Millian methods, but these methods are usually applied to sequences and processes, not whole cases as traditionally understood. For some sequences, such as ordered sequences, cross-case comparison is essential to the analysis because it allows the researcher to avoid having to depend on only counterfactual reasoning when making causal inferences. The comparison of sequences and processes also underscores the fact that CHA is typically focused on combinations of factors – causal configurations – rather than individual variables viewed in isolation.

For within-case analysis, process tracing is the central method used with the comparative sequential method. For analytic purposes, we distinguish inductive and deductive applications of process tracing. Inductive modes of process tracing are commonly used to identify key events and arrange them into coherent sequences and processes. Among other things, inductive process tracing allows the researcher to carry out an in-depth analysis of the unfolding of events when the events are not presumed to be causally linked or when they follow an ongoing process of self-reproduction, such as amplification or erosion. Process tracing tests, such as hoop tests and smoking gun tests, are at the core of deductive uses of process tracing. These tests are routinely used in conjunction with causal sequences and reactive sequences, given that these kinds of sequences are composed of tightly coupled events whose causal linkages can be established through specific pieces of within-case data. Process tracing tests are often applied after the analyst has carried out inductive process tracing and initially specified tentative linkages among events in sequences.

CHA is a field that is centrally concerned with – indeed, centrally animated by – the study of both time and causality. These two components of CHA become thoroughly integrated and work together with the comparative sequential method. By fusing these two elements, the comparative sequential method arguably merits the distinction of being the principal overarching methodology for CHA in general.

References

Abbott, Andrew. 2001. *Time Matters: On Theory and Method.* Chicago: University of Chicago Press.

Ahmed, Amel. 2013. *Democracy and the Politics of Electoral System Choice: Engineering Electoral Dominance.* New York: Cambridge University Press.

Aminzade, Ronald. 1992. "Historical Sociology and Time." *Sociological Methods and Research* 20:456–80.

Arthur, W. Brian. 1994. *Increasing Returns and Path Dependence in the Economy.* Ann Arbor: University of Michigan Press.

Barrenechea, Rodrigo, Edward Gibson, and Larkin Terrie. Forthcoming. "Historical Institutionalism in Democratization Studies." In *The Oxford Handbook of Historical Institutionalism*, edited by O. Fioretos, T. G. Falleti, and A. Sheingate. Oxford: Oxford University Press.

Beach, Derek, and Pasmus Brun Pederson. 2013. *Process Tracing Methods: Foundations and Guidelines.* Ann Arbor: University of Michigan Press.

Bennett, Andrew. 2008. "Process Tracing: A Bayesian Perspective." In *The Oxford Handbook of Political Methodology*, edited by Janet Box-Steffensmeier, Henry E. Brady, and David Collier, 217–70. Oxford: Oxford University Press.

Bennett, Andrew, and Jeffrey Checkel, eds. 2015. *Process Tracing: From Metaphor to Analytic Tool.* Cambridge: Cambridge University Press.

Bennett, Andrew, and Colin Elman. 2006. "Complex Causal Relations and Case Study Methods: The Example of Path Dependence." *Political Analysis* 14:250–67.

Campbell, Donald T. 1975. "'Degrees of Freedom' and the Case Study." *Comparative Political Studies* 8:178–93.

Caraway, Teri L. 2004. "Inclusion and Democratization: Class, Gender, Race, and the Extension of Suffrage." *Comparative Politics* 36 (4): 443–60.

Castiglioni, Rossana. 2014. "Paths to Welfare: Class Coalitions, Ideas, and Party Politics in Chile and Uruguay." Paper presented at the REPAL Annual Conference, Instituto de Ciencia Política, Universidad Católica de Chile, Santiago, Chile.

Chibber, Vivek. 2003. *Locked in Place: State-Building and Late Industrialization in India.* Princeton, NJ: Princeton University Press.

Collier, David. 1993. "The Comparative Method." In *Political Science: The State of the Discipline II*, edited by Ada Finifter, 105–19. Washington, DC: American Political Science Association.

　2011. "Understanding Process Tracing." *PS: Political Science and Politics* 44 (4): 823–30.

Collier, David, Henry E. Brady, and Jason Seawright. 2010. "Sources of Leverage in Causal Inference: Toward an Alternative View of Methodology." In *Rethinking Social Inquiry: Diverse Tools, Shared Standards*, 2nd ed., edited by Henry E. Brady and David Collier, 161–99. Lanham, MD: Rowman and Littlefield.

Collier, Ruth Berins, and David Collier. 1991. *Shaping the Political Arena: Critical Junctures, the Labor Movement, and Regime Dynamics in Latin America.* Princeton, NJ: Princeton University Press.

Dahl, Robert A. 1971. *Polyarchy: Participation and Opposition.* New Haven, CT: Yale University Press.

David, Paul A. 1985. "Clio and the Economics of QWERTY." *American Economic Review* 75:332–7.

Ertman, Thomas. 1997. *Birth of the Leviathan: Building States and Regimes in Medieval and Early Modern Europe.* Cambridge: Cambridge University Press.

Falleti, Tulia G. 2010. *Decentralization and Subnational Politics in Latin America.* New York: Cambridge University Press.

Falleti, Tulia G., and Julia Lynch. 2009. "Context and Causation in Political Analysis." *Comparative Political Studies* 49 (9): 1143–66.

George, Alexander L., and Andrew Bennett. 2005. *Case Studies and Theory Development in the Social Sciences.* Cambridge, MA: MIT Press.

Gerring, John. 2007. *Case Study Research: Principles and Practices.* New York: Cambridge University Press.

Gerschenkron, Alexander. 1943. *Bread and Democracy in Germany.* Ithaca, NY: Cornell University Press.

Goldstone, Jack A. 1998. "The Problem of the 'Early Modern' World." *Journal of Economic and Social History of the Orient* 41:249–84.

Griffin, Larry J. 1992. "Temporality, Events, and Explanation in Historical Sociology: An Introduction." *Sociological Methods and Research* 20:403–27.

Grzymala-Busse, Anna. 2011. "Time Will Tell? Temporality and the Analysis of Causal Mechanisms and Processes." *Comparative Political Studies* 44:1267–97.

Hacker, Jacob S. 1998. "The Historical Logic of National Health Insurance: Structure and Sequence in the Development of British, Canadian, and U.S. Medical Policy." *Studies in American Political Development* 12 (1): 57–130.

　2002. *The Divided Welfare State: The Battle over Public and Private Social Benefits in the United States.* New York: Cambridge University Press.

Hall, Peter A. 2013. "Tracing the Progress of Process Tracing." *European Political Science* 12:20–30.

Humphreys, Macartan, and Alan Jacobs. 2013. "Mixing Methods: A Bayesian Integration of Qualitative and Quantitative Inferences." Paper presented at the Annual Meeting of the American Political Science Association, Chicago.

Jacobs, Alan M. 2008. "The Politics of When: Redistribution, Investment, and the Politics of the Long Term." *British Journal of Political Science* 38 (2): 193–220.

2010. "Policymaking as Political Constraint: Institutional Development in the U.S. Social Security Program." In *Explaining Institutional Change: Ambiguity, Agency, and Power*, edited by James Mahoney and Kathleen Thelen, 94–131. New York: Cambridge University Press.

Kohli, Atul. 2004. *State-Directed Development: Political Power and Industrialization in the Global Periphery*. New York: Cambridge University Press.

Lieberman, Evan S. 2005. "Nested Analysis as a Mixed-Method Strategy for Comparative Research." *American Political Science Review* 99 (3): 435–52.

Luebbert, Gregory M. 1991. *Liberalism, Fascism, or Social Democracy: Social Classes and the Political Origins of Regimes in Interwar Europe*. New York: Oxford University Press.

Mahoney, James. 1999. "Nominal, Ordinal, and Narrative Appraisal in Macrocausal Analysis." *American Journal of Sociology* 104 (4): 1154–96.

2000. "Path Dependence in Historical Sociology." *Theory and Society* 29:507–48.

2010. *Colonialism and Postcolonial Development: Spanish America in Comparative Perspective*. New York: Cambridge University Press.

2012. "The Logic of Process Tracing Tests in the Social Sciences." *Sociological Methods and Research* 41:566–90.

McKeown, Timothy J. 1999. "Case Studies and the Statistical Worldview: Review of King, Keohane, and Verba's Designing Social Inquiry." *International Organization* 53:161–90.

Moore, Barrington Jr. 1966. *Social Origins of Dictatorship and Democracy: Lord and Peasant in the Making of the Modern World*. Boston: Beacon Press.

Onoma, Ato Kwamena. 2010. "The Contradictory Potential of Institutions: The Rise and Decline of Land Documentation in Kenya." In *Explaining Institutional Change: Ambiguity, Agency, and Power*, edited by James Mahoney and Kathleen Thelen, 63–93. New York: Cambridge University Press.

Pierson, Paul. 2000. "Increasing Returns, Path Dependence, and the Study of Politics." *American Political Science Review* 94:251–67.

2004. *Politics in Time: History, Institutions, and Social Analysis*. Princeton, NJ: Princeton University Press.

Prasad, Monica. 2012. *The Land of Too Much: American Abundance and the Paradox of Poverty*. Cambridge, MA: Harvard University Press.

Ragin, Charles C. 2000. *Fuzzy-Set Social Science*. Chicago: University of Chicago Press.

2008. *Redesigning Social Inquiry: Fuzzy Sets and Beyond*. Chicago: University of Chicago Press.

Riofrancos, Thea. 2014. "Contesting Extraction: State-Making, Democracy and Large Scale Mining in Ecuador." PhD diss., Department of Political Science, University of Pennsylvania, Philadelphia.

Rohlfing, Ingo. 2014. "Comparative Hypothesis Testing via Process Tracing." *Sociological Methods and Research*, 43 (4): 606–42.

Rosenblatt, Fernando. 2013. "How to Party? Static and Dynamic Party Survival in Latin American Consolidated Democracies." PhD diss., Instituto de Ciencia Política, Pontificia Universidad Católica de Chile.

Rueschemeyer, Dietrich. 2003. "Can One or a Few Cases Yield Theoretical Gains?" In *Comparative Historical Analysis in the Social Sciences*, edited by James Mahoney and Dietrich Rueschemeyer, 305–36. New York: Cambridge University Press.

Rueschemeyer, Dietrich, and John D. Stephens. 1997. "Comparing Historical Sequences – A Powerful Tool for Causal Analysis." *Comparative Social Research* 17:55–72.

Rueschemeyer, Dietrich, Evelyne Huber Stephens, and John D. Stephens. 1992. *Capitalist Development and Democracy.* Chicago: University of Chicago Press.

Rustow, Dankwart A. 1970. "Transitions to Democracy: Toward a Dynamic Model." *Comparative Politics* 2 (3): 337–63.

Sewell, William H. Jr. 1996. "Three Temporalities: Toward an Eventful Sociology." In *The Historic Turn in the Human Sciences*, edited by Terrence J. McDonald, 245–80. Ann Arbor: University of Michigan Press.

Skocpol, Theda. 1979. *States and Social Revolutions: A Comparative Analysis of France, Russia, and China.* Cambridge: Cambridge University Press.

   1999. "Why I Am a Historical Social Scientist." *Extensions: Journal of the Carl Albert Congressional Research and Studies Center*, pp. 16–19.

Smith, Benjamin. 2007. *Hard Times in the Lands of Plenty: Oil Politics in Iran and Indonesia.* Ithaca, NY: Cornell University Press.

Soifer, Hillel David. 2012. "The Causal Logic of Critical Junctures." *Comparative Political Studies* 45:1572–97.

Spruyt, Hendrik. 1994. *The Sovereign State and Its Competitors: An Analysis of Systems Change.* Princeton, NJ: Princeton University Press.

Stinchcombe, Arthur L. 1968. *Constructing Social Theories.* Chicago: University of Chicago Press.

Tannenwald, Nina. 2008. *The Nuclear Taboo: The United States and the Non-Use of Nuclear Weapons Since 1945.* New York: Cambridge University Press.

Thelen, Kathleen. 1999. "Historical Institutionalism in Comparative Politics." *Annual Review of Political Science* 2:369–404.

   2003. "How Institutions Evolve: Insights from Comparative-Historical Analysis." In *Comparative-Historical Analysis in the Social Sciences*, edited by James Mahoney and Dietrich Rueschemeyer, 208–40. New York: Cambridge University Press.

Van Evera, Stephen. 1997. *Guide to Methods for Students of Political Science.* Ithaca, NY: Cornell University Press.

Wood, Elisabeth Jean. 2000. *Forging Democracy from Below: Insurgent Transitions in South Africa and El Salvador.* New York: Cambridge University Press.

Nested analysis: toward the integration of comparative-historical analysis with other social science methods

Evan S. Lieberman

In the decade following publication of the original edited volume, *Comparative Historical Analysis in the Social Sciences* (Mahoney and Rueschemeyer 2003), multimethod research became an important strand of comparative-historical analysis, which now warrants attention and reflection. Almost one-third of books published between 2003 and 2013 at leading university presses using comparative-historical analysis (CHA) also employ some form of quantitative analysis. In this chapter, I review the motivation for multimethod research and focus on a single variant, which I call "nested analysis." I use that discussion as a point of departure for considering the possible integration of CHA with other forms of empirical analysis, including matching analyses and experimental methods.

The integration of multiple methods is not merely a defensive strategy to address the "few cases, many variables" critique that has long been leveled at canonical "small-N" comparative scholarship, such as Moore (1966), Skocpol (1979), Hall (1986), and Collier and Collier (1991). Mahoney and others have written extensively on the underappreciated leverage associated with the detailed over-time analyses contained in these seminal volumes and in CHA more generally (Gerring 2004; Lieberman 2001; Mahoney 1999). And Collier, Brady, and Seawright (2004) provide useful vocabulary with their notion of "causal process observations," and contributors to their volume offered a balanced view to methodology in political science. Building on these strengths, the integration of methodological approaches has sought to leverage additional synergies for identifying causal mechanisms, addressing plausible rival explanations, and providing additional testable implications of central propositions. When done well, mixed methods research ought to substantially enhance the credibility of the social scientific claims being made.

My goal in this chapter is to review the prospects for successfully integrating CHA with other types of empirical methods, especially quantitative and experimental approaches. But before I proceed any further, let me make clear three key points that structure the discussion.

First, the benefits of the methods I discuss herein are for the uncovering of general patterns that transcend just a few historically specific cases. For all sorts of obvious reasons, scholars may be primarily motivated by an interest in key cases – for example, countries of interest – but the approaches discussed here assume that a larger set of cases can both inform and be informed by the analysis of just a few. Whereas the analyst must specify the scope of the relevant universe of cases, the approaches discussed here assume that the larger set is sufficiently large to make in-depth investigation of all cases a practical impossibility.

Second, and relatedly, I consider probabilistic, not deterministic, causal relationships. In particular, I consider the sweet spot for nested analysis to be the overlapping research space Mahoney (2008) describes in which causation is understood in terms of likelihoods and probabilities: "a cause increases the probability that an outcome will take place" (415) – a notion of causation generally associated with Holland and Rubin (e.g., Holland 1986; Holland and Rubin 1988). This is a generally unrestrictive condition, as most comparatively oriented theory is structured around a logic of at least partial indeterminacy and assumes that most social and political processes are stochastic ones. Rare is the political scientist or sociologist who would fail to translate Moore's claim of "no bourgeoisie, no democracy" as "without a bourgeoisie, democracy is unlikely." Notwithstanding, much conventional small-N analysis, relying on Mill's methods or related Boolean logic, is designed to facilitate making inferences concerning the necessary or sufficient conditions for particular outcomes. The types of mixed methods approaches I discuss in this essay are not well suited for testing such strong deterministic claims.

And, third, while this essay does not attempt to provide a full primer on CHA methods (see other contributions to this volume; Gerring 2004; Lijphart 1971; Mahoney 1999; Mahoney and Reuschemeyer 2003), I assume that what constitutes CHA is much more than a superficial description of the names of the main actors and key variables of interest. The value of CHA is rooted in a scholar's mastery of sufficient source material to be able to speak with some confidence about the quality of available data (see Lieberman 2010) and the motivations and strategies of key actors within a particular context (Falleti and Lynch 2009). A high-quality CHA should attempt to explain why a particular account of a sequence of events is the correct one, addressing, for example, concerns about historiographical debates (Lustick 1996), highlighting moments and periods considered to be highly consequential, perhaps as critical junctures (Collier and Collier 1991, Pierson 2000), or doing both. Whereas the inclusion of "mini" case studies alongside large-N results may provide some additional value added in terms of heuristic understandings of the theory or evidence, the analytic gains are minimal and my focus here is on richer, more scholarly and authoritative accounts of particular historical processes unfolding over time.

In the remainder of this chapter, I provide a sketch of the nested analysis approach, consider and respond to some critiques of the approach, and conclude with some views about the potential frontiers for multimethod comparative-historical research and analysis. Throughout this discussion, I take the position that CHA continues to have the potential to enhance the body of scholarship, particularly in the subfield of comparative politics. The clear juxtaposition of macrolevel outcomes of substantial interest in just one or a few cases against other cases with contrasting outcomes continues to be a key source for motivating the most important questions in the field. Detailed and semistructured comparisons also continue to be a rich source of discovery and theoretical innovation; the plausibility of claims ultimately requires commensurate illustration through careful historical research. While quantitative, microlevel, and experimental approaches are also critical for uncovering key patterns about the social and political worlds, our ability to carry out such studies and to interpret our findings demands some attention to the qualitative, macrolevel understanding of how history has actually unfolded in different times and places.

Overview of research strategies and a focus on nested analysis

In Figure 9.1, I highlight what I take to be three critical dimensions of variation in empirical social science research analyses: (1) level or unit of analysis: whether the primary objects of analysis are individuals (micro) or collective or institutional outcomes and patterns, in which the researcher analyzes aggregates of individuals (macro); (2) sample size and mode of analysis: the extent to which the research focuses on just one or a few key cases (qualitative/small-N) or uses statistical methods to analyze many cases (quantitative/large-N); and (3) source of variation in key explanatory variables: the extent to which the research relies upon investigator-randomized treatments (experimental) or not (observational).[1] Archetypal single-method approaches are those that

---

[1] Much of this section is condensed from Lieberman (2005).

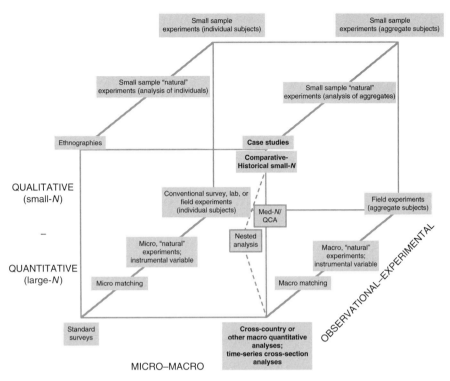

Figure 9.1   A typology of contemporary social science

can be usefully classified in one of the corners, while a hybrid approach such as Ragin's Fuzzy-Set Qualitative Comparative Analysis[2] or other "medium-N" approaches (i.e., Glynn and Ichino 2014) fall somewhere between two corners on a single axis. (Indeed, to the extent that CHA employs several cases and many time periods, such an approach is more accurately located as falling somewhat below the upper-right-front corner.) Similarly, the identification and analysis of "natural" experiments, in which some treatment can be plausibly interpreted as having been assigned "as if" random (Dunning 2012), is a method that falls somewhere in the middle of the axis distinguishing observational from experimental research. (Later in this chapter, I discuss some key distinctions among studies labeled as "natural experiments.")

Within the schema presented in Figure 9.1, each dimension could be further nuanced (for example, making distinctions between "big data" analyses

---

[2] See Schneider and Rohlfing (2013) for a discussion of combining process tracing/small-N analysis with qualitative comparative analysis.

of data sets of more than a million observations and "standard" quantitative analyses). It is beyond the scope of this chapter to fully describe each of these dimensions and each of the identified research methods and strategies. The larger point to be made is that CHA plays a critical role in agenda setting within the broader corpus of politically oriented social science research. Studies employing CHA have helped to motivate the big questions such as "Why are some countries democratic and others are not?" "Why are some states stronger/weaker than others?" and "Why have some countries grown more rapidly than others?" primarily by juxtaposing contrasting cases. Research located in the other corners of the cube use distinctive strategies for uncovering patterns related to these larger questions.

And within this framework, "mixed methods" approaches are those that *combine* strategies, typically from two or more points along the edges of the cube. As such, *multimethod analysis* implies a broad family of approaches to research that may include studies that combine different measurement strategies (i.e., surveys and focus groups) as well as studies that approach different *levels* of analysis in different ways – for example, a case study of electoral law in a single country that also considered quantitative analysis of survey data.

Nested analysis is one such approach that combines quantitative and qualitative analyses at the same macro level of analysis, such that the case study units are also observations within the quantitative data set (for example, country case studies and a data set of country cases). It gains analytic leverage by combining small-N analysis (SNA) and large-N analysis (LNA) of observational data within a single framework (summarized in Figure 9.2). I define LNA as a mode of analysis in which the primary causal inferences are derived from statistical analyses; I define SNA as a mode of analysis in which the primary causal inferences are derived from qualitative comparisons of cases or process tracing of causal chains within cases across time and in which the relationship between theory and facts is captured largely in narrative form. Using alternative strategies, both attempt to ascertain whether the value of the outcome variable(s) of interest would have been different with different values on the "treatment" or causal variable(s). In both cases, claims about the causal influence of X on Y rest on the ignorability assumption that once we have controlled for a certain set of observable factors, the particular value of X for any given case was generated more or less randomly and, importantly, is not itself a function of the outcome of interest. Of course, experimentalists tend to charge that both approaches rest on shaky grounds with respect to that assumption, which in turn can be addressed only through randomization

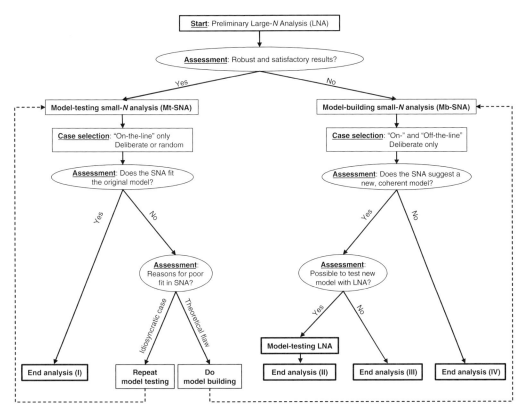

Figure 9.2   Overview of the nested analysis approach
Source: From Lieberman (2005).

of assignment, whereas observationalists would counter that, for practical or ethical reasons, a great many questions of interest cannot be studied through experimentation and that we ought to slog through as best as we can, even if we must sometimes rest heavily on such assumptions (Gerring 2011).

The strategy of combining the two approaches aims to improve the quality of conceptualization and measurement, analysis of rival explanations, and overall confidence in the central findings of a study. The promise of the nested research design is that both LNA and SNA can inform each other to the extent that the analytic payoff is greater than the sum of the parts. Not only is the information gleaned hopefully complementary, but each step of the analysis should provide direction for approaching the next step. Most prominently, LNA provides insights about rival explanations and helps to motivate case selection strategies for SNA, while SNA helps to improve the quality of measurement instruments and model specifications used in the LNA.

As a thumbnail sketch, the approach involves starting with a preliminary LNA and making an assessment of the robustness of those results. If the model is deemed to be well specified and provides robust results, one proceeds to model testing small-*N* analysis, and if not, to model building small-*N* analysis. In each case, as shown in Figure 9.2, the analyst must again make assessments about the findings from such analysis, using directions and insights gleaned from the SNA. Those assessments provide a framework for either ending the analysis or carrying out additional iterations of SNA or LNA. Although not all small-*N* analysis is of the comparative-historical variety, CHA is a particularly useful approach when trying to answer the types of macrohistorical questions described by Thelen and Mahoney (Chapter 1, this volume).

Nested analysis is resolutely "catholic" in its assumptions and objectives. It assumes an interest in *both* the exploration of general relationships and explanations as well as specific explanations of individual cases and groups of cases. For example, a nested research design implies that scholars will pose questions in forms such as "What causes social revolutions?" while simultaneously asking questions such as "What was the cause of social revolution in France?" Nested analysis helps scholars to ask good questions when analyzing their data and to be resourceful in finding answers.

Starting the analysis: preliminary large-*N* analysis

While scholars typically engage new research projects with varying levels of background information about a specific case or set of cases, and indeed may be motivated by the findings of a case study analysis, the nested analysis formally *begins* with a quantitative analysis, or preliminary LNA. Thus, a prerequisite for carrying out a nested analysis is availability of a quantitative data set, with a sufficient number of observations for statistical analysis,[3] and a baseline theory. Particularly for scholars who would have carried out SNA exclusively, the preliminary LNA requires explicit consideration of the universe of cases for which the theory ought to apply and identification of the range of variation on the dependent variable. It also provides opportunities to generate clear baseline estimates of the strength of the relationship between variables, including estimates of how confident we can be about those relationships.

---

[3] There is no clear lower bound for the number of cases that can be analyzed through a statistical analysis, but fewer cases obviously reduce the degrees of freedom and intrinsic power of the analysis. It is rare to see quantitative analyses of fewer than twelve cases in cross-country regression analyses.

A core strength of LNA relative to SNA is its ability to simultaneously estimate the effects of rival explanations and control variables on an outcome of interest. To a large extent, SNA in the field of comparative politics has relied upon variants of Mill's methods in order to address country-level rival explanations – that is, scholars identify cases that score similarly on several key variables, using shared traits as a basis for analytical equivalence approximating statistical control.[4] While the strategy of identifying cases with relatively similar scores on such variables can be a powerful one, in a nonexperimental setting important differences between cases can almost always be identified, and these emerge as possible rival explanations. Depending upon the question or the cases under investigation, LNA may be able to lend a hand. Assuming that the LNA is conducted as regression analysis, the relevant dependent variable can be regressed on measures of the rival explanatory variables under investigation in order to assess the strength of a relationship, particularly when the SNA is not able to shed light.

At least as important as its ability to address rival explanations is LNA's relatively stronger capacity for assessing the strength of partial explanations or control variables. Because country-level outcomes tend to be the product of several factors, preliminary LNA is likely to find that some variables *are* significant predictors of the outcome under investigation, even if they can account for only a limited portion of the large sample variance. Much small-N research involves the comparison of "similar" cases. However, because we only observe cases in which there is little to no variation on key control variables, we have weak leverage for making inferences about the need to condition our analyses on those variables or about how strong an influence we should expect those variables to have on the outcomes under investigation within a broader population of cases. The "puzzle" of a particular case or set of cases can be made clear when we have some estimate of predicted outcomes given a set of parameter estimates and the case scores on those variables.[5] Unlike in large-sample experiments, where we might be fairly confident that the control and treated groups are relatively similar owing to randomization, when it comes to small-N research, we can make no such assumptions and LNA provides some leverage for identifying relevant controls. (But, again, as I

---

[4] See Gerring (2001, 209–14) for a summary of these methods, often understood as "most similar" and "most different" systems research designs.

[5] While it is true that these initial parameter estimates are likely to be biased because of model misspecifications, including missing variable bias, our presumption is that when we do not have a fully specified or complete theoretical model, it is useful to gain a sense of what can be explained by the theory and data that *are* available.

discuss later, the introduction and proliferation of *matching* methods seek to specifically address the lack of balance between treatment and control groups in many regression-based studies.)

Assessing the findings of the LNA: are the results robust and satisfactory?

Beyond providing insights into the range of variation on the dependent variable, and estimates of the strength of rival hypotheses and control variables, LNA also provides important information about how to carry out the next stage of the analysis – intensive examination of one or more cases. First, the scholar must assess the findings: did the preliminary LNA lend credibility to the initial theoretical model?

As noted above, it is not possible to provide absolute criteria for answering the question about the robustness of the LNA results because subjective assessments about the state of knowledge and what constitutes strong evidence weigh heavily.[6] Depending upon the nature of the LNA, standard assessments about the strength of parameter estimates must be used to evaluate goodness of fit between the specified model and the empirical data. Nonetheless, one important tool is central to the nested analysis approach: the actual scores of the cases should be plotted graphically relative to the predicted scores from the statistical estimate,[7] and with proper names attached. This provides an opportunity to make specific assessments of the goodness of model fit with the available cases.

In combination with the parameter estimates generated from the LNA, the scholar must decide whether the unexplained variance is largely the product of random error or if there is reason to believe that a better model/explanation could be formulated. As in any statistical analysis, diagnostic plots may highlight suspect patterns of nonrandom variation in one or more cases – the identification of outliers. However, unlike in surveys of individuals, where case identities are anonymous, in the study of national states and many other macrolevel outcomes, the location of specific cases with respect to the regression line may strongly influence one's satisfaction with the model. For example, a scholar may feel unsatisfied with a model that cannot explain a case perceived to be of great significance within the scholarly literature (e.g., the French Revolution in the study of revolutions), or the identification

---

[6] For a classic statement on the use of common sense and professional judgment in the use of quantitative analysis, see Achen (1982), especially pp. 29–30.

[7] At the extreme, if no statistical relationship is found between any of the explanatory variables and the outcome of interest, one could simply use a central tendency of the data, such as the mean, as a baseline model, and country cases could be plotted as deviations from the mean.

of an outlier case may immediately suggest a new theoretical specification with potentially broader application. If a scholar enters the research project with specific hunches about seemingly anomalous outcomes, analysis of the actual-versus-predicted-scores plot may demonstrate that one or more cases are indeed outliers that may warrant more theoretical attention.

Using such analyses, the scholar can answer the questions, "Were all of the most important hypotheses tested? And were the results robust/satisfactory?" The answers to these questions inform the approach to the nested case analyses, or SNA, as described below.

Nesting intensive case studies (SNA) into the analysis

The second major step of the nested analysis involves the intensive analysis of one or more cases, typically using the types of CHA discussed throughout this volume. It is important to recall that the goal of a nested analysis is ultimately to make inferences about a broader population, which is typically larger than the small sample *and* the large sample. In pursuing this goal, a nested analysis requires a *shifting* of levels of analysis because the SNA component demands an examination of *within*-case processes or variation.[8] The SNA should be used to answer those questions left open by the LNA – typically, questions about causal processes but also important questions about the fit between data and concepts. For example, in a hypothetical study of the determinants of government policy, in which the LNA confirmed a hypothesized relationship between institutional form and policy outcome, the SNA would likely provide detailed and nuanced characterizations of those policies and investigate the specific actions of groups and individuals within a given country. This would be done in an attempt to find specific evidence that the patterns of human organization and action hypothesized to have been influenced by the institutional form were actually manifest in reality. Moreover, the SNA is particularly useful for investigating the impact of rival explanations for which we lack good data for the larger sample of cases. Historically oriented comparisons provide a powerful analytic strategy for evaluating the alignment between theory and data, again in ways that are often left open following the presentation of even confirmatory statistical evidence.

LNA and SNA can provide distinct and synergistic insights for analysis of a common problem, working together in pursuit of making inferences about causal relationships. Here, it is extremely useful to highlight the distinction

---

[8] See Gerring (2004) for a discussion of within-unit analysis in case studies, and for a more general discussion of contrasting case study research and cross-case study analysis.

between a "dataset observation," which responds to a row in a rectangular data set, and a "causal-process observation," which is "the foundation for process-oriented causal inference. [It] provides information about mechanism and context" (Collier, Brady, and Seawright 2004, 253). We can say that LNA is, by definition, rooted largely in the analysis of data set observations, while the hallmark of SNA is typically a much smaller number of data set observations *and* a host of causal process observations. The number of rows in a data set is generally understood to be the number of country cases, or N, that distinguishes small-N and large-N research. By now, most methodologists agree that even a small-N – that is, two-country study – will have many more than just two observations, and as Collier, Brady, and Seawright (2004) point out, different inferential strategies are used to interpret such data. In an analogous manner (thanks to Richard Nielsen for making this point), statistical analyses of data sets almost always incorporate some additional contextual knowledge in order to make inferences about relationships between variables, especially with respect to causation. Most important, scholars are called upon to defend claims about "assignment to treatment," or the degree to which values on causal variables were generated by random chance.

The focus of SNA is to investigate within-case processes and patterns, which, in turn, generally entail the scrutiny of a heterogeneous set of materials, including printed documents, interviews, and visual observations. These provide important information about the social phenomena we seek to understand. Because such materials are produced in such different shapes and forms across time and space, it is often impossible to specify a priori a set of very precise coding rules that would allow for an easily repeatable data collection and analysis process. (However, certain contemporary forms of communication and expression via the Internet are beginning to break down such barriers.) These materials provide more fine-grained measurements of a host of events and behaviors, at both the micro and macro levels and often in close temporal proximity to one another. For certain problems, and given the nature of various historical records, such data may be virtually impossible to capture across large numbers of countries in a consistent manner. Scholars gain analytic leverage when they scrutinize the theoretical implications of these observations, either by testing existing hypotheses or by inductively developing new propositions about general relationships between causes and effects.

What constitutes sufficient evidence? Currently, small-N scholars lack the analog of a priori power analyses. The very nature of "causal process observations" is that they are highly heterogeneous: some documented observations may serve as particularly powerful smoking gun evidence linking cause to effect, while others may simply serve as incremental steps that increase the plausibility of a set of theoretical claims. Small-N analysis provides the opportunity to implement various quasi-experimental explorations by looking at the impact of various shocks or treatments within the historical record (Lieberman 2001). Heterogeneity of approach tends to imply that quality of evidence will be problem- and even case-specific. But in an analogous manner, most quantitative analyses of social science data are also subject to highly subjective review of how we ought to interpret the substantive significance and reliability of findings.

Particularly if one were to follow the recommendations of King, Keohane, and Verba (1994) to increase the number of observations, scholars might incorrectly conclude that the best strategy for the SNA component of the nested analysis would be to analyze as many country (or relevant unit) cases as possible. On the contrary, such a strategy tends to lead to a diminution of the core strengths of the SNA. Increased degrees of freedom are provided by the LNA, and nested analysis should rely on the SNA component to provide more depth than breadth – that is, given a fixed amount of scholarly resources, more energy ought to be devoted to identifying and analyzing causal process observations within cases rather than to providing thinner insights about additional cases. Since the inherent weakness of SNA is its inability to assess external validity, there is little value in trying to force it to do so when the LNA component of the research design can do that work. Notwithstanding this advice, it almost always is useful to evaluate more than one case in the SNA; the elaboration of concepts and mechanisms can best be accomplished through *comparison*. A great strength of small-N analysis is the juxtaposition of similar and contrasting cases, helping to make transparent the operationalization of concepts that are largely hidden in the analysis of a statistical data set. Furthermore, comparison provides an empirical basis for making narrative assessments of counterfactual claims – that is, that an event would have happened a different way had the score on a key variable or set of variables been different.

Beyond emphasizing the general complementarities, it is also important to focus the SNA on the specific findings and analysis of the LNA. In regard to the question posed at the end of the previous section – namely, the analyst's assessment of the robustness of the preliminary LNA – SNA then proceeds along one of two tracks. If the answer is "yes, the results were robust," as indicated in Figure 9.2, then the goal of the SNA is almost exclusively focused on *testing* the model estimated in the LNA. On the other hand, if the findings were not deemed to be robust, or if one or more important hypotheses could not be explored, including if the analyst believes that the appropriate theoretical model has not yet been specified, the SNA is oriented toward model *building*. The decision about whether to proceed with a model-testing small-*N* analysis (Mt-SNA) or a model-building small-*N* analysis (Mb-SNA) informs the scope of the analysis, the case selection strategy, and the analysis-ending criteria for the SNA. Practitioners may respond that SNA is itself a mix of model building and model testing, and they may argue that the dichotomy is a false one. While it is true that these may be "ideal-type" approaches, there is enormous benefit to being self-conscious about the *central* intention of one's research in the SNA stage, particularly because the nested approach provides distinct sets of guidelines for the respective strategies.

While SNA is almost always more open-ended than LNA, given its primary interest in the details of case histories and the heterogeneous nature of causal process observations, a scholar's approach to case analysis can differ remarkably depending on his or her analytic goals. Assessment of the preliminary LNA constitutes an important decision point in how the nested approach will be carried out (as depicted in Figure 9.2), providing important guidelines for an appropriate analytic scope for the SNA.

Scholars can leverage their preliminary findings to make decisions about whether they have a sufficiently promising theoretical model that is worth testing – through case study research or additional quantitative analysis or both. Depending on the assessment of model fit at each level of analysis, the scholar can decide whether to focus on the unexplained "noise" – such as outliers from the regression – or to probe more deeply into the mechanisms that undergird well-predicted "on-the-line" cases. Ultimately, the analysis concludes with assessments of confidence in a particular theoretical model based on inferences drawn from the SNA and LNA when viewed together.[9]

Considerations and critiques

I cannot definitively answer the question of whether multimethod analysis yields substantive gains over single-method research.[10] But it is important to

---

[9] Further detailing of the approach can be found in Lieberman (2005).

[10] At the very least, scholars can provide some assessment of the costs versus value added from using mixed approaches in their research. In this regard, Kauffman (2012) and Verghese (2012) provide nicely detailed accounts of how multimethod approaches were at the core of their doctoral dissertations.

point out that more than a few scholarly articles and excellent contributions to the American Political Science Association's *Qualitative and Multi-Method Research* newsletter have raised questions about multimethod research more generally and nested analysis in particular. One "folk" critique is simply that it is difficult to do both quantitative and small-N analysis well. I suppose if the demand were to combine quantum physics and ethnography, the charge might be a fair one, but my general response, which I return to in the next section, is that it is quite fair to expect contemporary comparatively oriented social scientists to be reasonably fluent in both case-specific materials and methods *and* modern quantitative techniques. At the very least, we should expect that scholars with sufficient understanding of the basic vocabulary and inferential strategies associated with different methods can then engage in fruitful collaborations that recognize the complementarities of approaches and engage in a division of labor that captures the benefits of specialized skills and best practices. Not all will be successful and not all historically oriented studies will lend themselves to mixed methods approaches, but books such as Dunning's (2008) *Crude Democracy* and Mahoney's (2010) *Colonialism and Postcolonial Development* reveal the power of combining in-depth within-case study analyses with both thoroughgoing and more modest cross-case statistical analyses.

Scholars have also challenged the approach with more extensive critiques, such as Rohlfing's (2008), which goes so far as to argue that, "under certain circumstances, nothing is gained from a nested analysis. On the contrary, one might lose more than one gains compared to single-method designs." What are his concerns? The main one is that "ontological misspecification has methodological implications that are difficult, if not impossible, to detect in a nested analysis in its current form" (1493). To support this claim, he identifies various areas where he believes that the nested approach might lead to traveling errors across levels of analysis and inadvertent confidence that one might not have within a single-method approach.

For example, he argues that initial specification of a regression model – the preliminary LNA – is likely to omit a key variable of interest and that such estimates are biased and inconsistent if the omitted variable is correlated with others in the model, which is a likely pathology (Rohlfing 2008, 1498–9). As a result, "depending on the severity of the bias and inconsistency, the residuals thus may prove misleading indicators for the status of a case." More generally, Rohlfing's point is that virtually by design, the preliminary LNA is misspecified, and as such, we ought to be somewhat skeptical of the conclusions we can draw from the associated parameter estimates. I think this is a reasonable concern – we almost surely initially misspecify our models. However, what is the superior alternative in single-method LNA or SNA? The ever-present challenge with regression *and* case study diagnostics is that missing variable bias may lead to faulty inferences. But the hope of nested analysis is that such omitted variables might be identified and models reestimated with their inclusion.

Rohlfing (2008) claims that the inherent weakness of a nested approach is the possible *amplification* of analytical mistakes across types of analysis. However, this is presented as a hypothetical pitfall, and I think the more persuasive tendency is that multimethod analysis is more likely to detect mistakes and spurious associations than it is to replicate inferential errors. In many ways, I think Rohlfing's critiques lose sight of the fact that comparative-historical analysis is not useful for explaining relatively marginal differences between cases. It is difficult to imagine how we could illuminate through qualitative research the factors that led to, say, a difference of 1–2 percentage points in per capita income growth or tax collection as a share of GDP. While consequential, such differences are usefully detectable only in large sample studies. CHA is better suited to the study of *major* differences, including the occurrence or not of a relatively rare event or wide divergences in economic trends. As such, the pitfalls of slight over- or underfitting of models is much less consequential than the critique would lead us to believe.

Others have raised important questions about the possible *incompatibility* of CHA and quantitative approaches that might give us pause when contemplating strategies that involve mixing methods. For example, Hall (2003) highlights misalignments between methodology and ontology, and Mahoney and Goertz (2006) lay bare what they take to be quite distinctive "cultures" when comparing scholars who use qualitative or quantitative methods. However, despite their claim that "most researchers in political science will locate themselves predominantly in one column" (of their table differentiating research traditions), I find myself simultaneously sympathetic to large swaths of both "cultures," and I find little conflict here. While I agree that the ontologies of particular scholars and research projects *do* sometimes vary to a degree that they are operating in almost different research universes, I clearly take the position here that each method is *not necessarily* aligned with a particular ontology and that even methods located at opposite corners of the cube – notably case study research and conventional microlevel experimental research – can be successfully harnessed to answer a shared research question, a proposition I detail to a greater extent in the next section.

Frontiers in multimethod comparative-historical analysis: matching, experiments, and natural experiments

In the sections above, I have detailed one approach to multimethod CHA and responded to some of the critiques that have been leveled to date. But in this final section, I want to return to the original framing of this chapter and to consider other opportunities for multimethod research that combine CHA with other locations in the research space specified in Figure 9.1. In particular, such moves may be necessary in order to address, as discussed above, concerns about violations of the ignorability assumption – weaknesses that are characteristic of *both* the LNA and SNA anchors of the nested approach. In recent years, conventional regression analyses, and especially cross-national regressions, have come under increasing fire for their own intrinsic limitations,[11] and scholars have been introducing and implementing a host of new analytic tools. Importantly, I think that CHA could greatly enrich the quality of research and scholarship that is currently being conducted using these alternative approaches in isolation.

As I argued for nested analysis, careful CHA is useful for motivating big questions, inductively generating plausible theories, and helping to establish what we mean when we describe heterogeneous contexts. Some scholars may be rightfully suspicious of new field and survey experiments that simply parachute in a new research design, blind to context. And yet, the meat behind such concerns must be a clear and careful statement about how and why contexts vary so as to generate differential effects across cases.

The fundamental virtue of experimental research designs is that if treatment assignment is a function of a controlled, randomized process, such as a coin flip, we can be certain that treatment assignment is not even partially a function of some other factor that might be related to the outcome of interest. By contrast, CHA scholars generally try to make the argument that their cases are *sufficiently* comparable and that assignment on the values of key explanatory variables was *sufficiently* contingent that we can be *reasonably* confident in the independence of the cause or treatment from the outcome. But particularly when large macrolevel causes are being analyzed, it can be quite difficult to discount the role of other important factors that may have given rise to those values ("state strength," "coalitions," and "class relations,"

---

[11]   See, for example, Dunning (2010) and the symposium "Perfection Methodology, or Methodological Perfectionism?" in the Spring 2011 *Qualitative and Multi-Method Research* newsletter (vol. 9, no. 1).

for example, don't just emerge out of thin air). Standard regression analyses attempt to condition results on "pretreatment" covariates but proceed with essentially the same logic and increasingly tend to face similar challenges, particularly as skeptics raise possibilities of potential omitted variables, concerns about causal order, and shakiness of results depending on the model estimated.

Thus, it is worth considering at least three alternate methods for combining with CHA, options that are all located along the lower right axis of Figure 9.1.

The first is matching methods (e.g., Imai and Van Dyk 2004). This approach is most similar to standard regression-based LNA, as described above, in that matching analyses can be conducted with the same data sets. But a key difference is that matching tries to address heterogeneity in the treatment and control groups by sorting the data set in a manner that is as balanced as possible on covariates, which in turn reduces some of the sensitivities of model specification associated with standard regression analyses. In fact, the logic of matching methods is much closer to the character of standard CHA because, in the former, the goal of various matching algorithms is to find pairs of cases that are as similar as possible to one another on all covariates *except* the key treatment variable. Recently, Nielsen (2014) detailed an approach for doing exactly what I discuss here, identifying a set of strategies for qualitative case selection using various matching estimators. In many ways, matching methods are akin to the repetition of Mill's method of difference – a hallmark of the logic of SNA – many times over, and the final causal effect is calculated as an average of differences between treated and control observations. And as Nielsen's work nicely demonstrates, large-sample analyses provide us with much greater confidence in the quality of matches and, in turn, the inferences that can be generated from such analyses.

The analog to nested analysis, as presented above, is really quite straightforward in the sense that model-building SNA should help to identify the relevant treatment variable and variables for matching, whereas model-testing SNA would involve selecting matched pairs that generate the largest treatment effects. To the extent that scholars hypothesize outcomes for different causes or configurations of case characteristics, it is relatively straightforward to estimate a matching model with heterogeneous treatment effects.

From the most skeptical perspective (which is not a perspective I advocate to the extreme, but simply recognize that the revolution in causal identification has inculcated a *cadre* of extreme skeptics), matching methods do not fully address concerns about ignorability. Whatever doubt one might have about treatment assignment in a well-matched CHA carries over to the analysis of matched data, but in the latter, one can expect that a large sample will eliminate any idiosyncrasies of just a small number of cases and gain external validation with calculation of effects over the larger sample. On the other hand, the quality of matches, particularly with respect to unobserved characteristics, may decline in the large sample, and the quality of specific matches tends to be obscured in large-sample analyses. Again, I think the integration of matching methods with SNA is a very promising future avenue for scholars, but it is relatively easy to anticipate some of the concerns that will arise.

The more powerful strategies for addressing ignorability concerns are clearly bona fide natural experiments and field experiments. Again, I distinguish the former from examples of CHA that may describe themselves as akin to natural experiments in that CHA scholars tend to work backward from a matching process, arguing that cases are so similar on so many dimensions that differences in treatment assignment *must have been* random, and they may go on to further justify why it is plausible to believe that the key differences in the causal variable scores were not determined *ex ante*. This may be an attractive strategy, but it does ultimately require us to make a fairly strong assumption, or perhaps even a leap of faith!

By contrast, natural experiments, as generally understood today, are instances of a scholar identifying a naturally occurring or completely arbitrary set of circumstances and conditions that approximate random assignment. For instance, if election turnout were theorized to be a cause of governance outcomes, and in turn rainfall had a significant effect on voter turnout, we might be able to compare the effects of rainfall-induced turnout on governance outcomes across districts, proceeding under the assumption that within a climactic zone, rainfall on a particular day is a more or less randomly occurring phenomenon, not caused by other factors that might be related to other relevant variables of interest. In such analyses, rather than looking for the "causes of effects" – all the factors that explain variation in governance outcomes – we would focus more on the "effects of causes" – that is, the average treatment effect of different levels of turnout on quality of governance.[12] Along these lines, a small cottage industry of academic scholarship has developed around analyses of the effects of Gram Panchayat (village council) leadership assignment in India (Chattopadhyay and Duflo 2004; Dunning and Nilekani 2013, etc.), as the government of India has mandated randomly rotating rules that compel the reservation of leadership

---

[12] On the distinction between effects of causes and causes of effects, see Mahoney and Goertz (2006).

positions to previously underrepresented social categories. Through large-sample analyses, scholars have estimated the effects of such reservations relative to those control cases that have not yet been subject to the assignment of those quotas or reservations and have drawn inferences based on average treatment effects. So long as we can be convinced that assignment was *really and truly* random, that is, not somehow hijacked in the process of implementation, we can largely discount concerns about violations to our ignorability assumption.

The hallmark difference between such natural experiments and "true" experiments is that, in the latter, the investigator decides upon the treatment and assigns at random. From a research design perspective, this allows the investigator far more control, but this may not be feasible, and external validity is likely to be higher if we can draw inferences from naturally occurring phenomena.

So, what relevance is there for CHA and mixed methods research? A deep comparative-historical reading of the effects of the treatment variable ought to be leveraged as a source of theorizing and toward better design and implementation of both natural and standard experiments. For instance, in the case described above, one would want to draw on historical examples of the (presumably nonrandom) introduction of women or disadvantaged groups into political office and trace out the most likely effects prior to generating strong hypotheses about the effects of randomized reservations. In turn, if one identifies effects from the experimental analyses that were not initially evident in the SNA, one would want to consult the historical record to see whether (1) the experimental findings actually shed light on a previously missed understanding of the history; or (2) no such relationship exists in the record, and the scholar should try to ascertain whether this is simply a product of a mismatch or if the experimental findings demand some rethinking.

It is also important to highlight that the core competency of CHA is context. The core weakness of much experimental research is lack thereof. Too much field-based experimentation in political science seeks to test "universal" propositions about the determinants of important attitudes and behaviors, without much regard for how institutions and contexts are likely to structure cognitions and behaviors. As scholars attempt to replicate findings across countries, for example, they are likely to find important differences in treatment effects. In this regard, CHA may be able to shed some useful light, *ex ante*, on how individuals are likely to respond to various cues and incentives. In turn, such research should provide important tests for the findings of CHA.

Let me motivate a hypothetical example: a great deal of experimental research in the field of development has inquired about the effects of different types of cash transfers on individual behaviors, such as savings and investment (e.g., Rawlings and Rubio 2005). For the most part, those studies are at least written in a way that provides little context concerning the political history of development in the places where these experiments have been conducted. It is not very difficult to imagine that across countries, there may be substantial variation in the historical precedent of government- and donor-provided subsidies, such that the meaning and political implications of the very practice resonates in wildly different ways across contexts. In order to even begin to generate propositions about different treatment effects, one would need to have sufficiently mastered the historical record and be able to sensitively recognize possible differential implications of a treatment. To date, very little such research has been conducted, but I think this must be part of the ongoing agenda for both CHA and experimental methods.

Finally, and perhaps most importantly, our ability to identify compelling natural experiments and to develop meaningful experimental protocols for field experiments almost surely demands a solid, theoretically guided understanding of a country's social, political, and economic history in comparative perspective. The iterative process of moving between an inductive, structure-focused analysis of a small set of critical cases, which attempts to test particular implications of a theory in an experimental setting, strikes me as an exciting proposition for gaining a better understanding of how politics actually works in a manner that will allay skeptics from various corners.

Conclusions and next steps

Of course, the seminal comparative-historical works of Moore (1966) and Skocpol (1979) rightly deserve due recognition for their creativity and the power of their insights. As has been detailed elsewhere, such studies applied logical inferential frameworks that were generally absent from most prior macrolevel studies. And, of course, their contributions were made without any of the strategies discussed here, which might imply that such methodological advice is, to use a familiar lexicon, neither necessary nor sufficient to produce important comparative scholarship.

But several decades later, almost a half century since the publication of *Social Origins*, we find ourselves with exciting new possibilities for conducting research that helps us to understand both general patterns, and explanations that shed light on particular cases of interest. Reflecting on just a single decade, one can find a sea change in the availability of Internet-based databases, primary source archives, and quality scholarship. Gathering the facts of cases and constructing qualitative historical databases of events are substantially easier and can be more done comprehensively, almost incomparably different from what was available to scholars working in the CHA tradition a half century ago. Our access to electoral, social, and economic data; maps, GIS data on the location of events, boundaries, and local conditions; text-searchable newspaper archives; and a very wide range of other historical archives provides a radically distinctive terrain for conducting qualitative and quantitative analysis of both primary and secondary source materials. And modern tools continue to facilitate collaboration among scholars with complementary skills. While it may be tempting to let the availability of vast troves of data guide the selection of research questions, such practice would resemble the proverbial tail wagging the dog. Instead, such opportunities should be harnessed to fulfill the types of "big" research agendas frequently launched within the context of CHA.

In this essay, I have restricted my discussion to the right-side of the research space in Figure 9.1 – that is, to macrolevel research, which is at the heart of CHA. Certainly, many scholars (i.e., Campbell 2003) have already successfully combined macrohistorical and survey research, particularly in the context of American Political Development. Similarly, Cavaille (2014) provides a promising example in a study of redistributive politics and policies, highlighting that macrolevel outcomes depend heavily on attitudes and dispositions within the polity, and vice versa. Bridging the micro-macro divide is one of the central challenges of social science, and I do not claim to supply a solution in these concluding sentences. But I do think that a potentially valuable and practical strategy may be to combine more deliberately CHA with observational and experimental survey work, at both the elite and ordinary citizen levels.

While social scientists will continue to ask individual-level questions about household behavior, individual voting intentions, propensity to join wars, the consequences of particular social policies, and so on, we will also need to relate those findings to macrolevel questions about patterns of policymaking, why some parties or candidates win elections, and why wars occur. Using CHA within an integrated, mixed methods research design strikes me as a promising strategy for carrying out these important research agendas.

References

Achen, Christopher H. 1982. *Interpreting and Using Regression.* Beverly Hills, CA: Sage Publications.

Campbell, Andrea Louise. 2003. *How Policies Make Citizens: Senior Political Activism and the American Welfare State.* Princeton, NJ: Princeton University Press.

Cavaille, Charlotte. 2014. "Demand for Redistribution in the Age of Inequality." Unpublished PhD thesis, Department of Government and Social Policy, Harvard University, Cambridge, MA.

Chattopadhyay, Raghabendra, and Esther Duflo. 2004. "Women as Policy Makers: Evidence from a Randomized Policy Experiment in India." *Econometrica* 72 (5): 1409–43.

Collier, David, Henry E. Brady, and Jason Seawright. 2004. "Sources of Leverage in Causal Inference: Toward an Alternative View of Methodology." In *Rethinking Social Inquiry: Diverse Tools, Shared Standards,* edited by H. E. Brady and D. Collier. Berkeley, CA: Rowman & Littlefield and Berkeley Public Policy Press.

Collier, Ruth B., and David Collier. 1991. *Shaping the Political Arena.* Princeton, NJ: Princeton University Press.

Dunning, Thad. 2008. *Crude Democracy: Natural Resource Wealth and Political Regimes.* Cambridge: Cambridge University Press.

2010. "Design-Based Inference: Beyond the Pitfalls of Regression Analysis?" In *Rethinking Social Inquiry: Diverse Tools, Shared Standards,* 2nd ed., edited by H. E. Brady and D. Collier, 273–311. Berkeley, CA: Rowman & Littlefield and Berkeley Public Policy Press.

2012. *Natural Experiments in the Social Sciences: A Design-Based Approach.* New York: Cambridge University Press.

Dunning, Thad, and Janhavi Nilekani. 2013. "Ethnic Quotas and Political Mobilization: Caste, Parties, and Distribution in Indian Village Councils." *American Political Science Review* 107 (1): 35–56.

Falleti, Tulia G., and Julia F. Lynch. 2009. "Context and Causal Mechanisms in Political Analysis." *Comparative Political Studies* 42 (9): 1143–66.

Gerring, John. 2001. *Social Science Methodology: A Criterial Framework.* Cambridge: Cambridge University Press.

2004. "What Is a Case Study and What Is It Good For?" *American Political Science Review* 98 (2): 341–54.

2011. "How Good Is Good Enough? A Multidimensional, Best-Possible Standard for Research Design." *Political Research Quarterly* 64 (3): 625–36.

Glynn, Adam, and Nahomi Ichino. 2014. "Using Qualitative Information to Improve Causal Inference." *American Journal of Political Science.* doi:10.1111/ajps.12154.

Hall, Peter. 1986. *Governing the Economy: The Politics of State Intervention in Britain and France*. New York: Oxford University Press.

2003. "Aligning Ontology and Methodology in Comparative Politics." In *Comparative Historical Analysis in the Social Sciences*, edited by James Mahoney and Dietrich Rueschemeyer, chap. 11. Cambridge: Cambridge University Press.

Holland, Paul W. 1986. "Statistics and Causal Inference." *Journal of the American statistical Association* 81 (396): 945–60.

Holland, Paul W., and Donald B. Rubin. 1988. "Causal Inference in Retrospective Studies." *Evaluation Review* 12 (3): 203–31.

Imai, Kosuke, and David A. Van Dyk. 2004. "Causal Inference with General Treatment Regimes." *Journal of the American Statistical Association* 99 (467): 854–66.

Kauffman, Craig. 2012. "More Than the Sum of the Parts: Nested Analysis in Action." *Qualitative and Multi-method Research* 10 (2): 26–30.

King, Gary, Robert Keohane, and Sidney Verba. 1994. *Designing Social Inquiry: Scientific Inference in Qualitative Research*. Princeton, NJ: Princeton University Press.

Lieberman, Evan. 2001. "Causal Inference in Historical Institutional Analysis: A Specification of Periodization Strategies." *Comparative Political Studies* 34 (9): 1011–35.

2005. "Nested Analysis as a Mixed-Method Strategy for Comparative Research." *American Political Science Review* 99 (3): 435–52.

2010. "Bridging the Qualitative-Quantitative Divide: Best Practices in the Development of Historically Oriented Replication Databases." *Annual Review of Political Science* 13:37–59.

Lijphart, Arend. 1971. "Comparative Politics and the Comparative Method." *American Political Science Review* 65 (3): 682–93.

Lustick, I. S. 1996. "History, Historiography, and Political Science: Multiple Historical Records and the Problem of Selection Bias." *American Political Science Review* 90 (3): 605–18.

Mahoney, James. 1999. "Nominal, Ordinal, and Narrative Appraisal in Macrocausal Analysis." *American Journal of Sociology* 104 (4): 1154–96.

2010. *Colonialism and Postcolonial Development: Spanish America in Comparative Perspective*. Cambridge: Cambridge University Press.

Mahoney, James, and Gary Goertz. 2006. "A Tale of Two Cultures: Contrasting Quantitative and Qualitative Research." *Political Analysis* 14 (3): 227–49.

Mahoney, James, and Dietrich Rueschemeyer, eds. 2003. *Comparative Historical Analysis in the Social Sciences*. Cambridge: Cambridge University Press.

Moore, Barrington. 1966. *Social Origins of Dictatorship and Democracy: Lord and Peasant in the Making of the Modern World*. Boston: Beacon Press.

Nielsen, Richard. 2014. "Case Selection via Matching." *Sociological Methods and Research*. doi:10.1177/0049124114547054.

Pierson, Paul. 2000. "Increasing Returns, Path Dependence, and the Study of Politics." *American Political Science Review* 94 (2): 251–67.

Rawlings, Laura. B., and Gloria M. Rubio. 2005. "Evaluating the Impact of Conditional Cash Transfer Programs." *World Bank Research Observer* 20 (1): 29–56.

Rohlfing, Ingo. 2008. "What You See and What You Get: Pitfalls and Principles of Nested Analysis in Comparative Research." *Comparative Political Studies* 41 (11): 1492–514.

Schneider, Carsten Q., and Ingo Rohlfing. 2013. "Combining QCA and Process Tracing in Set-Theoretic Multi-Method Research." *Sociological Methods and Research* 42 (4): 559–97.

Skocpol, Theda. 1979. *States and Social Revolutions: A Comparative Analysis of France, Russia, and China.* Cambridge: Cambridge University Press.

Verghese, Ajay. 2012. "Multi-Method Fieldwork in Practice: Colonial Legacies and Ethnic Conflict in India." *Qualitative and Multi-Method Research* 10 (2): 41–4.

Epilogue
comparative-historical analysis:
past, present, future

Wolfgang Streeck

According to Mahoney and Rueschemeyer (2003), comparative-historical analysis looks for "historically grounded explanations of large-scale and substantively important outcomes" (4). It aims at the "identification of causal configurations that produce major outcomes of interest" (11), paying explicit attention to "historical sequences" while "take[ing] seriously the unfolding of processes over time" (12) and relying on "systematic and contextualized comparison of similar and contrasting cases" (13). In the same vein, Thelen and Mahoney, in their introductory chapter to the present volume, characterize comparative-historical analysis by "its focus on macroconfigurational explanation" and on "problem-driven case-based research" as well as "its commitment to temporally oriented analysis."

In this essay I undertake to place comparative-historical analysis in the context of the history of the social sciences, to show where it comes from and where not, what if anything is new or unique about it, and in what respects it differs from or resembles classical traditions of inquiry. My objective is to clarify some of the foundational assumptions underlying present-day comparative-historical analysis through comparison with similar but different approaches, historical and contemporary. My central claim is that comparative-historical analysis rests on a particular ontology of the social world that is historically new and characteristically unlike the ontologies underlying other, related modes of social science research and theory.

To begin with, comparative-historical analysis assumes that there are large ("macro") social structures in the real world ("societies") that can be classified into categories, or families, of "cases" similar in some respects while differing in others. Examples of families of cases for comparative-historical analysis are nation-states, supranational or subnational regions, local communities, sectoral or international regimes, local or national economies, and institutionalized religions, cultures, and value systems. Cases are seen as subject to a *historical dynamic*; rather than being fixed once and for all, they are changing over time. Furthermore, some of the differences between cases, cross-sectional as well as diachronic, are considered *fundamental*: they are assumed to matter in ways important enough to justify systematic efforts at understanding not just their present consequences but also their origins.

In comparative-historical analysis, present differences between comparable social structures, or among the events, behaviors, and proclivities to which such structures give rise, are assumed to have been caused by identifiable events or conditions *in a historical past*, long enough ago not to be contemporary with the effects to be causally explained by them. Differences between cases, conceived as different values on common but variable properties, are accounted for by other differences between the same cases as observed back in time – by different values of other "variables" in the past or by covariant historical differences. Also, the historical causes that are to account for present conditions – for why some conditions are found in some cases but not in others – are conceived as *contingent*: they happened to be present when they caused the differences that are today explained by them, but they might just as well have been absent – in which case the outcomes produced by them would not have materialized. *Fundamental* as the present differences attributed by comparative-historical analysis to past causes may be, that is to say, they are not *necessary*: had the past differences that account for them not existed – as they might well have – the present differences would not have come about. Moreover, comparative-historical analysis does not explain present and past differences as resulting from a common cause, in particular an underlying general logic of *historical development*. Past causal conditions explaining present differences are conceived as *exogenous* instead of endogenously predetermined. *Difference as a present fact* is seen on a background of *similarity as a past possibility*, contingently suppressed by specifiable causes identifiable by comparative causal analysis.

Finally, comparative-historical analysis assumes that the past causes it holds responsible for present differences were powerful enough to produce an impact of historical significance, one that is *durable, robust*, and *identity-defining*. Differences in outcomes, defined as "large-scale and substantively important," are attributed to past influences sufficiently strong to condition the future path of a society, by ruling out or rendering ineffective other influences militating toward similarity. Comparative-historical analysis, in summary, is concerned with relatively stable, lasting, nonincidental differences between social entities whose origins lie far enough back in time to require uncovering by systematic historical research.[1]

Contingent differences: the ontology of comparative-historical analysis

In the following I elaborate on the nature of comparative-historical analysis by comparing it to earlier, related but different approaches to the study of "large-scale and substantively important outcomes" in an attempt to locate it in the context of relevant traditions of empirical social inquiry. I argue that the idea of stable differences between social entities, produced by contingent events in a historical past overriding categorical similarities, is historically new as it requires discarding earlier conceptions of the social world that were either theoretically agnostic, at least with respect to social structures, or to the contrary informed by a substantive theory, or philosophy, of history. In fact comparative-historical analysis may itself be regarded as a historical phenomenon amenable to causal explanation: as a historically specific, twentieth-century, nonteleological way of viewing the world that has left behind earlier notions of predetermined evolutionary development or "progress."

To situate comparative-historical analysis in the tradition of social-historical scholarship, I begin by pointing out the way it differs from an *event-centered empirical historiography,* as seminally represented already by the inventor of secular history writing, the Greek general and historian of the Peloponnesian War, Thucydides (c. 460 to c. 395 BC). I believe that his ontology of the social world and his method are to this day the principal model of historiography and can as well as any other historian's be used to distinguish comparative-historical analysis as a type of social science from modern historical scholarship. Next, I look at the work of the founder of what is today called *policy analysis,* Niccolò Machiavelli (1469–1527). I argue that, where Machiavelli was not a historian in the mold of Thucydides – which in an important part of his work he was – his objective was to extract from political experience, past and present, a historically informed praxeology for political rulers on how to use power to retain it. This, too, created no need and left no place for causal explanation of social structures by systematic

---

[1] Time is a central concept in comparative-historical analysis, but in the sense of causal effects working and lasting over the *longue durée* rather than of evolutionary or developmental time (identical with a society's age). See Streeck (2010). For an outstanding example of the use of time, and sequence in time, as a causal mechanism, see Pierson's discussion of path dependence and power in Chapter 5, this volume.

historical comparison. From here I move on to the medieval Arab scholar, Ibn Khaldūn (1332–1406), who could arguably be considered one of the first sociologists, because of his interest in a substantive *theory of social change*. However, while Ibn Khaldūn stands at the beginning of a powerful tradition of social theory that conceives of societies as subject to *cyclical change*, that tradition is not the one of comparative-historical analysis. Nor, as I show at the end of this section, does comparative-historical analysis derive from another *teleological* or *linear* variant of historical philosophy, as embodied above all in (a simplified reading of) the historical materialism of Karl Marx (1818–1893) and the Marxist tradition.

I now characterize comparative-historical analysis by setting it off against – inevitably stylized – representations of the four traditions that preceded it, showing what it is concerned with, what it tries to offer, what sort of theory it aspires to, and what concept of causality it pursues. In particular, I argue that comparative-historical analysis is different in that it is concerned with structures rather than action (in other words, takes a macro as distinguished from a micro perspective); with theory rather than strategy (or praxeology); with explaining specific cases rather than explicating universal laws of history; and with contingent rather than necessary properties of societies.

Structure, not action

Scientific-empirical historiography, as first exemplified by Thucydides, is typically not interested in explaining differences among present societies by means of comparative evidence on past conditions constituting long-term structural constraints and opportunities for social change. Its world consists of actions – well-advised or foolish, calculated or emotional, advantageous or harmful, lucky or unlucky. Outcomes, "large" and "important" as they may be, are events – as unique as the actions that produce them, intentionally or not. Thus Thucydides presents a monographic reconstruction of the chain of decisions and occurrences that resulted in Athens losing the Peloponnesian War (431–404 BC) and its empire (Thucydides 1998 [c. 400 BC]). He is not concerned with explaining the differences between the social structures of Athens and Sparta by identifying past conditions or events that might have produced them or with establishing, by way of comparison, general principles governing the rise and fall of empires. Structures, as either explanans or explanandum, were not central to his world.[2] History for him was shaped

---

[2] Although they were invoked later, by more speculative observers such as Plato, in attempts to generalize on the rise and fall of political communities such as Greek city-states.

by human nature and human actions – the skills and the good luck of individuals. That Athens was in the end defeated was due ultimately to the bad attitudes and unfortunate choices of its leaders; there were no structural conditions strong enough to have protected or constrained them, nor was there any general "law" of history or divine intervention that would have favored their enemies.

Theory, not strategy

Modern political science, as distinguished from history writing, is often said to have begun with the Florentine politician and writer Niccolò Machiavelli. In part of his work, Machiavelli was an empirical, secular historian on the model of Thucydides.[3] In his *Florentine Histories* (1988 [1525]), Machiavelli recounts the sequence of events from the early Middle Ages to his own time that contributed to the rise of Florence as a European political and cultural superpower as well as for its failure to achieve the same greatness as Rome in antiquity. The book focuses on the intentions, decisions, and actions of the leading families and the populace of Florence. Central to its story are concepts such as *virtù* (the political skills of leading individuals), *fortuna* (their good luck and the occurrence of fateful, unpredictable events), *ambizione* (human egoism and pride), *necessità* (situations of emergency), and *occasione* (a window of opportunity, an auspicious moment to be recognized and used by skillful leaders) (Schröder 2004).

Machiavelli's concern with strategy, in particular political strategy, is even more present in his other, more popular writings. *The Prince* (1976 [1514]), the most prominent of these, draws on examples from what was in Machiavelli's time the entire known history of the world to answer questions such as how best to control a conquered city, how to procure truthful information from subordinates, "how flatterers should be avoided" (chapter XXIII), and "that one should avoid being despised and hated" (chapter XIX). Political rules of prudence are regarded as universally valid, being the same for King Solomon and Lorenzo il Magnifico, allowing for changes in matters such as military technology. Politics, the use and defense of public power, always follows the same principles. This is why practical advice can be based

---

[3] A parallel that was noted, by among others, Friedrich Nietzsche: "Thucydides and perhaps Machiavelli's *principe* are most closely related to me owing to the absolute determination which they show of refusing to deceive themselves and of seeing reason in *reality* – not in 'rationality,' and still less in 'morality'" (Nietzsche 1911, 114).

on the experience of all governments past and present, forming one big store of examples applicable to any problem a contemporary ruler might encounter. Rather than systematic comparison for the purpose of causal explanation, the job of Machiavellian policy science is to pick and choose from the unending supply of lessons history can teach political leaders, provided they are able to understand the relevance to the particular problems they are facing.

Specific, not universal

One of the most remarkable figures in early social science was the Andalusian Muslim historian Ibn Khaldūn, who lived in the fourteenth century in Spain and the Maghreb. Before the 1800s Ibn Khaldūn was hardly known in the West, and up to now only the smaller part of his massive work, written in Arabic, has been translated. Ibn Khaldūn's writings resemble those of Thucydides in that his historical narratives are secular and empiricist: human history is made by humans alone, and the historian is called upon to use commonsense critical judgment to distinguish the unlikely from the likely, rumor from fact, myth from reality, and speculation from what one can know about *"wie es eigentlich gewesen"* (Leopold von Ranke).[4] It was above all for this "scientific" approach to historiography that Ibn Khaldūn came to be appreciated by nineteenth-century historians in Western Europe, who saw in him an early forerunner.[5]

It was not only historians, however, who took, and continue to take, an interest in him. In his works one finds an astonishing wealth of highly sophisticated theoretical observations and reflections on a wide variety of subjects, including economic growth and development and, of all things, natural evolution.[6] Of particular interest here is Ibn Khaldūn's theory of history or, indeed, social change, which has earned him a reputation as one of the first sociologists. Most famous in the West is his *Muqaddimah*, or *Prolegomenon*

---

[4] In English: how things actually were.
[5] On Ibn Khaldūn, see the entries in Encyclopaedia Britannica (www.britannica.com/EBchecked/topic/280788/Ibn-Khaldun) and the English Wikipedia (http://en.wikipedia.org/wiki/Ibn_Khaldun).
[6] For a teaser, see: "The animal world then widens, its species become numerous, and, in a gradual process of creation, it finally leads to man, who is able to think and to reflect. The higher stage of man is reached from the world of the monkeys, in which both sagacity and perception are found, but which has not reached the stage of actual reflection and thinking. At this point we come to the first stage of man after (the world of monkeys). This is as far as our (physical) observation extends" (Ibn Khaldūn 1967 [1377], 75).

(Ibn Khaldūn 1967 [1377]) – the first of seven books of what is intended to be a universal history[7] – in which he suggests a *cyclical theory* of the rise and fall of human civilizations. As popularized by, among others, Daniel Bell (1976), the central concept of that theory is that of *asabiyyah*, translated as social cohesion or solidarity. The theory suggests a cyclical sequence that begins with migrant tribes among which *asabiyyah* is strong, conquering a territory where they settle down and become rich and civilized and hedonistic, as a result of which their social cohesion decays. At this point new barbarian tribes appear and conquer their predecessors, which restarts the cycle. Ibn Khaldūn believed this cycle to be a universal one, affecting all societies, at least as long as there are unsettled barbarians beyond their borders with the desire for the economic and cultural riches produced by a sedentary culture.

While Ibn Khaldūn does propose a theory, which makes him a sociologist as well as a historian,[8] that theory is not one that would be compatible with fundamental assumptions underlying comparative-historical analysis. Although it does provide for differences among societies, these are essentially differences *over time* – diachronic in nature rather than cross-sectional. Societies may differ, but only because they are in different stages of the *asabiyyah* cycle. Change takes place within an eternally recurring pattern that is continuously reproduced in and by all societies. The objective of theory of the Ibn Khaldūn sort is to look through apparent differences in order to recognize the similarities – the universal laws of development that are at the bottom of phenomena that are in fact no more than epiphenomena. Things change, but the forces responsible for this do not: the cycle always returns to square one. This is unlike comparative-historical analysis where differences between societies do not reflect different positions in a general societal life cycle but are explained by the historical presence and absence, respectively, of specific structures, actions, and events; where history is not orderly and general but contingent and diverse; and where change must be accounted for by formal theories devoid of substantive assumptions on a predetermined course of history.

---

[7] The title of the entire work is *Book of Lessons, Record of Beginnings and Events in the History of the Arabs and Berbers and their Powerful Contemporaries.*

[8] Or in any case identifies him as a *Historizist* (in English: historicist), in Karl Popper's definition: someone who believes in laws of history acting behind the backs of historical actors and determining their activities and the outcomes of these. See Popper (1957).

Contingent, not necessary

Unlike the Middle Ages, nineteenth-century sociological theory perceived history not as static nor cyclical but as a process of more or less linear and irreversible progress (Koselleck and Meier 1971–97). This holds true for Spencer in Victorian England as well as, by and large, for the French School from St. Simon to Comte and the young Durkheim.[9] Usually, Karl Marx is included among the ranks of historical progressivists and theorists of unilinear social development as, rightly or wrongly, his theory of human history as a "history of class struggles" tends to be presented as the model case of mechanistic determinism in the social sciences.[10] I will not debate this reading in detail but simply mention that one finds in the work of Marx, as it relates to the subject of this essay, at least three interestingly unorthodox ideas put forward by the very person alleged to be the founder of Marxian orthodoxy. First, in his early writing Marx for a while distinguished between England as the country of economics, France as the home of politics, and Germany, impotent both economically and politically, as the motherland of philosophy (Marx and Engels 1977 [1844]). Arguably, however, this never amounted to more than the notion of an international division of labor in a broad stream of political-economic development inside an emerging world society – of three springs feeding the same river. Second, and more importantly, in the case of at least one country, North America, Marx and Engels were apparently tempted for a while to modify their one-society unified model of history that has all societies moving through identical stages until they converge in a global world system, first capitalist and then socialist. Third, there was a highly political controversy in the twentieth century over Marx's notion, more or less systematically developed, of an "Asiatic mode of production," which was taken up in the 1950s by the Communist apostate Karl Wittfogel to explain why there was no democracy in Russia (Wittfogel

---

[9] Both Durkheim (1964 [1893]) and Spencer (2003 [1882]) speak of "progressive societies," to be distinguished from "primitive societies." Movement from the latter to the former was seen as universal, following a general law of development. This was essentially the same in Marx and, before him, Hegel.

[10] Marxian determinism, of course, includes an image of societal development that proceeds not continuously but in fits and spurts: periods of accelerated change, when a new societal configuration emerges, are followed by periods in which the contradictions characteristic of the respective stage of development slowly mature. Still, the movement of history, while discontinuous in this sense, is steadily upward, and the end is never in doubt. For a sophisticated, unorthodox, and, to this author, highly convincing reading of Marx, see Eagleton (2011).

1957). I return to Marx's view of the United States in the following section and to his Asiatic intuition in the third section.

In any case, open to interpretation as Marx's macrosociology may be, the standard Marxist account as it emerged in the first half of the twentieth century appears to leave little space for fundamental cross-sectional diversity among societies. This seems to result from its affinity to a notion of universal laws of history and historical progress, however momentarily modified by chance events, to be discovered and put to strategic-political use by "scientific socialism." History, in this reading, remains in the realm of necessity, with no serious contingency admitted. Here standard Marxism – and with it any other developmentalist or teleological theory, or "philosophy," of history – differs fundamentally from the comparative-historical analysis of today, which knows no historical laws and leaves it a priori open which causal explanations for observed societal differences may be uncovered in empirical investigation and what may become of such differences in the future.

Puzzling otherness: grounds for comparison

Up to here I have dealt with what comparative-historical analysis is *not*, in an effort to show what is specific about it, by identifying traditions in the social sciences from which it differs. In this section I reconstruct the rise in the nineteenth and twentieth centuries of a sociological concept of *genuine otherness among societies*. This presupposes a distinction between fundamental ("deep") and superficial ("shallow") differences, the latter soon to be eliminated in the course of history by "objective" forces of *convergence*, as in standard Marxism and simple versions of so-called modernization theory. Comparative-historical analysis, unlike a historiography of events, a universal political praxeology, or a cyclical or linear general theory of history, deals with genuine otherness among otherwise similar and therefore comparable societies – one could also say: with *multilinearity* as distinguished from *unilinearity* in the development of societies.[11] It is important to note that this

---

[11] Comparative-historical analysis also differs from what was called *Historismus* (not to be confused with *Historizismus*) in the nineteenth century, as it is concerned with different societies existing next to each other and simultaneously rather than with different epochs in the history of the same society. *Historismus* insists on the individual dignity of each epoch and aims at a holistic *Verstehen* of historical societies, not at causal explanations of differences between them. It also rejects the idea of historical epochs as stages of historical development or evolution, reducing them to be necessary forerunners of some subsequent "higher" state. As Leopold von Ranke put it, each epoch is *"unmittelbar zu Gott"* (directly to God).

does not forever rule out convergence, although brought about not by general laws of social development but by exogenous events as contingent as those having made a society differ from others in the first place. Such events may in fact be *political interventions informed by comparative-historical analysis* aimed at removing the historical obstacles, or correcting for the adverse historical events, that have prevented a society from developing in a particular direction. As we will see, theoretically informed political action to bring about convergence on a normatively desirable social model figures centrally in what one may regard as a sophisticated, nonmechanistic, multilinear variant of modernization theory.

I suggest that the notion of deep otherness of otherwise similar social structures, calling for explanation by different histories, arose first in the confrontation of Europe with the emerging New World society of North America. Even Marx seems sometimes to have entertained the idea that the United States might be a different type of society, not just a momentary variation on a set course of capitalist development. Thus in his discussion of "primitive accumulation," Marx noted that outside Europe, in the colonies, the formation of the capitalist mode of production was impeded by the free availability of land, enabling potential workers to refuse entering into wage labor and earn their living as independent farmers instead (Marx 1967 [1867]), 716ff.). It was only after access to land was restricted and immigration from Europe increased because of economic hardship there that a more or less stationary working class began to exist in the United States. Still, as Marx observed, "the lowering of the wages and the dependence of the wage-worker [were] yet far from being brought down to the normal European level" (Marx 1967 [1867], 724).

Contributing to this was another respect in which America differed from Europe, which was modern slavery, introduced precisely to compensate for the undersupply of "voluntary" wage labor in a colonial context. A side effect of slavery was that it impeded the formation of a revolutionary American working class by splitting labor in to two categories unable to organize collectively around a common interest. As Marx wrote famously in Volume I of *Capital*, "In the United States of North America, every independent movement of the workers was paralyzed as long as slavery disfigured a part of the Republic. Labor cannot emancipate itself in the white skin where in the black it is branded" (Marx 1967 [1867], 284). This is why Marx and Engels were ardent supporters of the Northern states in the American Civil War, as documented by the "Address of the International Working Men's Association to Abraham Lincoln, President of the United States of America," written by

Marx on the occasion of Lincoln's reelection in 1864.[12] However, while Marx had hoped for the abolition of slavery adding impetus to the organization of a revolutionary workers party in the United States, he and Engels soon were disappointed about the half-hearted pursuit and then the abandonment of Reconstruction under Lincoln's successors.[13] Although they were worried about revolutionary progress in America taking longer than expected, they eventually convinced themselves that, ultimately, American society would fall in line with the general, unilinear pattern, or "law," of capitalist development producing its socialist opposition and negation.

Marx and Engels were not the only ones to be puzzled by the contrast between Europe and the United States. Another main figure in this respect was, of course, Alexis de Tocqueville whose subject, obviously, was not capitalism but democracy. While Tocqueville delivered the most detailed account of his time of how the New World differed from Europe, continuously emphasizing the profoundness of such differences, in the end he also seems to have come down on the side of convergence – although in his case of Europe on America.[14] A third example in which observed differences between Europe and the United States that at first glance look quite fundamental are found to be in fact only temporary is Werner Sombart's explanation *Why There Is No Socialism in the United States* (Sombart 1976 [1906]) – a fine-grained report on historical and present diversity between European and American societies that ends up predicting identical outcomes in spite of different historical structures.[15] For Sombart, unlike Tocqueville but in line with

---

[12] See www.marxists.org/archive/marx/iwma/documents/1864/lincoln-letter.htm. The second-to-last paragraph reads: "While the workingmen, the true political powers of the North, allowed slavery to defile their own republic, while before the Negro, mastered and sold without his concurrence, they boasted it the highest prerogative of the white-skinned laborer to sell himself and choose his own master, they were unable to attain the true freedom of labor, or to support their European brethren in their struggle for emancipation; but this barrier to progress has been swept off by the red sea of civil war" (also in Marx and Engels 1971, 279–81).

[13] On Marx and his views on the American Civil War, see Blackburn (2011). A complete collection of the writings of Marx and Engels on the subject, including the respective correspondence between the two, is Marx and Engels (1971).

[14] With Europe learning from America by getting to know it better – and, in the process, adopting the lessons derived from comparison. "The laws of the French republic can be and, in many cases, should be different from those prevailing in the United States. But the principles on which the constitutions of the American states rest, the principles of order, balance of power, true liberty, and sincere and deep respect for law, are indispensable for all republics; they should be common to them all; and it is safe to forecast that where they are not found the republic will soon have ceased to exist" (Tocqueville 1988 [1835–40], xiv).

[15] Having asked whether "there [is] a tendency towards unity in the modern social movement, or must we deal with movements taking different forms in different countries? . . . Will the future social structures of Europe and America turn out the same or different?" (Sombart 1976 [1906], 24).

Marx, it is America that will be catching up with Europe rather than vice versa.[16]

The most explicit conceptual framework to accommodate deep, identity-defining, long-lasting differences between societies was, I suggest, developed by Max Weber – which would make him the true founding father of comparative-historical analysis, in addition to whatever else he may have founded. The *locus classicus* is Weber's account of the uniqueness of European culture and society, in particular its capacity to become the breeding ground of modern, rational capitalism. Combining economic history with cultural sociology, especially a sociology of religion, Weber's *Erkenntnisinteresse* was to understand the origins of the society of which he saw himself to be "a product."[17] That society, and the economic system it had given birth to, Weber considered exceptional among the several other, comparable civilizations that had arisen in the course of human history and had failed to produce the peculiar variant of capitalism that was in Weber's time embarking on a worldwide conquest.[18]

To understand why modern capitalism emerged in Western Europe and nowhere else Weber looked for an event in the past, including the very distant past, that had to be as unique as its outcome and could therefore explain it, provided the connection between the two could be plausibly reconstructed. The theory Weber came up with famously suggests a long line of causation that starts with ancient Judaism, in particular Jewish prophecy, and continues through its influence on Christianity, especially late-medieval Protestantism in whose worldview Weber saw something like a historical reappearance of the Jewish prophets. That worldview, according to Weber, was a "rational" one in that it was opposed to magic of all sorts, as practiced by the priesthood of early Palestine with which the prophets competed.[19] The – historically

---

[16] The book concludes, somewhat surprisingly given its meticulous enumeration of fundamental differences between American and European societies and economies: "All the factors that till now have prevented the development of Socialism in the United States are about to disappear or to be converted into their opposite, with the result that in the next generation Socialism in America will very probably experience the greatest possible expansion of its appeal" (Sombart 1976 [1906], 119). Perhaps Sombart's underlying grand theory, of a universal historical evolution of capitalism from *Früh-* to *Hoch-* to *Spätkapitalismus*, got the better of him at this point.

[17] "A product of modern European civilization, studying any problem of universal history, is bound to ask himself to what combination of circumstances the fact should be attributed that in Western civilization, and in Western civilization only, cultural phenomena have appeared which (as we like to think) lie in a line of development having universal significance and value" (Weber 1984 [1904/1905], 13) .

[18] In *Gesammelte Aufsätze zur Religionssoziologie* Weber dealt in particular with Confucianism and Taoism in China and Hinduism and Buddhism in India. The work remained incomplete.

[19] On prophecy, see *Economy and Society* (Weber 1979 [1922], 439–68), and in particular the section titled "The Nature of Prophetic Revelation: The World As a Meaningful Totality," pages 450ff.

contingent – victory of the prophets over the priests forever anchored in the culture of Judaism, and later in Christianity, a radically rationalist conception of the world that Weber saw as being at the heart of Western civilization. The connection of what Weber called the *Entzauberung der Welt* to modern capitalism is made in a famous passage in Weber's *General Economic History*:

Judaism was . . . of notable significance for modern rational capitalism, insofar as it transmitted to Christianity the latter's hostility to magic. Apart from Judaism and Christianity, and two or three oriental sects (one of which is in Japan), there is no religion with the character of outspoken hostility to magic. Probably this hostility arose through the circumstance that what the Israelites found in Canaan was the magic of the agricultural god Baal, while Jahveh was a god of volcanoes, earthquakes, and pestilences. The hostility between the two priesthoods and the victory of the priests of Jahveh discredited the fertility magic of the priests of Baal and stigmatized it with a character of decadence and godlessness. Since Judaism made Christianity possible and gave it the character of a religion essentially free from magic, it rendered an important service from the point of view of economic history. For the dominance of magic outside the sphere in which Christianity has prevailed is one of the most serious obstructions to the rationalization of economic life. Magic involves a stereotyping of technology and economic relations. (Weber 2003 [1927], 360ff.)[20]

In contemporary technical language, what Weber does here is compare the culture of Europe, with modern capitalism as its main outflow, with other cultures, that is, other "historical individuals" belonging to the same ontological category. To explain why one of the cases in that category differs from the others on a particular "variable" (namely, the presence as opposed to absence of rational capitalism), Weber searches its history for events crystallized in social structures that distinguish the case to be explained from the other, comparable cases (and in this sense covary with the outcome, or "dependent variable"). Looking back at the historical record, Weber then finds a critical juncture in the cultural history of occidental civilization that may be capable of accounting for the observed "variance." What he finds is the eradication of magic and the institutionalization of a rational (*entzaubert*) concept of the world among ancient Jewry that, Weber suggests, has placed Western civilization on a separate path: once rational monotheism was established, it became self-reproducing, as restoring magic became both socially costly and metaphysically risky.

---

[20] *General Economic History* is a 1927 English translation of a posthumously published volume, *Abriß der universalen Sozial- und Wirtschaftsgeschichte*, which appeared in 1923. The original volume is a compilation of manuscripts and lecture notes.

The "other" in Weber's *Religionssoziologie* is the East – a faraway world lacking the kind of rationalism and inner-worldly asceticism that had made Europe special. Although Weber was far from embracing a deterministic theory of capitalist modernization, one in which the whole world would ultimately become "like us," he does seem to have considered it a possibility that occidental capitalism might one day become a global economic order.[21] For this there was, in Weber's view of the social world, no need for other cultures to pass through the same religious experience and undergo the same cultural rationalization that ancient Jewry and early modern Protestantism had imparted to the Occident. The mechanism by which Weber saw contemporary capitalism survive and, potentially, diffuse was that of the "iron cage," as described in the final paragraphs of the "Protestant Ethic": once firmly established, capitalism no longer needed its "spirit" for its reproduction and expansion, as compliance with its prescripts would become a matter of rational adaptation to objective constraints.[22]

Unlike Marx, then, or the way he is usually read, that historically acquired differences between societies would ultimately disappear was not inevitable for Weber; it was, however, not impossible either. If this applied to societies as distant as Asia, it would be all the more true for differences within capitalism. Apparently, at the end of his life Weber still hoped that the rule of bureaucracy (*Herrschaft der Bürokratie*) he saw spreading in Europe might, *pace* Sombart, stop short of befalling North America, thus sparing from destruction what Weber considered the last bastion of bourgeois individualism and freedom, regardless of the powerful pressures he saw at work worldwide for capitalist rationalization turning into bureaucratic rationalization.[23] According to Claus Offe (2006), it was the United States where Weber was looking, perhaps desperately, for, in Offe's terms, "escape routes from the iron cage" (43), although he seems to have regarded their continued availability as contingent

---

[21] See his reference, in the first sentence of his Introduction to *Gesammelte Aufsätze*, to European "cultural phenomena" being potentially of "universal significance and value" (note 17, above).

[22] "The Puritan wanted to work in a calling; we are forced to do so . . . Since asceticism undertook to remodel the world and to work out its ideals in the world, material goods have gained an increasing and finally an inexorable power over the lives of men as at no previous period in history. To-day the spirit of religious asceticism . . . has escaped from the [iron] cage [of the modern economic order]. But victorious capitalism, since it rests on mechanical foundations, needs its support no longer" (Weber 1984 [1904/1905], 181ff.).

[23] In this sense, Weber may be regarded as a forerunner of today's Varieties of Capitalism perspective. The difference, however, would be that to the extent that Weber may have expected persistent diversity between local or regional capitalisms, he attributed these to social-structural and cultural historical factors rather than to strategic business choices between different but equal modes of efficiency. See Hall and Soskice (2001).

on the further existence of the open frontier (see Offe 2006, 57).[24] Interestingly, whereas for Marx the open frontier was an impediment to capitalist development, for Weber it stood in the way of postcapitalist bureaucratization and Sombart's transformation of capitalism into socialism – as long as it lasted.

Know your enemy: from Germany to the Soviet Union

The rise of comparative-historical analysis as an academic-scholarly pursuit – as an empirical-analytical macrosociology free of historical determinism and teleology – began with the reception of Max Weber in the United States in the course of the 1930s and 1940s. An important contribution was made by the emigration after 1933 of European, and in particular German, social science to North America. There European Marxists and Weberians met with an American Marxist tradition struggling to distance itself from Soviet-Communist orthodoxy after the purges and the Hitler-Stalin Pact. The political debates of the 1920s in Europe over democracy, socialism and liberalism, communism and fascism, and generally the politics and prospects of modern industrial societies were thus transplanted to the United States, where they continued in a dramatically evolving historical context.

In light of the social and political turbulences of the "Age of Extremes" (Hobsbawm 1994), it is not surprising that early arguments in the United States on the differences and similarities of contemporary modern societies and their historical roots, as in the Marxist and Weberian traditions, were highly politicized. If the emerging social science in nineteenth-century Europe had felt a need to understand the societies of America and Asia, in the 1930s the direction of observation was reversed, and the societies that were seen as posing questions in need of scientific answers were Nazi Germany and, later, the Soviet Union: two enemy states of the United States and, it was soon understood, of Western civilization generally. Why was there no democracy in Germany – a country leading in science and education and in so many other respects central to modern society? How could Germany have become fascist? Comparative-historical analysis began with America puzzling over

---

[24] Offe's book is a brilliant exploration of the double theme of the Americanization of Europe and the Europeanization of America, as seen by three European visitors to the United States, Tocqueville, Weber, and Adorno, with very different normative perspectives.

the *German enigma*,[25] soon to be extended to Soviet Russia and its viability as a competing version of industrial society challenging the American model.

Today's comparative-historical analysis may be regarded as an academic derivative of a social science originally deeply embedded in policymaking, especially the making of foreign policy, where it served as an advanced form of intelligence gathering and analysis on other societies. The sites where social science and intelligence joined forces during World War II and the early years of the Cold War were the Central European Section of the Office for Strategic Studies (OSS; the predecessor of the CIA),[26] the State Department, several large foundations, especially Rockefeller and Ford, and a number of well-funded research institutes at elite universities, such as the Russian Institute at Columbia and the Russian Research Center at Harvard. These were also the places where an astonishing number of German émigrés – among them Felix Gilbert, Otto Kirchheimer, Hans Meyerhoff, Herbert Marcuse, and Franz Neumann (Müller 2010) – contributed their theoretical acumen and local knowledge to the American war effort. Later they became involved in American discussions on how to deal with the Soviet Union, continuing in a different environment their often vitriolic controversies of the 1920s. With hindsight, it seems nothing short of remarkable to what extent European scholars of mostly radical-socialist conviction were given access to both the foreign policy establishment – located at the time on the East Coast and in New York City in particular – and the academy. When in the McCarthy years control over American foreign policy shifted and government agencies were purged of liberal experts with left leanings – with policy increasingly informed by game theory instead of historical macrosociology – comparative-historical analysis was both forced and allowed to retreat into the often luxurious protective setting of academia, where it was transformed into a politically purified, value-free methodology, decoupled from political purposes and relieved but also deprived of any requirement to be of practical use.

A pivotal figure in this story was Barrington Moore (1913–2005), who is the first of two forerunners-cum-founders of modern comparative-historical analysis that I introduce briefly in the following. Moore received his PhD in sociology in 1941 at Yale, from where he went to work for the OSS as a

---

[25] Such puzzling has in many ways continued: consider the extensive Varieties of Capitalism literature in which Germany figures as the foremost example of a nonliberal, non–Anglo American political economy (Hall and Soskice 2001; Streeck 2011). See also authors as different as Gerschenkron (1989 [1943]), Parsons (1945), and Lipset (1963 [1960]), each of whom contributed to the study, from an American perspective, of "Germany in comparison." On Parsons during World War II, see Gerhardt (1993, 1996).

[26] On the OSS, see R. Harris Smith (2007) and Bradley F. Smith (1983).

policy analyst. There he met Herbert Marcuse, who became a lifelong friend and collaborator. In 1945, when the OSS was dissolved, Moore went to the University of Chicago and in 1948 moved on to Harvard, where two years later he joined the Russian Research Center. Moore was a prolific scholar and teacher. Among his students at Harvard were Perry Anderson, Jeffrey Alexander, Theda Skocpol, Charles Tilly, and Immanuel Wallerstein, who each in his or her own way contributed to the kind of historical sociology that Moore had been instrumental in establishing in an American social science environment dominated at the time by Parsonian structural functionalism. In 1966 Moore published *Social Origins of Dictatorship and Democracy*, one of the most consequential works in twentieth-century sociology: a book that may be regarded as the exemplary postwar American synthesis of the Marxist and Weberian European traditions. It has also remained up to this day the principal template of what later came to be called comparative-historical analysis and to be codified as such.

Social Origins is about the three versions of contemporary societies that, according to its author, formed the "modern world" – capitalism-cum-democracy, fascism, and communism – and the distinct historical pathways that have produced them.[27] The book opens with extensive historical narratives of the "revolutionary origins of capitalist democracy" in England, France, and the United States. It then, in its second part, investigates "three routes to the modern world in Asia," as exemplified by Chinese communism, Japanese fascism, and Indian democracy. Each of the six narratives[28] focuses on social classes such as lords and peasants, burgers and artisans, capitalists and workers, rulers and bureaucrats and on institutions and organizations such as villages and estates, courts and cities, armies and guilds in an attempt to identify typical configurations between them that are associated with different outcomes in countries' move toward modernity. Germany and Soviet

---

[27] No exhaustive discussion of the book can, of course, be intended here. For this, see, among others, Dennis Smith (1983).

[28] In reading *Social Origins*, one finds a broad overlap between modern comparative-historical analysis and contemporary historiography, to the extent that the latter increasingly draws on comparison. Indeed, "comparative history" is now an important stream in historical research and in a way always has been, going back as it does to the likes of Otto Hintze and Marc Bloch. Recently, it appears to have merged into "global history," which seems to be about to become the new disciplinary frontier. How historians use comparison has been succinctly described by Hartmut Kaelble in a paper that is unfortunately available only in German (Kaelble 2012). Kaelble does mention the work of American "historical social scientists" (his term) such as Charles Tilly, Karl Deutsch, Reinhart Bendix, and Barrington Moore as having influenced comparative history writing. How comparative history differs from comparative-historical analysis cannot be discussed here in appropriate detail. One would, however, be safe in assuming that comparative-historical analysis would be distinguished by stricter emphasis on causality and causal explanation as well as, perhaps, by its more pronounced "macroconfigurational orientation" (Thelen and Mahoney, Chapter 1, this volume).

Russia are discussed in the third part of the book, "Theoretical Implications and Projections," not in separate case studies but, more importantly, as cases to be interpreted in light of the findings in the first two parts of the book.

It does not seem inappropriate to consider Moore's a theory of "modernization," although in major respects it differs from the mainstream of modernization theory in the 1950s and 1960s. Importantly, the causal explanations Moore offers for the rise of democracy, fascism, and communism are not deterministic; there is ample space in Moore's case histories for missed or suppressed alternatives that, had they been chosen, would have put a society on a different path. "Objective" tendencies of social development are conceived as potentially and indeed continuously modified by contingent effects of human agency, in particular in the form of revolutionary violence. That conflict, violence, revolution, and war are attributed such central significance for social development is another distinctive characteristic of Moore's historical macrosociology, strictly setting it apart from the functionalist system theory of its time.[29] It is true that the book is about "modernization" and convergence of its different varieties on a single modernity – "the ancient Western dream of a free and rational society" (Moore 1966, 508) – is not only not ruled out but is clearly held to be desirable. Unlike so much other social science in the 1950s and 1960s, however, one finds no American triumphalism. In fact democracy as it exists in the West is regarded in the book as incomplete and in need of defense, repair, and further development, requiring changes in American society as deep as those that, according to Moore, needed to be made in contemporary communism. "I would urge the view," Moore writes, "that both Western liberalism and communism (especially the Russian version) have begun to display many symptoms of historical obsolescence" (508). He continues:

As successful doctrines they have started to turn into ideologies that justify and conceal numerous forms of repression . . . Communist repression has been and remains so far mainly directed against its own population. The repression by liberal society, . . . again now in the armed struggle against revolutionary movements in the backward areas, has been directed heavily outward, against others. Nevertheless this common feature of repressive practice covered by talk of freedom may be the most significant one.

Emphasizing in the same breath the role of critical theory, political agency, revolutionary force, and historical contingency, Moore concludes:

---

[29] See, for example, Moore's doubts whether the peaceful transition of India to some sort of democracy, without revolutionary destruction of the country's traditional social order, can bring about progress toward a modern society.

To the extent that such is the case, the task of honest thinking is to detach itself from both sets of preconceptions, to uncover the causes of oppressive tendencies in both systems in the hope of overcoming them. Whether they can actually be overcome is dubious in the extreme. As long as powerful vested interests oppose changes that lead toward a less oppressive world, no commitment to a free society can dispense with some conception of revolutionary coercion. That, however, is an ultimate necessity, a last resort in political action, whose rational justification in time and place varies too much for any attempt at consideration here.

A second example of early comparative-historical analysis, also born of the ideological and international battles over fascism and communism in the first half of the twentieth century, is Karl Wittfogel's monumental work, *Oriental Despotism: A Comparative Study of Total Power* (Wittfogel 1957). The book is much less prominent and appreciated than *Social Origins*, but very likely more because of its politics than for a lack in scholarly merit. While Wittfogel is not well enough known to be considered among the official founding fathers of comparative-historical analysis, his work, with its strictly multilinear concept of social development, represents in almost pure form the characteristic theoretical and logical priors of this approach. It also illustrates like none other the profoundly political roots of modern comparative-historical analysis and its deep historical entanglement in the twists and turns of the politics and conflicts of the first part of the twentieth century.

Karl Wittfogel, born in 1896, was a German playwright and social scientist who was deeply engaged in Weimar radical-left politics. At age 24 he joined the newly founded Communist Party, and a few years later he abandoned drama to devote himself fully to social science, which he studied in Leipzig, Berlin, and Frankfurt. Under the influence of Max Weber (Wittfogel 1957, 5), he took an early interest in East Asia and how its societies, considered "stagnant" at the time, differed from Europe's. His main subject of study in his early years was China. In 1925 Wittfogel joined the *Institut für Sozialforschung* in Frankfurt. When the Nazis took power in 1933, he was interned in a concentration camp. A year later, following an international campaign on his behalf, he was released and left Germany for Britain and then the United States. Beginning in 1939, Wittfogel held successive appointments at Columbia University until in 1947 he moved to the University of Washington in Seattle. There he worked until 1966 as a professor of Chinese history at the Far Eastern and Russian Institute, later to be renamed the Henry M. Jackson School of International Studies. He died in 1988 at age 92.

Like many other German emigrants to the United States, Wittfogel turned anti-Stalinist in the second half of the 1930s. Unlike Marcuse and Neumann, however, who joined the then-liberal mainstream of American foreign policy-making and academic scholarship, Wittfogel became a fierce anti-Communist and cold warrior. In 1951, he turned informant before the McCarran Committee on some of his fellow emigrants and prominent American scholars on East Asia. Wittfogel's anti-Communism was consistent with the development of his theory, which culminated in his view of Stalinism as the most advanced case of what he called "oriental dictatorship": a political regime of bureaucratic totalitarianism matched to the peculiar, historically deeply engrained structure of "Asiatic" societies.

Oriental Despotism was the result of its author's lifelong scholarly-cum-political interest in Asia and its systems of political rule, beginning with but not confined to China and evolving under changing political auspices driven by the historical events of the first half of the century. Wittfogel's central claim in the postwar years was that Soviet Russia, unlike what liberals like Moore and Marcuse believed or hoped for, was not another version of an industrial society ultimately open to convergence with the West. Instead, he regarded it as a fundamentally different, "Asiatic" society in a line of social development distinct from Western Europe. Wittfogel traced the notion of "Asia" as a different society back to authors such as Montesquieu, Smith, and Mill; as his main anchor, however, he chose the various dispersed, more or less systematic remarks on Asian societies, briefly mentioned above, by Marx and Engels (Wittfogel 1957, chap. 9, "The Rise and Fall of the Theory of the Asiatic Mode of Production," 369–412). In a wide-ranging, detailed reconstruction, Wittfogel showed that the founders of Marxist theory at some point entertained the idea that the "Western" path of development, the three steps from slave owning to feudal to capitalist relations of production – and then from there to socialism – might not be the only one possible and that in particular the societies of Asia might have failed to give rise to the feudal form of social organization that was, according to Marxist theory, the condition of progress toward capitalism and, eventually, socialism. If Asian society, or more precisely, the "Asiatic mode of production," was indeed different – meaning, if contemporary Asian societies were not "feudal" in nature, implying that global social development was multilinear rather than unilinear – then their economic and political stagnation might be incurable. For these societies, there was no prospect of endogenous social progress driven by European-style class struggle; indeed, if they were to make progress at all, they would, as Marx had occasionally considered it possible for India, depend for their progress on external intervention, in the form of colonization by capitalist-imperialist Western powers.

What exactly was it that, according to Marx, Engels, and Wittfogel, made a society, or a mode of production, "Asiatic"? When Wittfogel used the term, he had in mind a system of centralized rule over a dispersed and disorganized society consisting of self-sufficient and isolated agricultural communities, without autonomous cities, independent local powers, and private property (including its predecessor, feudal property). Power in a society like this derived not from contestable feudal entitlements or private property rights but from the coordinating functions performed in a society incapable of coordinating itself by a ruling "managerial bureaucracy" that formed and served as a ruling class. Asiatic bureaucracies, according to Wittfogel, presided despotically over a passive society bound to stagnate because of its lack of social and institutional pluralism, and not least due to the high taxes their despotic rulers were able to extract from it.

The first time Wittfogel had encountered what he later identified as the Asiatic form of society had been in his study of China as a prototype of what he then called a "hydraulic civilization": one based and dependent on central regulation of its water supply by an autocratic ruler and his administrators.[30] In his early work Wittfogel became fascinated with the centralized allocation of water to villages that would otherwise be unable to provide for themselves. Where the collective regulation of a major waterway was at the origin of a society, Wittfogel saw it embarked on a path of development different from other, nonhydraulic societies – societies that had the option of becoming pluralist rather than monistic and despotic. Obviously, the hydraulic account of Asian backwardness represented an attractive materialistic alternative for a Marxist like Wittfogel to the more or less idealistic explanation offered by Weber in his *Religionssoziologie*. What the two approaches had in common was their emphasis on the long-lasting effects of formative events far back in history – which of course fits the theoretical template of comparative-historical analysis. Later, Wittfogel extended his studies to other "hydraulic" societies, ancient and contemporary, not just in Asia. He also gradually detached the notion of an Asiatic form of authoritarian rule from the specific case of water management, emphasizing instead the dispersed and isolated location of self-sufficient villages and the absence of institutions for independent, decentralized self-organization from below. In this way he managed to include Tsarist Russia in his category of Asiatic rule.

---

[30] The contingent formative event shaping such societies being their location on a big river, such as the Yangtze or the Nile, in an otherwise dry land, where local agricultural communities depended on regulated access to and protection from seasonal floodwater.

With his work on an "Asiatic mode of production," abstract and academic as it might at first glance appear, Wittfogel was right in the middle of a passionate political debate in the 1920s, in the aftermath of the Russian Revolution. As he shows in *Oriental Despotism*, Lenin and the other Bolshevist leaders were intensely aware of Marx's *Asiatic conjecture* and were deeply worried about it – in particular, who like Marx and Engels tended to attribute Russian backwardness to the country's Asiatic legacy. The issue this raised for him as a believer in scientific socialism was nothing less than whether the revolution he was planning made historical sense. If the Russian political economy was in fact Asiatic and not feudal, the preconditions of modern socialism, as spelled out by Marx and Engels, would be missing, and the Communist Party, after having seized power, would just replace the managerial bureaucracy of the Tsarist past, turning into another version of an Asiatic ruling class.

Eventually, it seems, Lenin settled on a view of Russian society as feudal, and of the February Revolution of Kerensky in 1917 as victory of bourgeois capitalism, allowing him to go ahead with his socialist revolution. But he remained concerned and for a while believed that a socialist transformation under the backward conditions of Russia required a simultaneous revolution in the more advanced countries of Western Europe, in particular Germany. When this failed and the task became to build "socialism in one country," the social theorists advising the Communist International began to puzzle over the nature of the Asian societies east of Russia. Lenin, for his part, uttered dire warnings in the years before his death about a possible deterioration of the "dictatorship of the proletariat" into one of a new bureaucracy. With the succession struggle between Stalin and Trotsky the social nature of the Soviet regime, and in particular that of its ruling party, became a central point of contention, until Trotsky was driven into exile and Stalin officially outlawed the multilinear view of history. By decreeing that there was no "Asiatic mode of production" and never had been, making the mere use of the concept a capital crime, Stalin tried to insure himself against the Trotskyite claim that he was in effect a new Tsar and old Asian despot at the same time.

In the 1950s at the latest, at the height of the Cold War, Wittfogel saw Stalin as exactly that and the Soviet-Stalinist bureaucracy as a new ruling class, much like Milovan Djilas in Yugoslavia and the heirs of Leon Trotsky worldwide, with the additional twist that he firmly located the Stalinist regime in the tradition of Asiatic society with its ruling managerial bureaucracy. For Wittfogel, the Soviet Union of his time was not a variant of European industrial society but a different society altogether, for deep historical reasons, a veritable Evil Empire, frozen in its path, with which there was no possibility of compromise – a new Persian enemy to the Western successor societies of democratic Greece, and an enemy that had urgently to be defeated so it could be reconstructed and prevented from in turn defeating the free societies of the West. Here there was truly deep diversity, uncovered by comparative-historical analysis, although even in Wittfogel's view, there was still a possibility of convergence. For it to be realized, however, it had to be brought about from the outside. Only external intervention could clear away the historical legacies of hydraulic society, by installing true pluralism through deep institutional rebuilding, bringing about convergence among profoundly different societies, not by societal evolution but by – scientifically informed – political agency.

By way of conclusion

"Big structures, large processes, huge comparisons" (Tilly 1984), a search for "historically grounded explanations of large-scale and substantively important outcomes" (Mahoney and Rueschemeyer 2003), a "focus on macro-configurational explanation," the pursuit of "problem-driven case-based research," and a methodical "commitment to temporally oriented analysis" (Thelen and Mahoney, Chapter 1, this volume) – this is how comparative-historical analysis began and how it will, hopefully, continue.

References

Bell, Daniel. 1976. *The Cultural Contradictions of Capitalism*. New York: Basic Books.
Blackburn, Robin. 2011. *An Unfinished Revolution: Karl Marx and Abraham Lincoln*. London: Verso.
Durkheim, Emile. (1893) 1964. *The Division of Labor in Society*. New York: The Free Press.
Eagleton, Terry. 2011. *Why Marx Was Right*. New Haven, CT: Yale University Press.
Gerhardt, Uta. 1993. *Talcott Parsons on National Socialism*. New York: Aldine de Gruyter.
    1996. "Talcott Parsons and the Transformation from Totalitarianism to Democracy in the End of World War II." *European Sociological Review* 12 (2): 303–25.
Gerschenkron, Alexander. (1943) 1989. *Bread and Democracy in Germany*. Ithaca, NY: Cornell University Press.
Hall, Peter A., and David Soskice. 2001. "An Introduction to Varieties of Capitalism." In *Varieties of Capitalism: The Institutional Foundations of Comparative Advantage*, edited by Peter A. Hall and David Soskice, 1–68. Oxford: Oxford University Press.
Hobsbawm, Eric. 1994. *The Age of Extremes: A History of the World, 1914–1991*. New York: Pantheon Books.

Ibn Khaldūn. (1377) 1967. *The Muqaddimah: An Introduction to History*, translated and introduced by Franz Rosenthal.

Kaelble, Hartmut. 2012. "Historischer Vergleich, Version: 1.0. Docupedia-Zeitgeschichte." 14.8.2012. http://docupedia.de/zg/.

Koselleck, Reinhard, and Christian Meier. 1971–97. "Fortschritt." In *Geschichtliche Grundbegriffe: Historisches Lexikon zur politisch-sozialen Sprache in Deutschland*, Bd. 2, edited by Otto Brunner, 351–423. Stuttgart: Klett-Cotta.

Lipset, Seymour Martin. (1960) 1963. *Political Man: The Social Bases of Politics*. Garden City, NY: Anchor Books.

Machiavelli, Niccolò. (1514)1976. *The Prince*, translated, introduced, and annotated by James B. Atkinson. Indianapolis: Bobbs-Merrill.
  (1525) 1988. *Florentine Histories*, translated by Laura F. Banfield and Harvey Mansfield. Princeton, NJ: Princeton University Press.

Mahoney, James, and Dietrich Rueschemeyer. 2003. "Comparative Historical Analysis: Achievements and Agendas." In *Comparative Historical Analysis in the Social Sciences*, edited by James Mahoney and Dietrich Rueschemeyer, 3–38. Cambridge: Cambridge University Press.

Marx, Karl. (1867) 1967. *Capital: A Critique of Political Economy*. Vol. I. New York: International Publishers.

Marx, Karl, and Frederick Engels. 1971. *The Civil War in the United States*. New York: International Publishers.
  (1844) 1977. "The German Ideology." In *Karl Marx: Selected Writings*, edited David McLellan, 157–91. Oxford: Oxford University Press.

Moore, Barrington. 1966. *Social Origins of Dictatorship and Democracy: Lord and Peasant in the Making of the Modern World*. Boston: Beacon Press.

Müller, Tim B. 2010. *Krieger und Gelehrte: Herbert Marcuse und die Denksysteme im Kalten Krieg*. Hamburg: Hamburger Edition.

Nietzsche, Friedrich. 1911. *Twilight of the Idols: Or, How to Philosophise with the Hammer; the Anti-Christ; Notes to Zarathustra and Eternal Recurrence*, translated by Anthony M. Ludovici. New York: Macmillan.

Offe, Claus. 2006. *Reflections on America: Tocqueville, Weber & Adorno in the United States*. Cambridge: Polity.

Parsons, Talcott. 1945. "The Problem of Controlled Institutional Change: An Essay in Applied Social Science." *Psychiatry* 8 (1): 79–101.

Popper, Karl R. 1957. *The Poverty of Historicism*. Boston: Beacon Press.

Schröder, Peter. 2004. *Niccolo Machiavelli*. Frankfurt am Main: Campus.

Smith, Bradley F. 1983. *The Shadow Warriors: O.S.S. and the Origins of the C.I.A.* London: André Deutsch.

Smith, Dennis. 1983. *Barrington Moore: Violence, Morality and Political Change*. London: Macmillan.

Sombart, Werner. (1906) 1976. *Why Is There No Socialism in the United States?* London: Macmillan.

Spencer, Herbert. (1882) 2003. *The Principles of Sociology*, 3 vols., edited by Hg. von Jonathan and H. Turner. New Brunswick, NJ: Transaction Publishers.

Streeck, Wolfgang. 2010. "Institutions in History: Bringing Capitalism Back In." In *Oxford Handbook of Comparative Institutional Analysis*, edited by Glenn Morgan, John

Campbell, Colin Crouch, Ove Kai Pedersen, and Richard Whitley, 659–86. Oxford: Oxford University Press.

2011. "E Pluribus Unum? Varieties and Commonalities of Capitalism." In *The Sociology of Economic Life*, 3rd ed., edited by Mark Granovetter and Richard Swedberg, 419–55. Boulder, CO: Westview.

Thucydides. (c. 400 BC) 1998. *The Peloponnesian War*, translated by Steven Lattimore. Indianapolis: Hackett.

Tilly, Charles. 1984. *Big Structures, Large Processes, Huge Comparisons.* New York: Russell Sage Foundation.

Tocqueville, Alexis de. (1835–40) 1988. *Democracy in America.* New York: HarperPerennial.

Weber, Max. (1922) 1979. *Economy and Society: An Outline of Interpretive Sociology*, 2 vols., edited by Günther Roth and Claus Wittich. Berkeley: University of California Press.

(1904/1905) 1984. *The Protestant Ethic and the Spirit of Capitalism*, translated by Talcott Parsons, introduced by Anthony Giddens. London: Unwin Paperbacks.

(1927) 2003. *General Economic History.* New Brunswick, NJ: Transaction Publishers.

Wittfogel, Karl A. 1957. *Oriental Despotism: A Comparative Study of Total Power.* New Haven, CT: Yale University Press.

Index